PAST IMPERFECT

Lawrence W. Towner

PAST IMPERFECT

ESSAYS ON HISTORY, LIBRARIES,

AND THE HUMANITIES

Lawrence W. Towner

EDITED BY ROBERT W. KARROW, JR.,

AND ALFRED F. YOUNG, WITH AN

INTRODUCTION BY ALFRED F. YOUNG

THE
UNIVERSITY OF CHICAGO
PRESS
Chicago & London

LAWRENCE W. TOWNER
1921–1992
Librarian and President of the Newberry Library from 1962 to 1986. A
historian, he taught at MIT, the College of William and Mary, and
Northwestern University. He was editor of the *William and Mary
Quarterly* from 1956 to 1962.

THE UNIVERSITY OF CHICAGO PRESS, CHICAGO 60637
THE UNIVERSITY OF CHICAGO PRESS, LTD., LONDON
© *1993 by The University of Chicago*
All rights reserved. Published 1993
Printed in the United States of America
02 01 00 99 98 97 96 95 94 93   1 2 3 4 5

ISBN: 0-226-81042-9 (cloth)

Library of Congress Cataloging-in-Publication Data

Towner, Lawrence W. (Lawrence William), 1921–1992.
    Past imperfect : essays on history, libraries, and the humanities
/ Lawrence W. Towner ; edited by Robert W. Karrow, Jr. and Alfred F.
Young, with an introducction by Alfred F. Young
      p.   cm.
    Includes bibliographical references.
    1. Research libraries—United States. 2. United States—History.
3. Humanities. I. Karrow, Robert W.   II. Young, Alfred Fabian,
    1925–   .   III. Title.
Z675.R45T68   1993
027.7'0973—dc20   92-32425
                                                              CIP

⊗The paper used in this publication meets the minimum requirements
of the American National Standard for Information Sciences—Perma-
nence of Paper for Printed Library Materials, ANSI Z39.48–1984.
This book is printed on acid-free paper.

For Rachel

CONTENTS

ILLUSTRATIONS

Frontispiece

Lawrence W. Towner

Following page 64

Increase Mather's *The Wicked Mans Portion* . . . (1675).
Cotton Mather's *Pillars of Salt* . . . (1699).
John Rogers's *Death the Certain Wages of Sin* . . . (1701).
A Brief Relation of Remarkables in the Shipwreck of Above One Hundred Pirates . . . (1717).
"The Last Speech and Dying Advice of Poor Julian," broadside (1733).
"Poor Julleyoun's Warnings to Children and Servants . . . ," broadside [1733].
"Advice from the Dead to the Living . . . ," broadside [1733].
"An Exhortation to Young and Old to Be Cautious of Small Crimes . . . " (1773).

Following page 122

A Surprising Narrative of a Young Woman Discovered in a Cave in the Wilderness, after Having Been Taken by the Savage Indians (1799).
American sheet music.
Look Here! Horses Wanted! For Winter Herding! J. P. McKissick and W. H. Moore Will Take Horses for Winter Herding, from any Point on Wood River . . . [188(?)].
Map of Hacienda de Santa Ines (1569).
Le secret du Jansenisme, de'couvert et refut par un docteur catholique (1653).
Floyd Dell, *An Old Man's Folly.* Author's autograph manuscript.
George Taylor and Andrew Skinner, *Survey and Maps of the Roads of North Britain or Scotland* (1776).
Selected editions of *Moby Dick.*
Rural Sport: Or, a Peep at a Lancashire Rush-Cart, 1821. Woodburytype in Richard Wright Proctor, *Memorials of Manchester Streets* (1874).

Jean Bellère, *Brevis exactaq[ue] totius novi orbis eiusq[ue] insularum descriptio* (ca. 1544).

Statutes Compiled for the Better Observation of the Holy Rule of the Most Glorious Father & Patriarch Sainct Benedict . . . Anno Dñi 1613. Manuscript.

Oszvald Pelbart Themesvari, *Pomerium Quadragesimale* (1502).

François Piquet, manuscript book, with prayers and hymns in the Mohawk language (1750–52).

Guillaume Del'Isle, *La France* (1703).

"God Presiding over the Fall of the Angels," in Jacques Legrand, *Livre de Bonnes Meurs*, illuminated manuscript (before 1478).

Autograph manuscript, Napoleon Bonaparte to his son, Prince Eugene de Beauharnais (14 May 1810).

Autograph letter, signed, Thomas Jefferson to George Watterston, (3 January 1816).

The Damnation of Theron Ware, or Illumination, by Harold Frederic. Poster by J. H. Twachtman.

Page 230

Lester Jesse Cappon

PREFACE

DURING HIS THREE DECADES as a historian, president of a major library, and national spokesman for the humanities, Bill Towner has left his mark on the American cultural landscape. It was the approach of his seventieth birthday in October 1991 that inspired a group of his friends and colleagues to make more widely available a selection of his most important writings, published and unpublished, that defines the man and his vision.

The material was chosen by a committee working in the tradition Bill helped to create at the Newberry Library—a community of scholars. This particular community comprised Richard H. Brown, academic vice-president; Charles T. Cullen, president and librarian; Robert W. Karrow, Jr., administrative curator of Special Collections and curator of maps; Kenneth Nebenzahl, trustee; Paul Saenger, George A. Poole Curator of Rare Books and Collection Development librarian; and Alfred F. Young, professor of history emeritus, Northern Illinois University, and senior research fellow, the Newberry Library.

Alfred Young and Robert Karrow assembled the body of Bill's writings from which the members of the committee reached a consensus on "the best of Bill Towner." Alfred Young wrote the general introduction and the introductions to the selections. Robert Karrow supervised the production and with Paul Saenger selected the illustrations from collections and funds acquired by the Newberry during Bill's tenure. Only when the editorial process was well advanced did we let Bill in on the game. He then became an active participant, reading the entire manuscript, suggesting new or alternative selections, filling us in on background, helping us get the names and dates right, and resisting the temptation to wield his editor's pencil. His writings are reprinted as they were originally written or delivered, except for a few typographical corrections.

For historical and biographical information we are indebted to William McGiffert, editor of the *William and Mary Quarterly*; Thad Tate, former director of the Institute of Early American History and Culture; Marcus McCorison, director of the American Antiquarian Society; and James M. Wells, former vice-president of the Newberry and custodian emeritus of the John M. Wing Foundation on the History of Printing. Margaret Chervinko and Joel L. Samuels assisted us is locating copies of Bill's writings, and Claudette Aho helped to prepare the typescript. It seems especially fitting that Lila Weinberg edited the manuscript for the University of Chicago Press. Lila and her late husband Arthur were Bill's ideal of independent scholars at the Newberry. Charles T. Cullen prepared the Index.

As this is Bill's book, it is fitting that the dedication is his too; we happily join him in extending our warm thanks to Rachel Towner for her assistance and encouragement. In this, as in all of Bill's endeavors, she has been an unfailing source of strength.

Bill died 13 June 1992 while the final manuscript was being edited. We have left the manuscript as he last saw it.

R. K. and A. Y.

INTRODUCTION: BILL TOWNER

LAWRENCE WILLIAM TOWNER—Bill Towner as he is known to all—
served as Librarian and President of the Newberry Library for
twenty-four years, from 1962 until his retirement in 1986. A year
later as people took stock of the institution on its centennial, it was
already clear, as Charles Cullen, his successor, put it, that Towner
had presided over "a spurt of growth unprecedented since the founding." The Newberry was a great library when he took over; when he
left, according to Stanley Katz, president of the American Council
of Learned Societies, the Newberry with its collections, research
centers, and fellowship programs was "an epitome of modern scholarly communication," an "incomparable resource," and a leader
among independent research libraries whose development was "integral to the emergence of rigorous modern scholarship in the humanities."[1]

And Bill Towner was recognized not only as a leader among librarians and the academic scholarly community by the foundations
and the National Endowment for the Humanities (NEH), but as a
public spokesman for all these constituencies—for the humanities
as a whole. It was appropriate when the National Endowment for
the Humanities, in response to his leadership, adopted its first programs of direct support for independent research libraries, and of
"challenge grants," that he should be invited to Washington to the
ceremonies at which Presidents Ford and Reagan announced the
programs.

The independent research libraries are a small minority among
America's libraries—free-standing institutions supported neither by
the endowments of universities nor by public tax moneys. And
among these Newberry is *sui generis*. But the issues Towner grappled with were not unique to the Newberry or to independent research libraries; others continue to grapple with them in a variety
of institutions. And his solutions had an impact not only on the
Newberry but on American research in the humanities. Taken together, they show him as a rare individual, a successful scholar/ad-
ministrator with a broad, coherent vision of the place of the humanities, libraries, and scholarship in American life.

1. Rolf Achilles, comp. and ed., *Humanities Mirror: Reading at the Newberry Library* (Chicago: Newberry Library, 1987), 7, 11.

Thus it seemed appropriate to a group of his colleagues and co-workers who have known or worked with Bill over many years to assemble a collection of his writings. The essays in this volume have been chosen to illustrate the range of his activity and thought as historian, librarian, and spokesman for the humanities as well as his views of his colleagues who were his mentors and coworkers. The essays are arranged under these four headings. Most of the pieces are known only to the specialized audiences for whom they were prepared, and a good number—several talks, an internal memorandum, a letter—have never been published before.

I have been asked to introduce the essays as someone who has known Bill since our graduate years in history at Northwestern University, and who has been a member of the Newberry "community of scholars" over the years of Bill's tenure and beyond. As a friend, I can hardly claim objectivity. But I can try, despite the limitations of my affection and admiration for Bill, to establish the outlines of a biographical and historical context that may illuminate the essays.

The issues facing Towner, it could be argued, are primarily of historical interest. What is remarkable, it seems to me, is how persistent and recurrent are the underlying issues Bill faced.

The essays address a wide range of issues on the future of the humanities in the United States. What is the role of the independent research library in the total world or research institutions? How viable is the independent research library? How should it define its collection policy in an age of diminished funding and competing internal demands? How can it assume the tremendous burden of the sheer physical preservation of ever-deteriorating books and manuscripts? Where will it find the financial resources for all these tasks?

Some questions are more directly the concern of scholars. Towner's vision of the Newberry was of a "community of scholars" pursuing research of their own choosing, supported by a fellowship program, of research centers, and long- and short-term sponsored projects. How much responsibility should (or can) the independent research library assume in promoting the use of its resources? What is the function of a research center in a library? What constitutes a "community of scholars," and what enables them to function as such?

Some are questions many scholars are still slow to entertain. What are the responsibilities of scholars in the humanities to American society? How can scholars best communicate their knowledge? How much "outreach" to the lay public should the academy attempt? The issue has been a persistent one among foundations and has been in the public eye in debates over the National Endowment for the Humanities since its founding in 1966. There the issue has been posed sometimes as a choice between supporting "public programs" or "pure" scholarship, and has often been caricatured by one side or the other as a "populist" as opposed to an "elitist" approach to the humanities. Towner argued against such a dichotomy. Where should the balance be struck?

This broad array of issues in the humanities continues to be debated. Indeed Towner, the Newberry, and the independent research libraries succeeded in placing many of them on the humanities agenda. Whether or not one agrees with the paths Bill Towner chose, there is no question that he has been a pathbreaker. And readers may share the pleasure of following the shaping of a major American institution of learning by a person with a coherent vision that flowed from a distinct core of convictions and values.

I

"You are a very lucky young man," Everett D. Graff, the president of the Newberry's Board of Trustees said to Bill in congratulating him on his appointment in 1962. Bill repeats the comment to hint at the skepticism some trustees may possibly have felt. He was forty-one, his Ph.D. degree only seven years old. He had ten years of experience as teacher, five as instructor and then assistant professor at M.I.T., five as associate professor at the College of William and Mary. He had no administrative experience save as editor of the *William and Mary Quarterly* with its staff of three. He had just spent a year on a fellowship at Harvard's new Center for the Study of the History of Liberty in America but had not completed the revision of his dissertation. In 1962 he published his first article, in the *Quarterly*, distilling a striking part of his superbly researched and written dissertation. But if the trustees had read this warmly empathic analysis of protest by the apprentices, indentured servants, and slaves of colonial Massachusetts, some might have raised their eyebrows. He had given one other striking demonstration of his capacities; as editor of the *Quarterly*, following a brilliant predecessor, Douglass Adair, he had stabilized the journal, beginning its reputation as one of the best-edited historical journals in the country. Entering the Newberry he had another hard act to follow: Stanley Pargellis, librarian from 1942 to 1962, who as Bill later wrote brought "imagination and verve to his self-appointed tasks" (selection no. 10).

In retrospect, it is easy to see the strengths someone brings to his job that accounts for his successes. Bill brought any number. He was a historian with unusual mastery of his craft who wrote very well. He worked in a field that put him at the crossroads of British and American history and a broad range of types of history. He does not fit easily into any mold by which students of historiography categorize scholars. He was a historian of the last glow of the progressive school that flourished in the years immediately after World War II before it was clouded over by the consensus school. His dissertation, "A Good Master Well Served: A Social History of Servitude in Massachusetts, 1620–1750," was a prescient example of "history from the bottom up," a good dozen years before Jesse Lemisch recoined the phrase and years before the French *Annales* school, English revisionist Marxists, or American social science historians had brought the "new social history" into fashion in the United States. He knew what it meant to be on the "cutting edge" of scholarship.

Unlike the progressives, he was keenly interested in intellectual history and, while he focused on the dissidents, he recognized the ties that bound together Puritan society. In his years of research Towner had found the secret of the successful historian: he had steeped himself in the original sources of Massachusetts as had few others, making the rounds of every county courthouse in the once-colony, reading every issue of every colonial newspaper, and every sermon, diary, and letter on his subject. He had a reverence for the stuff of libraries and archives. He loved rare books. He had experience in several contrasting communities of scholars, at the Institute of Early American History and Culture in Williamsburg and at the Center sponsored by Harvard's Department of History. And, as editor of the *Quarterly*, he had honed his ability to judge scholars and to nurture younger scholars.

Bill brought with him the marks of three remarkable mentors—Ray A. Billington, Clifford K. Shipton, and Lester J. Cappon—each very different from the other. Ray Billington at Northwestern was the personification of the progressive tradition in history (selection no. 18). His first book, his dissertation on American nativism in the nineteenth century, was written at Harvard under the direction of Arthur M. Schlesinger, Sr., founder of the first school of American social history. Billington became the country's leading historian of the frontier, studying under Frederick Merck who had been a student of Frederick Jackson Turner. Turner, Charles Beard, and Vernon Louis Parrington were the triumvirate who set the framework for progressive history with its emphasis on the conflicts of interests, classes, sections, and ideologies, its identification with the democratic tradition and, in the case of Beard, on historical relativism.

Ray, like Beard, assumed the historian had political responsibilities: as Henry Wallace moved toward the formation of the Progressive party in 1947–1948, Ray wrote and talked about the function of third parties as catalysts of change in American history; as the first wave of the witch-hunt broke he reminded scholars of the dangerous consequences of political hysteria. Bill sometimes reminds me of when he and I turned out leaflets at Northwestern against the Mundt-Nixon bill, an early harbinger of the witch-hunt; he claims I wrote them and made him crank the messy mimeograph machine in the history office (no Xeroxing then).

Bill had been politicized by his experiences in World War II. After all, it was a time when FDR spoke of the four freedoms, Henry Wallace of the "age of the common man," and Wendell Willkie of "one world." Bill served in the China-Burma-India theater as a pilot and returned with an abiding contempt for Chiang Kai-shek and bewilderment at America's postwar support for corrupt leaders who lacked support from their own people—the first in a long line of Cold War policies that would find the United States on the side of counterrevolution. George McGovern, our fellow teaching assistant, had tried to express his concern for social justice as a Methodist minister but found a more congenial outlet in history and then politics. We showed our progressivism by our choice of dissertation topics: Bill on the slaves, apprentices, and indentured servants of New England; George on the struggles of the Colorado miners with John D. Rockefeller; I on the Jeffersonians of New York whom I then thought of as the first successful farmer-labor party.

Ray Billington was a frontier historian and a sophisticated Turnerite, but he was not interested in building a "school" and encouraged his graduate students to pursue their own interests. Out of two dozen, two went into frontier history. Ray was delighted with Bill's interpretation of servitude as an English institution modified but hardly liberalized by New World conditions, as Turner would have it; just as he was pleased with my chapter that showed the New York frontier as a stronghold at first of Federalism and not Jeffersonian democracy. Ray was open to new interpretations, warmly supportive of his students, and an enthusiast of the Newberry on whose board he served. He was a model in more ways than one for Bill.

Bill does not call Clifford K. Shipton, director of the American Antiquarian Society, his second mentor, but his memoir leaves little doubt about his feelings (selection no. 19). Shipton could not have been more different from Billington. He was in the midst of what would become a fourteen-volume set of biographies of the graduates of Harvard College in the seventeenth and eighteenth centuries; every page breathed his empathy with the colonial elites and, when it came to the Revolution, with the Loyalists. Shipton, however, was a master of the sources of New England history and gave Bill the direction he needed, sending him into the court records. Shipton's ultimate monument was to take the vast collection of American imprints, some 40,000 titles in the bibliography compiled by Charles Evans, compile a new index (locating another 10,000 titles), and supervise the reproduction on microcard of every title, making available a collection of almost every pamphlet, book, and broadside published in America to 1800. As Bill remarked, by making it possible for libraries to acquire this collection (and a similar microcard edition of every issue of every newspaper published in early America), Shipton, the "elitist," had helped to "democratize" the scholarship of colonial America. He was a good model for thinking big about what an imaginative librarian could do for scholarship.

The influence of Billington and Shipton on Bill's scholarship is apparent in Bill's dissertation and four articles that distilled or grew out of it (selection nos. 1, 2, 3, 4), but the kind of history he wrote and the style is pure Towner. Always a question is posed: How did the "fondness for freedom" that Cotton Mather took for granted among servants manifest itself? Was Samuel Sewall's famous attack against slavery the beginning of an antislavery movement or, more likely, the end? What happened to the poorest of the poor, the children set out to apprenticeship by Boston's Overseers of the Poor? What were the patterns in the "true confessions" of criminals over the colonial period? Then the Towner trademark: a vast body of sources unobtrusively analyzed, without overwhelming the reader. Casually we learn that Towner has "recovered" some 7000 servants and tracked servants through 1500 court cases and every issue of every Massachusetts newspaper to 1750, or that he has analyzed 1100 Boston indentures, or read some 400 court confessions and 100 or more published broadside "true confessions." Halfway through "A Fondness for Freedom" we realize that Towner has boldly inverted the values of Puritan society by defining as protest "acts which today are described as delinquency or criminality." Acts of aggression against individuals he convinces us "were protests against society and its prescriptions." Or we realize that he has taken a genre of sources, the ritualized confessions of sin and contrition extracted by ministers (which other scholars have dismissed as formulaic) and distilled from them changing patterns of crime and criminals. Bill answers his question and leaves the reader with a sense of having evoked a piece of history beyond recovery.

The third layer of experience Bill drew upon when he became Librarian at Newberry was from his years at the Institute of Early American History and Culture whose director was Lester J. Cappon, his third mentor. Cappon chose Bill to be editor of the *Quarterly* the year Bill received his Ph.D. Bill had published some reviews, no articles or books, and Lester in his first year as director of the institute (and not a committee) made the choice. My guess is that Lester had read his dissertation, seen how skillful Bill was, especially as a writer, and knew what scholars he respected thought of Bill and his work. Lester saw in Bill the same lack of pretense and the same independence of judgment and candor, for which Lester himself was known. The institute was small: the director, an editor of the *Quarterly*, a book editor, several associate editors, and in time an annual Fellow turning a dissertation into a book. There was a council which was advisory; the money came from the College of William and Mary and Colonial Williamsburg, Inc. Combined with the scholars who did research for the restorations at Colonial Williamsburg this was a distinct community of scholars, and Bill knew the synergy they created.

As editor Bill was very much on his own. It was Lester's way of doing things which Bill would follow: choose a good person for a job and give him freedom to run his own show. The editorial board was advisory; manuscripts went out to referees, but the editor made his own decisions. Douglass Adair, Bill's predecessor, commissioned articles, often rewrote articles, published many of his own articles, rode his own hobbyhorses. He also let manuscript submissions go unacknowledged for inordinate lengths of time.

The historian who has written an analysis of Towner's editorship in the context of the twenty years of the *Quarterly* from 1944 to 1964 speaks of it as "a period of consolidation" in which the journal was "stabilized."[2] Towner was known for "an unobtrusive style of editing" despite the use of a "heavy blue pencil." In retrospect, it was a time when scholars were closing down one paradigm but had not yet opened up American history to new currents.[3] The book

2. Keith Berwick, "A Peculiar Monument: The Third Series of the 'William and Mary Quarterly,' *William and Mary Quarterly*, 3d ser., 31 (1964): 8.

3. Letters, Michael McGiffert to Alfred Young, 12 June 1990; Thad Tate to Alfred Young, 27 June, 20 July 1990.

review section edited by William W. Abbot kept open a sense of debate between the challengers to the Beardian interpretation and its defenders. Bill was willing to risk challenges from dissenters of a new breed such as William Appleman Williams on the age of mercantilism and Staughton Lynd on class conflict and to take a flyer with historians who drew on historical sociology or psychology. Bill paid homage to the democratic tradition by reprinting a little-known tract by a self-taught Massachusetts yeoman and tavern keeper, William Manning's "Key of Libberty," which depicted the struggle between "the few" and "the many." Unlike earlier progressives, he was keen to publish work in the history of ideas and the history of science. As an editor he was especially good in nursing along younger scholars. The *Quarterly* was a success.

Lester J. Cappon, the director of the institute, was the kind of person Bill called an "enabler," someone who enabled others to get big tasks done. Unwittingly he had taught Bill a very big lesson: you did not have to have experience as an editor to become a successful editor. Lester was a risk taker. So was Bill for the rest of his career.

II

Towner had grasped the essential character of the Newberry long before he arrived as director. We had both haunted it in graduate school; it was a conglomeration of collections of rare books plus all the secondary works and journals in the fields of its strength. It was a wonderful place to do the staggering bibliographic essay Ray Billington required as a preliminary to a Ph.D. dissertation. A few years after Bill got to the Newberry he began to popularize the defining phrase that has stuck; it was "an uncommon collection of uncommon collections."

"Unlike its nearest analogs, the Folger Shakespeare Library and the Huntington Library, both based on great collections gathered by their founders," Towner wrote later, "the Newberry began, from scratch, as a collection of money" (selection no. 10). The core of the library was an array of "massive subject-oriented collections," each focusing on a "broad subject field rather than on books as artifacts." Characteristic were the Wing Collection on the history of printing, the Ayer collection on American discovery and exploration and Indian-European relations, and the Greenlee collection on the Portuguese empire. All were gifts. The Ayer collection was the librarian's ideal: an initial gift which came with an endowment to buy books in the field and hire staff, with the result that an initial gift of 14,000 volumes had become 80,000 by 1962.

There was a pattern in all of this, if one focused hard. It was possible to make several general claims, as Bill did in a pamphlet introducing the Newberry. It was "a great research collection in the humanities, chiefly history, literature, music and philosophy." The Newberry "generally confines itself to Western Europe and the Americas, covering from the Middle Ages to the end of the Napoleonic era in Europe, to the revolutionary period in Latin America, and to World War I in North America—with excursions into nineteenth-century England and, in various areas to the present in the United States."[4] But even this claimed both too much and too little. There were vast lacunae from the fifteenth to the nineteenth centuries, and under Pargellis the Newberry had moved with both feet into the collecting of Chicago and Midwestern literary manuscripts and into business history, with two vast archives of railroad papers. It also had the largest collection of local and family history in the Midwest, making it a Mecca for genealogists, at the time the largest single body of Newberry users.

Towner also grasped the secret of the library's success in expanding. "The Library was not built according to a conscious architectonic plan," he wrote. "Instead, like almost all libraries, it grew; and it grew partly, at least, as the consequence of fortunate and often unforeseen opportunities seized upon when they presented themselves—there is no better time" (selection no. 12). Stanley Pargellis, his predecessor (1942–1962), had already moved in directions Bill wanted to continue. He had "nearly tripled the size of the collection," beginning the acquisition of manuscripts, and "literally inventing two new fields of the library, the history of the Chicago Literary Renaissance" and "the history of business." He had begun to bring the attention of the scholarly world to Newberry through "a modest fellowship program" and especially a series of exploratory conferences focusing on the areas of the library's greatest strengths, and through the creation of the *Newberry Library Bulletin*, publicizing these strengths.

By 1964, a year and a half into his tenure, Bill had created a Committee on the Future of the Library and drafted a preliminary "Statement on the Prospects before Us."[5] But he would not propose the first "architectonic plan" until 1971. In the early 1960s he had not so much a blueprint as a set of assumptions as to the directions in

4. Lawrence W. Towner et al., *An Uncommon Collection of Uncommon Collections: The Newberry Library* (Chicago: Newberry Library, 1970), 15.

5. Towner, "Memorandum to the Committee on the Future of the Newberry," 23 April 1964, Towner Papers, Newberry Library Archives.

which he wanted to go. First, to continue to build the collections by seizing "unforeseen opportunities" for *en bloc* purchases and gifts and through the day-by-day efforts of the Library's curators. Second, to come to grips with the long-neglected nightmare of the physical deterioration of the books, maps, and manuscripts and face the nearly overwhelming task of preservation and conservation. And third, to promote what he variously called "effective use" or "planned use" of the Newberry's rich resources by scholars and an expanded public.

These were by no means self-evident truths. The first—building the collections through major purchase—was based on pride, hubris if you will, a sense of the Newberry's mission. It just had to remain preeminent in the fields of its greatest strengths. The second goal, conservation, became self-evident only as Towner and others on the staff raised the consciousness of the Newberry community and, more important, the fund givers. The third was based on an assumption that the library "is directly useful and important to society at large" and that the "trickle-down theory of the distribution of knowledge by a few top scholars with exclusive access to the collections" was "no more satisfying today than is the trickle-down theory of the distribution of wealth that was so popular in the late nineteenth century." [6] It was based on the assumption that vast collections were "underused" or "lying fallow." [7]

In his first years a great deal of Towner's energies went into seizing "unforeseen opportunities," as his absorbing account of the acquisition of the Louis H. Silver Collection in 1964 makes clear (selection no. 12). The Silver Collection was rich in books and manuscripts of the Renaissance and English literature. It was costly: the purchase price was $2,687,000, which the Library did not have. This was what Bill called "a silver lining with a cloud." The strategy that he worked out with enthusiastic trustees was risk taking: sell the duplicates; also sell the duplicates in the collection of Western Americana which Everett D. Graff donated to the Library the same year; and launch the first fund-raising drive in the Library's history. It worked, and Bill had maintained the Newberry's reputation and established his own.

As Bill describes this purchase and those that followed—the Deering Collection of Indian captivity narratives (1967), the Novacco and

6. Towner, "The Virtue of Necessity" (address to Independent Research Libraries Association, 1980), typescript, Towner Papers, Newberry Library Archives.

7. Towner, "Address to the Society of Research Administrators, Chicago, 6 October 1980," typescript, Towner Papers, Newberry Library Archives.

Sack collections of maps from the sixteenth through the eighteenth centuries (1967–1968), the Driscoll collection of American sheet music (1967)—seizing opportunities as they appeared forced planning. In what fields should the Newberry build to strength? The inevitable corollary was what fields were "out of scope" and should possibly be disposed of? Bill acted on this too. The acquisitions process was one of further defining the Newberry.

It is characteristic that he should deprecate his own role in acquiring the big new collections. "It was the easy way, of course," he wrote. "Any damn fool with good advisors on his staff, bold Trustees, a little audacity, a little luck, good lawyers and a willingness to haggle, can do it." By contrast, paying tribute to the unsung staff of curators and librarians, "The real intelligence in building a library is applied in the day-by-day, week-by-week, year-by-year addition of one book at a time. There's the hard work: knowing the books, which ones to buy, at what prices, for what purposes."[8] Bill was especially mindful of James M. Wells—then associate director, later vice-president—"a great, great bookman," and Hans Baron, a Renaissance scholar and bibliographer in residence. Confessing to an "acquisitive instinct" through his entire tenure, Bill felt that "building collections is the quintessential act of this profession."[9]

The second area in which Towner moved, conservation, acquired the stature of a self-evident truth with a dawning consciousness of the dire consequences of failure to act. The great flood in Florence, Italy, in 1966 was to the field of library conservation what Sputnik was to American education. The Newberry had 5,000,000 manuscripts and 1,300,000 volumes of books, a large number of which were printed in the nineteenth and twentieth centuries on decaying, acidic paper. Moreover, the collections were kept in some twenty-seven different stacks of varying states of humidity and temperature scattered throughout the building. At the end of a busy Saturday in the section of the reading room inhabited by genealogists, the floor was scattered with a confetti of brittle paper.

Towner's strategy, which he summarized midway in his tenure, was threefold (selection no. 13). The first was "in-house conservation," in which a resident conservator would pursue a "full spectrum" of conservation techniques. Bill hired Paul N. Banks in 1963 and described him fondly as one of the three staff members in his

8. Towner, "The Library and the Collector: The Newberry Library," *Louisiana State University Library Lectures* (Baton Rouge, 1971): 14–23.

9. Towner, "The President's Corner," *Newberry Newsletter*, no. 17 (Summer 1979); ibid., no. 23 (Winter 1981).

first twelve years "who have really told me off." The second was prevention, to "stay the forces destroying our books," which meant nothing less than a new stack building in which temperature and humidity could be kept at ideal levels. The third was to lift the whole field of conservation by encouraging Banks to do research to develop the state of the art, write, and train other conservators. By the end of Bill's tenure the new stacks were built, in-house conservation a commitment, the first graduate programs in conservation launched, and the Newberry had earned a reputation as a pioneer in the field.

The third area of Bill's master plan—promoting "effective use" of the Library among scholars and an "outreach" to nontraditional users—was the least self-evident. Not all librarians were in agreement. Bill likes to tell the story of how James Wells "made a gift to him of an 1814 message from Isaiah Thomas, founder and President of the American Antiquarian Society that read '. . . our principle objects are to COLLECT and PRESERVE.' "[10] While, like other reformers, he could present his bold measures as carrying on the tradition of his predecessors—Stanley Pargellis sponsored conferences among scholars and funded fellowships, and even William Poole, the first librarian, had offered adult education courses in the 1890s— the ultimate Towner goal would change the character of the Newberry.

At the core of his thinking was what might be called a sociology of knowledge, if so pretentious a phrase was not so inappropriate for Bill Towner. Bill followed keenly the trends in scholarship of the 1960s. In a talk to the International Council of Librarians in Japan in 1969—a good vantage point from which to take a broad overview—he said he thought American studies was nothing less than "in the midst of a revolution": a technical revolution that made sources in microform widely available, a paperback revolution that made it possible for "students to afford libraries that their professors at one time could not get or afford," but above all a revolution in interpretation stemming from the conflicts in American society that had produced a generation of "New Left" challenges to "consensus history" (selection no. 8).

As Towner thought through the implications of the challenges of the 1960s he worked out a rationale for the centrality of the research library in American life (selection no. 9). "Knowledge of the past (literature, history, music, or philosophy) is indeed imperfect"; in

10. Ibid., no. 33 (Spring 1984).

fact, it was "always imperfect." Scholars were always discovering subjects that had escaped their attention. New sources were constantly being opened up. New techniques and new technologies made it possible to probe sources in new ways. But above all, "the emergence of social change drives our inquiries of the past." The awareness of contemporary social problems pushed scholars into a search for their "historical antecedents." As examples he cited the issues of violence, racism, Indian policy, and dissent. Anticipating the "heinous" charge of presentism ("judging the past by contemporary values"), he argued that seeking historical antecedents committed the scholar to no particular solution. Knowledge of the past will "always be imperfect" and the research library always necessary. It was a commitment to an unending process of revisionism as scholars responded to newly felt needs.

This was the imperative underlying Towner's vision of the "planned use" of the resources of the Newberry. That the times were ripe is a mild understatement. The number of graduate students and faculties were expanding exponentially. (Of 86,000 Ph.D.'s awarded in the humanities since 1920, he pointed out in 1980, 61,489 or nearly 72 percent had been granted since 1960.) By the late sixties history was breaking out of its old confines; new subfields were proliferating in social, ethnic, labor, urban, and later women's history. Foundations were responsive to the new trends; and in 1966 the National Endowment for the Humanities was founded.

The reason Towner could propose so bold a program for "effective use" in 1971 is that he had demonstrated the possibilities in programs he had already adopted at the Newberry. Since 1964 the Associated Colleges of the Midwest, a consortium of liberal arts colleges, had been conducting semester-long seminars in the humanities at the Newberry in which some twenty undergraduates took up residence in Chicago and pursued research around a common theme. Early on the trustees had set aside a fund for an expanded program of fellowships which was enlarged by several major grants from the Mellon foundation. Two scholarly projects were underway: the Northwestern-Newberry edition of *The Works of Herman Melville* and the *Atlas of Early American History* under the direction of Lester J. Cappon, since 1968 a scholar in residence at the Newberry.

And one research center, the Center for the History of Cartography, had come into being. The pieces just seemed to have fallen into place. The Newberry's collections of rare maps was already unique. In 1964 Kenneth Nebenzahl, an antiquarian bookdealer, later a trustee, endowed a lecture series in cartography in honor of his son. The inaugural lecturer in 1966, R. A. Skelton, Keeper of the Map Room at the British Museum, was asked to survey the Newberry's holdings and reported positively on the feasibility of a center. Two spectacular purchases, the Novacco and the Sack collections, followed in 1967 and 1968, making the map collection world-class. Then in 1969 Bill appointed David Woodward, a recent Ph.D. in geography from Wisconsin, Fellow and Bibliographer in Cartography. A center had come into being. In 1971 Hermon Dunlap Smith, chairman of the Board of Trustees and an avid collector of Midwestern maps, richly endowed the center which bears his name (selection no. 21).

With achievements such as these Towner had living demonstrations of what he now established as a principle in 1971. Positing two abstract extremes to define a library, either "(1) an inert mass of materials waiting patiently to be used by the regular or occasional scholar visitor on demand, [or] (2) an organized group of scholars in history and the humanities who happen to have a good library at their disposal," he clearly sought to locate Newberry toward the latter end of this spectrum. He thought of the library as "one of several varieties of educational institutions" whose objective was "the enlargement of mankind's knowledge and the sharing of that knowledge with as large an audience as is practical for the kind of institution it is" (selection no. 11).

He projected several "incipient programs" which rapidly became centers, the Center for the History of the American Indian (1971) and the Family and Community History Center (1973), and a Center for Humanities Education, which did not. And he tossed out ideas for centers for the History of the Book and another for the History of Linguistics. In 1980 the fourth and last center, devoted to Renaissance Studies, evolved out of a long tradition of conferences and seminars. Towner spelled out the criteria for a center: a "strong and growing collection of library materials in the field" as "an absolute prerequisite," "a demonstrable need," a "strongly felt interest on the part of the scholarly world," and, most practically, "an interested donor or donors."

Towner summed up the process in a colloquial talk using the Indian center as an example. "Here was a 95,000 volume collection, the Edward Ayer collection, plus 10,000 volumes on the history of the west, the Graff collection. The teaching of frontier history hardly exists east of the Mississippi except at Yale. The collections which dealt with the west were in our judgment, lying fallow. At the same time, here were peoples whose histories very badly needed to be rewritten. We combined the resources with the need and created a Center for the History of the American Indian."[11]

What Bill left unsaid was implicit in his choice for the first director of the center, D'Arcy McNickle, a distinguished scholar whom he regarded as its founder. McNickle, born on the Flathead Reservation, was a member of the Confederated Salish and Kootenai tribes. As Bill phrased it in his posthumous tribute, McNickle "was half Indian and half white, biologically. But in his essential self he was both totally Indian and totally 'European.'" He had been educated at a federal Indian boarding school, at the University of Montana, and then at Oxford. He was a man "with compassion for both sides in the historical tragedy of Indian white relations" (selection no. 22). What Bill also left unsaid was that he had taken two great Newberry collections that earlier generations of scholars had used primarily to tell the frontier story, following Turner, from the vantage point of American westward expansion, and turned them to the use of a new generation of scholars who were ready to look at the process from the vantage point of the Indians.

To Bill the Indian Center epitomized his ideal of the Newberry reaching out to a wide range of users. It publishes bibliographies, so far some thirty of them; it was home for the project that became *The Atlas of Great Lakes Indian History;* it offers fellowships for both pre- and postdoctoral scholars; and it sponsors scholarly conferences. It also runs an institute for high school teachers, particularly from areas where there are many Indians, and a program of fellowships to bring tribal historians to the Newberry to study their own histories.

Setting up the Family and Community History Center involved a similarly creative adaptation of Newberry collections to new scholarly interests. The Newberry's collections in genealogy and local history were first-rate, but the scholarship of genealogists rarely passed into mainstream history. In the late sixties one branch of the new social history took as its province the study of the history of the family, the small community, and the social basis of politics, applying the tools of quantitative analysis. Kenneth Lockridge, a young innovative scholar in the thick of such research, helped Bill conceptualize the Family and Community History Center which would turn collections gathered for one purpose to use for another.

11. Towner, "Address to the Society of Research Administrators, Chicago, 6 October 1980."

One by one the centers were "bought" by the scholarly communities they sought to serve; each did indeed fill a "felt need." At the same time the fellowship program for individual "random" scholarly use flourished, enhanced by support from the National Endowment for the Humanities. Under the leadership of Richard H. Brown, academic vice-president, the budget of the Division of Research and Education grew from $400,000 in 1973 to $1,600,000 in 1991. Not one "community of scholars" but a number of overlapping communities of scholars came and went, often achieving the critical mass Towner hoped for. One of the virtues of the centers was that they did not engage in what Towner called "programmed research," a term he put into quotation marks because he was uneasy with its implications for individual choice. Centers sponsored summer institutes, conferences, and seminars. If a center had its ups and downs, it had something to do with whether or not it was in sync with trends in scholarship in its field. By the time he retired in 1986 the Newberry had created in all but name the institute for advanced study in history and the humanities Towner had projected in 1971.

The renovated building dramatized the changes, a good "symbol of what the Newberry was all about," as Bill put it. Years of planning under the direction of Joel L. Samuels saw fruition. With all the books moved into the new ten-story stacks, space in the original building could now be apportioned to fit the needs of the new "educational institution." On the third floor is the general catalog with more than 3,000,000 cards, the computers that track everything catalogued since 1980, and an open reference and bibliography collection, a browser's paradise. The second floor holds the general reading room (with no invidious distinctions between genealogists and academic scholars) and enlarged space for microform reading. And on the fourth floor is a consolidated special collections reading room for manuscripts, maps and rare books, ample carrels for readers on fellowships, and space for the ongoing centers and long- or short-term projects. Six seminar rooms were created where there had been only one. The "communities of scholars" could flourish in the old Fellows Lounge (now the Lawrence W. Towner Fellows Lounge), or in a lounge and dining area on the fifth floor. The fifth floor also houses the conservation center. And on the first floor there are two large exhibition spaces to display the Newberry's riches, a bookstore, a large lofty room for lectures, concerts, meetings of the Newberry Associates or what-have-you, all tokens of the Newberry's outreach to larger publics. There too is the Office of Development, heart of the never-ending search for the support to sustain the new Newberry. The new internal architecture was proof that Towner's "architectonic" plan of 1971 had become a reality.

III

Bill Towner did not plan to become a spokesman for the country's independent research libraries in the 1970s and 1980s, much less a spokesman for the humanities community, testifying before congressional committees and making appearances in Washington. There was an air of necessity to the process. He was drawn into the public arena to create and extend new opportunities for funding the Newberry. With the creation of the National Endowment for the Humanities in 1966, new and unprecedented opportunities opened up for support from the federal government as well as an ongoing public debate as to how NEH money should be spent. Over time, as Newberry became one of the most frequent beneficiaries of NEH, Towner had a good deal to offer about the Newberry experience, and people were ready to listen.

In 1971 and 1972 Bill was the cofounder, with Marcus McCorison of the American Antiquarian Society and O. B. Hardison of the Folger Library, of the Independent Research Libraries Association (IRLA). It was an idea whose time had come. The fifteen libraries had common problems; they were hardly competitors. But in the vast post-Sputnik expansion of federal aid to education they had qualified for support neither as educational institutions nor public tax-supported libraries. In the early 1970s IRLA "began to lobby intensively for NEH support." By the mid-1970s NEH had set up a category of support explicitly for research libraries, and in the eyes of a former NEH staff member "much of the credit for establishing the program area should go to the research libraries themselves, especially the Independent Research Libraries Association," whose "chief spokesman" (and chairman from 1975 to 1977) was Bill Towner.[12]

Testifying in 1973 on behalf of both Newberry and IRLA, Towner said that "the National Endowment has become crucial to our [i.e., Newberry's] effective operation in meeting the growing opportunities to serve. . . . We need funds for almost every aspect of our operations—acquisitions, binding, conservation, construction, fellowships, and publications." When Senator Claiborne Pell asked him to

12. Stephen Miller, *Excellence and Equity: The National Endowment for the Humanities* (Lexington: University Press of Kentucky, 1984), 90–91.

establish priorities, Towner replied, "If I had to single out [one] overwhelming need . . . I think it would be to conserve what we already have . . . we are facing a crisis of major proportions . . . because of the deterioration of our books and manuscripts."[13] In the 1970s NEH began to allocate funds to the research libraries, but it did not earmark a fund for preservation until 1981, and then it was no more than a token for pilot projects. The problem remains staggering in its dimensions.

In the mid 1970s, as Bill began to speak out on humanities issues, it was clear how much had changed in American life and in academia. In retrospect, the 1960s and early 1970s were not only boom times but years of optimism. The turmoil over civil rights, the Vietnam War, or the counterculture was the result of movements that had posed questions for scholars to probe, created new fields of inquiry, and brought new blood into academic life. Moreover, the academic world, whatever its internal conflicts, was expanding, scholarly publishers were booming, and there was money. From the vantage point of the early 1990s it is clear how much Towner's bold plan for the future of the Newberry in 1971 reflected the opportunities and optimism of a period that had passed quickly. He had indeed seized the time.

If the late 1960s and early 1970s were a time of possibilities, the late 1970s and 1980s seemed to be a time of narrowing horizons. In 1978 when Towner testified in support of a White House Conference on the Humanities—an unlikely prospect which did not materialize—he drew a grim picture of American society:

> We as a people are confounded that the *Pax Americana* we thought we had established after the Second World War, a war so bravely and justly fought, could have been so quickly dissipated by the long, unjust, and undeclared war in Vietnam. And we are dismayed to find that our confident assumption that good intentions and dollars would earn us a just world at home has been proven wrong. The end results of the New Deal, the Fair Deal, the New Frontier, the Great Society, and the new Federalism seem to be a loss of faith in our national government; a ruinous inflation; an economy in neutral; high unemployment, a society divided on racial, sexual, and generational grounds; a people whose strongest institu-

13. U.S. Cong., Senate Committee on Labor and Public Welfare, House Committee on Education and Labor, Joint Hearings, *National Foundation on the Arts and Humanities Amendments of 1973*, 93d Cong., 1st sess., 6–8 March 1973, 797.

tion, the family, is in disarray and retreat; an urban culture whose urban centers are in decay; and an affluent society with great pockets of poverty. Bewildered we ask: Where did we go wrong, and what should be done to go right?

As he turned to the consequences for the humanities his picture was no less depressing:

> Enrollment in humanities courses and enlistment in humanities majors are down. . . . Liberal arts colleges, the traditional stronghold of the humanities, are caught in a vise of rising costs and declining enrollments. Underemployment and unemployment in academia are fast creating an academic proletariat. . . . University presses, one of whose chief functions is to publish the results of humanistic scholarship, are in deep financial difficulty. And finally libraries, those chief repositories of the sources for and results of humanistic scholarship, face seemingly insurmountable problems, the most devastating being the rapid physical deterioration of some seventy per cent of their collections.[14]

In 1981 the newly elected Reagan administration threatened drastic cuts in the budget for the NEH and proposed to eliminate funds for the National Historical Publications and Records Commission, the chief source of support for the great editorial projects on the founding fathers (on three of whose advisory boards Towner sat). Towner's congressional testimony bristled with indignation (selection no. 27). Towner spoke of the country's cultural and educational institutions as "besieged" and framed the question as "how shall we *defend* the humanities in the 1980s" (selection no. 28).

As he surveyed the scholarly publishing world he felt himself in the same rearguard action (selection no. 24). The heyday of the 1960s was over; within one year he had written letters to two universities to ward off dissolution of their presses. Changes in the commercial publishing world made university presses more important than ever: "The chain bookstores, the book clubs, and the ownership of publishing houses by monster corporations that often look only at the bottom line, threaten . . . the marketplace of ideas." It was the obligation of the presses "as plural agents in a pluralistic

---

14. "Statement by Lawrence W. Towner Regarding House Joint Resolution 639, Authorizing the President to Call a White House Conference on the Humanities," Chicago, 13 January 1978, typescript, Towner Papers, Newberry Library Archives.

society, to keep open to our society the free flow of ideas as expressed in books." Yet he did not spare those university press directors who had compounded the problem by "going big time," creating production lines that had to be fed, and placing "too much emphasis on prestige." Where, he asked, were the university presses in the "major, even revolutionary publishing ventures" of the past generation?

Even within the library world Bill wrote ruefully of "an end to innocence," including his own (selection no. 16). In the mid-1980s he called the emergence of "a wave" of thefts of library materials a "plague." Asking "How can this be happening?" he felt that "we librarians must certainly assume a significant part of the blame" as a result of "an indifference compounded by innocence, ignorance and complacency." As he described the Newberry's traumatic experiences and the security measures the Library had adopted, he wondered out loud at the "human costs" of creating an atmosphere of mistrust. "Will library security measures, like national security measures, possibly destroy the liberty we wish to defend?" It is an anguished reflection by someone who had poured so much energy into creating a community of scholars.

In the midst of these sea changes in American life, Bill saw the National Endowment for the Humanities as "a bright star in the often murky American skies." It was not just that the star shone so brightly on 60 West Walton Street, Chicago, but here was the federal government assuming for the humanities (and the National Endowment for the Arts for the arts) the same responsibility it had assumed decades before in the sciences.

The range of support NEH had given the Newberry was astonishing as Bill observed on the Endowment's twentieth anniversary.[15] The NEH had made major contributions to funding three of the four research centers (Indian History, Family and Community History, Renaissance Studies), it had funded two major atlases, and it had granted the Newberry funds for major fellowships to "regrant" to advanced scholars. These it could be said were all within the confines of traditional support for scholarship.

With the creation of its "Library Resources" program in the late 1970s, the NEH also made major grants to the Newberry for operational support of the Library: for acquisitions, construction, renovation, conservation. All of the latter grants were on the principle of the recipient finding matching funds, the Challenge Grant Program.

15. Towner, "The President's Corner," *Newberry Newsletter*, no. 36 (Winter 1986).

Thus in the spring of 1977 NEH offered Newberry $797,000 on a three-to-one basis, requiring the Library to raise $2,391,000 in three years from private sources. In January 1977 Towner was invited to Washington to receive the announcement of the new program, on behalf of the country's cultural institutions. In thanking President Gerald Ford, Bill expressed the opinion that the program would encourage support for "The Republic of Letters" by a "Democracy of Donors."[16] In December 1982 he was in the White House to receive notice from President Ronald Reagan of still another challenge grant of $750,000—for which the Newberry would have to raise $2,250,000—and this would be used to augment the Newberry's endowment, an unprecedented underwriting of the principle of ongoing federal support for the independent research library.

"Why the Newberry Library?" Bill asked out loud. "Why so much from the NEH over such a long stretch?" The first part of the answer I had heard given by an NEH program officer in response to the same question at a public meeting: "Let's face it, because their proposals are so good." The second part of the answer is less obvious: "because," as Bill put it, "our goals happily coincide with the goals of the National Endowment for the Humanities. In short we succeed with the NEH because we help the NEH meet its congressionally mandated goals and because we deserve it."[17]

NEH, to put it another way, needed the Newberry as much as the Newberry needed NEH. NEH could point with pride to Newberry as a model. Moreover, Newberry thrived whatever the political orientation of the NEH chairman. Bill was on close terms with the first three: Barnaby Keeney (1966–1968), Ronald H. Berman (1968–1976), and Joseph Duffey (1976–1980). Because Bill was a consistent and influential public supporter of NEH, the chairmen sought him out. When the full history of the NEH is written, scholars should find much to enlighten them in the numerous boxes in the Towner Papers at the Newberry labeled "N.E.H."

There was still another often-overlooked reason why the Newberry and NEH were a good fit. The Newberry, in Bill's words, provided "a bridge between the world of academe and the private, unaffiliated scholarly minded public." Newberry attempted to "reach out to wide lay audiences in successful attempts to involve them in the humanities."[18] Towner took part in a variety of public programs

---

16. Ibid., no. 9 (Spring 1977).
17. Ibid., no. 30 (Winter 1983); ibid., no. 36 (Winter 1986).
18. Ibid., no. 36 (Winter 1986).

funded by NEH. Beginning in 1973, he served on the Board of the Illinois Humanities Council with such success that the council elected him chairman and honored him after he left it in 1979 by establishing the "Lawrence W. Towner Award for the Best Risk-taking Proposal." They got him right.

From the first debates in Congress authorizing the establishment of the NEH and its twin, the NEA, there was a sharp difference of opinion between supporters of "public programs" and so-called pure scholarship. Leaders of the American Council of Learned Societies, the umbrella group in the humanities, saw the National Science Foundation as their model, supporting research by scholars. Senator Pell, often referred to as the "father of NEH," envisioned a major emphasis on "outreach" or public programs, and the congressional mandate ended up with both, the proportions changing under different chairmen.

The Newberry was unique in developing both kinds of programs, a clear reflection of Towner's long-standing rejection of the "trickle down" theory of knowledge. In its basic function as a research library, Towner, like his predecessors, maintained open access to a wide range of users. He could report with pride on the ever-increasing number of advanced scholars, Ph.D. candidates, and M.A. students who used the Library each year. But he could also rattle off the number of "user-days" by genealogists and was proud of the "service that came in out of the cold" (selection no. 15). He also was proud that a long line of nonprofessional scholars worked at the Newberry, and he kept a shelf of books in his office with Lloyd Lewis's biography of Grant, the works of Arthur and Lila Weinberg on Clarence Darrow, and of Ralph Korngold on Wendell Phillips, William Lloyd Garrison, and Toussaint L'Overture, among others.

Under Towner's direction outreach went further. The Indian Center had a program for tribal historians and another for high school teachers of Indian history. The Family and Community Center was the home of the Metro History Fair with its thousands of Chicago area high school students. And each semester the library sponsored a Lyceum of short courses for adults on Newberry-related themes. With the new exhibition halls it was possible to display the library's riches or traveling exhibits for the general public. And with the large multipurpose hall it was possible to present lectures or concerts based on the Newberry's vast collections of music.

Bill savored the headlines on two articles he thought caught the Newberry spirit: "The Swinging Dowager of Walton Street" (the headline on a story in the old *Chicago Daily News*), and "What Do a Cherokee Indian and a Polish Scholar have in Common? They Are Both Doing Research at the Newberry Library" (*Wall Street Journal*).[19] Towner had converted the Newberry into what very likely was the most nonelite scholarly institution in the country.

But when at intervals the pressure was on NEH to shift support from public programs at the expense of scholarship or to the state councils at the expense of national programs, and especially when the charge of "elitism" was leveled at support for scholarship, Towner was unequivocal in defense of scholarship. His letter to Senator Pell in 1976 is an eloquent refutation of the notion that advanced scholarship is inherently "elitist," arguing that "there is no real dichotomy between 'elite' studies on the one hand and public programs on the other" (selection no. 26).

On his retirement in 1986, as Bill looked back on his twenty-four years at the Newberry, he clearly had achieved the vision of the Library he had laid out in his 1971 plan. It is characteristic, however, that in the history of the Library he wrote on the occasion of its one-hundredth anniversary he sums up the last quarter of a century almost without mentioning his own role (selection no. 10). He had maintained the preeminence of the Newberry as an "uncommon collection of uncommon collections." He had taken two giant steps to preserve its resources by constructing a new stack building and making it a pacesetter in conservation. He had promoted "effective use" with what was at the time the largest fellowship program attached to a library and the largest program of research centers and special projects. And he had reached out to new participants in the humanities on an unusual scale. He had even found new ways to "pay for the whole shebang."

But just as his own achievements had been shaped by the context of the times and the problems and opportunities at the Newberry, so it was likely that the Newberry of the next quarter century would be shaped by forces both within and without the Library. Fundraising inevitably would have a high priority. As a library Newberry was most likely to grow, not by expensive spectacular purchases but one by one and day by day, especially as computer technologies allowed librarians to establish bibliographic control of what was already available at other libraries. Preservation would have to com-

19. Joseph Haas, "The Newberry: Our Swinging Dowager on the Streets of Academe," *Panorama, Chicago Daily News* (27–28 March 1971): 4–6; John Ryan, "Why Are a Cherokee and a Polish Scientist at Bughouse Square? They're Using the Newberry, a Chicago Library That Is One of the Nation's Finest," *Wall Street Journal*, 20 March 1978, 1–13.

mand an increasing share of the total budget. Fellowships were likely to be even more important as academic institutions retrenched. The research centers, built as they were on the *sine qua non* of extending use of Newberry collections, would be tested by their capacity to respond to changing needs as they were felt in their scholarly communities.

As to the outlook for the humanities in the American future, Towner, whatever his innermost disappointments at the bleak trends in American society, still offered a counsel of "turning problems into opportunities." The agenda he offered at the beginning of the 1980s for the "defense of the humanities" is arguably still an agenda for the 1990s (selection no. 28). Always the historian, Towner could put into perspective the gains he had seen over a lifetime. These were the resources: "the largest community of highly educated men and women ever known," an unprecedented number of people with advanced degrees in the humanities, the largest educational establishment in the world, new humanities centers—the Rockefeller Foundation identified some one hundred in 1980— "peerless library resources," the NEH in a period of "unimagined growth and maturity." With such resources, he thought, "we should see not a retrenchment of the humanities, but a regeneration; not a blight, but a flowering; not a fall, but a spring."

This was less a prediction than a statement of possibilities which left room for the variable of human agency. "To survive the eighties and beyond," Towner argued, "we will have to be like the shark— aggressive, tough and adaptable." "We" meant the humanities community as a whole. If "we" have not achieved the "regeneration" and the "flowering" that Towner saw as possible, perhaps humanist scholars should look within themselves to ask how aggressive and adaptable they have been. In Bill Towner's achievement at the Newberry they have an example of the difference human agency can make.

Alfred F. Young

I

HISTORIAN

★

"A FONDNESS FOR FREEDOM": SERVANT PROTEST IN PURITAN SOCIETY

Most of the assumptions scholars now take for granted about the persons in servitude in colonial America—slaves, indentured servants, apprentices, and criminals—were unproven when Towner wrote this article. At a time when historians assumed a consensual society, he established that there was social protest; that the attitudes and opinions of the "inarticulate" at the bottom of the society could be recovered; that acts authority categorizes as acts of criminality and delinquency could be interpreted as protest.

In this article, which expanded on a theme of his dissertation, Towner compressed some 1500 cases into one table placing it in one footnote (see n. 42). He analyzed "Servant Protest by Type of Servant and Kind of Protest, 1629–1750," breaking it down into four time periods. He recognized five categories of servants and three types of protest: legal (which was rarely recorded in specifics), unruly protest (recorded in cases in which masters took their servants to court), and runaways (found mostly through newspaper advertisements). Rarely has a scholar said so much with such economy.

The essay was successful and is still a standard, frequently cited. It helped to have the Reverend Cotton Mather on his side of the argument.

ON MAY 25, 1721, the prison on Boston's Queen Street lost a star boarder to the gallows: Joseph Hanno, emancipated Negro slave, was hanged for doing in his wife "in a very barbarous manner." Hanno had received a religious education, he had been baptized, and he had become a candidate for communion. Not unnaturally, the act of bashing in his wife's head spoiled his chances of joining the elect in

From *William and Mary Quarterly*, 3d ser., 19 (1962): 201–19. Reprinted with permission.

this world, but almost to the last and fatal moment hope was held out for his chances in the next.

Earlier in May, the Reverend Cotton Mather of North Church had noted Hanno's impending execution as an opportunity to do a good deed, and he thereupon visited, instructed, and counseled the poor prisoner in an attempt to lead him to salvation. While Hanno died repentant but unsaved, Providence so ordered it that his execution date coincided with Mather's midweek lecture. Following well-established custom, Mather preached an execution sermon, which he titled *Tremenda. The Dreadful Sound with which the Wicked are to be Struck* . . . and which, along with the hanging, attracted a large audience including Hanno and many slaves. The occasion demanded animadversions on the wicked sin of murder and exhortatory remarks on the proper behavior of husbands toward their wives. But Hanno's former status as a slave, the composition of the audience, and the fact that marriage and servitude both fell under family government led Mather to observations on slavery itself. Sorrowfully, he pointed out that Hanno had been emancipated "into a *Liberty*, which he had been too unthankful for." Turning to the slaves in his audience, he went on, "There is a *Fondness* for *Freedom* in many of you, who live Comfortably in a very easy Servitude; wherein you are not so *Well-advised* as you should be." "If you were *Free*," he said, "many of you would not *Live* near so well as you do." Even were your servitude very hard, you ought to live patiently under it, because slavery was "what GOD will have to be, *The Thing Appointed for you.*" Happily, "Your *Servitude* is *Gentle* . . . you are treated, with more than meer *Humanity*, and fed and clothed and lodged, as well as you can wish for, and you have no *Cares* upon you, but only to *Come when you are called*, and to *Do what you are Bidden.* . . . "[1]

If Mather had an inkling that having to "*Come when you are called*" and "*Do what you are Bidden*" was in any way connected with a "*Fondness for Freedom*," he did not reveal it. Nor could he be expected to do so. What was required were statements of the obvious and the accepted so that Hanno's execution would confirm in Mather's listeners the kind of behavior they ought to exhibit lest

1. Worthington C. Ford, ed., *Diary of Cotton Mather* . . . (Massachusetts Historical Society, *Collections*, Ser. 7, VII–VIII [Boston, 1911–12]), II, 618, 620, 623, and n. Cotton Mather, *Tremenda* . . . (Boston, 1721), passim, and especially 23–27; Worthington C. Ford and others, eds., *Journals of the House of Representatives of Massachusetts*. . . (Boston, 1919–), II, 286–287.

they follow Hanno to the gallows. To the modern reader, however, the juxtaposition of the idea of liberty, as expressed in the actions of the servants Mather was talking to, and the idea of authority, implicit in the subservience described so seductively, raises a whole series of questions. What were the obvious and accepted ideas that Mather voiced about slavery? If servitude was an accepted institution, how did it fit into society, and how was it rationalized? If Negroes had a "Fondness for Freedom," how did it manifest itself, and did it extend to other kinds of servants? Finally, what significance should be attached to this alleged "Fondness for Freedom"?

Servitude in Puritan Massachusetts included several different kinds or ranks of servants. "Some are more Free," said Samuel Willard, pastor of South Church, "and others more in Bondage. . . ." First came servants by compact or agreement, "most *honourable*" of all. He had in mind apprentices and indentured and hired servants, the servant elite. Next came those who entered servitude by "*self Alienation*," either by themselves or by their parents, or through debt or some pecuniary crime. These included poor-apprentices, debtors, and domestic criminals. Last were slaves, Indians and Negroes, either captured in war and sold into slavery or born into it, for, said Willard, "though Men are not naturally Servants as they are Men; yet Men may be born Servants, being descended of such Parents as are so."[2] Before the death of John Winthrop in 1649, each of these types had come into being in Massachusetts. There were a few Negro and Indian slaves and servants,[3] and a few debtors and criminals,[4] but the bulk of the servants were of the "most honourable" type who had emigrated to America

2. Samuel Willard, *A Compleat Body of Divinity in two Hundred and Sixty Expository Lectures on the Assembly's Shorter Catechism* . . . (Boston, 1726), 614. This book, the first folio volume published in British North America, was printed on several presses. As a result, an error was made in pagination so that page numbers 581–666 are repeated. The references to pages within that group of numbers in this article refers to the second set.

3. Negroes and Indians constituted less than 10 per cent of the bound labor force before 1650. See Lawrence W. Towner, A Good Master Well Served: A Social History of Servitude in Massachusetts, 1620–1750 (unpubl. Ph.D. diss., Northwestern University, 1955), Appendix J. Available on microfilm, University Microfilms, Ann Arbor, Mich.; hereafter cited as Towner, A Good Master.

4. See John Noble and John F. Cronin, eds., *Records of the Court of Assistants of . . . Massachusetts* . . . , 3 vols. (Boston, 1901–28), II, 32, 132; hereafter cited as Noble and Cronin, eds., *Assistants*. I could locate no cases for servitude for debt before the 1670's but the 1641 law making provision for such service suggests there may have been some. See William H. Whitmore, comp., *The Colonial Laws of Massachusetts* . . . (Boston, 1889), 123–124.

from England between 1629 and 1641.[5] For the most part they had come voluntarily and after relatively careful scrutiny as to their suitability.

Most of these servants were incorporated into the society through the agency of the family. A few came alone to Massachusetts to work for absentee masters,[6] a few score came as servants to the company under overseers,[7] and a handful worked as labor gangs for private individuals,[8] but most came as parts of families or were taken into families on their arrival.[9] They lived under their master's roofs, ate at their tables, shared their workaday world, joined in family prayers, and were disciplined under family government. Such an intimate relationship made it absolutely necessary that the master be concerned not only with getting labor from his servant, but with making the servant conform to the general behavior pattern sanctioned by himself and demanded by society. Otherwise his family would suffer materially and his family government would come under the suspicion of the authorities, who saw in the family the nursery for good Puritans and in family government the first line of defense against the unregenerate.[10]

This system of exacting labor and inculcating proper behavior from single persons by means of the authority of the head of a family was established in Massachusetts almost silently, with little or no rationalization in literature and very little definition in law. As Englishmen, the Puritans were well acquainted with apprenticeship and poor-apprenticeship as long-term forms of contract labor, and

5. See appendixes A (Apprentice Contracts) and B (Contract Servants) in Towner, A Good Master.

6. For examples, see John Humphrey to Isaac Allerton, Dec. 17, 1630, in Massachusetts Historical Society, *The Winthrop Papers*, 5 vols. (Boston, 1929–47), II, 334–335; Sir Matthew Boynton to John Winthrop, Jr., 1636, *ibid.*, III, 247; Thomas Hewson to John Winthrop, Mar. 7, 1636, *ibid.*, III, 234–235.

7. See Nathaniel B. Shurtleff, ed., *Records of the Governor and Company of the Massachusetts Bay* . . . , 5 vols. in 6 (Boston, 1853–54), I, appendix, passim; Thomas Hutchinson, *The History of the Colony and Province of Massachusetts Bay*, ed. Lawrence Shaw Mayo, 3 vols. (Cambridge, Mass., 1936), I, 19.

8. See the agreement between William Tyng and John Reade in Thomas Lechford's "Notebook," American Antiquarian Society, *Archaeologia Americana*, VII (Cambridge, Mass., 1885), 94–100.

9. The handiest list of emigrating families, with their servants, is in Charles Edward Banks, *The Planters of the Commonwealth . . . 1620–1640* (Boston, 1930), Pt. ii, passim. See also Towner, A Good Master, 50–60.

10. See Edmund S. Morgan, *The Puritan Family . . .* (Boston, 1956), passim, but particularly chap. 4.

the Statute of Artificers and the Elizabethan poor law had accustomed them to hiring agricultural labor by the year.[11] Moreover, the concept of rank and order in society was generally accepted and needed no special elaboration in terms of servitude. John Winthrop, on board the *Arbella*, had prefaced his design for Massachusetts, *A Modell of Christian Charity*, with the since often-quoted assumption that "God Almightie in his most holy and wise providence hath soe disposed of the Condicion of mankinde, as in all times some must be rich some poore, some highe and eminent in power and dignitie; others meane and in subieccion."[12]

The responsibility a master had concerning the way a servant fitted into society was also taken for granted. Thus when a correspondent in England recommended an Irish Catholic boy to the Winthrops, he devoted only a sentence to what the servant could do; the rest of the recommendation concerned the boy's salvation. "This is a verie tractable fellowe," the letter said, "and yet of a hardie and stout corage. . . . At his first comminge over [to England] he would not goe to church; nor come to prayers; but first we gatt him up to prayers and then on the lords day to catachise, and afterwards very willingly he hath bin at church 4 or 5 tymes; he as yet makes conscience of fridayes fast from flesh; and doth not love to heare the Romish rel[igion] spoken against, but I hope with gods grace he will become a good convert. . . . As for his fittnesse to be a member of your church; it's well if the Lord worke it in 3 or 4 yeare, yet he can doe it sooner if he please. . . ."[13]

By the end of the seventeenth century, however, times had changed. The family was not performing the functions it was supposed to perform, or at least not so well as was desirable.[14] The servants, difficult enough when they had been rather carefully selected, had changed to a melange of Indians, Negroes, non-English whites, debtors, and colonial criminals thrown in with the local young men and women. By the 1720's and 1730's Negroes and non-English whites would outnumber the imported labor and, with the Indians,

11. Richard B. Morris, *Government and Labor in Early America* (New York, 1946), 3–16; Margaret Gay Davies, *The Enforcement of English Apprenticeship . . . 1563–1642* (Cambridge, Mass., 1956), 1–14, et passim.

12. John Winthrop, "A Modell of Christian Charity . . . ," *Winthrop Papers,* II, 282. For a later expression see William Hubbard, "The Happiness of a People," in Perry Miller and Thomas H. Johnson, eds., *The Puritans* (New York, 1938), 247–250.

13. Edward Howes to John Winthrop, Jr., 1633, *Winthrop Papers*, III, 133–135.

14. For legislation reflecting this see *Mass. Recs.,* III, 355 (1654), IV, Pt. ii, 34–35 (1661), 43 (1662), 395–396 (1668), V, 59–64 (1675), 240–241 (1679), 373 (1682).

possibly all forms of bound labor.[15] In this situation, laws and rationalization defining the system and ordering it in society were called for. In response, Cotton Mather published one book on the family and three on servitude; the Reverend Benjamin Wadsworth published a book on the family; and Samuel Willard, preaching 246 sermons on the greater catechism, devoted five of them to family relationships, including one to masters and servants.[16]

Willard's work, later published as *A Compleat Body of Divinity*, does the best job of fitting servitude into the family, the family into society, and society into the complex framework of Puritan ideology. He sketched out a great chain reaching from God's awful majesty through the ranks of angels and men and animals down to inanimate objects. "One part of the Harmony in Heaven," he said, "is the Order there is among the Angels; and were there not something of it upheld among the Rebel Rout of Devils, Hell must disband."[17] Under the rubric of the Fifth Commandment, Willard analyzed the "*Ranks and Orders among Mankind in this World*," which "*God hath appointed*," including the relationships embraced within that "first foundation of Humane Societies," the family. Within the family, the servile relationship was the least natural. Here Willard took exception to the pagan philosophers who saw dominion and servitude as an expression of natural law. They were ignorant, he said, of man's primitive "State of Perfection." Man had been created in "a State of Liberty" and had been expected, once having reached the age of reason, to be "at his own dispose." Like government itself, however, the dominion of master over servant was made necessary by man's fall from Grace. "All Servitude," said Willard, "began in the Curse. . . . And such is the Condition of some that they do fall unavoidably under this State, and are made Servants of others."[18]

15. See Towner, A Good Master, Appendix J. This shows, on a basis of 7,066 servants recovered from 1620–1750, that bound whites, for example, decreased from 95 per cent of the servants, 1620–40, to 58 per cent in 1711–20, to 25 per cent in 1741–50, while Negroes increased from less than 5 per cent, to 35 per cent, to 70 per cent in the same period.

16. Cotton Mather, *A Good Master Well Served* . . . (Boston, 1696); *The Servant of Abraham* . . . (Boston, 1716), no known copy in existence; *The Negro Christianized.* . . (Boston, 1706); *A Family Well-Ordered* . . . (Boston, 1699); *Family Religion.* . . . 2d ed. (Boston, 1707); Benjamin Wadsworth, *The Well-Ordered Family* . . . (Boston, 1712, 1719); Willard, *A Compleat Body of Divinity*, 601–617, 647–649.

17. Willard, *A Compleat Body of Divinity*, 107–129, quotation on 598.

18. *Ibid.* The sermons on the Fifth Commandment fall on pages 597–655; on the family, pages 601–617, and 647–649; on servants particularly, 613–617. The quotations above are from pages 597, 598, 609, 613–614.

Servitude, like marriage, could be made to work only when the rules were observed. These were variously grounded in custom, in law, in oral and written contracts, and in the Bible. But Willard turned to the *"Law of Nature, or the Moral Law,"* as expressed in Matt. 7:12: *"Therefore all things whatsoever ye would that men should do to you, do ye even so to them. . . ."* From it came general laws of behavior embracing servitude. Masters must have love for their servants shaping their commands over them and their care for them. In governing they should avoid unlawful commands and "undue threatenings," and they should correct their servants with humanity, allowing them full opportunity to plead their innocence of wrongdoing. In caring for their servants they should nurture both soul and body. Servants, in turn, had reciprocal duties. They were to show a reverential fear of their masters, obey them cheerfully, serve them diligently, and be patient and submissive, even under those who were hard. If these rules were obeyed, servitude would prosper families and be a bulwark to society.[19]

It was unfortunate for the well-ordering of servitude, for good government in families, and for society as a whole that there was, as Willard put it, a "disorderly Disposition in Men . . ." that "makes those in Superiour Order apt to be Boundless and Arbitrary, and so Tyrannical; and such as are Inferiour to be uneasy, and not willing to bear the Yoke, or be under any Command."[20] Here was the root of servant protest as the Puritans saw it: the wickedness of some masters which led them to become little tyrants imposing a thousand petty cruelties and indignities upon their servants and thus forcing them to protest; and a like wickedness on the part of some servants which led them to a thousand petty violations of their obligations to their masters.

Experience and ideology made the Puritans well aware that mankind was corrupt and likely to run into diverse enormities, and they allowed for that fact even on the part of masters. The Body of Liberties in 1641 provided protection for servants who should flee from the "Tiranny and crueltie of their masters," by permitting them to seek refuge with neighbors so long as the masters and the nearest magistrates were notified.[21] If a servant is "injuriously treated," wrote Willard, "he may make his orderly application to the Civil Magistrate, whose Duty it is impartially to afford him a redress upon

19. *Ibid.,* 614–617.
20. *Ibid.,* 598.
21. Whitmore, comp., *Colonial Laws,* 51.

a clear Proof of it. . . ."[22] Protests of this sort, against abuses by the master, were quite legitimate; and failure to behave himself properly toward one under his authority left a master subject to censure by the community, punishment by the courts, and possible loss of his servant.[23]

Most cases of legal protest were based on physical abuses and on contract violations. Many were suits for freedom, which, because they could not be based on an inalienable right to liberty, an idea not yet accepted, though it was available, had to be based on violations of the accepted conditions of servitude. These included an ingenious variety of beatings and sexual abuse by masters, mistresses, and sons of the family; denial of adequate food, clothing, shelter, and care in time of sickness; removal of a servant from the colony or his transfer to another master contrary to his indenture; failure to teach a trade as promised; employment at menial tasks unconnected with a trade; arbitrary extension of the time of service; and in one instance the sale of an Indian servant's three children as slaves.[24]

One poor petitioner, William Henwood, had come to Massachusetts, paying his own way, but had been sold, he said, for thirty shillings to one Thomas Peachey. His master's family, he complained, "is so disordered as I can never expeckt to learn any good of him

22. Willard, *A Compleat Body of Divinity*, 616–617.

23. See the case of William Franklin in John Winthrop, *The History of New England. . .*, ed. James Savage (Boston, 1853), II, 225–227, master excommunicated and hanged for causing his servant's death. For loss of a servant, see case of James Harmon in Suffolk County Court Records, photostat copy, "Suffolk 1680–1692," 2 vols., I, 39 (1680), Office of the Clerk for Civil Business, Superior Court, Suffolk County Court House, Boston; hereafter cited as Suffolk County Court. For others see Towner, *A Good Master*, 258–269.

24. The following examples will illustrate my point. George F. Dow, ed., *Records . . . of the Quarterly Courts of Essex County . . .*, 8 vols. (Salem, 1911–21), I, 83 (1645, beating); *ibid.*, I, 111 (1646, not teaching trade); *ibid.*, III, 172 (1664, transfer to other masters); hereafter cited as *Essex County Court*. Noble and Cronin, eds., *Assistants*, I, 199 (1681, rape). Suffolk County Court, I, 182 (1683, inadequate food and clothes). Records of the Suffolk County General Sessions of the Peace, IV, 410 (1732, put out in midwinter while pregnant), Office of the Clerk of the Supreme Judicial Court, Suffolk County Court House; hereafter cited as Suffolk Sessions; *ibid.*, IV, 113–115 (1727, time added, master leaving country). Samuel E. Morison, ed., *Records of the Suffolk County Court, 1671–1680* (Colonial Society of Massachusetts, *Publications*, XXIX–XXX [Boston, 1933]), Pt. I, 155 (1672, failure to teach trade, employment at menial tasks); hereafter cited as *Suffolk County Court*. Records of the Plymouth County General Sessions of the Peace, III, 67 (1726/7, children of servants bound out), Office of the Clerk of Court, Plymouth County Court House; hereafter cited as Plymouth Sessions. Winthrop, *History*, II, 225–227 (1644, murder and abuse).

nither for soule nor body: he did ingage to teach me his traid of a Tailourr: but for his other Traides I hope god will give me more grace then to learn. His humour is such that I am afraid of my life if I shold be forced to abid out my Tim with him. . . ."[25] Protests of this kind, if properly voiced by "orderly application to the civil magistrate," gained the ear of society, and if proved, resulted in redress. Roughly 55 per cent of the cases which arose out of abuses by masters were decided in favor of the servants.[26]

Not all protests arose from the disorderly disposition of masters, however. Many come out of the same disposition on the part of "such as are inferiour," which led them to be "uneasy, and not willing to bear the yoke, or be under any command." Such protests found expression in unruly, often vicious, and usually illegal behavior. In one way or another, most acts of unruly protest were anticipated by the do's and don't's of the typical indenture of apprenticeship: his master he shall well and truly serve; his secrets he shall keep; all his commands he shall everywhere do and perform; hurt unto his master he shall not do, nor consent to be done; taverns or ordinaries he shall not frequent; fornication he shall not commit; unlawful games he shall not play; the goods of his master he shall not waste; from his master's service he shall not absent himself either by day or night; and he shall behave himself in all his term as a true and faithful servant ought to do.[27]

These rules were the norm to which all servants were expected to conform. To the extent that they did not, they violated their duties as servants, weakened family government, and threatened to reduce society to a rout. By doing what they wanted to do instead of what they were supposed to do, they were consciously or unconsciously asserting that "Fondness for Freedom" which Mather found so ill advised. Their masters described them as stubborn, disrespectful, disorderly, incorrigible, self-willed, rebellious, sullen, insulting,

25. Petition of William Henwood, Oct. 1681, Middlesex County Court Files, File 95, Office of the Clerk of Court, Middlesex County Court House, Cambridge, Mass.; hereafter cited as Middlesex Files.

26. Based on approximately 200 cases to be found largely in printed and manuscript court records and cited in Towner, A Good Master, 258–269.

27. For an apprentice indenture see sample in Morgan, The Puritan Family, 71–72. Contracts of indentured servants were simpler than those for apprentices and did not spell out in detail the kind of behavior expected. For an easily accessible servant indenture see Abbot Emerson Smith, Colonists in Bondage . . . (Chapel Hill, 1947), 18. It is almost identical with one dated 1717 from Massachusetts to be found in the Public Notary Books of Stephen and Mitchell Sewall, I, 141, Office of the Clerk of Courts, Essex County Court House, Salem.

abusive, saucy, and wicked. They were also called useless, unfaithful, lazy, rude, unmannerly, desperate, neglectful, and untoward. Moreover, they were found to be of wicked disposition, inclined toward crossness and disobedience, and worst of all, quite capable of resisting authority.[28] The acts which generated such enthusiastic recrimination were many and varied. They included tavern keeping and drunkenness; theft and burglary; sexual aberration such as seduction of masters' daughters or sons, homosexuality, bestiality, rape, and miscegenation; striking masters or other responsible adults; running away; arson; murder; and suicide.[29]

Such behavior was a far cry from that of the servant recommended to Margaret Winthrop as one who would be "as absolutely, and humbly at your command as any that ever you could have,"[30] and equally far from the ideal Cotton Mather set forth in his book, *A Good Master Well Served*. "Servants," Mather said, "You are the *Animate, Separate, Active Instruments* of other men. *Servants*, your *Tongues*, your *Hands*, your *Feet*, are your *Masters*, and they should move according to the Will of your *Masters*."[31] A far cry, but it may be questioned whether the acts which today are described as delinquency or criminality deserve to be ennobled by the term, protest. Fornication, for example, might have some other motivation! Yet fornication and other offenses hardly signified contented acceptance of the obligations inherent in the servant role. Violations of the mores of servitude, in fact, were active refusals to abide by the duties of one's condition. Murder and stealing, for example were (and still are) not only acts of aggression against individuals but protests against society and its prescriptions. And servitude, it must be re-

28. These terms are taken from actual cases in the period 1629–1750.
29. See the following cases for examples, "Deposition of William Knapp and Hugh Tilley," *Winthrop Papers*, IV, 131 (1639, drunkenness, filthy railing speeches). *Boston Gazette*, July 17, 1750 (tavern keeping). Suffolk County Court, I, 207 (1684, night walking, abusive speech, propositioning a woman). Records of the Superior Court of Judicature, I, 2 (1686, riot and assault), Office of the Clerk of the Supreme Judicial Court, Suffolk County Court House. Bristol General Sessions of the Peace, II, 96 (1706, fornication with master's daughter), Office of the Clerk of Court, Bristol County Court House, Taunton; hereafter cited as Bristol Sessions. *Ibid.*, I, 46–47 (1699/1700, buggery). Dow, ed., *Essex County Court*, I, 44 (1642, "unseemly practices" between two maids). *Ibid.*, I, 133n (1647, striking master with pitchfork). Noble and Cronin, eds., *Assistants*, II, 121 (1643, theft and fornication). *Ibid.*, II, 100. (1640, arson). *Ibid.*, I, 30, 32 (1674, murder of master). *New England Weekly Journal* (Boston), Oct. 27, 1729 (suicide).
30. John Winthrop, Jr., to Margaret Winthrop [1638], *Winthrop Papers*, IV, 68–69.
31. Cotton Mather, *A Good Master Well Served*, 38.

membered, was not simply an obligation to labor but a complex set of obligations involving every aspect of daily life.

In a number of instances, unruly behavior quite clearly arose out of specific discontents with the condition of being a servant. An early case concerned two servants who drowned while seeking oysters. "One of them," Winthrop said, "being reproved for his lewdness, and put in mind of hell, answered, that if hell were ten times hotter, he had rather be there than he would serve his master. The occasion was, because he had bound himself for divers years, and saw that, if he had been at liberty, he might have had greater wages, though otherwise his master used him very well." In the second case, a servant suicide, Winthrop recorded that the servant had been addicted to cursing and was a thief. "His discontent," said Winthrop, arose "from the long time he was to serve his master, (though he were well used)." [32] In a later instance, one of two servants who had murdered their master confessed that "His *Pride* had been his *Bane;* For, he thought much of it, that such a one as *he,* should be a *Servant;* and he would sometimes utter such words as these, *I am Flesh and Blood, as well as my Master, and therefore I know no Reason, why my Master should not obey me, as well as I obey him.*" [33]

The Puritans themselves taught a connection between unruly behavior and an uneasiness in servitude. A reading of the various execution sermons and broadsides leads one to this conclusion quite readily. Sin was all of a piece, and minor sins led almost inevitably to other, and worse, sins. According to Cotton Mather, the one sin which most dying malefactors bewailed was "Oh my Disobedience to my Parents, . . . and my Ungovernableness, under such Parents, and Masters, as God had given me!" Thus, in an execution sermon one Hugh Henderson, an Irish servant who confessed to drinking, stealing, cursing, Sabbathbreaking, gaming, whoring, and housebreaking, for which latter sin he was about to die, was quoted as saying: "I would solemnly Warn all *Children and Servants* that they be sure to be obedient to their Parents, and Masters and Mistresses: Disobedience being a dangerous Inlet to much other wickedness." [34]

32. Winthrop, *History,* I, 126 (1633), 216–217 (1635).
33. Cotton Mather, *Pillars of Salt* . . . (Boston, 1699), 68.
34. *Ibid.,* 55; John Campbell, *After Souls by Death are Separated from their Bodies. . .* (Boston, 1738), 34–36. For others, see: Increase Mather, *The Wicked Man's Portion. . .* (Boston, 1675, 1685); Cotton Mather, *Pillars of Salt,* passim; Samuel Danforth, *The Cry of Sodom Enquired Into* . . . (Cambridge, Mass, 1674); Samuel and Joseph Moody, *A Faithful Narrative* . . . (Boston, 1738); *Declaration and Confession*

But the best statement of the connection between unruly behavior and a "Fondness for Freedom" was written by another minister, Benjamin Wadsworth, in his twice-printed book on the family. After cataloguing the servant sins of disobedience, idleness, lying, stealing, and running away, he asked, rhetorically: why do servants behave as they do? "Possibly," he answered, "some Servants are very high, proud, stout, they'll scarce bear to be commanded or restrained; they are for much liberty. They must have liberty for their tongues to speak almost what and when they please; liberty to give or receive visits of their own accord, and when they will; liberty to keep what company they please; liberty to be out late on nights, to go and come almost when they will, without telling why or wherefore; such liberty they contend for, they wont be ruled, governed, restrained; or it may be the work they are set about, they reckon 'tis beneath and below them, they wont stoop to do it, but will rather disobey Masters or Mistresses." Such servants, he said, "are very wicked. They are daring in their plain disobedience to God, [in] their abominable rebellion against him: they trample God's law, his Authority, under their feet."[35]

A good example of this daring disobedience to authority is the case of Jerathmeel Bowers, which Professor Edmund S. Morgan found in the Middlesex County Court for the seventeenth century. Bowers, a servant to a patient and long-suffering family man, was in 1669 hailed into court after having been taken to the local minister for counseling and to the selectmen, twice, for reprimands. He had been persistently absent without permission, neglectful of his duties, bothersome to other men's servants, and destructive of his master's property. He had celebrated the leniency of the selectmen, who accepted his plea of ignorance of the law, by drinking the rest of the day in a tavern and by staying out all night. He had been rude and threatening, "as if he would a knotk his Master in the head"; and his mistress, whom he called an "[ordin]ary whore, burnt-taile

---

of Jeffrey, A Negro . . . (Boston, 1745). For examples of broadsides in connection with crime see the three published in 1733 commemorating the execution of "Poor Julian," an Indian servant. Towner, A Good Master, following page 308.

35. Wadsworth, Well-Ordered Family, 117–118. The second edition (Boston, 1719) rearranges the word order of "for much liberty" making it "much for liberty," a far stronger statement. However, regardless of Wadsworth's intent, as he defined servant behavior, it rejected an essential characteristic of servitude, the control over the hourly behavior of the servant by the master.

Bitch and hopping Toad," was afraid to be alone with him. He ended up stealing a pair of shoes and a mare, and running away.[36]

That such a servant as Bowers ended up running away came as no surprise to the Puritans. That particular sin had been a minor nuisance ever since the Puritans first brought servants to Massachusetts Bay, and the masters' reactions found expression in law, diplomacy, servant contracts, and the literature of the times. An early law provided that the authorities should raise a hue and cry and impress boats or horses to take after wayward servants, and the return of runaways had been an early subject of diplomacy between the English and the Indians.[37] At least one servant was sold in the seventeenth century with the cautionary phrase "living or dying staying or running" in his purchase agreement.[38] In literature, Michael Wigglesworth's *Day of Doom* placed runaways on judgment day "At Christ's left hand [where] the Goats do stand. . . ."[39] And, at the turn of the century, Willard, Wadsworth, and Mather all damned running away as a sin. Servants, said Willard, disobey the Fifth Commandment when they are "Unfaithful *to their Masters and do them wrong* . . . [by] Running away . . ."; they "*do very wickedly,*" wrote Benjamin Wadsworth, "*when they run away from their Masters*'; "A Run *away* Servant," said Cotton Mather, "is a Dishonest and Disgraced sort of Creature, among all the sober Part of Mankind."[40] This crime, above all others, was the single most persistent form of protest.[41]

Judged by their numbers, servant protests in Puritan society do not seem terribly impressive. Altogether only some fifteen hundred cases survive for the period from 1629 through 1750, an average of about 115 per decade, or less than a dozen a year.[42] Quite clearly

36. See Morgan, *The Puritan Family*, 75. The case and my quotation are to be found in Middlesex Court Files, File 53, May–June 1669.

37. *Mass. Recs.*, I, 157 (1635); Winthrop, *History*, I, 237–238 (1636).

38. See case of William Warrener, *Essex County Court*, III, 28 and n. (1663).

39. "The Day of Doom," vv. 27–28, in Miller and Johnson, eds., *The Puritans*, 592–593.

40. Willard, *A Compleat Body of Divinity*, 649; Wadsworth, *The Well-Ordered Family*, 119; Cotton Mather, *A Good Master Well Served*, 32.

41. Runaways are to be found chiefly in the court records and in the newspapers. I searched all the extant county court records for the 17th and 18th centuries and all the newspapers through 1750. For Massachusetts I found 676. See n. 42, below.

42. This and the following paragraphs are based on the table below. It is important to understand that while I consider these figures the best available, they are, at best, very faulty. The assignment of a servant to one category or another, such as "Other

these figures indicate neither a mass movement aimed at a servile rebellion nor a total rejection of the system. Apparently the rewards

English" instead of "Apprentice" was often for lack of evidence that the servant was an apprentice. Similarly, the category "Non-English Whites," usually comprised of Irish or Scots, is hardly infallible. Finally, there is neither an absolute number of servants to compare the rate of protest against, so that the rate of apprentice protest, for example, may be far above or below his relative numbers in society, nor any satisfactory continuity of records, so that runaways, which were advertised in 18th-century newspapers may have been far more frequent in the early period when there were no newspapers. With these caveats in mind, the table is useful only to indicate possible trends; it does not prove them.

SERVANT PROTEST BY TYPE OF SERVANT AND KIND OF PROTEST, 1629–1750

	Apprentices	Other English	Non-English Whites	Indians	Negroes	Totals
1629–59						
Legal	12	33	—	—	—	45
Unruly	5	109	11	1	7	133
Runaways	3	52	1	1	6	63
Total	20	194	12	2	13	241
1660–89						
Legal	19	29	7	1	1	57
Unruly	3	98	29	13	83	226
Runaways	13	51	23	7	14	108
Totals	35	178	59	21	98	391
1690–1719						
Legal	21	11	3	10	7	52
Unruly	7	27	16	17	86	153
Runaways	3	6	9	8	3	29
Totals	31	44	28	35	96	234
1720–50						
Legal	20	4	6	10	5	45
Unruly	4	13	17	8	94	136
Runaways	14	68	139	55	200	476
Totals	38	85	162	73	299	657
Grand Totals	124	501	261	131	506	1523

Total Legal 199   Total Unruly 648   Total Runaway 676

The above table is based largely on court records and newspapers. I searched all the extant county court records for the 17th century and all the extant records of the

PART ONE/HISTORIAN

for apprentices and indentured servants and the sanctions for those less fortunate were sufficient to make the system workable, though not perfect.

Yet, if the figures are analyzed, they yield some rather interesting, if unspectacular, results. They show that all types of servants were engaged in legal protest, unruly behavior, and running away. Consequently, Mather's characterization of Negro slaves as having a "Fondness for Freedom" applied to all ranks of servitude. But the phrase did not fit all ranks equally well. Those servants from Massachusetts or England who were protected by contracts and who had friends or relatives in the community to speak up for them tended to protest more to the courts or by unruly behavior than by running away. Conversely, foreign indentured servants and Indians and Negroes, while occasionally having recourse to the courts, protested most often as unruly servants or runaways. They account for only 25 per cent of legal protest, but for 57 per cent of unruly behavior and for 69 per cent of the cases of runaways.

The figures also show that only a small proportion of servants with real or imagined grievances took them to the courts. Only about two hundred cases, or less than 13 per cent, were orderly applications to the magistrates. Unruly behavior, with about 650 cases, accounted for 42 per cent, and running away, with about 680 cases, for 45 per cent of the total protest. Apparently most servants could not afford to take their cases to court, had no cases which the courts would recognize, or were protesting blindly and from the belly or the heart rather than from the head. Moreover, as the colonial period progressed, illegal protests increased both absolutely in terms of numbers and relatively with regard to the kinds of protest. There was an average of about 200 per cent more illegal protest per decade in the thirty years between 1720 and 1750 than in the three decades between 1629 and 1659, while in the same periods legal protest remained constant. Thus, looked at as a whole, servant protest appears to have shifted from English whites protesting legally or by unruly behavior in the seventeenth century to non-English servants—white, Indian, or Negro—protesting by unruly behavior or running away, in the eighteenth.[43]

county General Sessions of the Peace through 1750. I also used the vast collection of court papers known as the Suffolk Files in the office of the Clerk for the Supreme Judicial Court, Suffolk County Court House, all published court records, including *Mass. Recs.*, and extant files of all Massachusetts newspapers through 1750. See Towner, A Good Master, Bibliography.

43. Compare the data in nn. 42 and 15, above.

This data, of course, reflects the changing composition of the servant class and the fact that by the eighteenth century there was some place besides New England hamlets and Virginia to run away to. But it also reflects the fact that servitude as a system was working less well than was desirable and increasingly less well as the years passed. This fact in turn suggests that the family, charged with integrating the servant with society, was doing an increasingly inadequate job. A boy from Massachusetts or a young man or woman from England of Puritan background might be persuaded to accept the mores of Puritan society and his temporary status in that society. But the verminous Irish, as James Franklin's newspaper called them, or the Negroes of "extravasat Blood" who can "never embody with us," as Samuel Sewall complained, were less apt to accept those mores and the temporary or permanent status of servant or slave.[44] John Winthrop, with his retinue of servants, his large family, and his impressive personal and public authority, might contemplate converting an Irish Catholic boy to Puritanism, but the average master was not a John Winthrop, and he could not always count on his authority as head of a family to keep his servants in line.

This development is hardly surprising. The Puritans in Massachusetts had placed heavy social burdens on the family at the very time that, in the process of migration, it was stripped of some of its most important sources of authority over the individual. In leaving behind the traditional home, the traditional lands, the established church with its graveyard full of ancestors, the extended network tying it to other branches of the family, the neighbors of generations, and the extensive hierarchy of the state with its traditional forms and trappings, the family was exposed much more nakedly to the world than it had been. This nakedness was only partially covered by raw houses on raw lands in raw communities, by new churches with untraditional forms, and by a new state which, while it had power and exercised it, lacked the rich tapestry of the English monarchy. In America, moreover, the family lost much of its near monopoly over the economic future of its members. The individual's economic dependence on his family was lessened by the general

44. See the *New England Courant* (Boston), Jan. 4–11, 1725, where "Homespun Jack" complains of the Irish "vagabonds" brought over as servants, "Fellows and Wenches brought up to no other Employments than the *picking* St. Patricks Vermin. . . ." For Sewall's remarks, see "The Selling of Joseph . . . ," in Mass. Hist. Soc., *Proceedings*, Ser. 1, VII (Boston, 1864), 161–165, first published in Boston in 1700. Quotations from page 162.

availability of land, by the relative freedom to enter trades, and by the increased opportunity for employment in a labor-hungry economy.[45]

To the Puritans, at least, the family seemed to be failing in its functions. While the halfway covenant, for example, strengthened the formal authority of the family by allowing baptized but unsanctified parents to have their children baptized in turn, it was in fact a confession of the family's failure to pass on its religious zeal to the rising generation. Later in the seventeenth century, the Puritans laid other sins of society, like foundling children, at the doorstep of inadequate family government.[46] Gradually, as society became richer and more complex, other institutions—poorhouses, workhouses, houses of correction, schools—supplemented, if they did not replace, the family as a socializing agency.[47] Eventually, labor, like education, would be separated as an institution from the family, and free labor would become as characteristic of society as bound labor once had been.

Until more is known about the changes in the family and the demise of servitude in Massachusetts, a significant role for servant protest in affecting either development can hardly be claimed. Yet, two suggestions may be made. The first is that the misbehavior of servants made the system of servitude unattractive to those who were expected to profit most from it, the masters. Samuel Sewall, for example, pointed out that the Negro's "continual aspiring" after his "forbidden Liberty" made him an unwilling servant.[48] Cotton Mather claimed that the term *servant* had become almost synonymous with knave or villain.[49] But the best illustration comes from Robert Auchmuty, Roxbury lawyer, who was willing to sell his slave

45. Despite Professor Edmund S. Morgan's excellent work, *The Puritan Family,* which I have constantly drawn on, much more work remains to be done on the New England family, especially since Morgan barely ventures into the 18th century. An historical sociology of that family would be a real contribution. See Bernard Bailyn, *Education in the Forming of American Society: Needs and Opportunities for Study* (Chapel Hill, 1960), particularly pages 21–40, for a stimulating discussion of the changing colonial family.

46. See n. 14, above, and the numerous works on the family around the turn of the century, some of which are listed in n. 16, above.

47. For example, Boston, in 1682, set up a workhouse for poor families and for idle persons and families under enabling legislation enacted earlier that year. See *Mass. Recs.,* V, 373, and Record Commissioners of the Town of Boston, *Reports,* 39 vols. (Boston, 1881–1909), VII, 157–158. See also Bailyn, *Education,* 29–36.

48. "The Selling of Joseph," in Mass. Hist. Soc., *Proc.,* VII, 162.

49. *A Good Master Well-Served,* 31.

at a loss just to get rid of him. "For sale, on easy terms," went his advertisement in the *Boston Weekly News-Letter,* "provided he is transported to North Carolina and there sold, his Master having experienced that what with the Charge and Trouble of sending Negroes to the House of Correction, and the Lenity of the Laws, and Punishment when there, the Master has his slave returned to him in a more wicked Disposition than at first."[50]

The second suggestion is that servant protests helped force Puritan society to search its conscience for justification of the institution of servitude and, in at least one instance, to find there arguments rejecting its most extreme form, the enslavement of Negroes. Samuel Willard, as we have seen, justified slavery by stating that, while the liberty to be at one's own disposal was the natural condition of man before the Fall, Adam's apostasy had made it necessary that some men should be under the personal dominion of others. Willard, to be sure, pointed out that there were some who held it "unlawful for any to take unto himself the Authority of a Master, or for any to submit to the Condition of a servant,"[51] but he no more accepted the idea that liberty was natural after the Fall than that servitude had been natural before it.[52] Adam's sin had changed everything. It was Samuel Sewall who demonstrated that natural liberty had not been tarnished by Adam's sin. The occasion which called forth this demonstration was the protest of a servant. He was a Negro slave. Appropriately, his name was Adam.

John Saffin, merchant and occasional dealer in slaves, had in 1694 rented out a farm and assigned Adam to the tenant for seven years. Adam was promised his freedom at the end of this period if he behaved himself, but after six years he was returned as intractable. Adam took his case to the courts, where Judge Samuel Sewall, who had occasion to pass on it and who had been "long much dissatisfied

50. July 9–16, 1741.

51. *A Compleat Body of Divinity,* 613.

52. John Winthrop's classic statement on liberty (see Miller and Johnson, eds., *The Puritans,* 205–207) distinguishes between natural or corrupt liberty (corrupted by the Fall), the exercise of which "makes men grow more evil, and in time to be worse than brute beasts," and civil or federal liberty, which is "maintained and exercised in a way of subjection to authority." He did not relate it directly to servitude, however. Actually, a strict application of covenant or federal theology would exclude slavery, except—and this is an important exception in the 17th century—where the fiction of consent on the part of the slave could be maintained. Thomas Hooker, for example, asserted that without consent of both parties, the master-servant relationship did not exist. (*A Survey of the Summe of Church Discipline. . . .* [London, 1648], Pt. I, 68 ff.)

with the Trade of fetching Negroes from Guinea," was prompted to write and publish his tract, *The Selling of Joseph*.[53] Its premise is that since "Liberty is in real value next unto Life: None ought to part with it themselves, or deprive others of it, but upon most mature Consideration."[54] Its references are almost entirely Biblical, and much is made of the traditional Puritan opposition to slavery as a product of manstealing, a capital offense in the collected laws of 1641, 1648, and 1660.[55] At the same time, natural liberty is stripped of its corrupt connotations as a consequence of man's fall. "It is most certain," Sewall wrote, "that all Men, as they are the Sons of *Adam*, are Coheirs; and have equal Rights unto Liberty, and all other outward Comforts of Life." Moreover, "through the Indulgence of GOD to our First Parents after the Fall, the outward Estate of all and every [one] of their Children, remains the same, as to one another. So that Originally, and Naturally, there is no such thing as Slavery."[56]

After extensive litigation, Adam won his freedom from Saffin and lived in Boston thereafter as a free man. But he won his freedom because it could not be proved that he had actually violated the terms of his conditional manumission, not because the court or the society accepted Sewall's redefinition of natural liberty.[57] The time of that idea had not yet come; and after 1700 slavery and other forms of servitude flourished in Massachusetts. Meanwhile, the servants' "Fondness for Freedom" in a "very easy Servitude" continued to demonstrate that, for masters and servants alike, no servitude was easy.

53. Abner C. Goodell, Jr., "John Saffin and His Slave Adam," Col. Soc. of Mass., *Publs.*, I, 85–112.

54. Sewall, "Selling of Joseph," in Mass. Hist. Soc., *Proc.*, VII, 161. Sewall had read Richard Baxter in his search for an authoritative statement on slavery. He might better have read William Ames who denied that even voluntary "perfect servitude" (i.e., slavery) was legal because while the prospective slave might be willing, the master in "procuring and exercising the authority" would violate the injunction laid on mankind in Matt. 7:12. As for slavery imposed for a crime, this could be justified only by "some hainous offence, which might deserve the severest punishment, to wit, death: *because our liberty in the naturall account, is the very next thing to life it selfe, yea by many preferred before it.*" (*Conscience with the Power and Cases Thereof....* [London, 1643], Bk. IV, 160. Italics mine.)

55. Whitmore, comp., *Colonial Laws*, 55 (1641), 128 (1660); Max Farrand, ed., *The Laws and Liberties of Massachusetts* . . . (Cambridge, Mass., 1929), 6.

56. Sewall, "Selling of Joseph," in Mass. Hist. Soc., *Proc.*, VII, 161–162. Italics mine.

57. Goodell, "John Saffin and His Slave Adam," in Col. Soc. of Mass., *Publs.*, I, 100.

2

THE SEWALL-SAFFIN DIALOGUE ON

SLAVERY

Since Towner wrote this article historical scholarship has been blessed by monumental studies on American racism by Winthrop Jordan and on abolition by David B. Davis among others, which have helped set in perspective the sparse evidence on these subjects for the early eighteenth century. When Towner was writing, the study of antislavery suffered from the fallacy of the "Whig" interpretation of history in which everything that came before was a "forerunner" of the progress that came afterward.

In this essay Towner rigorously examines the texts of two participants in an argument over slavery in New England: Judge Samuel Sewall and John Saffin, setting the terms of the debate in stark outline. Through his command of the context, Towner establishes that the winner was neither Sewall nor Saffin but Cotton Mather, whose views a few years later "removed the final Christian barrier to slavery . . . [asserting] that baptism did not change the temporal status of a slave."

BY 1700, THE YEAR Samuel Sewall published his now famous attack on slavery, *The Selling of Joseph*, Negroes had been coming to Massachusetts and New Englanders had been engaged in the slave trade for sixty or seventy years. Although the questions of when Negroes were enslaved in New England and why they were made slaves instead of being treated as indentured servants are still troubling historians, there can be no question that by the end of the century Negro slavery had taken root there. The morality of the slave trade and probably of slavery itself had become a public issue as early as 1645,[1] but it was not until after the monopoly of the Royal African

From *William and Mary Quarterly*, 3d ser., 21 (1964): 40–52. Reprinted with permission.

1. See Nathaniel B. Shurtleff, ed., *Records of the Governor and Company of the Massachusetts Bay* . . . (Boston, 1853–54), III, 46; hereafter cited as *Mass. Recs.*

Company was broken in 1696, that enough Negroes were living in the colony to make them the subject of published controversy. Samuel Sewall's contribution to this dialogue has often been considered the beginning of the eighteenth-century antislavery movement in Massachusetts. An alternative view is that it was a seventeenth-century Puritan response to a sudden increase in the slave population, particularly in Boston, and to a growing awareness that slavery was becoming important and was likely to become more so. "The Numerousness of Slaves at this day in the Province," Sewall wrote, "and the Uneasiness of them under their Slavery, hath put many upon thinking whether the Foundation of it be firmly and well laid; so as to sustain the Vast Weight that is built upon it." [2] When the brief dialogue was over between Sewall and his antagonist, John Saffin, the proslavery argument seemed to have had the best of it, and, indeed, within five years New England's leading divine had put his seal of approval on the institution. The way was cleared for slavery to flourish so far as the limits of Massachusetts's need for unskilled labor would permit.

For some time before 1700, Sewall had been troubled by the existence of slavery in the colony. As a merchant he was familiar with the "Trade of fetching Negroes from Guinea," and it was this part of slavery which first raised doubts in his mind. He noted in his diary that he had had a "strong Inclination to Write something about it; but it wore off." [3] This unease was sharpened in 1700, he tells us, by four events. A friend showed him a petition he wished to present to the General Court about a Negro man and wife "unjustly held in Bondage." [4] At the same time, public agitation began in favor of an

2. Samuel Sewall, *The Selling of Joseph: A Memorial* (Boston, 1700).

3. June 19, 1700, in *Diary of Samuel Sewall, 1674–1729* (Massachusetts Historical Society, *Collections*, 5th Ser., V–VII [Boston, 1878–82]), II, 16. Sewall probably owned slaves, as is apparent from Saffin's remarks quoted below, page 48, and from Sewall's *Diary*, index under "Scipio." A Samuel Sewall, probably the diarist's nephew, offered slaves for sale in the Boston newspapers. See: *Boston News-Letter*, Sept. 13, 1714; *Boston Gazette*, Aug. 12–19, 1723; July 26–Aug. 2, 1725; Aug. 2–9, 1725; May 23–30, 1726.

4. June 19, 1700, in Sewall, *Diary*, II, 16. The petition is not to be found in the Massachusetts Archives. In "'A Fondness for Freedom': Servant Protest in Puritan Society," *William and Mary Quarterly*, 3d Ser., XIX (1962), 217–219, I follow the suggestion of Abner C. Goodell, "John Saffin and His Slave Adam," Colonial Society of Massachusetts, *Publications*, I (Boston, 1895), 85 and *n.*, that *The Selling of Joseph* was written in response to the case of the slave, Adam. However, since there is no evidence that Adam had a wife, and since he did not come to Sewall for help until after the publication of Sewall's pamphlet, there seems to be no original connection between Adam and the pamphlet.

impost on Negroes "to discourage the bringing of them." Sewall also learned that Cotton Mather planned to "publish a sheet" urging that slaves be converted to Christianity. These events were brought into focus when Sewall read Paul Baynes's *An Entire Commentary Upon the Whole Epistle of the Apostle Paul to the Ephesians . . .* (London, 1643), particularly the section on masters and servants, which describes "blackamores" as "perpetually put under the power of the master."[5]

The result of Sewall's soul searching, *The Selling of Joseph*, is similar in form to hundreds of Puritan sermons he must have heard and read: a statement of the text; an elaboration of the text, studded with Biblical and other authorities and Latin quotations; a series of objections with their answers; and a conclusion or "use" backed up by a quotation from an accepted Biblical scholar.[6]

Sewall's text was "*Forasmuch as* Liberty *is in real value next unto* Life: *None ought to part with it themselves, or deprive others of it, but upon most mature Consideration.*" In a cautious, undogmatic way, he elaborated this text. Using Joseph as his model, he proceeded to equate Joseph's experience with manstealing and then manstealing with slavery, proving the moral liability of the last from the known immorality of the first.

Because all men, as sons of Adam, are coheirs, he wrote, they "have equal Right unto Liberty, and all other outward Comforts of Life." The last Adam, by His sacrifice, had indeed improved man's title to the earth, making him a leaseholder instead of a tenant at will, and He had also improved man's relationship with God; but that sacrifice did not alter the relationship of man to man. The "outward Estate of all and every of their [our first parents'] Children, remains the same, as to one another." Neither man's fall nor Christianity justifies slavery. Consequently, Joseph was enslaved unlawfully. Liberty was his natural state, and the sale price did not alter that condition in law. "There is no proportion between Twenty Pieces of Silver, and LIBERTY." Any person who thinks there is "seems to have forfeited a great part of his own claim to Humanity."

We are more careful, Sewall complained, in buying a horse or a bit

5. The reference to "blackamores" occurs at Chapter VI, Verse 5, of Baynes's work. The editors of Sewall's *Diary*, II, 16n, wrongly infer from Sewall that his brief reference to Baynes was to his "'Commentary on the First Chapter of Ephesians,' 1618."

6. Sewall's pamphlet was apparently reprinted only once in the 18th century and not again until 1864. (Mass. Hist. Soc., *Proceedings for 1863–1864* [Boston, 1864], 161–165.) The only known copy is in the Mass. Hist. Soc. The following summary and quotations are taken from Sewall's *The Selling of Joseph*.

of Arabian gold—a reference to the treasure that Captain Kidd brought with him and part of which Sewall had had charge of[7]—than in buying humans whose liberty is more precious than gold. In buying humans, moreover, we run the risk of violating the Biblical injunction against stealing men (Exodus 21:16), an injunction which had been included among the capital offenses in the Massachusetts Body of Liberties of 1641 and in subsequent compilations under the old charter. "This Law being of Everlasting Equity," wrote Sewall, "wherein Man Stealing is ranked amongst the most atrocious of Capital Crimes: What louder Cry can there be made of that Celebrated Warning, *Caveat Emptor!*"

While purchasing slaves resulted in sharing the guilt of Joseph's brothers and possibly breaking the Old Testament injunction against manstealing, the mere owning of slaves was also full of hazards, for society and for individuals. Negro slaves did not strengthen society, but weakened it. They were unsatisfactory as servants because they were always hungering after their freedom. Few masters would free them, however, because, said Sewall, they could "seldom use their freedom well." By taking the places of white servants who might marry local girls, increase the population, and build up the militia, they left Massachusetts weaker than if they had not come at all. This was not a temporary, but a permanent condition: "there is such a disparity in their Conditions, Colour and Hair, that they can never embody with us, and grow up into orderly Families, to the Peopling of the Land: but still remain in our Body Politick as a kind of extravasat Blood."

The masters not only weakened society by peopling the land with permanent aliens, they also endangered their own souls and incited crimes by having slaves. By separating men from their country, husbands from their wives, and parents from their children, "That which GOD ha's joyned together men do boldly rend asunder." And, because masters would not provide married mates for their slaves, they encouraged fornication, both a sin and a crime. Other crimes, such as theft, were encouraged too, for masters failed to report them to the authorities for fear of having to pay the fines of their slaves.

Sewall ended the first half of his attack by touching on a current local problem. He himself had been engaged in prolonged negotiations leading to the release of New Englanders held as slaves in Af-

7. Memorandum, Mar. 2, 1699/1700, in *Letter-Book of Samuel Sewall* (Mass. Hist. Soc., *Colls.*, 6th Ser., I–II [Boston, 1886–88]), I, 219. An inventory of Kidd's goods certified by Sewall and others appears in Graham Brooks, ed., *Trial of Captain Kidd* (Edinburgh and London, 1930), Appendix III.

rica.[8] "Methinks, when we are bemoaning the barbarous Usage of our Friends and Kinsfolk in *Africa:* it might not be unseasonable to enquire whether we are not culpable in forcing the *Africans* to become Slaves amongst our selves."

In the second half of *The Selling of Joseph,* Sewall lists four likely objections to his attack on the foundation of slavery and provides a suggested rebuttal for each. The first objection offered is that the Negroes as descendants of Ham were condemned to slavery for Ham's having seen the nakedness of his father, Noah. Sewall countered this by arguing that no one "Uncalled for" should be the "Executioner of the Vindictive Wrath of God"; by questioning, with the help of David Pareus of Heidelberg,[9] the extent to which all of Ham's posterity were included in the curse; and by raising doubts about the descent of the Negro race from Ham. The second of the four objections is that slavery brought Negroes out of a heathen country to where they might be reached by the Gospel. Against the implication that it was better to be an enslaved Christian than a free heathen, Sewall did not argue. He merely stated that "Evil must not be done, that good may come of it." The fact that Joseph and the "Church" were better off as a result of Joseph's enslavement did not justify his brothers' selling him.

The third objection is that the Negroes were sold into slavery as captives in just wars between Africans. Sewall's memory of the recent war against King Philip, when many Indians had been sold into slavery, may have made him hesitate to deny the right;[10] instead, he suggested that perhaps the African wars, like the "war" of Joseph's brothers against him, were in fact not just wars, because they were started for the purpose of acquiring slaves. In any event, he argued, every war "is upon one side Unjust," and "An Unlawful War can't make lawful Captives." How could a Bostonian know that the slaves he bought from distant Africa were lawful captives from just wars? Suppose, Sewall argued, "some Gentlemen should go down to the *Brewsters* to take the Air, and Fish: And a stronger party from *Hull*

8. For examples, see letters from Sewall to John Ive, May 31, July 15, Sept. 4, 1686, Mar. 30, July 9, 1687, Mar. 31, 1688, and Memoranda, Sept. 25, 1690, all referring to Joshua Gee, a captive in Algiers whom Sewall helped free between 1686 and 1690, in Sewall, *Letter-Book,* I, 28, 34, 38, 45, 49, 76–77, 112, and letter of June 10, 1700, to John Ive, *ibid.,* 234–235.

9. Sewall says, *"Vide Pareum."* He must be referring to the Protestant theologian David Pareus (1548–1635) of Heidelberg. See John Watkins, *The Universal Biographical Dictionary* . . . (London, 1823), 826–827.

10. Nov. 3, 1675, and Sept. 16, 1676, in *Mass. Recs.,* V, 68, 115; Certificate of John Leverett, Sept. 12, 1676, Miscellaneous Manuscripts, Mass. Hist. Soc.

should Surprise them, and Sell them for Slaves to a Ship outward bound: they would think themselves unjustly dealt with; both by Sellers and Buyers."

The fourth objection Sewall raised against his antislavery argument is that Abraham had had slaves born in his own house and bought with his own money. If the man of the covenant could own slaves, surely slavery was permissible. Sewall could not refute this directly. The evidence—for example, Genesis 17:27, "all the men of his house, born in the house, and bought with money of the stranger"—was incontrovertible. All Sewall could say was that he did not know all the circumstances of the purchase and he must assume it was lawful because Abraham did the purchasing. But, there had been restrictions concerning slavery placed on the Jews: they could not enslave fellow Jews, only non-Jews, the uncircumcised, the strangers (Leviticus 25:44–46). The distinction between Jew and Gentile, however, had been removed by Jesus Christ. Paraphrasing Ephesians 2:14, "For he is our peace, who hath made both one, and hath broken down the middle wall of partition *between us,*" Sewall argued in effect that all men were now Jews and fell under the prohibition in Leviticus against enslaving Jews. "Christians," he said, "should carry it to all the World, as the *Israelites* were to carry it one towards another."[11]

Sewall ended his argument with a final plea. He sought to touch those who still labored, as he did, under the awful Puritan doubt about whether they were saved and the extent to which their own behavior was a reflection of their state of grace. For men to hold their fellow men in bondage, he warned, "seems to be no proper way of gaining Assurance that God ha's given them Spiritual Freedom."

The Selling of Joseph closes with two quotations from the early seventeenth-century Puritan divine, William Ames. His book, *De conscientia, et eius iure, vel casibus,* did not flatly prohibit slavery, but, like Sewall's work, it made of slavery an extremely doubtful institution, particularly for the slaveholder. While slavery between Christian and Christian, said Ames, was legal on the part of the slave, if it were necessary (that is, if a man sold himself into slavery out of necessity); on the part of the master, who has to buy the slave and exercises the authority of the master, it is unlawful because his

11. Paul Baynes's commentary on Ephesians 2:14 emphasizes that man was a "war with man, wolves to one another" prior to the coming of Christ. However: "Now Christ hath put an end to all these wars." By inference, slavery is a form of warfare of man against man and no longer allowed to Christians. *Commentary upon . . . Ephesians,* Chapter II, Verse 14.

actions violate the Golden Rule. Involuntary penal servitude is justified only for those who had committed some "hainous offense" (in which category captives were apparently not included), "because our liberty in the naturall account," wrote Ames, "is the very next thing to life itselfe, yea, by many is perferred before it."[12]

At the publication of *The Selling of Joseph*, Sewall was an important figure in Massachusetts. He was forty-eight years of age, a Harvard graduate, an established merchant, and a son-in-law of the late John Hull, goldsmith, merchant, and mintmaster of the colony. By 1700 he had already had a distinguished political career. Under the old charter he had been a deputy to the General Court, and from 1684–86 he had served as a member of the Council. During a visit to England he had appeared before the King, and he had aided Increase Mather in his efforts to restore the Massachusetts Charter. Under the new charter of 1691 he was appointed to the Council, to which body he was thereafter regularly elected until his resignation in 1725. In 1692, Governor William Phips had appointed him to the special commission of oyer and terminer which tried the witchcraft cases, and it was Sewall who later had the courage to confess publicly his share in the judicial murder of the witches. In 1692, he was also appointed a Justice of the Superior Court, from which position he afterwards rose to become Chief Justice, in 1718. He accepted appointment as commissioner of the Society for the Propagation of the Gospel in New England in 1699, later becoming that organization's local secretary and treasurer.

Despite his prominent position, Sewall was roundly criticized for arguing as he did. In 1701, Cotton Mather became enraged because Sewall had opposed Increase Mather's plan to live in Boston while continuing to hold the office of president of Harvard. In cowardly fashion Mather berated Sewall, not to his face, but through Samuel, Jr., then only an apprentice. Mather told the younger Sewall that, while the Judge "pleaded much for Negros," he had used Increase Mather "worse than a Negro." He spoke so loudly, said Sewall, "that people in the street might hear him."[13] As late as 1706, the Judge was still smarting from his wounds. In a letter that year to Reverend John Higginson of Salem, Sewall sent thanks for Higginson's being

12. Sewall refers to and quotes from a Latin edition of William Ames's *Conscience, with the Power and Cases Thereof* . . . (London, 1643), Bk. IV, 160. In my "A Fondness for Freedom," n.54, I made the grievous error of advising Sewall to read Ames, whom he did quote and cite, instead of Baxter, whom he did not. I trust the good Judge will forgive me, as he was forgiven, on this, my public acknowledgment of error.

13. Oct. 20, 1701, in Sewall, *Diary*, II, 43.

his "Abettor," his "Brest-work," in the cause for which he had received many "Frowns and hard Words."[14] Even so, for nearly a score of years Sewall distributed his *Selling of Joseph* to members of the legislature, friends, casual acquaintances, and correspondents as far away as New York and England.[15]

"Frowns and hard Words" were not the only response. Late in 1701, John Saffin, merchant, occasional dealer in slaves, deputy, speaker of the house of deputies under the old charter, sometimes councilor under the new, justice of the peace, and, as of August 1, 1701, member of the same court as Sewall, published an argument against Sewall's views. He was a resourceful opponent.[16]

What provoked Saffin's attack was the case of his Negro slave, Adam. In 1694 Saffin had let out a farm stocked with cattle and sheep and one Negro named Adam to a Thomas Shepherd, promising Adam his freedom effective after seven years' faithful service. Despite the fact that Adam had proved unsatisfactory to Shepherd, the Negro insisted when his seven years were up that he was free, while Saffin insisted that Adam was still bound. In March 1701, the case came up, first before Judge Sewall, then before Sewall and Penn Townsend, and then before the Superior Court to which, in the meantime, Saffin had been appointed.[17]

From the first Sewall had advised Saffin to free Adam, probably handing him a copy of his *Selling of Joseph*. In addition to giving this gratuitous advice, Sewall was openly critical of Saffin's role as a judge. Saffin had not only refused to disqualify himself in the case of Adam, he had, according to Sewall, also tampered with the jury.[18] Sewall's attitude and the decision of the court to continue the case for a year stung Saffin to write his rejoinder.

A Brief and Candid Answer to a Late Printed Sheet, Entituled, The Selling of Joseph . . . (Boston, 1701) is divided into two main

14. Sewall, *Letter-Book*, I, 326.
15. Sewall to Paul Dudley, Nov. 20, 1700, to Nathaniel Byfield, Jan. 4, 1705/6, to Rev. John Higginson, Apr. 13, 1706, to Henry Newman, Aug. 9, 1711, and Dec. 18, 1714, to Addington Davenport, July 20, 1719, all in *ibid.*, 245, 322, 325–326, 412; II, 39, 101; and Dec. 24, 1705, in Sewall, *Diary*, II, 150.
16. While much is known of Sewall, relatively little biographical material is available on Saffin; however, see Goodell, "John Saffin and His Slave Adam," 85n and 90, and a biographical sketch in Harvey Hunter Pratt, *The Early Planters of Scituate* . . . ([Scituate, Mass.], 1929), 236–258. Saffin left an interesting commonplace book which was published as *John Saffin: His Book (1665–1708)* . . . (New York, 1928), with an introduction by Caroline Hazard.
17. Goodell, "John Saffin and His Slave Adam," 85 ff.
18. Sept. 9 and 11, 1701, in Sewall, *Diary*, II, 41.

sections.[19] The first is a powerful attack on Sewall's *Selling of Joseph*. The second, and longer section, is a defense of Saffin's actions with regard to Adam and includes several documents from the case submitted to the Superior Court in Bristol that fall. It is the first part with which we are chiefly concerned. Its main theme is that the selling of Joseph, manstealing, and slavery are not parallel and, therefore, Sewall's argument could not stand. At the end of the section he published a verse underscoring that between the cases of Joseph and the Africans there was no "congruiety therein."

The Negroes Character.
Cowardly and cruel are those Blacks *Innate,*
Prone to Revenge, Imp of inveterate hate.
He that exasperates them, soon espies
Mischief and Murder in their very eyes.
Libidinous, Deceitful, False and Rude,
The Spume Issue of Ingratitude.
The Premises consider'd, all may tell,
How near good Joseph *they are Parallel.*

In between Saffin's statement of his theme and his concluding verse, he attacked Sewall's argument point by point with considerable success. To Sewall's claim that slavery was questionable because Adam's seed were coheirs, Saffin countered that this did not put all men on a parity. To suggest "that all men have equal right to Liberty, and all outward comforts of this life . . . seems to invert the Order that God hath set in the World, who hath Ordained different degrees and orders of men, some to be High and Honourable, some to be Low and Despicable." How else could there be kings, masters, governors, if there were none to obey? There had to be "Servants of sundry sorts and degrees, bound to obey; yea some to be born Slaves." Here Saffin likened Paul's comparison of the human body and the church (I Corinthians 12:13–26) to society at large where "God hath set different Orders and Degrees of men in the World, both in Church and Common weal." It would be a "breach of good manners," wrote Saffin, "to treat a Prince like a Peasant. And this

19. The material and quotations which follow are drawn from the first 5 pages of the 16-page quarto. Saffin's *Answer* apparently dropped out of sight until George H. Moore discovered a copy when his book was in page proof. He published part of it in an appendix. (See George H. Moore, *Notes on the History of Slavery in Massachusetts* [New York, 1866], 88, 251–256.) Part was also published in Goodell, "John Saffin and His Slave Adam," 103–112. It has not been reprinted in Clifford K. Shipton, ed., *Early American Imprints, 1639–1800* (Worcester, Mass., 1956–), but there is an incomplete copy in the New-York Historical Society, New York City.

worthy Gentleman would deem himself much neglected, if we should show him no more Defference than to an ordinary Porter."

Having stretched Sewall's equal rights into equality of wealth and position, an appeal directly to some of the strongest underlying assumptions of the time, Saffin turned to Sewall's rating of white servants over black: "who doubts that?" But, did this preference imply that Negroes could not be enslaved or that slaves could be set free lest the owners "live in any known sin?" This seemed to be Sewall's opinion, said Saffin, "but it is a Question whether ever it was the Gentlemans practice?" Since not even Sewall, let alone those who saw no wrong in slavery, had freed his slaves, the only choice open to society was to indemnify the owners and—because freed Negroes "will be a plague to this Country"—ship the Negroes back to Africa, a choice that was no choice at all, as Saffin realized.

Sewall's opponent then linked liberty for slaves to liberty for temporary white servants. If it were wrong to deprive heathens, lawful captives, of liberty, how much more wrong, "to deprive our Brethren, of our own or other Christian Nations of the Liberty, (though but for a time) by binding them to Serve some Seven, Ten, Fifteen, and some Twenty years, which oft times proves for their whole Life." This argument would undermine either the established bound labor system or Sewall's argument against slavery: Saffin knew which would fall.

As for the Biblical injunction against manstealing, Saffin admitted the provision, but he underscored the difference between stealing and buying: "in that very Chapter" of the Bible where manstealing is prohibited, he wrote, "there is a Dispensation to the People of *Israel*, to have Bond men . . . even of their own Nation in some case." To clinch his argument, he quoted Leviticus 25:44, *"Both thy Bond men, and they Bond maids which thou shalt have shall be of the Heathen . . . of them shall you Buy Bond men and Bond maids."*

Having disposed of Sewall's general arguments, Saffin proceeded to reestablish the objections that Sewall had dismissed. The ancestry of the Negroes was irrelevant, he said, for "any lawful Captives of other Heathen Nations may be made Bond men." It was not evil, but good to bring the Negroes out of heathen country to where they might be "Eternally Saved." Just war or unjust, captives can be bought "without contracting the guilt of the *Agressors*." And, finally, Abraham's case merely proves the point—"our Imitation of him in this his Moral Action, is as warrantable as [in] that of his Faith; *who is the Father of all them that believe."*

Saffin's arguments emphasize the significance of Sewall's use of Ephesians 2:14. Nowhere did Saffin mention the passage, yet he four times made the careful distinction between God's people enslaving their own kind, which was ordinarily illegal, and their enslaving Heathens, which was legal. The partition wall between peoples was still up, and the distinction, for example between Christian and heathen, was valid. So valid was it, in fact, that it represented a major concern of the time. What should happen if a Negro were to be Christianized? Would he then be free? Neither Sewall nor Saffin came to that point in print.

It must have appeared at the time that Saffin had bested Sewall on grounds that the latter had chosen. Not for four years did Sewall make an attempt to answer Saffin's counterblast; not until he was again forcibly reminded of the issue. In early December 1705, a bill was introduced by the deputies designed to prevent miscegenation between the whites, on the one hand, and Negroes and Indians, on the other. "If it be passed," Sewall wrote, "I fear twill be an Opression provoking to God, and that which will promote Murders and other Abominations."[20] The bill was enacted, but Sewall claims it was less severe than in the original form thanks to his efforts. Negroes, male or female, convicted of fornication with whites, were to be whipped severely and sold out of the country; performing a marriage ceremony between white and Negro was thereafter punishable by a £50 fine; and a £4 duty was to be levied on all Negroes imported into the province. The penalties had been worse in the draft bill, said Sewall, and Indians had been included. Moreover, he had been able to get a clause inserted which prohibited any master from unreasonably denying "marriage to his negro with one of the same nation."[21]

Before the law was enacted, Sewall published a question copied from John Dunston's *Athenian Oracle*. Sewall's edition or printing was a four-page pamphlet, also entitled the *Athenian Oracle* [Boston, 1705], printed by Bartholomew Green and sold by Samuel Phillips.[22] The question was *"Whether Trading for Negroes i.e., carrying*

20. Dec. 1, 1705, in Sewall, *Diary,* II, 143.

21. An Act for the Better Preventing of a Spurious and Mixt Issue, Dec. 5, 1705, in *Acts and Resolves . . . of the Province of the Massachusetts Bay . . . ,* I (Boston, 1869), 578–579. Dec. 1, 1705, in Sewall, *Diary,* II, 143.

22. Moore, *Notes,* reprinted the wrong question from the *Athenian Oracle,* one dealing with Christianizing the slaves. See pp. 90–94. The quotations and analysis which follow are taken from Sewall's pamphlet. (Vols. I–III of John Dunston's *Athenian Oracle* were published in 1703, vol. IV, in 1710, all in London.)

them out of their own Country into perpetual Slavery, be in it self Unlawful, and especially contrary to the great law of CHRISTIAN-ITY?" The answer was emphatically yes, but the argument was largely repetitious of what Sewall had already said on the matter. It pointed out, however, that the Africans had come to hate Christianity because of the Christians engaged in the slave trade; that the so-called just wars between Africans were actually instigated by slave traders; and that the argument that slavery improved the Negro by bringing him to Christianity, ought if it were true to result in the Negro's coming freely. If so, "what need a Cargo . . . to purchase 'em? What need of Chains, and Bolts, and Fetters?" Why do so many prefer suicide to slavery, and why do they celebrate when one of their fellows dies, "as foolishly concluding he is happily returned to his own Country?"

At one point, however, the *Athenian Oracle* burst from the circle of the Sewall-Saffin dialogue. Saffin had agreed that the moral law prohibited Christian enslaving Christian; but, he had argued, "any lawful Captives of other Heathen Nations may be made Bond men." What happens, however, when the heathen is Christianized? Does he become free? Yes, said the *Athenian Oracle*. "The Law of our Land is so far from allowing it [slavery]; that if an Infidel be brought into this Kingdom, as soon as he can give an Account of the Christian Faith and desires to be Baptized; any Charitable lawful Minister may do it, and then he is under the same Law with other Christians [i.e., he is free]."

This was a critical issue in Massachusetts. In 1694 a group of ministers, exercised over the failure to provide baptism for slaves, had petitioned the General Court for clarification: "It is Desired," the petition read, "That the well knowne Discouragement upon the endeavors of many masters [to] Christianize their salves may be removed by a Law which may take away all pre[text] to Release from just servitude, by receiving of Baptisme." [23]

This petition was without legislative results. However, in 1706, the year following publication of Sewall's *Athenian Oracle*, Cotton Mather provided an answer. Mather, it must be said, was vigorously opposed to the slave trade, which he regarded as piracy, and as "One of the worst kinds of Thievery in the World." [24] His chief concern,

23. Quoted in Lorenzo Johnston Greene, *The Negro in Colonial New England, 1620–1776* (New York, 1942), 267.
24. *Theopolis Americana: An Essay on the Golden Street of the Holy City . . .* (Boston, 1710), 21–22. Those who ignore their slaves' salvation, said Mather, "are fitter to be called, *Incarnate Devils, than Christians.*"

however, was not to stop the traffic, but to save the slave. In *The Negro Christianized*, published in 1706, he argued that slavery placed an obligation on the master for his Negro's soul, that he was obligated to lead his slave to Christianity. He then made the significant point that the act of becoming a Christian would not free the slave, as many people feared, *but would instead make him a better slave.* "Christianity," he said, "directs a *Slave*, upon his embracing the *Law of the Redeemer*, to satisfy himself, *That he is the Lords Freeman*, tho' he continues a *Slave.*"

"What *Law* is it, that Sets the *Baptised Slave at Liberty?*" Mather asked. "Not the *Law of Christianity:* that allows of *Slavery.* . . . Will the *Canon-law* do it? No; The *Canons* of Numberless *Councils*, mention, the *Slaves* of *Christians*, without any contradiction. Will the *Civil Law* do it? No: Tell, if you can, any part of *Christendom*, wherein *Slaves* are not frequently to be met withal. But is not *Freedom* to be claimed for a *Baptised Slave*, by the *English* Constitution? The English *Laws*, about *Villains*, or *Slaves*, will not say so; for by those *Laws*, they may be granted for *Life*, like a *Lease*, and passed over . . . like other *Goods or Chattels.*" "These English *Laws* were made when the *Lords* and the *Slaves*, were both of them *Christians*; and they stand still unrepealed. If there are not now such *Slaves* in *England* as formerly, it is from the *Lords*, more than from the *Laws*. The *Baptised* men are not thereby entitled unto their *Liberty.*" [25]

It cannot be claimed that *The Negro Christianized* was published in particular response to the opinion in Sewall's *Athenian Oracle*. Actually, as we have seen, Mather had been thinking of this book, or this problem, since 1700. According to him, the invasion of the West Indies by a French fleet, recorded in his diary on May 3, 1706, led him to send his manuscript to the press in June, in order to ward off a similar visitation of God's wrath on New England.[26] Whatever the particular reason, Mather's small book was a response to the same conditions that provoked Sewall to write his *Selling of Joseph*—the growing numbers of Negroes in the colony. And, it was Mather's views, and Saffin's, not Sewall's, that were representative of the times. Mather's position, in fact, removed the final Christian barrier to slavery; and it found general support in an opinion ren-

<hr>

25. *The Negro Christianized* . . . (Boston, 1706), 26–27. This sermon was part of a long series of arguments in this direction dating back at least to 1660. See Greene, *The Negro in Colonial New England*, 263–267.

26. May 3 and 31, 1706, in *Diary of Cotton Mather, 1681–1724* (Mass. Hist. Soc., *Colls.*, 7th Ser., VII–VIII [Boston, 1911–12]), I, 561, 564–565.

dered by the King's Attorney and the Solicitor General in England in 1729—published in a Boston newspaper—that baptism did not change the temporal status of a slave.[27]

The little vocal opposition to slavery that remained after the Sewall-Saffin dialogue accepted only Sewall's *social* argument against the Negroes and opposed only the slave trade. In 1706, for example, an article appeared in the *Boston News-Letter* attacking slavery essentially on the grounds that the Negroes were thieves, liars, and "eye servants," and that whites were preferable.[28] Slavery as such, however, experienced little opposition until the decades of the Revolution.[29]

27. The opinion was dated Jan. 14, 1729, and was published in the *Boston Gazette,* Aug. 31–Sept. 7, 1730. It ruled that slaves, merely by virtue of their being brought to England or Ireland, or by being baptized, did not become free.

28. June 3–10. Similar views were expressed, briefly, in a currency tract, in 1716, and at length in an article reprinted in 1736 from the London monthly, *Political State of Great Britain.* See Col. Soc. Mass., *Publs.,* VIII (Boston, 1906), 288, and the *Boston Evening-Post,* Nov. 15, 1736. In 1708/9 an act authorized, for three years, a 40 shilling bounty for each white male servant imported. (An Act to Encourage the Importation of White Servants, Feb. 26, 1708, in *Acts and Resolves,* I, 634.)

29. The *Athenian Oracle* was reprinted in the *New-England Weekly Journal* (Boston) for June 21, 1737, and, of course, the Quaker, Elihu Coleman, published his attack on slavery in this period, *A Testimony Against that Anti-Christian Practice of Making Slaves of Men* . . . (Boston, 1733). Against this slender evidence of continued antislavery sentiment must be weighed the massive fact of the institution itself.

3

THE INDENTURES OF BOSTON'S POOR

APPRENTICES, 1734–1805

The private contract, or indenture, between most masters and apprentices was a document that did not have to be filed in court. Only a handful of them have survived. But for one group of servants, the children bound out by the Overseers of the Poor in Boston to servitude as a form of poor relief, the indentures had to be filed with the local magistrates and have survived.

This essay is the introduction to Towner's tabular summary of 1100 indentures filed by Boston's Overseers of the Poor from 1734 to 1805. We reprint at the end an excerpt from this "Table of Indentures" which gives the name of the apprentice, the dates of servitude, the name, trade, and town of the master. Analyzing this data, Towner was able to draw conclusions as to the kinds of trades boys and girls were put out to, where they were sent, and the social status of the masters. Where he could, he fleshed out his statistical data with materials that would bring these youths alive and suggest what might have happened to some of them.

EARLY IN JUNE 1756 Zachariah Fowle, Boston printer and bookseller, took as apprentice a seven-year-old boy, one of some 1,100 boys and girls bound out by Boston's Overseers of the Poor between 1734 and 1805.[1] In signing the indenture of apprenticeship, Fowle bound him-

From Colonial Society of Massachusetts, *Publications* 43 (1966): 417–33. The entire table, based on the indentures themselves, is to be found on pages 435–68 of *Publications*. Reprinted with permission.

1. There were more indentures, but the rest have disappeared. At present there is only one between 1734 and 1739. Between 21 April 1756, and 1 November 1773, there were 483 children bound out, but only 390 indentures are extant. Thus, there may have been as many as 25 per cent more than the 1,100 apprentices, 1734–1805. But between 2 April 1785, and early January, 1790, the lists and indentures correspond exactly in numbers. Hence, all that can be said for sure is that there were at least 93 more children bound out than there are indentures for the whole period. Compare the indentures abstracted below with the fragmentary lists in "Admissions, 1760–

self, his wife, and his heirs to feed, clothe, and shelter the boy until he reached the age of twenty-one years; to teach him to read, write, and cipher; and, having taught him the "Art and Mistery" of a printer, to release him with "two good Suits of Apparrell for all parts of his Body one for the Lords Days the other for working days Suitable to his Degree." In turn, the apprentice promised to obey Fowle's lawful commands, to keep his secrets, to absent himself only with his master's leave, to avoid fornication and matrimony, to shun taverns and alehouses, and to stay away from cards, dice, and other forms of gaming. He was, in short, to behave as a "good and faithfull Apprentice" ought to behave. The indentures were witnessed by eight Overseers of the Poor and, a month later, assented to by two of his majesty's justices of the peace.[2] The apprentice was Isaiah Thomas, one of five children of the indigent and possibly widowed Mrs. Thomas. Isaiah's grandfather, Peter Thomas, had been a merchant in Boston and had held such minor civic posts as tithingman, constable, wharfinger, purchaser of grain, and assessor. Isaiah's father, however, had fallen on evil days and had abandoned his family, leaving his wife the responsibility of raising the children. Between the ages of two and six years, Isaiah had been cared for by a family in the country. Now, after a year and a half at home, he was being apprenticed.[3]

His indenture was saved, along with the others executed by the Overseers of the Poor, in what is the largest collection of indentures for any kind of bound servant in New England. From these indentures can be learned something about the ethnic background of Boston's poor in the eighteenth century, the kinds of trades that were open to poor children, the extent to which Boston supplied a colony- or state-wide labor market, and the kinds of persons who were willing to take poor boys and girls into their farms, homes, and shops.

74," Records of the Boston Overseers of the Poor, Massachusetts Historical Society. Hereafter cited as Overseers Records.

2. The copy of Thomas's indenture abstracted below carries only the signatures of Fowle, two overseers, and two justices. Thomas's personal copy, now at the American Antiquarian Society, has the signatures of eight overseers and two justices.

3. See Clifford K. Shipton, *Isaiah Thomas, Printer, Patriot, and Philanthropist, 1749–1831* (Rochester, 1948). For Peter Thomas's offices, see Robert Francis Seybolt, *The Town Officials of Colonial Boston, 1634–1775* (Cambridge, Mass., 1939), 124, 149, 156, 182. Mr. Marcus McCorison, librarian of the American Antiquarian Society, kindly allowed me to consult the typescript of the recently located "Diary" of Isaiah Thomas, soon to be published. Thomas recorded that his grandfather had also been an Overseer of the Poor.

They provide information for the historian of education, of the family, of the poor, and of the bound labor system. They also provide a starting point for the student of specific trades in eighteenth-century Massachusetts as well as rich genealogical material for researchers in family history. They are reproduced in abstract form in the table, below.

Poor apprenticeship was but one of several forms of servitude in early Massachusetts. Although in the early decades of settlement, indentured servants and apprentices had been most typical, after the 1650's other kinds became important. Debtors, criminals, poor apprentices, and slaves were added to the servant categories, so that by the eighteenth century there were more than a half-dozen types. The composition of the servant class changed also. In the early years most servants were born either in England or in America of English parents. With some serious exceptions, they fit in well with the Puritan community, some becoming landowners, church members, and freemen of the colony. Gradually at first, but with increasing swiftness, new religious, social, racial, and national groups were introduced. Irish and Scottish prisoners from the English civil wars came in the 1650's. Indians and Negroes became servants and slaves—Indians particularly following the Pequot War and King Philip's War, Negroes particularly after the restoration of the Stuarts and the penetration of the slave trade by the English. By the eighteenth century the servant class was a marvelously polyglot group. Irish in goodly numbers, and Scottish, Jersey, Guernsey, and continental whites were sold as indentured servants. Spanish and New England Indians were bought or hired as slaves and servants and the latter were used frequently in fishing and whaling in what had been Plymouth colony. Negroes from the West Indies and the Guinea Coast were sold regularly and came to be the largest single group of imported bound labor by the 1730's and 1740's.[4]

The growth of this complicated and diverse system of bound labor cannot be explained in terms of custom alone. Most of the types of servitude had been part of the English experience before the Winthrop fleet sailed for America,[5] but more than the transplanting of

4. Lawrence W. Towner, "A Good Master Well Served, A Social History of Servitude in Massachusetts, 1620–1750," Ph.D. Dissertation, Northwestern University, 1955, appendix J.

5. Even in the case of slavery, the English were not without recent experience. English ships had dabbled in the slave trade, and Paul Baynes, who died in 1619, spoke familiarly of Blackmoor slaves. See his *An Entire Commentary Upon . . . Ephesians . . .* (London, 1643), 694.

English institutions was involved. The general availability of land, the widespread opportunities for labor, the necessity of importing labor, all made bound labor an apparent necessity if men were to have help in building homes, clearing land, and engaging in crafts and commerce. Moreover, servitude, which was modeled on the family in Massachusetts, provided an effective means of socializing the young, the unregenerate, and the criminal. By means of a contract, which bound the worker to his employer, or, through outright ownership, the slave to his master, both the economic and the social needs of society could be met.[6]

The relationship between Puritans and their poor is an excellent example of this combination of a customary institution with their immediate economic and social needs as they understood them. The seventeenth-century Puritans had a highly developed social consciousness set within a religious framework. They believed that the welfare of the individual should be subordinated to the religious and secular needs of the community, and in turn, that the community had a responsibility for the individual's welfare. This sense of moral responsibility led them to a broad definition of poverty, one which went well beyond the mere question of pounds, shillings, and pence. While the truly poor were not considered morally dangerous merely because they were poor, their poverty might be a warning of God's displeasure at secret evil actions not yet discovered to the community. On the other hand, financially solvent violators of the Commandments were, under the Covenant Theology, already moral liabilities and might well be on the road to becoming economic liabilities as well. Both groups presented an open invitation to God to visit his wrath upon the entire community. The solution to this problem was to make sure, as Professor Edmund S. Morgan has demonstrated, that every individual was subordinated to proper family government.[7]

Consequently, it was not merely those in need of alms who were subject to having their children taken from them under what might be called legislation for the poor. Parents or masters who failed to raise their children or servants in a properly religious atmosphere, who neglected their instruction in reading, who failed to teach them the catechism, or who were not bringing them up to a secular calling were equally likely to lose their wards to some other master. Single individuals of whatever age were required by law to place

6. Towner, "A Good Master," Ch. I.
7. Edmund S. Morgan, *The Puritan Family* . . . (Boston, 1956), Chs. IV–V.

themselves under good family government, and even a few married persons—those whose family government had failed—were placed under the jurisdiction of other families. The idle as well as the indigent; the loose liver as well as the lame, the halt, and the blind; the profligate as well as the poor orphan were trapped in the fine-meshed net of legislation for the poor.[8]

Ruben Guppy of Salem is a good example of how poverty of spirit was considered as dangerous as a thin purse. Guppy was in and out of court on charges at least fourteen times between 1641 and 1674. He got himself severely whipped in 1641 for abandoning his pregnant wife, and for theft, lying, swearing, and blasphemy. Among other things, he had said that the pairings of his nails were as acceptable to God as were days of Thanksgiving. In 1644, having already been in court six times, he was fined for not paying his rent and for using a neighbor's fence for firewood. A year later he was again hailed into court for fence stealing. At the same court he accused his wife of "wanton dalliance" with a neighbor. Shortly thereafter the community ordered Guppy's two oldest children apprenticed. Guppy was subsequently in court in 1649 for defamation of character, in 1651 for more fence stealing, and again in 1657 for accusing a neighbor of buggery. Obviously Guppy fitted well into the Puritan's definition of a moral liability.[9]

It was in the late 1660's, the 1670's, and the 1680's, however, when the pressure from England exacerbated the growing divisions within Massachusetts and when King Philip's War threatened the very existence of the colony, that the emphasis on family government as a means of social control reached its climax. In 1668, the Massachusetts government embarked on a vigorous campaign to enforce conformity. Printed instructions were sent to all towns repeating the laws relating to children, servants, and single adults living "dissolute lives" and requiring that their names be reported.[10] In Middlesex county alone, seven towns listed twenty-six persons living disorderly lives outside family government and three persons who

8. For representative legislation, see *Records of the Governor and Company of . . . Massachusetts Bay . . .* , ed., Nathaniel B. Shurtleff, 5 vols. in 6 (Boston, 1853–1854), 1 (1633), 109, (1636), 186; 11 (1646), 180. Hereafter cited as *Mass. Recs.* See also *The Laws and Liberties of Massachusetts . . .* , ed. Max Farrand (Cambridge, Mass., 1929, p. 11).

9. *Records and files of the Quarterly Courts of Essex County Massachusetts*, ed. George Francis Dow, 8 vols. (Salem, 1911–1921), I–V, *passim.* For the particular instances cited see: I. 25, 68, 82–83, 158, 209; II. 60. for the order to bind out Guppy's children see the Essex Institute Historical *Collections*, IX (1869), 151.

10. *Mass. Recs.*, IV. part ii, 395–396.

needed watching.[11] In other counties, too, families and single individuals were carefully scrutinized for the next two decades. In 1672, for example, twelve families of Muddy River were warned to put out their children as "servants to serve by Indentures."[12] In 1680, the Hampshire County Court found Cornelius Merry of Northampton to be a "very vicious" person and his care over his little children to be such as he "Rather Learnes them Irreligion rather than any good Literature. . . ." It ordered the selectmen to apprentice his two children.[13] In the same year, Robert Lyman and his wife, also of Northampton, were found incapable of maintaining their family. When they appeared in court, "showing their earnestnes that their children should not be put out," the Court ruled "that what the said Parents Spoke, [was] more out of fond affection and sinful Indulgence than any Reason or Rule." The two youngest Lyman boys and one of the girls were subsequently apprenticed.[14]

Adults also were subjected to family government following the 1660's. One Abigail Roberts, for example, was presented for dressing in clothing finer than her station in life warranted and for living outside of family government. However, several neighbors appeared in court and testified that she now lived in service and had reformed her dress.[15] A more serious charge, against a widow having a child three years after her husband's death, resulted in her being whipped ten stripes and ordered "into some good Family where shee may be under government."[16] Charges of idleness, drunkenness, "idle reports to amuse the people," playing cards and keeping bad company, stubborn and wicked notions, and the wearing of men's clothes by a girl, thus "seeming to confound the course of nature," all resulted in persons being placed under family jurisdiction.[17] In one case, that of an aged deacon and militia captain named James Johnson,

11. File 49 (1668), Files of the Middlesex County Court (Middlesex County Court House, Cambridge, Mass.).

12. Record Commissioners of the Town of Boston, *Reports*, 39 vols. (Boston 1881–1909), VII. 67. Hereafter cited as *Boston Records*.

13. Records of the Hampshire County Court, I (1680), 36, Hampshire County Court House, Northampton, Massachusetts.

14. *Ibid.*

15. *Records of the Suffolk County Court, 1671–1680*, Colonial Society of Massachusetts, *Publications*, XXIX–XXX (1933); II (1676), 751. Hereafter cited as *Suffolk County Court*.

16. *Ibid.*, I (1674), 442.

17. *Ibid.*, I (1672), 184, (1673), 258; II (1677), 870–871; Records of the Middlesex County Court, III (1679), 290; case of Mary Henly, 1691/92, *ibid.*, vols. 1689–1699, n.p.

"disorderly carriages" in his family resulted in an order to break up housekeeping and to "dispose of himselfe into some good orderly Family within one Fortnight. . . ."[18]

In 1679 the General Court summed up its conception of secular and spiritual poverty in its instructions for the newly created office of tithingman. These officials, to be chosen annually from among the "most prudent and discreet Inhabitants," were "diligently to inspect the manner of all disorderly persons, and whereby more private admonitions they will not be reclaimed, they are . . . to present their names [to the proper authorities] . . . who shall proceed against them as the Law directs, as also they are in like manner to present . . . all single persons that live from under Family Government, stubborne and disorderly Children and Servants, night-walkers, Typlers, Sabbath breakers, by night or by day, and such as absent themselves from the publick Worship of God on the Lords dayes, or whatever else course or practice of any person or persons whatsoever tending to debauchery, Irreligion, prophanness, and Atheisme amongst us, whether by omission of Family Government, nurture and religious dutyes and instruction of Children and Servants, or idle, profligate, uncivil or rude practices of any sort. . . ."[19]

The very intensity of this drive to emphasize family government was a measure of the changes that were taking place in society. Between 1660 and 1720, as Professor Perry Miller has shown, the religiously oriented, homogeneous community was becoming a secular, diverse, and commercial society.[20] As a result, the area of agreement on what was right and wrong was slowly narrowing, and the broad religious and moral concept of poverty was giving way to a definition based primarily on the lack of measurable wealth. At the same time, the society, growing richer and more complex, was turning gradually to institutions of brick and mortar as a means of caring for its criminals, its idle, and its poor. Increasingly, adults ended up at the house of correction, the workhouse, or the almshouse, and by and large, after 1692, only poor children, not poor or wayward adults, were subjected to family authority other than their own.[21]

18. *Suffolk County Court*, II (1675), 646–647.

19. *Mass Recs.*, V. 240–241. I have followed the wording of this law as reproduced in *The Colonial Laws of Massachusetts . . .* , ed. William H. Whitmore (Boston, 1887), 270.

20. Perry Miller, *The New England Mind: From Colony to Province* (Cambridge, Mass., 1953), *passim*.

21. Criminals, particularly thieves, and a few poor debtors were exceptions. See Towner, "A Good Master," Ch. IV. In 1756 a law was enacted, for three years, allowing

Eighteenth-century legislation concerning the binding out of poor children, then, was more sharply based on economic considerations than in the seventeenth century, although it still allowed some leeway in defining exactly who were the poor. The basic law came in 1692. By its terms the selectmen or Overseers of the Poor could bind out poor children with the consent of two justices of the peace, the boys to age twenty-one, the girls to age eighteen "or time of marriage." All children, or at least those "not having estates otherwise to maintain themselves," were subject to scrutiny to make sure they were being brought up to honest callings. No definition of poverty was provided, but presumably only those receiving alms were considered as falling within the jurisdiction of the law.[22]

The acts which followed were largely explanatory in nature and sought an effective definition of what constituted poverty. In the Act of 1704 the poor were defined as those who were not rated for town or province taxes. Such persons, whether receiving alms or not, were liable to having their children bound out by the authorities. This act also required that apprentices be taught to read and write, a provision subsequently restricted to males in 1711, the girls to be taught reading only. While being rated for taxes would protect one from losing his children under ordinary circumstances, a law in 1722 made idle, dissolute, or vagrant parents, whether rated for taxes or not, subject to having their children "put out into orderly families."[23]

The climax to this legislation came in 1735 in the form of a special act for Boston, where the numbers of the poor had been increasing alarmingly. Since the 1690's local taxes had been raised regularly "for relieving the poor and other charges"; three private charitable societies now existed; and at least one minister saw the danger of a growing class of idle poor. In 1742, out of a population of 17,756, there were 110 persons in the almshouse and 36 in the workhouse.

---

the overseers or selectmen of a town to bind out a poor adult for one year, his wages to be used to support his family. In 1759, a law was enacted for five years allowing the mother of a bastard child to be indentured for five years if her charges had been born by the town or if her child became a charge to the town before it was five years of age. Neither law was re-enacted. *Acts and Resolves . . . of the Province of the Massachusetts Bay . . .*, 21 vols. (Boston, 1869–1922), III. 926–928; IV. 178–179. Hereafter cited as *Acts and Resolves.*

22. *Acts and Resolves,* I. 67.

23. *Ibid.,* I. 538–539, 654–655; II. 242. These acts were usually temporary, renewed from time to time, but not always soon enough to avoid lapsing.

Of 1,200 widows, 1,000 were not rated for taxes.[24] Under these circumstances, the legislature, by the Act of 1735, allowed Boston to appoint twelve Overseers of the Poor, one for each ward. These men were to supervise the poor, to commit persons to a workhouse, which by the act they were empowered to erect, and to enforce the laws with regard to apprenticing the children of the poor. Unless a parent were rated for personal estate or faculty (i.e. a trade or profession), he was subject to having his children bound out. Furthermore, children who, at the age of six years, did not know the alphabet, were to be bound out "as when parents are indigent and rated nothing to the publick taxes. . . ."[25] This latter provision notwithstanding, there is little or no evidence to indicate that any criterion other than poverty was actually used. Isaiah Thomas and the other poor children bound out between 1734 and 1805 seem to have been truly children of the poor.

The numbers of boys and girls apprenticed under the Act of 1735 and other laws modeled on it varied from year to year. The high year was 1768 with forty-six apprentices, the low, 1776, with but one. The average number per year was seventeen. The peak decades were between 1760 and 1780 when, for all but five years, more than the average number of apprentices were bound out. The decades of war and revolution, obviously, created serious social problems. By contrast, in the decades between 1780 and 1805 there were only three above-average years. The ratio of boys to girls remained fairly steady at three to two throughout the period.[26]

The duration of the contracts varied, of course, with the age and sex of the individual apprentice. About one-half of the children were

24. *Boston Records*, VIII. *passim*; Carl Bridenbaugh, *Cities in the Wilderness* . . . (New York, 1938), 393–394; Clifford K. Shipton, *Sibley's Harvard Graduates* (Cambridge, Mass., 1873–), VI. 448. Massachusetts Historical Society, *Collections*, 3rd Ser., I (1825), 152.

25. *Acts and Resolves*, II. 756–758. Except for a law in 1771, which required that boys be taught reading, writing, and ciphering, no significant change was made in this law during the colonial period. In 1778 and 1794 the state of Massachusetts empowered all towns to appoint overseers of the poor and the overseers to bind out the children of the poor as apprentices or servants. The educational provisions were the same as revised in 1771. Parents who were assessed town or district taxes were not liable to having their children bound. *Ibid.*, V. 161–162; *The General Laws of Massachusetts from the Adoption of the Constitution to February, 1822*, ed., Theron Metcalf, 2 vols. (Boston, 1823), I. 438–449.

26. This and the following paragraphs concerning the poor apprentices are based on the table of indentures below.

bound out between the ages of five and nine. The median age was nine. Some, like Edward Holin who was apprenticed in 1745 at the age of eighteen months to serve Robert Anderson, housewright of Chester, New Hampshire, were very young and served long terms. But only thirty-seven apprentices, 3 per cent of the total, were placed out under the age of five. At the other end of the scale, a few served for very short terms. Bathsheba Rogers, for example, was apprenticed at the age of seventeen for one year to James Mason, a farmer in Bristol County, in 1742. However, only 1.7 per cent served for less than three years, and less than 25 per cent served terms of less than seven years.

Boys were apprenticed to sixty different trades, ranging from apothecary to victualler, from bricklayer to goldsmith. The maritime trades (sailors, navigators, and shoremen), the shipbuilding trades (mastmakers, ship carpenters, ropemakers, sail makers, shipwrights, and sparmakers), and the leather trades (cordwainers, saddlers, leather dressers, tanners, and leather drapers) each accounted for about 8 per cent of the boys. Coopers absorbed 5 per cent, and tailors about 3 per cent. House trades and metal trades each took about 4 per cent. There was little observable fluctuation in demand for apprentices in the various crafts, except in the 1760's. Then, coopers, shipbuilding trades, and maritime trades—all related fields—more than doubled their demand following the French and Indian War when the seas were again safe for Massachusetts shipping.

About 40 per cent of the boys were not apprenticed to crafts but were put out to learn husbandry. Prior to the 1770's, agriculture, although it was the leading field to which poor boys were apprenticed, drew fewer apprentices than did the crafts, and it actually declined to about 5 per cent of the total in the 1760's. But in the 1770's and thereafter, agriculture once again became the leading field and, in fact, took more poor boys than all the crafts put together—60 per cent of the boys in the 1770's and 1780's, 55 per cent in the 1790's, and 86 per cent in the first six years of the nineteenth century.

Girls were apprenticed chiefly to serve as household maids. During the 1740's and 1750's, most of their indentures specified the trade of a spinster, but about a third of them were simply apprenticed to learn housewifery, and even the spinsters probably spent most of their time doing household work. In the 1760's the term, "spinster," was dropped and "housewifery" took its place. From 1770 to the end of the century, knitting, sewing, and spinning were usually added to housewifery. Only two girls were taught another trade, that of manteau or mantua maker.[27]

The demand for poor apprentices, particularly in farming but also in housewifery, drew many boys and girls out of Boston. In the 1740's about 67 per cent of the children were sent out of town. By the 1780's this had increased to 89 per cent, only to drop back to 82 per cent in the 1790's. In the first six years of the nineteenth century more than 90 per cent left Boston. All told, Boston sent away about 74 per cent of its poor apprentices—all but 126 girls and 162 boys. These country apprentices were distributed throughout Massachusetts in twelve counties and in the present state of Maine, and a few went to New Hampshire and Connecticut. About 70 per cent of all apprentices, however, were absorbed by the two eastern counties of Suffolk and Middlesex and the two western counties of Hampshire and Worcester.

The masters who took these poor children as apprentices were as varied in trade and occupation as the arts or mysteries the boys and girls were supposed to learn. There were sixty-four crafts, trades, and occupations, and three professions represented among the masters. Mariners and cordwainers took more apprentices than any other craftsmen or tradesmen, but yeomen, husbandmen, and farmers, all of whom were presumably engaged in agriculture, took more than any other occupation. Several masters, it should be noted, agreed to teach, or have taught, trades with which they were not familiar, or which they were themselves apparently not practicing.

Considerable variation in social rank existed among the masters. At the top of the scale were persons of some social prominence in their own communities. They included such Boston worthies as the Reverend Andrew Eliot; Josiah Warren, Gent.; Nathaniel Loring, merchant; the Reverend Oxenbridge Thatcher; and Samuel Otis, merchant. There were also such persons of standing as the Reverend John Hancock of Braintree; Robert Treat Paine, Esq., of Taunton; John Oliver of Malden; Daniel Oliver and Levi Lincoln of Worcester; James Warren, Esq., of Plymouth; and John Langdon of New Hampshire. More than 125 masters claimed honorifics; and there were seventeen merchants, seventeen physicians, twelve ministers, two schoolmasters, and thirty or more men of officer rank in the military among the masters.

The indentures, in fact, suggest a good bit about the existence of social classes in eighteenth-century Massachusetts. From the regu-

27. See Ann Cromartie (1769) and Ann Wilkinson (1784), below.

larity with which honorifics were entered with the names of the Overseers, for example, it can be assumed that men took their "Hon.," "Gent.," and "Esq." quite seriously.[28] The masters, too, were careful about their social ranking or occupational designations, although they were less so after the start of the Revolution. In the case of those engaged in agriculture, the exact social weight of the terms "Yeoman," "Husbandman," and "farmer" is not clear. Yet their weights relative to each other seem clear enough. "Yeoman" still retained its concept of social worth, while "Husbandman," used far less frequently, and "farmer," used hardly at all, seem to have been of lower rank. After 1777, however, "Yeoman" and "Husbandman" drop out of use, occupational designations even in the trades are recorded only infrequently, and "Mr." comes into general but not universal use.

If honorifics and occupational designations were of social significance, then the bulk of the masters were drawn from the middling and upper strata of the various towns—successful craftsmen and tradesmen, securely established farmers, and a sprinkling of local leaders. Only occasionally, if at all, was a master drawn from among those who were of doubtful financial responsibility or questionable social respectability. The screening of potential masters was, as we shall see, the purpose behind a requirement that they be recommended to the Overseers by the officials who knew them best, the selectmen in the towns where they lived.

Many masters, particularly those in the smaller towns, took two apprentices, usually one to learn husbandry, the other housewifery. Paul Mandell, Gent., of Hardwick, took ten between 1760 and 1778, usually two at a time. The most he had at one time was eight. That was in February 1778 when he apprenticed William Dunn and Sarah Granger, ages seven and six years, respectively. With these two added to his household, he had a total of five girl apprentices, between the ages of six and sixteen, and three boys, between the ages of seven and sixteen. Mandell was the first person in Hardwick to take poor apprentices from Boston, but within a dozen years of his first apprentice's arrival in town, eight other residents had taken boys or girls from the almshouse. His contentment with his Boston servants, as measured by his return trips to the almshouse, must have communicated itself to his neighbors.

Not a great deal more can be known about most of the apprentices other than what their indentures reveal. How they were chosen,

28. In some cases, where they had been left off, they were inserted afterwards.

who they were, the actual conditions of life with their masters, how well they learned their trades, how well they were educated, are all questions which for the most part cannot be answered with any assurance.

The Overseers regularly perambulated their wards looking for poor people who ought to be in the workhouse or in the almshouse and, presumably, checking up on the condition of dependent children.[29] Undoubtedly they apprenticed many children directly from their homes, but many others were taken from the almshouse. Some arrived there with one or both of their parents, some alone, and some were born there, often the illegitimate children of wayward girls.[30] Quite a few were apparently the children of recent immigrants. While most, 57 per cent, appear to have come from families of English ancestry, about 15 per cent were from families of Irish background, about the same percentage were Scots, 5 per cent Welsh, 4 per cent French, and the rest were German, Italian, and Negro.[31]

Once a child was in the almhouse, it was to the advantage of the Overseers to get him apprenticed quickly to avoid the cost of food, clothing, and housing. It was also to the advantage of the child to get out as quickly as possible. The almshouse, like other eighteenth-century public institutions, was probably not an attractive place to be.

Cotton Mather wrote in the records of the Second Church for 4 April 1697, that one Abigail Day had complained bitterly about the food at the almshouse, saying that "she would thank neither God nor Man for such Victuals," and about the master of the house, who, she said, "had several Times made Attempts upon her Chastity." More than a century later the almshouse was still having difficulty. A committee, charged with constructing new vaults for the privies reported that they had had to construct new sewers. "The drain from the pump and kitchen," the report said, "being originally turned

29. See the Miscellaneous Files (by date) of the Overseers of the Poor, Department of Public Welfare, Boston, Massachusetts.

30. "Admissions, 1768–1774," Overseers Records.

31. This estimate is based on a random sampling of the names of four hundred apprentices checked against Elsdon C. Smith, *Dictionary of American Family Names* (New York, 1956). In 1790, it may be pointed out, Massachusetts' population was composed roughly of the following linguistic and national stocks: English, 82 per cent; Scotch, 4.4 per cent; Ulster Irish, 1.6 per cent; Irish, 1.3 per cent; German, .3 per cent; Dutch, .2 per cent; and French, .8 per cent. See "Report of the Committee on Linguistic and National Stocks in the Population of the United States," American Historical Association, *Annual Report* for 1931 (Washington, D.C., 1932), I. 124.

through the privies, opened a direct communication into the body of the house for the foul air, not only of the drain but that air was surcharged with the fetidity of the vaults, so that on the rising of the tide, especially when accompanied with an east wind, the stench was not only diffused through the yard, but entered thro' the sink into . . . the body of the house."[32]

Whether or not these pictures indicate the true nature of the food, the morals, and the smells of the almshouse, they suggest that getting out was a good thing. The chance came when a prospective master applied for an apprentice. If he lived in Boston, he needed no written recommendation, for presumably he was known to the Overseers of the Poor. But if he was from out of town, he had to have a letter of recommendation from the majority of his selectmen. By 1758 these recommendations had been printed with blanks for names and dates. According to the printed formula, the master was to be "a Man of sober Life and Conversation; and in such Circumstances [that the selectman could] recommend him as a fit Person to bind an Apprentice to."[33]

If the master found a child to his liking, he might take him home on trial before signing the indentures. The selectmen of Rehoboth, for example, wrote the Overseers on 8 November 1776, about one Elizabeth Barber, a poor girl of Boston who had been living with James Thurber, Esq., for some time. "As she proves to be an Industrious likely girl and is Very desireous to Tarry with the family and they well affected towards her," she would be happily situated if she could be bound out to Thurber. On 9 December 1776, the Overseers signed her indentures, binding her for four years.[34] Other children were not so fortunate as to like and be liked. Esther Burgean, ten years old in 1773, was one of these. Her master, David Durfee of Dartmouth, had apparently not completed the process of apprenticing her two years earlier when indentures had been drawn binding Esther to him for ten years. On 27 November 1773, he sent her back to Boston with a letter saying that he found her "not to Answer my expectations in any respect she being so Dull and Stupid Capacity

32. *The Diary of Cotton Mather, 1681–1724*, ed., Worthington C. Ford, Massachusetts Historical Society, *Collections*, 7th Ser., VII–VIII (Boston, 1911–1912), I. 226n. Report of Committee of Repairs, 25 September 1819, "Register of Letters, etc., 1817–1834," 2, Overseers Records.

33. Completed copies of this form are scattered throughout the volumes in which the indentures, below, are bound. Boston Indentures, 1734–1805, 6 vols., City Clerk's office, City Hall, Boston.

34. *Ibid.*, IV. 143.

as not to be capable of doing any Service of account, nor to be Learnt to any Tolerable degree either to Work or Read as hath been declared by her Tutors. . . ."[35]

Once a child was bound, he was not ordinarily cause for further concern on the part of the Overseers until the time came to exchange indentures at the end of his term of service. Only occasionally did the Overseers have to bind out an apprentice anew or make some other arrangement for him. So far as the records reveal, for example, only one apprentice was freed to enlist in military service, although there were probably others whose masters did not bother to let the Overseers know.[36] Even the death of the master did not ordinarily require that the apprentice be bound out again, for the indentures almost invariably specified that the servant was being bound to the master, his wife, and his heirs. In fact, since the contract bound both parties, the one to service, the other to provide keep and training, the master's estate was liable for fulfillment of the terms. A letter of 3 November 1789, from Samuel Cutler, administrator of the estate of one William Atkins, Esq., of Newburyport, shows the problems that could arise because of these conditions. He reported that Peggy Kilgore, bound out on 8 June 1782, for eleven years, was ill, and the heirs wanted to return her to the almshouse. "I can assure you, Gentlemen," Cutler wrote, "that it will be a great hardship upon the Heirs to maintain her, the Estate being but small and three unmarried Daughters to be maintained by it. I do not conceive by the Indentures that the Estate is obliged to maintain her after she is rendered incapable, by sickness, to perform what she was bound to do. Should I be mistaken We rely on your Charity and generosity to grant this our petition."[37]

Other children, for reasons mostly unknown, were turned over to different masters before their terms were up, but that too was a rare occasion. In 1770, for example, one Thomas Banks, after nine years with William Williams, Gent., of Hatfield, was apprenticed to a cordwainer named Belding of that town to learn his trade. Apparently all parties, the masters, the servant, and the Overseers were satisfied with the change. Most relieved, was Williams, who had written the Overseers about his unhappy experiences with Banks. "For the first four years," he said, "I schooled him constantly at the Town school here, and a considerable part of every year since, except

35. *Ibid.*, IV. 63.
36. John Ruggles to Overseers, n.d., *ibid.*, IV. 103.
37. *Ibid.*, V. 22.

of last. He is now seventeen years . . . old and about as big as an ordinary Country boy of thirteen . . . and . . . scarcely able to perform the service of one of our boys of that age—I have been sensible some time that it would by no means answer to bring him up to husbandry. He will never be capable to perform the Labour or to endure the fatigues that are the unavoidable lot of the husbandman—I therefore attempted more than a year ago to get him a Trade, but the notion which then generally (and with too much foundation in truth) prevailed of his being a Rogue in grain prevented the success of these attempts at that Time—"[38]

Information is even more lacking on what happened to the apprentices after they completed their service than it is on their condition while servants. What happened to them? Were they incorporated into the society, or were they likely to become dependent again? In short, how successful was the system as far as the apprentices themselves were concerned? This is an extremely difficult question, one susceptible of definitive answer only if a representative sample of the apprentices could be followed throughout their lives.

What can be done at this point, however, is to lay out the extremes of success and failure and hazard a guess as to what happened to those in between. Isaiah Thomas is the success story. Although he ran away from Fowle at the age of eighteen, he returned to Boston in 1770 and rejoined his former master, this time as a partner in publishing the *Massachusetts Spy*. In 1771, he took an apprentice, another poor boy put out by the Overseers of the Poor. The rest of his story is well known.[39]

At the other extreme was Mary Butcher. Mary became an apprentice of Richard Storkney, yeoman of Staughton, in 1754 when she was but an infant. For fifty years thereafter she left no record; but in 1804 she turned up in Canton, poor, unmarried, and lame. The Overseers there, after keeping her fed and housed awhile, wrote to the Overseers in Boston. "She is," they said, "a person whom nature has not been over bountiful in furnishing her mental faculties. . . ." Should they keep her there at Boston's charge, or send her home? On the back of this letter is an endorsement by a resigned Boston Overseer: "Ansd. 3 July and said, send her in."[40]

38. William Williams to Royall Tyler, 23 January 1770, *ibid.*, IV. 15.
39. The apprentice was Anthony Haswell (1771), below. For Thomas, see note 3 [this selection,] above.
40. Overseers of the Poor of Canton, Massachusetts, to Overseers of Boston, 25 June 1805, "Papers, 1733–1854," Overseers Records.

Between these two extremes fell the mass of the apprentices. All had learned to read and write, or, at least, were promised reading and writing, and all males were promised ciphering as well.[41] All were exposed to the skills or the routine tasks whereby they could earn their livings as artisans, farmers, or housewives. Their formal and practical training was the equivalent of that of the average maid of eighteen or youth of twenty-one in eighteenth-century Massachusetts. They were prepared to enter life, not as wards of society, but as individuals whose economic lives and social statuses would be determined in part by their own efforts. Yet, unlike other young adults, they did not have families standing behind them prepared to provide assistance in getting a start in life. Their freedom dues, which might have served that purpose, were usually limited to two suits of clothing. Except in a very few instances, indentures did not specify a gift of tools or other tangible assets. Only in the case of boys apprenticed to farming, beginning in the 1760's, did indentures specify a cash payment as part of the freedom dues. At first this payment amounted to £13:06:08. In the 1770's, 1780's, and early 1790's it was £20, and thereafter it amounted to about $70.

To the males given training in a craft, the future must have seemed fairly bright. Craftsmen of all kinds were generally in short supply in eighteenth-century America, and the skilled worker of industrious habits and a little luck could easily find work as a journeyman in the cities, towns, and villages.[42] There were, for example, more than 140 different trades being practiced in Boston in the 1790's.[43] On the other hand, the chances of being apprenticed to a trade instead of to husbandry were considerably less by the 1780's and 1790's than they had been in the middle of the century. Moreover, without freedom dues in cash or tools, a good many years of service as a journeyman probably awaited the poor apprentice when he was freed. Out of seventy boys apprenticed to tradesmen in Boston between 1760 and 1790, for example, only three are listed as masters of their own trades in the Boston Directory for 1796. They are Joseph Lilly, apprenticed in 1771 and working as a tailor on

41. Isaiah Thomas claimed that his master did not instruct him in reading or writing. In fact, he claimed that Fowle was unable to spell or punctuate. See Thomas's "Diary," American Antiquarian Society. Between 1786 and 1792, most girl apprentices were to be taught reading, writing, *and* ciphering.

42. Carl Bridenbaugh, *The Colonial Craftsman* (New York and London, 1950), 135–137.

43. "The Boston Directory . . . ," (1796), *Boston Records*, X. 221–296.

Middle Street; William Pierce, apprenticed in 1761 and working as a hairdresser with a shop on Marshall's Lane and a house on Union Street; and James McCleary, apprenticed in 1771 and working as a tobacconist with a shop at number 8 Butler's Row and a house on Windmill Walk.[44] The others had either left Boston for other towns or were still working as journeymen or laborers.

The same pattern probably existed among the boys apprenticed to husbandry. With luck, a boy might marry the farmer's daughter and be set up by the family on new land or inherit the house and land of the family into which he had married. But without luck, he probably had to serve for years as a hired hand before he would be in a position to farm for himself. The freedom dues in cash, about the equivalent of a half-year's wages, would hardly sustain a man as a farmer if he were starting from scratch. Without a family behind him to ease the burden of the first years, a man starting farming even in those relatively simple times probably required more capital than he had at his disposal.[45]

As for the girls, there was no likelihood or expectation that they would become independent. Their choices were limited to continuing as paid household servants or getting married. In this they differed little from their sisters who were fortunate enough to have families to sustain them. Their choice of husbands was limited, however, by the fact that they had no dowries to bring to their marriages and no one but their masters to seek marriage matches for them.

At its worst, poor apprenticeship was only a temporary condition, not a permanent status. It provided a means not only of reintegrating the poor into society as useful working members but also of reducing the cost of supporting public institutions. In a day when manufacturing was largely in the hands of craftsmen, when most people worked on farms, when women had few opportunities anyway, and when education beyond primary school level was the province of the few, it was probably as workable a system as could be devised. What had begun in the seventeenth century as a means of insuring moral and religious conformity had ended up as a valuable and workable

44. *Ibid.*, X. 263, 274, 267.
45. Only one apprentice was assured land in his indentures. Francis Dizer (7/22/66), who was apprenticed to both husbandry and surveying, was promised twenty acres of unimproved land and, if he behaved himself, a set of surveying instruments. Two boys were promised cattle: Richard Caswell (8/3/48), a yoke of oxen or £40 O.T.; and Barzallai Eddy (10/10/98), two three-year-old oxen and a heifer of the same age.

social institution. Unlike slavery, which died out in the 1780's and 1790's in Massachusetts, poor apprenticeship seemed to fit the needs of a free society.

The table of indentures of poor apprentices which follows is based on the original printed forms bound in six volumes located in the City Clerk's office, City Hall, Boston, Massachusetts. Several years ago Dr. Stephen T. Riley of the Massachusetts Historical Society told me about them. Subsequently they were microfilmed for the Institute of Early American History and Culture, Williamsburg, Virginia. The indentures through 1776 were transcribed in tabular form by Mr. W. Graham Millar, who kindly gave me a copy of his tables.[46] Those from 1777 on were transcribed by Mrs. Beverly Schell, secretary at the Institute, largely on her own time and as a labor of love for history. I have subsequently proofread the new table, here presented, against the originals.

The table [see p. 55] is an abstract and does not carry all the information available on the indentures. Conspicuously absent are the freedom dues, discussed above. There is such a regularity in these dues that it does not seem worthwhile to take the space to list them. Variations in formal educational requirements have also been discussed in the text, and they are omitted in the table except for an occasional footnote. No column has been provided for the master's occupations, but a careful reader will find those occupations if he understands that from 1734 to 1779, the period when occupations were almost always listed, the master's occupation was the same as that being taught unless otherwise indicated by footnote. From 1780 to 1805, when occupations for masters were rarely given, every master whose occupation is on the indenture has his occupation listed by footnote. Finally, to conserve space I have abbreviated trades in the table by leaving out vowels. Except in such cases as prk mkr (peruke maker) and mntu mkr (manteau maker), this should cause no serious difficulty.

46. W. Graham Millar, "The Poor Apprentices of Boston; Indentures of Poor Children Bound Out by the Overseers of the Poor of Boston, 1734–1776 . . . ," M.A. Thesis, College of William and Mary, 1958.

Apprentice	Date Bound	Date Free	Trade	Master	Town
William Croxford	6/5/49	6/7/66	hsbndry	Daniel Chase, Yeo.	Sutton
Veronica Vantiber	7/31/49	7/15/55	spinster	Isaiah Barrett	Boston
John Bedson	8/1/49	4/4/57	cooper	Samuel Smalledge	Boston
Jeremiah Field	9/6/49	7/1/57	farmer	William Richardson, Gent.	Lancaster
Asa Soper	9/7/49	10/22/55	shopkpng	Thomas Paine	Boston
Francis Orne (?)	9/16/49	3/6/67	hsbndry	Alexander Campbell	Boston
Miles Hubbard	10/2/49	9/10/61	chrmkr	Samuel Ridgway, Jr.	Boston
Hannah Martin	12/28/49	4/15/62	spinster	Isaac Bauldin	Sudbury
Charles Richardson	12/28/49	5/31/65	hsbndry	Charles Snell	Bridgewater
Mary Hermon	5/2/50	5/1/63	spinster	Joseph Langret	Lebanon, Conn.
Sarrah Wakefield	5/10/50	8/1/65	spinster	Henry Spring, Yeo.	Weston
Charles Whitewood	6/5/60	1/18/65	farmer	John Ryan, Yeo.	Sturbridge
Judith Simons	6/24/50	2/15/57	spinster	Moses Arnold	Boston
Mary Hyland	7/3/50	10/20/57	spinster	John Liddell, Gent.	Boston
Elizabeth Timberle	8/13/50	7/22/61	spinster	Joshua Bramhall	Plymouth
James McConnel	8/22/50	7/15/63	crdwnr	Joseph Fitch, Gent.	Boston
Farnell Chamberlane	9/26/50	8/21/67	farmer	Daniel Alger	Bridgewater
Susanna Vail	9/26/50	9/15/62	spinster	Thomas Gleason, Yeo.	Oxford
Elizabeth Stamers	9/26/50	3/15/62	spinster	James Packard, Yeo.	Bridgewater
John Badson	10/2/50	4/10/57	cooper	Benjamin Sault	Boston
Lidia Richardson	10/2/50	5/15/61	spinster	Jabez Fisher, Yeo.	Wrentham
Sarah Croutch	11/5/50	4/14/64	spinster	James Brown, Yeo.	Western
Ezekiel Clisby	11/5/50	4/15/65	hsbndry	Nathan Ames	Bridgewater
William Perry	12/3/50	9/18/59	prk mkr	John Gyles	Boston
Mary Engerson	12/31/50	5/15/58	spinster	Thomas Bacon, Yeo.	Wrentham
William Roberts	4/30/51	4/30/58	gunsmth	Samuel Clough	Boston
Simeon Pery	4/30/51	5/15/66	cooper	Oliver Wyman	Leominster

>4<

TRUE CONFESSIONS AND DYING

WARNINGS IN COLONIAL NEW

ENGLAND

This is a wonderful example of a piece of scholarship that began as a lark and ended as a serious examination of an important though neglected genre of social history. Towner's forays into servitude had led him to crime as a form of protest, and that led him to the large body of literature in which the criminal (through his amanuensis) confessed his crime in "a grand design of sin, remorse, confession, presumptive salvation, and death."

Over the years Towner examined some 400 court confessions in the published records of seventeenth-century Massachusetts and then some 100 broadsides, the characteristic eighteenth-century form, often crudely illustrated. He continued his earlier efforts to use the confessions to analyze the changing social character of criminals and crime. But he also grappled with the question of "declension" in Puritan society that Perry Miller had raised. The genre has since become commonplace in the new wave of social history in England, France, and America.

From *Sibley's Heir: A Volume in Memory of Clifford Kenyon Shipton*, Publications of the Colonial Society of Massachusetts, vol. 59, *Collections*, 523–39 (Andover: Colonial Society of Massachusetts, 1982). Reprinted with permission.
[*Author's note:*] I am delighted to have this essay accepted for Ted Shipton's memorial volume. It was written originally at his request as the keynote speech (titillating but not substantial) for a conference he organized in 1963. I have since revised it extensively and in the process bored several kindly audiences with it. Now, I gladly give it up as no longer readable aloud. Meanwhile, two friends have helped me with it: Ms. Sandra Peterson took the idea, and in altered form, traced it in American literature up through Dreiser's *An American Tragedy*, earning the Ph.D. in English on the way; more recently, Charles G. Steffen, while a doctoral candidate in history at Northwestern University, tracked down lost footnotes, checked quotations, reminded me of recent literature I should read, criticized the whole, and made solid suggestions for significant improvements based on his review of the cases. Sigmund Diamond, the late Max Savelle, and at least two Northwestern University graduate English seminars also aided and abetted me in this crime.

I

LATE IN JULY 1701, Esther Rodgers of Ipswich, Massachusetts, died on the gallows. "The manner of her Entertaining DEATH," said the account published that year by the Reverend Mr. John Rogers, was "astonishing to a Multitude of Spectators," who numbered some four to five thousand souls. Her "Composure of Spirit, Cheerfulness of Countenance, pleasantness of Speech, and a sort of Complaisantness in Carriage towards the Ministers who were assistant to her, . . . melted the hearts of all that were within seeing or hearing, into Tears of affection. . . ."[1]

Poor Esther had been born in Kittery sometime in May of 1680. At thirteen, she was apprenticed in Newbury, where she was taught to read and required to learn John Cotton's catechism. She forgot it, however, for at the age of seventeen she found herself pregnant by "a *Negro* Lad living in the same House."[2] Remarkable as it may seem, she delivered the baby herself without anyone suspecting her condition and immediately buried the child, after suffocating it, in her master's garden.

Esther came out of her apprenticeship at eighteen and worked in a public house in Piscataqua, returning within a year to her former master, only to leave him again, for a position in Ipswich. There she again strayed from the narrow way, and again became pregnant by a black servant. This child she delivered in a field and again immediately did away with it. Her crime was soon discovered, however, and the court convicted her of murder. Some eight months later, she was turned off into eternity.

The Reverend Mr. Rogers' account of Esther's life is entitled *Death The certain Wages of Sin to the Impenitent: Life The sure Reward of Grace to the Penitent: Together with the only Way for YOUTH To avoid the former, and attain the latter.* It comprises an introduction by the Reverend Mr. William Hubbard, *three* lectureday sermons by John Rogers, and—from Esther—a detailed confession, an account of her experiences in jail, two statements, a final dying warning, and a last prayer; altogether 154 pages. This, in short, is the classic True Confession and Dying Warning.

In these pages we see the grand design of sin, remorse, confession, presumptive salvation, and death. Esther had been introduced to re-

---

1. John Rogers, *Death The certain Wages of Sin to the Inmpenitent: Life The sure Reward of Grace to the Penitent: Together with the only Way for YOUTH To avoid the former, and attain the latter* (Boston, 1701), 153.
2. *Ibid.*, 121–122.

ligion at an early age, but in sabbath-breaking and evil-company-keeping she had run afoul not only of God's law but of man's. She hid from man her first infanticide; but in typical Puritan fashion, God's punishment confirmed her in the very same crime. Sin begot sin. In jail her hardened heart rejected the words of the visiting ministers—including the famous Mr. John Wise—and "other Christians of the Town and Neighbourhood."[3] Ultimately, however, through the good offices of an "Ambassador of Jesus Christ"—presumably our author—she repented, confessed, and threw herself on the Lord's mercy. She "approved the Verdict and Sentence, that they were just and right."[4] In church, shortly before her execution, she was told that she was a "Dead Woman; not only that she was dead in Trespasses & Sins, but . . . in Law, and by a Sentence of Condemnation must be put to Death before another Sabbath come about. . . ." And yet, argued the Reverend Mr. Rogers, "there is more than a possibility through Grace, that she may Live again; though not in this World. . . ."[5]

On the scaffold, Esther's last words were taken down in short-hand. She would die a shameful death, she said, and a justly deserved one. From it, let all young people take warning: "I beg of all to have a Care. Be Obedient to your Parents and Masters; Run not out at Nights, especially on Sabbath Nights, Refrain bad Company for the Lord's Sake. . . . Keep God's Sabbaths, mind the Word of God, and let good People be your Company. . . ."[6]

Finally, the account concludes, "being bid to lean her head back upon the Ladder, to receive the Halter, She readily does it; and Cryes, . . . *O Come Lord Jesus by Thy Pardoning Mercy, to Save me Now, or I perish for ever. My Blessed Jesus, O Lord Jesus, have Pity upon me, O Good Lord. . . .*"[7]

II

As it was with so many aspects of New-England culture, the literature of True Confessions and Dying Warnings had its antecedents in old England. As the late Clifford K. Shipton first pointed out many years ago, in gentle opposition to the Turner thesis, what may have been notable about colonial New England was not so much the influence of the frontier in shaping its institutions, but rather the de-

3. *Ibid.*, 127.
4. *Ibid.*, 143, 132.
5. *Ibid.*, 135.
6. *Ibid.*, 147.
7. *Ibid.*, 152.

gree to which the colonists were able to reproduce on the frontier what they had known in old England.[8]

The precedent for True Confessions and Dying Warnings can be traced at least as far back as the distinguished Puritan divine, William Perkins, whose name is referred to several times in the works we are about to examine. As late as 1713, for example, Cotton Mather wrote of "the famous Mr. *Perkins* . . . who dealt much with Condemned Prisoners. . . ."[9] A check on the writings of this Puritan forerunner, the father of so many ideas carried to New England, reveals no titles that sound like True Confessions and Dying Warnings, but he had been concerned with prisoners in old Cambridge and often accompanied them to their executions.[10]

Execution sermons and confessions were quite common in England in the sixteenth and seventeenth centuries.[11] By the eighteenth, they had become a staple crop in John Applebee's *London Weekly Journal.* "*Mr.* Applebee," wrote Eustace Budgell, a contemporary, "*takes Care to purchase from all our dying Criminals the private Memoirs of their Lives and Conversations; and though many of these pieces have been wrote or dictated under great Perturbation of Mind, and consequently have not been very Coherant, they still incite the Curious and Inquisitive to peruse Mr.* Applebee's *Journal.*"[12]

True Confessions and Dying Warnings found a rich and ready soil in the lives of New-England Puritans, where confession already flourished. That phenomenon appears as early as the pre-migration writings of the greatest Puritan of them all, John Winthrop. It was only after the most rigorous examination of his evil ways that Winthrop could find relief from the nagging suspicion that he was damned; that, on taking his spiritual temperature, he could believe he was not running a fever after all. These confessions, confided to paper in his "Christian Experienca,"[13] were private of course, as

8. Clifford K. Shipton, "The New England Frontier," *The New England Quarterly,* X. (March 1937), 25–36.

9. Cotton Mather, *The Sad Effects of Sin* (Boston, 1713), 56.

10. *Dictionary of National Biography, s.v.,* William Perkins.

11. See Alfred William Pollard, comp., *A Short-title Catalogue of Books Printed in England . . . 1475–1640* (London, 1926), and Donald Goddard Wing, comp., *Short-title Catalogue of Books Printed in England . . . 1641–1700* (3 vols., New York, 1945–1951).

12. Michael Shugrue, "Applebee's Original Weekly Journal . . . ," *The Newberry Library Bulletin,* VI. (March 1964), 111–112.

13. "John Winthrop's Christian Experienca," *Winthrop Papers* (5 vols., Boston, 1929), I. 154–160. I think the figure is Edmund S. Morgan's, but I forget from where.

were those much later that can be read only with agony in the diaries of such worthies as Michael Wigglesworth and Cotton Mather.[14]

In Mather's Diary, confessions begin on 16 April 1681, his nineteenth year, and carry on for two volumes, almost without relief. There are some 250 there, and the most vivid image one gains is of his groveling on the floor of his study confessing unworthiness and begging forgiveness. He wrote on 7 February 1707: "I sett apart this Day, to humble myself deeply before the Lord, for my horrible Corruptions and Miscarriages. I could plainly discern on myself, grevious Marks of a Man abhorred of the Lord. And as one even ashamed to approach unto Heaven, I lay prostrate in the Dust afar off, crying out, *God be merciful to me a Sinner.*"[15] As David Stannard has emphasized in his "Death and Dying in Colonial New England," "The best sign . . . [of salvation] . . . was to be unsure."[16] By admitting his wickedness, Mather was assuring himself he was unsure of assurance and therefore more than likely still among the assured!

Private confession before God alone, however, was only one aspect of its role in the Puritan's religious life. Public confession in church, not only of one's faith (and an examination thereof by the elect) was a commonplace occurrence. To a good Puritan, this was deadly serious business, as is revealed in the Reverend Mr. John Fiske's *Notebook* of the transactions of the church at Wenham, Massachusetts, in the early seventeenth century.[17]

True, later in the century, these confessions of faith became more nominal, or are at least recorded more perfunctorily. Thus, at the First Church of Beverly, Massachusetts, dozens of brief entries appear, such as that for 26 July 1674: "Goody Trask was baptized upon a profession of faith and repentance."[18] But where a person's *particular* sin was known, he or she was expected to confess openly before being admitted, or readmitted, to membership.

---

14. Edmund S. Morgan, ed., "The Diary of Michael Wigglesworth," Colonial Society of Massachusetts, *Publications,* XXXV. 311–444; Cotton Mather, "Diary," Massachusetts Historical Society, *Collections,* Seventh Series, VII–VIII.

15. Mather, *ibid.,* 584.

16. *American Historical Review,* 78. (December 1973), 1311.

17. Robert G. Pope, ed., "The Notebook of the Reverend John Fiske, 1644–1675," Colonial Society of Massachusetts, *Publications,* XLVII. See the early pages, especially.

18. "Beverly First Church Records," Essex Institute, *Historical Collections,* XXXV. (July 1899), 194. In this and following quotations from the records, most abbreviations and thorns have been silently expanded.

Scores of examples showing the importance of this kind of confession can be found in the church records for the seventeenth century. On 16 August 1669, for example, Bethia Stanly of the First Church of Beverly, "a childe of the Covenant having before marriage committed Fornication with him who is since her husband & the fact evident by her having a childe soon after marriage & confessed by herselfe was sent for to apeare publickly before the Church to give account to them of her sinne & repentance. . . . Shee owned that God had of late made her to see from his word the greatness of her sin against God & desire that God would humble her truly. . . ." The church deliberated, decided she needed more time, and told her that her confession would be considered truly genuine if and when it showed in her behavior. Four years later, she was finally "reconciled to the Church upon her professing repentance for her offence for which shee had been under admonition." [19]

It is interesting to note that there was a tendency in the eighteenth century to make even the church confession of a *particular* sin a more purely formal act than it had been.[20] Thus, in Groton in 1740 it was "Voted that Whereas it has been (for a Considerable time) a Sort of Rule: & the Practice in this Church: respecting Persons Suspected of Fornication: That such of them as had been married seven months before they [produced a child, the church would not] . . . Compel *them* Publickly to acknowledge, what is . . . next to Impossible to Convict them of: Therefore tis desired that for the future . . . in such like Cases; the Pastor of this Church, admitt them to desired Priviledges: without Compelling them to [confess] . . . and That he will bring them to declare that they have Humbly Begg'd of God the Pardon of all known Sins: & Promise that they will . . . Study to *know* [God's will]." [21]

Confession was as common in the courts as in the churches. An early case, certainly the most notorious, occurred in Plymouth Colony in 1642 when a young servant boy, Thomas Granger, blotted his copybook. The account in the saintly William Bradford's *History* reads as follows:

19. *Ibid.*, 188, 193. Also see, for examples, Richard D. Pierce, ed., *Records of the First Church in Boston, 1630–1868*, Colonial Society of Massachusetts, *Collections*, XXXIX. (Boston, 1961), *passim.*

20. See Emil Oberholzer, Jr., *Delinquent Saints: Disciplinary Action in the Early Congregational Churches of Massachusetts* (New York, 1956), 135–141. This trend was especially noticeable in extramarital sexual relations.

21. "The Earliest Church Records in Groton," *Groton Historical Series*, I. No. 10, 41–42.

He was this year detected of buggery, and indicted for the same, with a mare, a cow, two goats, five sheep and a turkey. Horrible it is to mention, but the truth of the history requires it. He was first discovered by one that accidentally saw his lewd practice towards the mare. (I forebear particulars.) Being upon it examined and committed, in the end he . . . confessed. . . . And this his free confession was not only in private to the magistrates (though at first he strived to deny it) but to the sundry, both ministers and others; and afterwards, up on his indictment, to the whole Court and Jury; and confirmed it at his execution."[22]

In the some four hundred court confessions in the published records of seventeenth-century Massachusetts, there appear to be three main types. The first, and most frequent, was the simple admission of guilt at the time of trial. In 1674, for example, one Alice Clarke was convicted "by her own confession" of selling strong beer without a license. She was thereupon sentenced to pay five pounds and fees of court, remaining committed in jail until the sentence was performed.[23]

The second, and far more interesting, type was the public acknowledgment of crime often required of a convicted offender as part of the sentence imposed upon him. In 1649, in the Essex Quarterly Court, one George Norton was convicted of lying and of suborning witnesses to scandalize the church at Wenham. He was sentenced to pay a twenty-shilling fine and to confess his sin in the meetinghouse. If he refused, he was to sit an hour in the stocks.

Norton's prescribed confession was as follows: "I doe confess and acknowledge that I have sinfullie indeavored to Justifie my self and my turbulent and factious agitations against the Just and orderlie proceedings of the church against me for my sin in that I have uncessantly laboured out of the pride of my hart to gather up witnisis of all sorts to testifie against the dealinge of the Church with me seekinge thereby to lay a scandall uppon the Church which cannot but greatly tende to the dishonor of god and the reproch of religion."[24]

22. Samuel Eliot Morison, ed., William Bradford, *Of Plymouth Plantation 1620–1647* (New York, 1952), 320.

23. *Records of the Suffolk County Court*, Colonial Society of Massachusetts, *Publications*, XXIX. 491 (28 July 1674).

24. George F. Dow, ed., *Records and Files of the Quarterly Courts of Essex County, Massachusetts* (Salem, Mass., 1911), I. 156.

The third type of civil confession came after trial and sentencing, but *before* the sentence had been fully carried out. Often this was associated with an appeal for clemency, with a hope that part of a fine, or part or all of a corporal or other punishment, including banishment, would be remitted.[25]

Thus, in 1648, the Massachusetts General Court favored confession in the case of one John Dand. What his crime was does not appear, but in answer to his petition for forgiveness, the court said: It was "meete (on his acknowledgment hereto annexed . . .) that he should be freed from his imprisonment, & his fine is readily remitted him, to manifest the Courts ready inclination to shew all due incuragment to delinquents to confes their errors, and acknowledg the justice of the Courts proceedings, rather than put any to such temptation as should either dishonor God or wound their owne consciences, by hardening them selves in their evill courses."[26]

The most famous *series* of court confessions in colonial New England, of course, was that connected with the witchcraft cases in Salem Village in 1691 and 1692. Here, according to Charles W. Upham, some fifty-five persons declared themselves guilty of having made pacts with the devil in order to become witches.[27] One obvious reason that so many confessed was that it was the only sure way to escape the scaffold. It was confess or die, and they knew it. Yet some there were, undoubtedly, who believed what they confessed. Esther Forbes, in her *A MIRROR FOR WITCHES*, has persuasively demonstrated this in her imaginative reconstruction of the spirit of the time.[28]

With private diaries, church meetings, and court sessions rich in the act of confession, it would have been astonishing had no published literature appeared focusing on this act of contrition.

III

The first True Confession and Dying Warning published in New England was Increase Mather's execution sermon for two men who had murdered their master in 1674, a quarter of a century before the

25. Jules Zanger, "Crime and Punishment in Early Massachusetts," *The William and Mary Quarterly*, 3rd Ser., XXII. (July 1965), 471–477.

26. Nathaniel B. Shurtleff, ed., *Records of the Governor and Company of Massachusetts Bay* (5 vols., Boston, 1853–1854), II. 241; III. 125–126.

27. Charles W. Upham, *Salem Witchcraft, With an Account of Salem Village and A History of Opinions on Witchcraft and Kindred Subjects* (2 vols., Boston, 1867), II. 397.

28. Esther Forbes, *A MIRROR FOR WITCHES* (Boston, 1928).

genre reached its classic expression. Entitled *The Wicked mans Portion*, this publication has many of the elements of John Rogers' later and longer work, but only in rudimentary form.[29] Mather had visited the condemned men in jail, elicited partial confessions from them, and expressed some hope for their salvation: "The Blood of Christ [he said] can satisfie for the blood which you have shed. Jesus doth deliver from wrath to come. And he doth not exclude you from salvation by him, if you doe not by Impenitency & Unbelief exclude your selves." But, warned Mather, the criminals had not yet completely confessed, for they "accuse and impeach one another" of the deed itself.[30] Only with complete confession and true penitence would Jesus save.

Taking his text from Ecclesiastes 7:17, "Be not overmuch wicked, neither be thou foolish: why shouldest thou dye before thy time," Mather canvassed the field of wickedness using the condemned malefactors as horrid examples. He was particularly concerned with the sin of disobedience. Magistrates and ministers were not honored, schoolmasters were despised and disobeyed, and, he said, "Look into Families, and O what disobedient Children? O what unruly servants may we find there? . . . If there be any prevailing iniquity in *New-England* this is it. And therefore no marvell that such an awfull Providence doth come to rebuke and humble us, that servants have conspired together to Kill their Master. . . . And mark what I say, If ever *New-England* be destroyed, this very sin of disobedience to the *fifth Commandment* will be the ruine of this Land."[31]

Between Increase Mather's first published example (which went to two editions)[32] and the classic example by John Rogers twenty-five years later, a dozen True Confessions and Dying Warnings were published in New England. Only three, however, add new literary elements that are fully developed in Rogers' book in 1701. These appear in three accounts about the same man, one James Morgan.

The first occurs in Increase Mather's *A Sermon, Occasioned by the Execution of a Man found Guilty of Murder. . . .* Published in Boston in 1686, this work was much more elaborate than Mather's initial book in the genre. It includes sermons by three ministers, all uttered the day of execution, and the complete confession of the condemned Morgan as allegedly taken down in shorthand.

29. (Boston, 1675).
30. *Ibid.*, 23.
31. *Ibid.*, 17.
32. The second has the title *A Sermon (preached at the Lecture in Boston . . . When two men were Executed . . .)* (Boston, 1685).

John Dolbeare

entered

The Wicked mans Portion.

OR

A SERMON

(Preached at the *Lecture* in *Boston* in *New-England* the
18th day of the 1 Moneth 1674. when two men
were *executed*, who had *murthered*
their Master.)

Wherein is shewed

*That excesse in wickedness doth bring
untimely Death.*

By *INCREASE MATHER*, Teacher
of a Church of Christ.

Prov. 10. 27. *The fear of the Lord prolongeth dayes, but the years
of the wicked shall be shortned.*

Eph. 6. 2, 3. *Honour thy Father and thy Mother (which is the first
Commandment with promise) that it may be well with thee,
and thou mayst live long on the Earth.*

Pæna ad paucos, metus ad omnes.

BOSTON,
Printed by *John Foster*, 1675

Increase Mather's *The Wicked Mans Portion . . .* (1675). Courtesy, American
Antiquarian Society, Worcester, Massachusetts.

Pillars of Salt.

An HISTORY

OF SOME

CRIMINALS Executed in this Land,

FOR

Capital Crimes.

With some of their Dying

Speeches ;

Collected and Published,
For the WARNING of such as *Live* in
Destructive *Courses* of Ungodliness.

Whereto is added,
For the better Improvement of this History,
A Brief Discourse about the Dreadful
Justice of God, in Punishing of
S I N, with S I N.

By Cotton Mather.

Deut. 19. 20.

*Those which remain shall hear & fear, and shall hence-
forth commit no more any such Evil among you.*

BOSTON in *New-England.*
Printed by B. *Green*, and *J. Allen*, for *Samuel Phillips*
at the Brick Shop near the Old-Meeting-House. 1699.

Cotton Mather's *Pillars of Salt . . .* (1699). Courtesy, American Antiquarian
Society, Worcester, Massachusetts.

Death

The certain *Wages of Sin*
to the Impenitent:

Life

The sure *Reward of Grace*
to the Penitent :

Together with the only *Way* for

YOUTH

To avoid the former, and attain
the latter.

Deliver'd in three **Lecture Sermons** ;
Occasioned by the *Imprisonment, Condemnation* and *Execution,* of a Young
Woman, who was guilty of Murdering
her Infant begotten in Whoredom.

To which is added,
An *Account* of her manner of Life & Death,
in which the Glory of free Grace is displayed

By Mr. **John Rogers**, Pastor of
the Church of *Ipswich.*

i Tim. 1. 16

Boston : Printed by **B** *Green,* and *J. Allen,*
for *Samuel Phillips* at the Brick Shop. 1701.

John Rogers's *Death the Certain Wages of Sin . . .* (1701). By courtesy of the Trustees of the Boston Public Library.

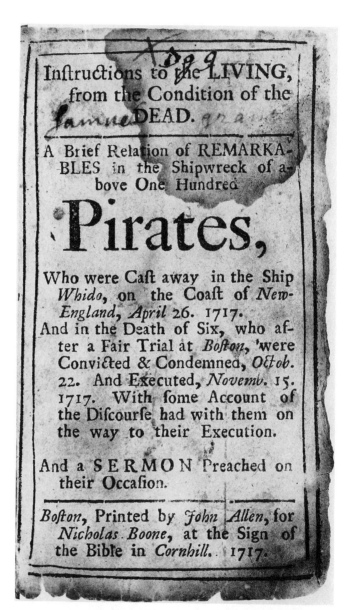

Inſtructions to the LIVING,
from the Condition of the
DEAD.

A Brief Relation of REMARKA-
BLES in the Shipwreck of a-
bove One Hundred

Pirates,

Who were Caſt away in the Ship
Whido, on the Coaſt of *New-
England*, *April* 26. 1717.
And in the Death of Six, who after a Fair Trial at *Boſton*, 'were
Convicted & Condemned, *Octob.*
22. And Executed, *Novemb.* 15.
1717. With ſome Account of
the Diſcourſe had with them on
the way to their Execution.

And a SERMON Preached on
their Occaſion.

Boſton, Printed by *John Allen*, for
Nicholas Boone, at the Sign of
the Bible in *Cornhill*. 1717.

*A Brief Relation of Remarkables in the Shipwreck of Above One Hundred
Pirates . . .* (1717). Massachusetts Historical Society, Boston.

Pſal. LI. 14. *Deliver me from Blood-Guiltineſs, O God, thou God of my Salvation: and my Tongue ſhall ſing aloud of thy Righteouſneſs.* Iſa. I. 18. *Come now and let us Reaſon together, ſaith the Lord: though your Sins be as ſcarlet, they ſhall be as white as ſnow: though they be red like crimſon, they ſhall be as wool.*

The laſt SPEECH and dying ADVICE of

poor Julian,

Who was Executed the 22d of *March*, 1733. for the Murder of Mr. *John Rogers* of *Pembroke*. Written with his own Hand, and delivered to the Publiſher the Day before his Execution.

FRom my Childhood to Twenty Years of Age, I liv'd in a Family where I was learnt to Read and ſay my Catechiſm, and had a great deal of Pains taken with me.—— And in my younger Years I was under ſome Convictions and Awakenings, and concern'd about the Condition of my Soul ;—— and I had many Warnings in the Providence of God to turn from my Sins—— But I have (and I deſire to lament it) abuſed God's Patience and Goodneſs to me, and apoſtatiſed from God and good Beginnings, and now I have forſaken God, he has forſaken me, and I acknowledge he has been juſt in leaving me, ſo that I have gone from bad to worſe, till for my Sins I am now to die.

Whereas I have been charged with and tried for burning my Maſter's Barn, I now declare as a dying Man that I did not do it, nor was I any way privy to it.

I acknowledge I deſerve to die, and would confeſs eſpecially my Drunkenneſs and Sabbath-breaking, which have led me to this great Sin for which I now die.

I deſire therefore that all, and eſpecially Servants, would take Warning by me ; I am a dying Man, juſt going to leave this World, and the Thoughts of it terrify me, knowing how unfit I am to appear before my Judge.

O beware of ſinning as I have done— Beware of Drunkenneſs, of Sabbath-breaking, and of running away from your Maſters, and don't put away the Thoughts of Death and of Judgment : I once put theſe Things far away, but now they are near, and I am going to appear before my great and terrible Judge, which ſurprizeth me beyond what I am able to expreſs.

If you have been inſtructed and catechized from your Childhood, and joined your ſelves to Aſſemblies in which the Lord Jeſus Chriſt is moſt purely worſhipped, then let me warn and charge you to beware of caſting off the Things that are good, leſt God leave you to your ſelves, and you go on in Sin till you come to the greateſt Wickedneſs.

O take Warning by me all of you, I intreat you—— See and fear and do no more ſo wickedly as I have done.

O let me once more intreat you all, eſpecially Servants, to beware of the Sin of Drunkenneſs, and be obedient to your Maſters ; don't run away from them, nor get Drunk, for if you do it will bring you to Ruine as it has done me.

I call to you now as one come from the Dead, to turn from your evil Ways while you have Time, and not put off your Repentance to another Day, leſt you then call and God will not anſwer you.

My Maſter often told me that my Sins would bring me to this, but I little thought that it would be ſo.

I return my hearty Thanks to the Rev. Miniſters who have taken Pains to aſſiſt me in preparing for my latter End. And as I deſire to be forgiven, ſo I forgive all Mankind.

Theſe Things I declare freely and voluntarily, and deſire Mr. *Fleet* to Print the ſame for the Benefit of the Living : And I do hereby utterly diſown and diſclaim all other Speeches, Papers or Declarations that may be printed in my Name, as Witneſs my Hand this 21ſt. of *March*, 1733.

Julian.

Witneſs
Zach. Treſcott.

Printed and Sold by *T. Fleet*, at the *Heart* and *Crown* in *Cornhill*, *Boſton*.

"The Last Speech and Dying Advice of Poor Julian," broadside (1733). By courtesy of the Trustees of the Boston Public Library.

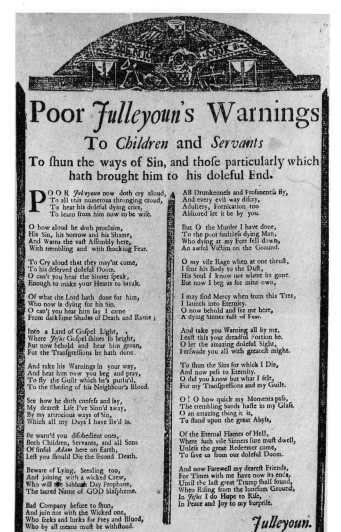

"Poor Julleyoun's Warnings to Children and Servants . . . ," broadside [1733].
By courtesy of the Trustees of the Boston Public Library.

Advice from the Dead to the Living:

OR, A

Solemn Warning to the World.

Occasioned by the untimely Death of

poor Julian,

Who was Executed on *Boston* Neck, on *Thursday* the 22d. of *March*, 1733. for the Murder of Mr. *John Rogers* of *Pembroke*, the 12th of *September*, 1732.

Very proper to be Read by all Persons, but especially young People, and Servants of all Sorts.

THIS Day take warning young and old,
By a sad Sight we here behold,
Of one whom Vengeance in his Chase
Hath taken in his sinful Race.

Here we behold amidst the Throng,
Condemned *Julian* guarded strong,
To Gallows bound with heavy Heart,
To suffer as his just Desert.

Where we for Warning may observe
What cruel Murder doth deserve,
Also the sad procuring Cause
Why Sinners die amidst their Days.

Here now we have a lively View,
Of *Cain's* vile Action fresh and new,
That old Revenge is by Permit
Prevailing in our Natures yet.

Revenge is sweet, we often hear,
How bitter now doth it appear?
It leads to Ruine, Death and Fate,
And bitter Mourning when too late.

We often hear Men to complain,
Their Punishment like guilty *Cain*,
Which justly falleth to their Share,
Is great, and more than they can bear!

The Prisoner owns the bloody Act,
And faith the Sentence on his Fact,
Was pass'd on him impartially,
And therefore doth deserve to die.

By his Account he first was sold,
When he was not quite three Years old;
And by his Master in his Youth,
Instructed in the Ways of Truth.

Was also taught to Write and Read,
And learn'd his Catechise and Creed,
And what was proper (as he faith)
Relating to the Christian Faith.

His pious Master did with care,
By Counsels warn him to beware
Of wicked Courses, that would tend
To his Destruction in the End.

When Twenty Years were gone and past,
By his Account he took at last

To Drinking and ill Company,
Which prov'd his fatal Destiny.

No timely Warnings would he hear,
From kind Reproofs he turn'd his Ear,
Provoked God for to depart,
And leave him to an harden'd Heart.

Since he despis'd the Ways of Truth,
And good Instruction in his Youth,
God then withdrew restraining Grace,
And let him run his wicked Race.

From Sin to Sin advancing thus,
By sad Degrees from bad to worse,
He did at length commit the Crime,
For which he dies before his Time.

He prays his sad untimely Fall,
May be a Warning unto all,
That they no such like Steps do tread,
Nor lead such Life as he has led.

That Children and all Servants they
Would in their Stations all obey,
Parents and Masters every one,
And not to do as he has done.

Obey them with a willing Mind,
Be always honest, just and kind,
And pray to God to give them Grace,
To do their Duty in their Place.

He thanks good Preachers heartily,
For all their Helps of Piety,
Which to his Soul they did extend,
To fit him for his latter End.

So here we leave his pitious Case,
In tender Arms of sov'reign Grace,
Altho' his Crimes are great and sore,
Grace can abound and pardon more.

Now may the Congregation hear,
This awful Voice, and stand in fear,
And being timely warn'd thereby,
may do no more so wickedly.

F I N I S.

BOSTON: Printed and Sold at the *Heart* and *Crown* in *Cornhill*.

Note. There being a foolish Paper printed, called *Julian's Advice to Children and Servants,* said to be published at his Desire; this may certify, that the said Paper is false and spurious, and disowned by the said *Julian* in the Presence of three Persons.

"Advice from the Dead to the Living . . . ," broadside [1733]. By courtesy of the Trustees of the Boston Public Library.

An Exhortation to young and old to be cautious of small Crimes, left they become habitual, and lead them before they are aware into thofe of the moft heinous Nature. Occafioned by the unhappy Cafe of *Levi Ames*, Executed on *Bofton*-Neck, *October* 21ft, 1773, for the Crime of Burglary.

I.

BEWARE, young People, look at me,
  Before it be too late,
And fee Sin's End is Mifery :
  Oh ! fhun poor *Ames*'s Fate.

II.

I warn you all (beware betimes)
  With my now dying Breath,
To fhun Theft, Burglaries, heinous Crimes ;
  They bring untimely Death.

III.

Shun vain and idle Company ;
  They'll lead you foon aftray ;
From ill-fam'd Houfes ever flee,
  And keep yourfelves away.

IV.

With honeft Labor earn your Bread,
  While in your youthful Prime ;
Nor come you near the Harlot's Bed,
  Nor idly wafte your Time.

V.

Nor meddle with another's Wealth,
  In a defrauding Way :
A Curfe is with what's got by ftealth,
  Which makes your Life a Prey.

VI.

Shun Things that feem but little Sins,
  For they lead on to great ;
From Sporting many Times begins
  Ill Blood, and poifonous Hate.

VII.

The Sabbath-Day do not prophane,
  By wickednefs and Plays ;
By needlefs Walking Streets or Lanes
  Upon fuch Holy days.

VIII.

To you that have the care of Youth,
  Parents and Mafters too,
Teach them betimes to know the Truth,
  And Righteoufnefs to do.

IX.

The dreadful Deed for which I die,
  Arofe from fmall Beginning ;
My Idlenefs brought poverty,
  And fo I took to Stealing.

X.

Thus I went on in finning faft,
  And tho' I'm young 'tis true,
I'm old in Sin, but catcht at laft,
  And here receive my due.

XI.

Alas for my unhappy Fall,
  The Rigs that I have run !
Juftice aloud for vengeance calls,
  Hang him for what he's done.

XII.

O may it have fome good Effect,
  And warn each wicked one,
That they God's righteous Laws refpect,
  And Sinful Courfes Shun.

"An Exhortation to Young and Old to Be Cautious of Small Crimes . . . " (1773). The Historical Society of Pennsylvania.

The next year a second edition appeared, to which had been added the second new element—a discourse between the prisoner and a minister. It was prefaced by a note from the printer to the reader: "The general *Usefulness & Acceptableness* of this Book, together with the *speedy sale of the 1st* Impression, as also some *gain to my self & good to others*, has enclined me to renew the Impression. . . ."[33] The printer went on to point out that he had added the new element on his own.

In this obvious attempt to introduce a note of realism, the condemned Morgan overheard a man mocking him when he stumbled: "I have mocked & scoffed like that man," he said, "and see what it hath brought me to: *he* may come to the like." Next, poor Morgan sighted the scaffold: "Oh what a huge Multitude of people is come together on this occasion!" he exclaimed. Finally, they reached a "*miery way.*" Said the minister: "*I'm sorry so small a thing as a* plashy Street *should make me lose one minute of this* more-than-ordinary *precious time. . . .*"[34]

The third new literary element is a verbatim report of the Dying Warning. This first appears in Cotton Mather's *Pillars of Salt. An HISTORY OF SOME CRIMINALS Executed in this Land; for Capital Crimes. With some of their Dying Speeches; Collected and Published, For the WARNING of such as Live in Destructive Courses of Ungodliness . . .* (Boston, 1699). It was subsequently reprinted in his *Magnalia Christi Americana.*

The first fifty-eight pages of *Pillars of Salt* are devoted to an analysis of the way God punishes sin with sin, based on an account of "a *Young Woman, but an Old Sinner*" hanged for the murder of her baseborn child.[35] Towards the end of this section Mather generalizes on the kinds of sin that led most of the malefactors to their deaths: "*Apostasy from Good Beginnings in Religion . . . Notorious Unprofitableness under the Means of Grace . . . Evil Company Keeping . . . and Disobedience to Parents.*" The latter, a violation of the Fifth Commandment, was the sin most frequently lamented, and in these words: "*Oh my disobedience to my Parents, my Disobedience to my Parents, and my Ungovernableness, under such Parents and Masters, as God had given me.*"[36]

The last fifty pages or so of *Pillars of Salt* are given over to ac-

33. Three printings (under different titles) were issued in 1686 and 1687. A fourth occurred in London in 1691. The quotation is from the 1687 edition, 114.
34. *Ibid.,* 121, 122.
35. [Mather], *Pillars of Salt,* 106.
36. *Ibid.,* 52–55.

counts of thirteen hangings for adultery, sodomy, and murder. In the midst lies the case of poor James Morgan, now with the full paraphernalia of the True Confession and Dying Warning—the sermon, the discourse between the minister and the condemned, the confession, and the "verbatim" dying warning. As Morgan ascended the gallows, said Mather, his last words, hitherto unreported, had been recorded in shorthand. They are a not-unexpected catalogue of sins to avoid—swearing, drinking, whoring, evil-company-keeping, sabbath-breaking, and murder. "O take warning by me," Morgan concluded, "and beg God to keep you from this sin which has been my ruine."[37]

With the publication of Cotton Mather's work in 1699, John Rogers had available to him all the elements for emulation and elaboration in his book about poor Esther Rodgers to be published in 1701. Thereafter, down to the Revolution, no new elements were added, although the total works in this genre reach over one hundred. They vary in the numbers of sermons included, and thus in length, but the basic pattern remains the same, either complete with all the elements or published in attenuated form. Some were published as broadsides, with woodcuts, and no doubt achieved wide circulation. Further changes are to be found on somewhat subtler levels such as the origins of the confessors themselves and the meanings of the confessions they uttered.[38]

IV

At an average of little more than one a year from 1674, published True Confessions and Dying Warnings hardly constitute a major literary contribution, even without reference to their literary quality.

37. *Ibid.*, 83–85.

38. The statements in this paragraph and below are based on a reading of the True Confessions and Dying Warnings listed in the following sources: Charles Evans, *American Bibliography* (14 vols., Chicago, 1903–1955); Thomas M. McDade, *The Annals of Murder: A Bibliography of Books and Pamphlets on American Murders from Colonial Times to 1900* (Norman, Oklahoma, 1961); *Broadsides, Ballads Etc. Printed in Massachusetts 1639–1800*, in Massachusetts historical Society, *Collections*, 75; and Ola Elizabeth Winslow, *American Broadside Verse from Imprints of the 17th & 18th Centuries* (New Haven, Conn., 1930). After this essay had been accepted for publication by the late Walter Muir Whitehill, my colleague, Richard Colles Johnson, brought to my attention Ronald A. Bosco's "Early American Gallows Literature: An Annotated Checklist," in *Resources for American Literary Study*, VIII (Spring 1978), 81–105. In his introduction, Bosco cites Wayne C. Minnick, "The New England Execution Sermon, 1630–1800," in *Speech Monographs*, XXXV (1968), 67–89. It is an interesting article, but I did not change mine because of it.

But if they did not shape the past, they at least provide a clue to it and therefore provoke curiosity.

Initially, at least, one can accept this literature at face value, particularly in view of the historical record regarding confessions in private, in church, and in court. The New Englanders *did* commit crimes, and for one reason or another, they *were* led to contrition. This fits well with the Puritans' view of themselves. Wrote Samuel Willard of Boston's South Church: a new life discovers itself "By a free and hearty *Confession* of . . . Sin. And this, though not always to Men, in regard of some particular Sins; yet always to God, whose Law is broken. . . . This is always a proper adjunct of true repentance and it waits upon it; so that he who upon Conviction of Sin, doth not freely Confess it to God . . . , hath sufficient reason to fear that he never repented of it. The very burden which his Conscience is distressed with, by reason of it, will make him to seek relief. . . ."[39] Undoubtedly it was partly the importance which Puritan thought placed on the role of confession in achieving a restored conscience and ultimate salvation that led to its emphasis in the private lives and public literature of the time.[40]

Even at face value, True Confessions and Dying Warnings raise a question, although they do not provide an answer, about Puritan ideas versus Puritan practice. How could Puritans who believed strongly in predestination—a belief that no act of a man can affect his salvation—reconcile that belief with the necessity of holding out some hope for salvation so that man would try to live according to God's law? The ministers had worked out a very sophisticated covenant theory that barely fell within the doctrine of predestination. But in actual practice, when confronted by a simple layman, they taught, I suspect, a doctrine dangerously close to "good works." It was necessary that men be good, or at least that they act as though they were good, in spite of themselves. As the late Perry Miller put it: the elect "are covenanted to sainthood, not forced into it, and they are to be saved for trying, not for succeeding, whereas the reprobate are eternally damned, not for failing, but for not trying."[41]

Thus in parish work as distinguished from scholarly debate, the Puritan minister possibly placed less emphasis on election as an arbitrary act of God, than upon the individual sinner's seeking God

39. *A Compleat Body of Divinity* (Boston, 1726), 802–803.
40. See George Lee Haskins, *Law and Authority in Early Massachusetts: A Study in Tradition and Design* (New York, 1960), 91–93, 204–211.
41. *The New England Mind: The Seventeenth Century* (New York, 1939), Chapter XIII, *passim*. Quotation from page 384.

through repentance and confession. As we have seen in the case of Esther Rodgers, the ministers were almost, if not quite, persuaded of her chances for salvation. Later, in an execution sermon delivered in 1721, while admitting that God's grace is necessary for salvation, Cotton Mather argued that a serious and sincere repentance, a seeking for God's grace, creates a hope, a sign, that God will grant it.[42] Did his listeners go one step further and see cause and effect?

The Reverend William Cooper's preface to an execution sermon by Thomas Foxcroft in 1733 does take that step. "It may be," he wrote, that "there is no Place in the World, where such Pains are taken with condemned Criminals to prepare them for their Death; that *in the Destruction of the Flesh, the Spirit may be saved in the Day of the Lord Jesus.*" Time, he said, sometimes a month, is always given by "compassionate *Judges*" so that the prisoner *might achieve salvation.*[43] Thus, the sermons not only warned that the gallows lay at the end of evil behavior, but also that damnation lay on the other side of the gallows. By inference, good behavior, or true repentance for bad, would result in escaping the gallows and, perhaps, in achieving salvation as well.

But acceptance at face value—even with presumptive salvation thrown in—does not totally satisfy as an explanation of the meaning of True Confessions and Dying Warnings. It is only the outer and most obvious layer. To go beyond one needs only to ask why they were published at all once the confessors and dying warners were dead.

The obvious answer is that the genre was a form of hortatory literature consciously designed to make the criminal acts detestable and to induce proper behavior in society as a whole. And since most of the listeners to the sermons and readers of the True Confessions and Dying Warnings were not criminals, but rather, at worst, doers of minor evils, it was necessary to trace the criminal career back to its origins and to generalize about the nature of crime itself. Then one's auditors and readers could see where their small peccadillos were leading them. Mighty oaks of crime from little acorns of disobedience would grow. Death and damnation would be the results.

Almost invariably the root cause of wickedness was found in a breaking of the Fifth Commandment—"Honor thy father and mother—that thy days may be long in the land which the Lord thy God giveth thee"—usually as disobedience to parent or master. Oc-

42. Cotton Mather, *TREMENDA. The Dreadful Sound WITH WHICH The Wicked are to be Thunderstruck* (Boston, 1721), 35–40.
43. Thomas Foxcroft, *Lessons of Caution to Young Sinners* (Boston, 1733), i.

casionally the miscreant's life of crime is traced back to an early theft, or, later in the eighteenth century, to drink, but throughout the period the Fifth Commandment is invoked with regularity. This may indeed be significant, for it is under this Commandment that Samuel Willard, for example, organized his entire analysis of society: the relationships between parents and children, husbands and wives, masters and servants, magistrates and people, rulers and subjects, and ministers and flock. Without obedience to the Fifth Commandment, order would disappear and society would collapse.[44]

Rather than being only, or even primarily, verbalized acts of individual religious piety, then, True Confessions and Dying Warnings were also social acts consciously designed as a necessary cement to hold society together. This was particularly true in the period of their emergence as a New England literature, 1674–1701. Whether or not one accepts Perry Miller's idea and timing of Puritan declension, these years saw some awesome events in the transition from the God-oriented community of Winthrop's "Modell of Christian Charity" to a secular and commercial society. I doubt that it was pure coincidence that the emergence of confession literature occurred during the period of King Philip's devastating war and subsequent Indian troubles, the loss of the Massachusetts Charter, the imposition of royal control under the new charter, the introduction of the Anglican church into Boston, the witchcraft trials of the 1680s, and the progressive decline of the influence of the clergy.[45]

In the midst of Cotton Mather's greatest Jeremiad of them all, the *Magnalia Christi Americana* (1702), lies his explanation for publishing *Pillars of Salt* in 1699: "One of the *New-English ministers,* [he wrote, referring to himself, characteristically in the third person] beholding *vice* besieging his country as an enemy, singled out a company of *dead wretches* to set upon the walls, in hopes that the horrible sight would cause that worst enemy to fly before it."[46] Here was a row of antiheroes, negative symbols for the godly community.

The social utility of, and even necessity for, confessions is underscored by the apparent lengths society went to to get them. We have

44. *A Compleat Body of Divinity,* 597–655 (second pagination).
45. See Perry Miller, *The New England Mind: From Colony to Province* (Cambridge, Mass., 1953) *passim.* For two works that question Miller's theme of declension, see Darrett Bruce Rutman, *Winthrop's Boston: Portrait of a Puritan Town* (Chapel Hill, N.C., 1965), and Michael Zuckerman, *Peaceable Kingdoms: New England Towns in the Eighteenth Century* (New York, 1970).
46. *Magnalia Christi Americana or, THE Ecclesiastical history of NEW ENGLAND* (London, 1702), Book VI, 37.

seen that Esther Rodgers was visited by several ministers, that Increase Mather rebuked the two murderers of their master for incomplete confession, and that James Morgan's True Confession and
Dying Warning grew in size and complexity over three editions published over a period of twenty years. That Morgan's words may have
been put into his mouth, is suggested by Robert Calef's admittedly
hostile account of the witchcraft trials.

Wrote Calef: "besides the powerful Argument of Life (and freedom
from hardships and Irons not only promised, but also performed to
all that owned their guilt), There are numerous Instances . . . of the
tedious Examinations before private persons, many hours together;
they all that time urging them to Confess (and taking turns to persuade them) till the accused were wearied out by being forced to
stand so long, or for want of Sleep, etc., and so brought to give As-
sent to what they said; they then asking them, 'Were you at such a
Witch meeting,' or 'have you signed the Devil's Book?' etc. upon
their replying 'yes,' the whole was drawn into form as their Confession."[47]

It is doubtful that the New-England malefactors were aware of the
implications of their confessions, doubtful even that society was
fully aware of them. Yet, it is evident that for reasons of state as well
as soul the Puritans had a need to exact confession and acceptance
of the meteness of the punishment from those who had violated the
mores of the community. This was especially so in the time of crisis.
In admitting their guilt, in giving detailed accounts of it, and in admitting the justice of the sentences imposed upon them, New England's confessors and dying warners acquiesced in the laws they
had broken, and they reinforced the role of society in exacting conformity.

The case of Hugh Stone, convicted of murdering his pregnant
wife, is instructive in this regard. In the course of several visits by a
minister, Stone finally admitted that his sins were so abominable
that, even were he to be pardoned by the court, he would insist that
the sentence be carried out. He agreed that by breaking one commandment he had literally broken them all, not in the figurative

47. Robert Calef, "More Wonders of the Invisible World," in George Lincoln Burr,
ed., *Narratives of the Witchcraft Cases* (New York, 1914), 375–376. The obvious parallel between this statement of the situation and Arthur Koestler's *Darkness at Noon*
suggests that societies in crisis, regardless of their differences, tend to act alike. A
further and striking parallel is to be found in Tudor Society described by Lacey Bald-
win Smith, "English Treason Trials and Confessions in the Sixteenth Century," *The
Journal of the History of Ideas*, XV. (October 1954), 471–498.

sense that Saint James used, but literally. Society was just in executing him for his crime.[48]

Thus by confessing, and consenting, the early True Confessors found social as well as spiritual salvation. It was the final act of exercising the liberty of which John Winthrop had spoken, the liberty to obey God's law by "subjection to authority."[49]

If the True Confessions and Dying Warnings were at least partially symbolic as well as historic in the early period, and if they held a social meaning as well as a private meaning, did the phenomena persist down to the Revolution? The answer is a complicated and qualified yes. It is complicated and qualified by two significant changes in the literature.

First, there was a remarkable change in the cultural and social origins of the confessors themselves. While in the seventeenth and early eighteenth centuries the confession-seeking minister would find himself walking down a "plashy" way with a wayward member from *within* the society, in the eighteenth century he was more than likely to accompany a black, an Indian, an Irishman, or a foreign pirate. Just as most illegal protests in the servant class then arose from the blacks, whom Samuel Sewall described as being of "extravasat blood" who can "never embody with us," from the "Verminous Irish," as James Franklin's *Courant* called them, or from other outsiders,[50] so among the hanged confessors, the majority then came from outside the community. Internal deviants to pray with, and for, were replaced by external enemies to be rid of.[51]

This change in personae explains, or at least leads to, the second change in the eighteenth century. Earlier, the self-doubting Puritan knew, as he watched the dying throes of a condemned malefactor,

48. Cotton Mather, *Magnalia Christi Americana*, Book VI, 43–47. I was happy to have Mr. Charles G. Steffen point out to me Kai T. Erikson's statement, on pages 194–195 of his *Wayward Puritans . . .* (New York, 1966), supporting this view. "To repent," he wrote, "is to agree that the moral standards of the community are right and that the sentence of the court is just."

49. Winthrop, speech to General Court 3 July 1645, in Perry Miller and Thomas H. Johnson, eds., *The Puritans* (Boston, 1938), 207.

50. Lawrence W. Towner, "A Fondness for Freedom: Servant Protest in Puritan Society," *The William and Mary Quarterly*, 3rd Ser., XIX (April 1962), 213–215. The quotations are from page 215.

51. I am indebted to Mr. Charles G. Steffen for the following data and for suggesting their importance to me: In the early years of the literary genre, through 1701, the eleven confessors were all members of the community. But between 1702 and 1776, while nineteen were members of the community, sixty-six were outsiders, among them sixteen Indians, ten blacks, eleven Irish, and twelve pirates. See note 2 [this selection], above, for the sources.

that very little separated himself from the almost sacrificial victim on the gallows. He too had started sinning with disobedience and might not stop in time. Had not his neighbor, there on the gallows? But in the eighteenth century, the victim was often outside his ken, and the literature as well as the event, while still instructive, could become primarily diverting, even entertaining.

Thus, the tone of True Confessions and Dying Warnings seems gradually to change from one of moral suasion to an increasingly popular one of titillation. New editions designed to capitalize on a readers' market were issued. Rival works were published dealing with a particular malefactor. And, in at least one instance, a condemned prisoner repudiated one confession attributed to him and issued an "authorized" confession with another printer.[52]

This exploitation of the genre reached the point where in 1773 eleven separate publications were issued dealing with one condemned prisoner, Levi Ames, executed for burglary. Most were not, however, sermons, and conversations, and confessions published in pamphlet form; instead, they were broadsides.[53]

It is the change to broadside publication, in fact, that is the most significant alteration in *form* for True Confessions and Dying Warnings in the eighteenth century. With that change came the introduction of woodcuts, usually with the gallows prominently featured, and the use of verse. When, for example, an Indian named Julian was hanged for murder, three broadsides were issued;

> The last SPEECH and dying ADVICE of poor Julian . . . (Boston, [1733]).
> Poor Julleyoun's Warnings To Children and Servants To shun the Ways of Sin . . . (Boston, [1733]).
> Advice from the Dead to the Living; OR A Solemn Warning to the World. Occasioned by the untimely Death of poor Julian . . . (Boston, [1733]).

Two of these broadsides came from the same printer, two were in verse, each has a different woodcut: a death's head, a cut of the hanging, and a representation of the murder itself. One warning from poor Julian ends as follows:

> And now Farewell my dearest Friends,
> For times with me have now its ends,
> Until the last great Trump shall sound
> When Rising from the lonesome Ground,

52. *Advice from the Dead to the Living . . . poor Julian . . .* (Boston, [1733]).
53. *Ibid.*

In *Jesus* I do Hope to Rise,
In Peace and Joy to my Surprise.[54]

Finally, the sub-genre had become so secularized by populariza-
tion and the use of burlesque-like broadsides that the form could be
borrowed in 1750 not to illuminate the sins of man, the necessity of
confession, the hope of salvation, or the terrors of damnation, but
rather to express the desire for a more stable currency! In that year,
two broadsides lamented the passing of the paper currency known
as Old Tenor. One, entitled *The Dying Speech of Old Tenor, on the
31st of March 1750; being the Day Appointed for his Execution*,
ends with these lines:

> Altho' this Day looks dark, and Hearts are sad,
> Mind not the Frowns of wicked Men who're glad;
> Shortly they'll say, *Old Tenor* come again,
> But then, Alas! 'twill be too late for them.[55]

It is symbolic that paper currency had taken the place of—or at
least taken a place with—salvation as a central problem of the day,
for New England by the mid-eighteenth century had completed the
transition from a religious community to an essentially secular society.

54. These broadsides are in the Boston Public Library and are cited in *Broadsides,
Ballads, op. cit.*, Nos. 628–630.
55. Winslow, *American Broadside Verse*, 167; and *Broadsides, Ballads, Etc.*, 128
(No. 912).

5

ARS POETICA ET SCULPTURA:

POCAHONTAS ON THE BOSTON

COMMON

As editor of the *William and Mary Quarterly*, Towner inherited the "Trivia" section to which historians sent in those amusing nuggets of original sources they did not know what to do with in their scholarship. Some were funny, some condescending, the best were bawdy, and Towner did his best to cultivate them.

This essay, which Towner published in the *Journal of Southern History* about a Bostonian's proposal in 1734 to erect a statue to Pocahontas on the Boston Common, was distinctly not bawdy. But in his remarks Towner revealed incidentally that for years, as editor of the *Quarterly*, he had "kept under the blotter of my desk, a graphic description of a delightful game allegedly played at mixed gatherings in the eighteenth century, merely because I hadn't the nerve to publish it." Readers hungry for the denouement of this story may move on to selection 6.

EARLY EIGHTEENTH-CENTURY NEW ENGLAND newspapers are mostly dull affairs (always with the exception of Benjamin Franklin's *New-England Courant*); their news columns are filled with the "latest" advices from England and Europe, several months old, rather than with colonial news, and their local stories concern themselves largely with the coming and going of ships. Only the advertisements can be counted on to give a picture of domestic events: whose servant or slave had run away, whose house was for sale, who were the active merchants in town. Once in a while, of course, a choice item, amusing then as now, got printed and today delights the eye of the dullards who plod through the papers seeking this or that.

From *Journal of Southern History* 28 (1962): 482–85. Copyright 1962 by the Southern Historical Association. Reprinted by permission of the Managing Editor.

Some of these eye catchers are so embarrassingly lewd or down-right vulgar by modern standards that they could not be reprinted even in a column in the *William and Mary Quarterly* devoted to humorous and often slightly salacious trivia of the seventeenth and eighteenth centuries. For years, as editor of that magazine, I kept, under the blotter of my desk, a graphic description of a delightful game allegedly played at mixed gatherings in the eighteenth century, merely because I hadn't the nerve to publish it.[1]

But the trivialities published in the early newspapers reveal much more than that our forefathers had stronger stomachs (or their editors more courage) than we. They reveal a refreshing innocence about journalism that is found today only in a smalltown weekly gazette. This, in effect, the early colonial newspapers were, except that having no news of their own they relayed others' news, at length, and in serial form. Where but in such a newspaper could be found the engaging admission that the filler being printed was as good as if not better than "many Occurrences we are obliged to insert for want of more material News"?

The letter printed below from the Boston *Gazette* for June 17–24, 1734, however, has more to recommend it than the salaciousness of some entries or the innocence and candor of its publisher-editor, Bartholomew Greene, Jr., son of the then late publisher and printer of the Boston *News-Letter*.[2] It was, in all likelihood, the first proposal published in America urging the elevation of Pocahontas to the status of American folk heroine. Thus, if it was a Yankee author and a Yankee publisher who first attempted to destroy the Smith-Pocahontas "legend" in the nineteenth century, it was also a Yankee who in the eighteenth century first published a recommendation to memorialize that story in verse and in stone on the Boston Common. Here is a kind of poetic justice, even if in reverse.

As the letter's introduction reveals, however, it was an English correspondent of someone in Boston who first made the suggestion that the figure of Pocahontas be "set up in the beautifullest Places of the Publick Walks where your Company meets." He had been stimulated by reading a "Piece of Poetry" sent to him from Boston. The verses, he said, revealed a "Beauty in the Composition . . . and a tender and affectionate Mind in the Author." Who this poet was we can not know. Boston was cursed in the early eighteenth century by some versifiers, many of whom, according to the acid pen of

1. *New England Courant*, January 15–25, 1725.
2. Clarence L. Brigham, *History and Bibliography of American Newspapers, 1690–1820* (2 vols., Worcester, Mass., 1947), I, 297.

Moses Coit Tyler, were enchanted by Alexander Pope and aped him with unfortunate results.[3] The manner in which the author of the letter describes his subject—the "shine" of Pocahontas "interceding with her Rigid Father for the life of the *English* Captain"—suggests that the poem which stimulated his letter was one of these. It is even possible that the verse had been composed by the author of another poem, "*On the celestial* Parthanissa," published anonymously in the Boston *News-Letter* for May 2–9, 1727, and accompanied by the comment that "there breaths a wonderful softness and delicacy thro' the lines, at the same time that the author's intellectuals seem to be impared and weakened."

Where the English correspondent got his story of Pocahontas is not entirely clear. He could have read it, of course, in John Smith's *General History of Virginia.* More than likely, however, he used Robert Beverley's classic *History and Present State of Virginia.* This is suggested by the fact that the three newspaper columns following the letter are filled with a long selection from Beverley's work. The passage reproduces the history for the years 1612–1616 and includes John Smith's petition to James I's wife, Queen Anne, concerning Pocahontas.[4]

Thus, in 1734, readers of the Boston *Gazette* were treated not only to a proposal for community support of the arts, poetic and graven, but were also given a good introduction to the Smith-Pocahontas story. The proposal is published below, but without the accompanying text from Beverley.

*

Accidentally hearing read a Paragraph in a LETTER *from a Gentleman in* ENGLAND *to his Friend here, We thought if a Copy could be obtain'd, the Publishing of it, with the* STORY *it alludes to, might be as agreeable (if not more so) then many Occurrences we are obliged to insert for want of more material News. The Letter bears Date from Colchester, 13th of July, 1733. wherein the Gentleman among other things (speaking of* America*) says,*

"*YOUR New England* POETRY gives me a great deal of Pleasure, as it discovers (besides a Beauty in the Composition) a tender and affectionate mind in the Author; if the humanity shewn in that Piece

---

3. Moses Coit Tyler, *A History of American Literature, 1607–1765* (Ithaca, N.Y., 1949), 296 ff.

4. The passage is copied, almost exactly, from R[obert] B[everley], *The History and Present State of Virginia . . .* (London, 1705), pt. 1, pars. 26–29. Smith's petition was copied by Beverley, probably from John Smith, *The Generall Historie of Virginia . . .* (London, 1624), 121–22.

(referring to a Piece of Poetry sent from hence) be any thing of the General Temper there, the People must be happy unless something AB EXTRA disturbs their Social Virtue. If your Poets will indulge their Muse, there's no want of Subjects in that part of the Globe. What a glorious Figure wou'd the Princess Pocahontas make, Painted by a fine hand? How charmingly wou'd she shine interceeding with her Rigid Father for the Life of the *English* Captain, and when that wou'd not prevail, throwing her own Neck upon him and by that means intercepting the Fatal Blow.

"How beautiful wou'd she appear afterwards a Captive in the hands of the Countrymen of him that she had saved? The Treachery of the *Indian King* that betray'd her, and the steady behaviour of her Father, who wou'd not comply with terms to the disadvantage of the Country, even for the sake of a beloved Daughter, whom he doated on with utmost tenderness wou'd be incidents as great in their kinds to any the *Greeks* and *Romans* wrote of. Then her Marriage with an English Gentleman, her graceful and majestick Behaviour in the Court of K. J. 1st, and her Sickness and Death at *Gravesend*, wou'd be an ample Field to shew all that can be lovely or great in a Female Character, and all that can be lamented in the loss of such a one. For my own part I don't recollect any of the celebrated Heroines of Antiquity of half so just a behaviour or that any way exceed her in virtue or true greatness of Mind. How many Statues and Medals would have been made by the *Romans* in memory of such a Lady? Not a Woman of Fashion but wou'd have had her Impression on a Jewel or a Seal: To shew your selves the most Elegant of all the Settlements, you shou'd Subscribe for her STATUE, to set up in the beautifullest Places of the Publick Walks where your Company meets."

6

POCAHONTAS ON THE BOSTON

COMMON, REVISITED

> We here resolve the mystery of the document Towner "hadn't
> the nerve to publish." For the first time in any modern publica-
> tion we reprint the account by "Sylvia" of "the delightful game
> played at mixed gatherings" from the *New England Courant* of
> 1725 which he had written up but suppressed for thirty years.
> May all those who cling to misguided notions of the meaning of
> "Puritan" in eighteenth-century America profit from it.

IN AUGUST 1962, whilst moving my very pregnant wife, unborn
twins, and four children from Williamsburg, Virginia (where I was
giving up the *William and Mary Quarterly*), to Chicago (where I was
taking up the Newberry Library), I sent off to the *Journal of Southern
History* final copy of a short piece for the "Notes and Documents"
section.

My good friend, W. W. Abbot, then editor of the *Journal*, who had
seen the penultimate draft, immediately published it as *"ARS Poetica et Sculptura:* Pocahontas on the Boston Common," *Journal of
Southern History*, 28:482–485, following a far more weighty note
concerning "The Rehabilitation of Captain John Smith," by Laura
Polanyi Striker and Bradford Smith, pp. 474–481.

My little note was mostly fun, and it would have escaped comment entirely had I not made a mistake in a citation to the *New-
England Courant*. "Early Eighteenth-Century New England newspapers are mostly dull affairs . . . ," I wrote (I had read all extant
through 1750, so I *knew*.) But "Once in a while, of course, a choice
item, amusing then as now, got printed and today delights the eye of
the dullards who plod through the papers seeking this or that.

"Some of these eye catchers [I continued] are so embarrassingly
lewd or downright vulgar by modern standards that they could not
be reprinted even in a column in the *William and Mary Quarterly*

devoted to humorous and often slightly salacious trivia of the seventeenth and eighteenth centuries. For years, as editor of that magazine, I kept, under the blotter of my desk, a graphic description of a delightful game allegedly played at mixed gatherings in the eighteenth century, merely because I hadn't the nerve to publish it."

It was one of my "fathers," the late Clifford K. (Ted) Shipton of the American Antiquarian Society, who caught the error. Apparently titillated by the description, and fond of the TRIVIA section of the *Quarterly*, he looked up the reference in the *Courant*. "Your citation is wrong," he wrote. "Where is the story?"

I have only recently looked it up (forgive me, Ted), in the very microtext edition of the *New-England Courant* that, along with so many newspapers and books, became available to all scholars, everywhere, through Shipton's intelligent labors. There, for February 15–22, 1725 (not as I had reported it, dated January 15–25, 1725), lies the "graphic description" of this "delightful game" that I hadn't the nerve to publish then but *do now.*

I feel free not only because, as I retire from my entrepreneurial and administrative job to become a scholar again, I renew my license to run ahead of the crowd, not afraid of being fired for "lewd and lascivious behavior," but also because in the intervening quarter century times have changed.

Even as recently as ten years ago *Hustler* magazine could (justifiably) post an advertisement in Grand Central Station—"HUSTLER, THE MAGAZINE NOBODY QUOTES." But not today: somebody must have quoted it by now. On the other hand, taking into account the women's movement, I'm not sure I would still call the *Courant*-described activity a "delightful game." The tide moves both ways. Anyhow, to set the story straight, here it is:

> *To the venerable doctor JANUS*
> SIR,
>
> It is with no little Difficulty that I take upon me this Task of writing to you, to notify your Female Readers especially, of a certain new coin'd Wedding Game, the Discovery of which would better become the Pen of some generous Youth, than that of a Virgin. But since the Want of such Discovery may encourage further Injuries to the Modesty of my Sex. I must venture upon a Relation of the Fact.
>
> Know then, That I being not long since at a certain Wedding, where the Company consisted of a considerable Number of both Sexes, and of single and married Persons,

some Beaux of Pleasure invented the following Game. In playing of Pawns, a Man was first oblig'd to sit down ou [sic] the Floor, with his Feet extended as far as possible; next him a Woman was order'd to sit down and have one of her Feet ty'd to the Man's and next her another Man with one of his Feet ty'd to the other of her's [sic], she still keeping her Feet close; and after this manner about half the Company were ty'd to one another, in a strait [sic] Line from one end of the Room to the other. This being done, an opposite Line was drawn in the same manner; and it was so contriv'd, that every Man in each Line had a Woman seated opposite to him. A Number of Candles were then brought, and set down in a Row between each Line, and two Constables, one at each end of the Lines, stood to see something perform'd, but those of my own Sex knew not what. The Men, we thought, extended their Feet on Purpose that we might keep ours close, and to let us see that they had no Design upon our Modesty. For our Parts, the worst we could dream of, was to get up and dance round the Candles. But presently a Signal was given, and the Men of one Line clos'd their Feet, fell backwards with the Womens [sic] Arms link'd their's, and as they fell, rais'd their Feet a considerable Distance from the Floor; and there—Oh!—there they held them, till the dismal Shrieks of their injur'd Partners forc'd them to be as they were. After which the Opposite Line of *Barbarians* did the like, notwithstanding the Struggles and Entreaties of the fair ones to whom they were ty'd, who now saw their Doom at Hand. You may easily conceive the dire Confusion we were in at this inhumane Treatment from those who call themselves Men of Honour. Oh! my Hand trembles in writing and every Letter is accompany'd with a Blush! But the ill Consequences that may attend such another Frolick forces me to discover this, that my own Sex may for ever after be upon their Guard against such unheard of and worse than Brutish Insults. Believe me, Sir, the Noise that was raised by those base Men, resembled rather the Screamings of a *Bedlam* than the Mirth of a *Wedding Chamber*, and some of us very narrowly escap'd Distraction. That the like Affront to the fair Sex may never more be heard of in *New-England* shall be the hearty Prayer of,

SIR,
Your Humble Servant,
Sylvia

>7<

THE MAPPING OF THE AMERICAN

REVOLUTIONARY WAR IN THE

NINETEENTH CENTURY

Towner apologized for this essay as the work of a "hurried and harried pinch-hitter" for a scholar who had agreed to deliver one of the Kenneth Nebenzahl, Jr. Lectures in the History of Cartography and had reneged at the eleventh hour.

The first lecture in the series, by J. B. Harley, was devoted to the contemporary mapping of the American Revolution. The final lecture, by Barbara B. Petchenik, cartographic editor of the Newberry-sponsored *Atlas of Early American History* edited by Lester B. Cappon, dealt with the Revolution in twentieth-century cartography. Bill's lecture was the bridge between the two, the efforts of nineteenth-century historians to depict the Revolution cartographically.

The topic was totally unstudied, and Towner dove into it with characteristic energy and thoroughness. Casually, as usual, he mentioned that he had looked at 700 maps in ninety-four books and fifteen periodicals for the nineteenth century and eight military histories for the twentieth century. He zeroed in on three

From J. B. Harley, Barbara Bartz Petchenik, and Lawrence W. Towner, *Mapping the American Revolutionary War* (Chicago: University of Chicago Press, 1978), 111–24. © 1978 by The University of Chicago Press. All rights reserved.

[Author's note:] This essay is a foray into unknown and dangerous territory for a hurried and harried pinch hitter. Without the help of many people, I would have had even less to say than is said, and there would be more errors of fact and interpretation than there are. My first helper was my daughter Elizabeth (see note 11). Charles Steffen, doctoral candidate at Northwestern University, did a lot of research and drafting for me, including a visit to the Huntington Library where he searched the Lossing Papers. David Woodward introduced me to cartographic printing and reproduction; Kenneth Nebenzahl lent me the proofs of two of his works (see note 2); Robert Karrow's excellent exhibit, set up for the lectures, was most instructive; and Don Higginbotham of the University of North Carolina, Chapel Hill, counseled me by telephone in my occasional desperation. None of the above can be blamed for this study's deficiencies, alas.

major nineteenth-century makers and users of maps of the revolutionary era. There was no need to apologize. The pinch hitter got a base hit.

THE DISTINGUISHED SCHOLAR Hans Kohn, while comparing European and American nationalism at the Massachusetts Institute of Technology in the 1950s, contrasted Swiss and American attitudes toward resident aliens. My recollection is that he said the Swiss were suspicious of any alien who wished to become a citizen; Americans, on the other hand, were suspicious of aliens who did not. To the Swiss, he went on, being Swiss means being several generations a native of the soil, with bloodlines reaching back into the dim and unrecorded past, sharing one or more common languages, and having a cultural identity that could not be conferred by legislative act. To the Americans, however, being American means voluntarily choosing to share certain loosely defined common values variously described as freedom, democracy, free enterprise, or Americanism. Underscoring his point, Professor Kohn doubted that there would ever be a Swiss counterpart of the then Un-American Activities Committee.

The reasons for this emphasis on values rather than on origins lie in American history and the unique developments of the Revolutionary generation. The United States of America were a new nation and, as in a new marriage, they had very little common history. Out of thirteen former colonies strung out along some fourteen hundred miles of seacoast, and out of a population comprising some four million souls of British, European, African, and Amerind origin (a more diverse people in one nation than the world had ever seen), that remarkable first generation created a nation almost overnight. By inventing the constitutional convention at the state level and then at the national, the Founding Fathers developed a way to legitimize a revolutionary government, one that succeeded in transferring power, not only from one political party to another, but also from one generation to another. In short, they solved the constitutional problem of sovereignty, at least until the Civil War.

During the nineteenth century, the American nation took away from the Indians, the Spanish, the French, the Mexicans, and the English a territory more than four times its original size. The nation survived one of the bloodiest civil wars in history; it freed its vast slave population (which had grown naturally more rapidly than any other slave population in the Americas); it absorbed immigrants from Europe numbering nearly five times its original population; and it changed from a society that was primarily rural, agricultural, and commercial into a vast industrial power.

THE AMERICAN REVOLUTION AS MYTH

Lacking the "natural" ties that bound more ancient peoples together, Americans early turned to the history of the American Revolution and to biographies of their Founding Fathers for a substantial part of their national myth. George Washington, for example, became the American Ulysses, and during the nineteenth century dozens of biographies of that hero were published—in some of which he would not have recognized himself.

Ironically, in the earliest years of the new nation, its best histories—David Ramsay's two-volume masterpiece, *The American Revolution;* William Gordon's *The History of the Rise, Progress, and Establishment of the Independence of the United States;* and even John Marshall's four-volume *Life of George Washington*—relied heavily for fact, interpretation, organization, and a good deal of text on a British publication edited by Edmund Burke and known as the *Annual Register.*[1]

Even for the maps and charts that illustrate the war of the American Revolution, the new nation depended heavily on English and French cartographers and map publishers contemporary with the Revolution.[2] For years, the British author Charles Stedman's *History of the Rise, Progress, and Termination of the American War* (published in London in 1794) provided the most useful military text and maps of that war. Even as late as the 1840s, Benson J. Lossing, when writing his popular *Pictorial Field Book of the Revolution*, visited the battlefields with Stedman's work in hand.[3]

Soon, however, the new nation was ill content to rely on its early histories and its early historians, just as it was unwilling to rely on a non-American language and literature. As Noah Webster put it in 1789: "Our honor requires us to have a system of our own, in language as well as government. Great Britain, whose children we are,

1. R. Kent Newmyer, "Charles Stedman's *History of the American War,*" *American Historical Review* 63 (1958): 924–25.
2. Two works by Kenneth Nebenzahl are fundamental to assessing contemporary mapping of the war. They are: *Atlas of the American Revolution* (Chicago: Rand McNally & Co., 1974) and *A Bibliography of Contemporary Printed Battle Plans of the American Revolution: 1775–1795* (Chicago and London: University of Chicago Press, 1975).
3. Benson J. Lossing to Henry B. Carrington, 13 April 1875, Box 6, Henry B. Carrington Papers, Yale University Library.

and whose language we speak, should no longer be *our* standard; for the taste of her writers is already corrupted, and her language on the decline."[4] Similarly, Ralph Waldo Emerson, writing half a century later argued that: "Perhaps the time is already come . . . when the sluggard intellect of this continent will . . . fill the postponed expectation of the world with something better than . . . mechanical skill. Our day of dependence, our long apprenticeship to the learning of other lands, draws to a close."[5]

As in language and literature, so also in history: Americans early generated a great deal of historical activity, on various levels, much of it focused on the Revolution and on the War for Independence. The Founding Fathers had known they were participating in great events, and they left to the nation a remarkable corpus of papers. Learned societies, such as the Massachusetts Historical Society, the American Philosophical Society, the New-York Historical Society, and the American Antiquarian Society, began to gather, preserve, and publish the nation's historical record. Even the Congress created its own library. Soon, gentlemen antiquaries were filling volumes of "proceedings" with accounts of every battle, skirmish, and encounter; new historical journals were created and carried stories of the Revolution; and general magazines, such as *Harper's Monthly*, printed extended accounts of that war.

Probably the most popular historian of the nineteenth century, and the most effective myth creator in the larger sense of the word, was George Bancroft. His monumental ten-volume *History of the United States*, 1834–1874, devoted six volumes to the Revolutionary period, 1763–1782, including two volumes on the war. In this history—based on a wide use of manuscript and other source materials—European as well as American—Bancroft depicted the Revolution, according to Page Smith, as "the golden age, the time of giants, the opening act of the extraordinary drama of American democracy."[6] "History, for Bancroft, was the working of Divine Wisdom, and God's eternal principles were discoverable through its study. . . . Seen in this light, the Revolution appeared as part of God's plan: it was intended for the edification of man and the improve-

4. Noah Webster, *Dissertations on the English Language* . . . (Boston: I. Thomas and Co., 1789), p. 20.

5. Ralph Waldo Emerson, *An Oration, Delivered before the Phi Beta Kappa Society, at Cambridge, August 31, 1837* [Usually entitled "The American Scholar"] (Boston: James Munroe & Co., 1837), p. 1.

6. Page Smith, "David Ramsay and the Causes of the American Revolution," *William and Mary Quarterly*, 3d ser., 17 (1960): 60.

ment of society; it ushered in a new and brighter age of human progress."[7]

Despite Bancroft's sweeping panoramic vision—with its foundation in the Puritan view that Americans were God's chosen people—he, like other historians, wrote intensively on purely military aspects of the Revolution, criticizing this commander and that and delighting in the controversy his words engendered. Indeed, as Don Higginbotham has said, military history in the nineteenth century was, "on the whole, narrowly conceived to mean the field of combat. Captain John Parker mustering his company on Lexington Common, Washington crossing the ice-filled Delaware, Greene struggling through fog at Germantown . . . young Alexander Hamilton seizing a redoubt at Yorktown—all this, and little more, was military history."[8]

HARD TIMES FOR HISTORICAL CARTOGRAPHY

Given the nationalistic need for a historic myth, this intense interest in the battlefield, and the remarkable series of nobly conceived and executed contemporary maps already available, one would not be surprised to find in American histories an extensive and imaginative use of cartography as an adjunct to the history of the War for Independence as written in the nineteenth century. Similarly, in Europe, given the emergence during the American Revolution of both a citizen army, or armies, and very successful partisan or guerilla warfare, one would expect that the Revolutionary War—and the maps of the war—would have been extensively written about and studied in nineteenth-century Europe.

Unfortunately, in neither Europe nor America was that the case. Peter Paret, in his "Colonial Experience and European Military Reform at the end of the Eighteenth Century," finds that the colonial wars, in America and India, provided little but emotional examples, not hard case studies for tactical reform. "The decisive innovation in infantry fighting," he said, ". . . consisted in the acceptance of open order tactics by the line infantry. Close order methods—the line, the attack column, fire by volley—were now combined as a matter of course with skirmish groups and individual, aimed fire."[9] But the examples were not found in America: "many of the great and minor figures in the military reform movements of the time

7. Ibid., pp. 60–61.
8. Don Higginbotham, "American Historians and the Military History of the American Revolution," *American Historical Review* 70 (1965): 20, 24.
9. *Bulletin of the Institute of Historical Research* 37 (1964): 51.

showed little special interest in colonial wars—Scharnhorst and Clausewitz are two examples."[10] Consequently, there was apparently no great demand in Europe for either the military annals or the maps of the American Revolution showing our ragtag and bobtail military tactics.

As for American histories, there were many. But with few exceptions, if maps were used at all extensively (Bancroft, for example, printed none in his war volumes, nor did he cite any), they were ill used and they added little to an understanding of the text they accompanied. In the history of cartography, they represent a retreat from, rather than an advance over, the maps of the eighteenth century.

To be sure, there were many maps produced or reproduced during the period. With the help of David Sanders Clark's "Index to the Maps of the American Revolution," I looked at some seven hundred maps in ninety-four books and fifteen periodicals. They began appearing in the first decade of the century and they reached a numerical peak just before the Civil War, when the Revolution became at once a part of the controversy between the North and South and, as myth, a possible cement for the disintegrating nation. They peaked again, predictably, in the 1870s, the centennial of the Revolution, and their production stayed at a fairly high level to the end of the century.[11]

As one might expect, the methods of reproduction evolved parallel to the printing history of the century. The largest percentage down to 1850 were copper or steel engravings, with lithography and wood engravings frequently used for large foldout maps and small maps in books, respectively. By the end of the century, line cuts predominated, although lithography and wax engraving were still in use.

The average size of these maps was 24.5 square inches, or not quite 5-by-5 inches. For the most part, it appears, map size was technically a function of how large a map the page size would allow, for maps were mostly reproduced in books and periodicals. Intellec-

10. Ibid., p. 59.
11. David Sanders Clark, "Index to Maps of the American Revolution in Books and Periodicals Illustrating the Revolutionary War and Other Events of the Period 1763–1789," mimeographed (Washington, D.C.: n.p., 1969). Elizabeth G. Towner spent a tedious month using Clark's "Index," identifying works I should examine, writing the call slips, locating the maps, measuring them, putting them in chronological order of publication, and the like. This work could not have been written without her intelligent help.

tually, it is just barely too harsh to say that map size seems to have been a function of keeping the maps small enough to be virtually unintelligible.

The use of symbols (which in eighteenth-century maps often involved the use of different colors) also deteriorated. Examination of eighteenth-century maps reveals a score of more conventional symbols, such as a man-of-war, a ferry boat, a watch boat, cavalry, troop encampments, troop movements, redoubts, cannon, and the like. There was very little development in these symbols in the nineteenth century. Troops, ships, fortifications, and troop movements were simplified and standardized, but the loss of color greatly reduced what a given map could tell. Troop encampments and troop movements are usually indistinguishable, and many of the ornamental features of the earlier maps were lost. In short, no notable advances were made in the difficult art of depicting movement in space over time.

The publishing company Matthews-Northrup was an exception. In 1891 there appeared John Fiske's two-volume, *The American Revolution*, which contained eleven maps designed and printed in color by means of wax engraving by the publishers. Matthews-Northrup continued to produce maps of unrivaled quality in the twentieth century, culminating in Elroy McKendree Avery's *History of the United States and Its People* (7 vols., 1904–1910). Indeed, Barbara Petchenik has called this latter work "a landmark in American mapmaking" and "the only real contribution to the 20th-century mapping of the War of the American Revolution."[12]

Finally, concerning the technical features, one has to deal with map compilation. Again, with some notable exceptions, there were few advances in the period. Most of the maps printed in the nineteenth century were old maps. To the extent they were redrawn, redrawing was to simplify detail for reproduction in a smaller size rather than for accuracy. Apparently little effort was made to compare maps with battle terrains, with the manuscript or printed accounts of the participants, or with each other. As a single example of what could have been done, the Historical Society of Pennsylvania in 1846 commissioned a survey of the terrain of the Battle of Brandywine. The map was designed by one Joseph Townsend and has since been used at least three times, most recently in an adaptation by Douglas Southall Freeman in his *Life of Washington*. It

12. John Fiske, *The American Revolution*, 2 vols. (Cambridge, Mass.: Riverside Press, 1896). See below, Barbara B. Petchenik, "The Mapping of the American Revolutionary War in the Twentieth Century."

embraces more territory than the famous Faden map, it shows roads along which troops moved, and it is, or was at least intended to be, geographically more accurate.[13]

In short, the historical cartography of the Revolutionary War during the nineteenth century lacked a systematic foundation in both theory and technique, and this was especially true for the mapping of the Revolution. Revolutionary battles in general were not seen as case studies in military tactics and strategy; still less were they viewed in light of the wider problem of the relationship between geography and human behavior. The Revolution was an episode to be celebrated, not analyzed. It is not surprising, therefore, that maps of the war were limited to reproductions within books, serving as illustrations rather than integral parts of the text.

But if historical cartography was in a rudimentary state, cartography was not. One has only to look at John Melish's *Atlas of the War of 1812* (published in 1813) to know that good maps could be, and were being, produced in America. This work includes five handsomely-engraved 16-by-21-inch maps: three are by the distinguished cartographer Henry Schenk Tanner, one is an eighteenth-century map, and one is based on a British engineer's sketch of the fighting on the Detroit River.[14] The fact is that cartographic energy was being devoted more to contemporary maps than to historical maps. America was expanding into uncharted lands: following the Louisiana Purchase, the Lewis and Clark expedition, and the emerging conquest of the West, American cartographic enterprise was more challenged by mapping a new nation than by an old war.

THREE CONTRIBUTORS TO REVOLUTIONARY CARTOGRAPHY

An account of the nineteenth-century mapping of the American Revolution could stop right here, were it not for three men. They, however, make a major difference in the story, not only because they each made a significant contribution to the cartography of the Revolution, but also because each is interesting in himself.

13. Joseph Townsend, "Plan of the Battle of Brandywine, September 11th 1777" in "Some Account of the British Army . . . and of the Battle of Brandywine . . . ," *Bulletin of the Historical Society of Pennsylvania* 1 (September 1846): opp. p. 8. See also an adapted version of the same map in Douglas Southall Freeman, *George Washington: A Biography,* 7 vols. (New York, Charles Scribner's Sons, 1948–1957), 4 (1951): 473. John Long of the staff of the Newberry Library's Hermon Dunlap Smith Center for the History of Cartography brought this map to my attention.

14. John Melish, *A Military and Topographical Atlas of the United States . . .* (Philadelphia: printed by G. Palmer, 1813).

Benson J. Lossing

The first of these men is Benson J. Lossing, 1813–1891, publisher, editor, wood-engraver, and author. His most important writings are a series of volumes called *Field-Books*—of the Revolution, of the War of 1812, and of the Civil War. The first, *A Field-Book of the Revolution*, was published in thirty parts by Harper's during 1851–1852, then as a book in two volumes, which he twice revised.[15]

Lossing's first *Field-Book* is a narrative account of his eight-thousand-mile, five-month journey to the scenes of the Revolutionary battles, then rapidly changing. He was really more interested in depicting scenes and views and buildings than drawing maps, alas. Of the nearly twelve hundred illustrations, only seventy-six are maps and, truth be told, even the maps are often more illustrative than militarily informative. They are miniscule, the largest being about 3-by-5 inches, and they provide very little information for the general reader.

What contribution, then, did Lossing make? First, he made an effort to compare standing maps with the actual terrain. As he told a correspondent years later, he visited the battlefields with Charles Stedman's maps in hand, carrying as well a camera lucida and a drawing board to record his impressions on the spot.[16] He also interviewed aged survivors of the war. His research was necessarily unsystematic, but Lossing did gain access to many private manuscript holdings.[17] Moreover, even though the rise of the historical profession was another half-century in the future, Lossing was in touch with the leading scholars of the time. "Mr. Irving, Mr. Sparks, Mr. Force, Mr. Frothingham and many others," he wrote, "genuinely expressed their desire to contribute all in their power to my work. . . ."[18]

Lossing, we must remember, was not an objective historian-

---

15. Benson J. Lossing, *The Pictorial Field-Book of the Revolution . . .* , 2 vols. (New York: Harper & Brothers, 1851–1852); *The Pictorial Field-Book of the War of 1812 . . .* , (New York: Harper & Brothers, 1868); *The Pictorial Field-Book of the Civil War in the United States of America*, 3 vols. (New York: T. Belknap, 1868–1869; first published as *The Pictorial History . . .* Philadelphia: G. W. Childs, 1866–1868).

16. Alexander Davidson, Jr., "How Benson J. Lossing Wrote His 'Field Books' of the Revolution, the War of 1812, and the Civil War," *Papers of the Bibliographical Society of America* 32 (1938): 63.

17. Lossing to Helen Lossing, 5 October 1858, Lossing Papers, Henry E. Huntington Library and Art Gallery.

18. Lossing to J. J. Smith, 23 December 1850, Lossing Papers.

cartographer. His *Field-Book* and his maps were designed to play a symbolic role, to build American nationality by appealing to its glorious Revolutionary past. Perhaps Lossing believed that the sectional conflicts of the 1850s could be quieted through a timely invocation of the Revolution. As an admirer wrote, the *Field-Book* was "peculiarly opportune in these foppish and degenerate days when we appear to be losing sight of our revolutionary landmarks in the fogs of partyism." [19] And when civil war came, Lossing began a new Field Book—"a Great National work"—which might help provide a new foundation on which to rebuild American unity." [20] His "unflinching national sentiments," in Lossing's own words, ran throughout his work.[21] Only at the end of the nineteenth century, with the advent of "scientific history," environmental determinism, and a greater appreciation for the interplay between geography and history, would historical cartography become more objective and scholarly.

Henry B. Carrington

Lossing provides a direct link to the second figure worth remembering, Henry Beebe Carrington, 1824–1912, for whom Lossing's onsite inspections and publishing success were an inspiration. The two men frequently corresponded in the 1870s, the older man, Lossing, being unstinting in his support, suggestions, and praise. Carrington's claim on our attention rests chiefly, of course, on his *Battles of the American Revolution, 1775–1781*, which went through at least five editions and from which was published, as a separate work, his *Battle Maps and Charts of the American Revolution* (New York, 1881).

There were several impulses that led to Carrington's interest in the military history of the Revolution. His great-grandfather had served in the colonial army, and some of his military gear was still around when Carrington was a child. Carrington tells of his youthful anger at a hired man who sharpened up the old soldier's sword "for the purpose of cutting corn stalks. . . ." "My mother," he wrote, reproved "my wicked" outburst that "I wish it had cut his head off." [22] On the annual training days in Wallingford, Connecticut, Carrington recounted:

19. Josiah D. Channing to Lossing, 11 April 1853, Lossing Papers.
20. Amos Dean to George W. Childs, 12 April 1862, Lossing Papers.
21. Lossing to Helen Lossing, 22 April 1861, Lossing Papers.
22. Henry B. Carrington, "E. Yale, 1841–1845: A Glance at College Life by Carrington" (Typescript), Box 10, 5, Carrington Papers.

Just after sunrise, there passed by the old home two soldiers of the Wallingford Light Infantry. This Company retained the uniform . . . worn during the Revolutionary War as a part of Lafayette's Special Light Infantry Division, with which he marched . . . to command the campaign against Cornwallis. . . . The hats of these soldiers were surmounted with a tall white feather, nearly eighteen inches in length, and tipped with red. The swallow-tail coat was also a fiery red, while the trousers were white. On the Training Days, several carriages, or large wagons, brought to the view of the people large and small the presence of surviving Revolutionary Veterans, and two or three of them used to visit the Tavern and rehearse stories of their war experience.[23]

Carrington's childhood interests in the Revolution and the military were reinforced by the career of his grandfather, James C. Carrington, who had been a partner of Eli Whitney in the manufacture of arms at Whitneyville, Connecticut, from 1800 to 1825, and was subsequently superintendent for the United States of the manufacture of arms there and inspector of works at the arsenals at Springfield and Harper's Ferry.[24]

In fact, young Carrington's interest in the military would have led him to West Point had lung trouble not prevented it. Instead he decided for Yale, where his maternal grandfather and great-grandfather had studied. Upon graduating in classics, he taught at the Irving Institute in Tarrytown, New York, for two years. There he came to know Washington Irving, who had just returned from being United States Minister to Spain. "His acquaintance," wrote Carrington, "laid the foundation for my years of subsequent labor in preparing *The Battles of the American Revolution.*"[25] Irving himself followed the same course by publishing his four-volume biography of Washington between 1857 and 1859.[26]

One final influence on Carrington must be mentioned. That was John Brown, the radical abolitionist. Before attending Yale in the early 1840s, Carrington heard John Brown preach and became an immediate convert to the cause of abolitionism. After college and

23. Ibid.
24. *Dictionary of American Biography,* s.v. "Carrington, Henry Beebee."
25. Carrington, "E. Yale," Carrington Papers, pp. 6–7.
26. Washington Irving, *Life of George Washington,* 5 vols. (New York: G. P. Putnam & Co., 1855–1859).

after teaching at the Irving Institute, Carrington moved to Ohio to practice law and there played an important role as an antislavery man in organizing the Republican Party. In 1857, he jumped at the chance to enter the military, and he reorganized the Ohio militia, becoming adjutant general. At the outbreak of the Civil War, he rushed nine regiments across the Kentucky border, saving that state for the Union, and earned a federal commission as colonel. His vigorous Republicanism and abolitionism led him to try several Copperheads or Sons of Liberty (Democrats who opposed the war) by military tribunal, but the convictions were later reversed by the United States Supreme Court. After the war, Carrington participated in various military campaigns in the West against the Indians: he built Fort Phil Kearney in Nebraska, he took part in the Red Cloud War, and he defended the Union Pacific against Indian marauders. He was severely wounded in one of those engagements and in 1869 was detailed to teach military history at Wabash College in Indiana.[27]

Reflecting later on his Indian fighting, in a speech delivered in England, he revealed the same kind of manifest-destiny nationalism that led him to participate so zealously in the Civil War. These same sentiments are everywhere evident in his book on the Revolution:

> The Anglo-Saxon, in his westward match, still meets the red man. It is the old story of an issue of races in the expansion of the stronger. The inferior must perish. Bloody issues have been evoked, and earnest efforts have been made to harmonize the conflicting elements; but the waste goes on. On the one hand, all passions are stimulated to annihilate the savage as a beast, because he tears and tortures in the throes of his death struggle; and, on the other hand, we yearn for his rescue from that oblivion which buried his earlier ancestors, because we feel that his destinies, like his possessions, are in our hands.[28]

Carrington's real work on *The Battles of the American Revolution* began when he started teaching at Wabash College. As he wrote George Bancroft: "During my labors at this college for nearly five years, I have given a course of lectures upon the battlefields of the Revolution: using maps compiled from all known sources, excluding so far as possible civil history and presenting Washington,

27. See note 24 above.
28. Unidentified British newspaper account, "Indians of North America," Box 12, Scrapbook, 38, Carrington Papers.

Greene, etc. as military men through the actual field operations of the War. . . . Neither at West Point nor elsewhere," he added, "has a similar enterprise been attempted."[29]

During the last year of Carrington's work before publication, there was a flurry of activity. He sent outlines, some maps, and some text to Bancroft and Lossing, both of whom encouraged him to go on, as he did Generals Sherman and Sheridan. Bancroft urged him to use the New-York Historical Society, the Lenox Collection, and the Library of Congress. Lossing encouraged him, saying that his work "cannot fail to be exceedingly interesting to all scholars, and especially to students of American History, whether in military circles or not, and I hope you will carry out your plan, successfully. A Knowledge of the topography of the battlefield, is a very great help in rightly understanding a report of the battle. . . ."[30]

Sherman was particularly interested in the military value of Carrington's work: "I have no doubt in your studies to illustrate your lectures on the Military Science you must collect much valuable material that would warrant presentation in the form of a Book. I know of nothing of the kind about the Revolutionary War—should you desire you may use my name for I am sure such a book as you describe would be most valuable to military men and to professors engaged like yourself in the effort to save our profession from sinking clear out of mind."[31]

The climax to Carrington's research was a trip to England and Europe in 1875, recorded in his scrapbook. There he visited the British Museum, the Bodleian, the Royal Geographical Society, and the Bibliothèque Nationale. At the British Museum he checked out Stedman's *History*, Clinton's *Narrative of the Campaign of 1781* (Philadelphia, 1865), and Faden's plan of Newport, Rhode Island, 1777. To his hometown newspaper he wrote on 28 July 1875, "My time has fastened itself to regular hours, between the War Office, British Museum, and Hall of Records. Generous courtesy meets my work, and from ten to twelve, and one to five, I am at maps and books, old watercolor sketches of Charlestown in flames, pen and ink plans of battles, and even pencil plans. . . ."[32]

On his return from Europe, Carrington completed the maps and

29. Carrington to George Bancroft, 26 March 1875, Massachusetts Historical Society.
30. Lossing to Carrington, 13 April 1875, Box 6, Carrington Papers; and letters from Bancroft, Sherman, and Sheridan, ibid.
31. Sherman to Carrington, 29 March 1875, Box 6, Carrington Papers.
32. Box 12, Scrapbook, Carrington Papers.

the text and, with the help of Lossing, finally found a publisher, A. S. Barnes and Company, who printed it in parts during 1876. By November of that year, General Sherman had read the third part and wrote to tell him that he would "call the attention of the officers to it, that they may Encourage you in the long effort to systematize and arrange American military history so that it may be studied."[33]

In December came a letter from George Bancroft filled with praise, but revealing a little pique that Lossing might have caught him out in an error: "I have just received your splendid volume, which I see at once is the fruit of much toil and careful research, & the advantage of military experience. One matter caught my eye: pray do not think it ungracious if I enclose to you a little memorandum on a point, where you think me in the wrong: but where I hope you will find reasons to reverse your opinion."[34] Unfortunately, the little memorandum is lost.

Using the same maps, Carrington then prepared a slim volume, *Battle Maps and Charts of the Revolution*, published in 1881. It is an ugly book, with the one page of text for each map, printed in alternating lines of red and black ink. But, as did his earlier volume—which was priced at five dollars, a high price for those days—it sold well. Carrington helped; for example, he urged it on Secretary of War Robert Todd Lincoln in 1882. Wrote Lincoln in reply: "With reference to your suggestion that said work would be of value, as a text book, for the Military Academy, I beg to state that 36 copies for the use of the military schools at West Point, Willetts Point, Fort Monroe, and Fort Leavenworth were purchased by the department in July last."[35]

Since this essay is supposed to be about maps, not chaps, it is not enough that Henry Beebe Carrington was a colorful character who happens to deserve a biography of at least article length. Instead, we now have to address the question, just what did he contribute to the history of historical mapmaking, in particular of the Revolution? Several observations, it seems to me, can be made.

First, the *Battles of the American Revolution* grew out of a felt need for maps with which to teach the history of the war. The contemporary maps were already scarce, widely scattered, and probably unavailable at Wabash College where Carrington was teaching. He

33. Sherman to Carrington, 17 November 1876, Box 6, Carrington Papers.
34. Bancroft to Carrington, 7 December 1876, Massachusetts Historical Society.
35. Robert Todd Lincoln to Carrington, 11 November 1882, Box 6, Carrington Papers.

moved to supply that need, perhaps only coincidentally, in time for the centennial in 1876. Thus the maps were presented as deliberately patriotic history, not news.

Second, the maps are newly-compiled, not reproductions, and they are based on several sources. These include some on-site visits, research in old maps, and research in the written records of the combatants. Carrington visited at least six map repositories in the United States, and his bibliography cites three hundred sources, European as well as American. (Unfortunately, there is no record for any single map of whether Carrington visited the site, of what other maps he used, or of what written materials he consulted. The bibliography for the *Battles* is a general one.)

Third, while the book includes text as well as maps, the maps are of primary importance and the book was designed with them in mind. It is a historical atlas. As we have seen, the maps were later published separately in a small atlas, and they are quite able to stand on their own.

Fourth, as a military man experienced in topography and mapping, Carrington kept his maps uncluttered and readable, even understandable. Bancroft commented on the value of Carrington's military experience, and Lossing said that Carrington's "topographical maps will be the next best, in giving clearness to history, to an actual visit in person."[36]

Finally, a new method of map reproduction, wax-engraving, had been developed, allowing maps of considerable clarity, compared with other maps of the period. This method was invented in the United States by Sidney Edwards Morse in the 1830s. By the 1870s, a number of large map publishing companies had begun to use the process.[37] It was wax-engraving, including the use of set type for the lettering, that Carrington's publishers used. (The total costs for illustrations, composition, and plates, by the way, was $2,569.)

Justin Winsor

Despite the real advances made by Henry Beebe Carrington, the culmination of nineteenth-century and the beginning of twentieth-century cartography of the American Revolution came with Justin Winsor, Librarian of Harvard College. This formidable scholar, who

36. Lossing to Carrington, 13 April 1875, Box 6, Carrington Papers.
37. David Woodward, *The All-American Map* (Chicago and London: University of Chicago Press, 1977), p. 30.

became the century's leading student of the history of cartography, was born in Boston in 1831.[38] He attended Boston Latin School and there acquired a distaste for organized instruction that, at Harvard, led him to near revolt and near suspension. Winsor spent two years in France and Germany instead of finishing his college courses, and got his degree only several years later. His attitude was not mere youthful rebelliousness against all authority, however, for on his return from Europe, he lived happily with his parents—even after he was married—until his forty-ninth year. It was rather that he thought classwork got in the way of an education that was proceeding very well on its own. He was probably right, for in his freshman year he had published his first book, *A History of the Town of Duxbury:* he was then eighteen years old.[39]

Winsor turned his back on American history for some twenty years, devoting himself to literary criticism, poetry, commentary, and fiction. For fourteen of those years he worked on a monumental study of the life and times of David Garrick, the eighteenth-century actor and playwright. When he completed it, in 1864, it comprised ten folio manuscript volumes. Never published, it sits with forty other volumes of Winsor manuscripts at the Massachusetts Historical Society.

Winsor returned to writing history after becoming head of the Boston Public Library in 1868, and he continued in that field as Librarian of Harvard College, where he succeeded John Langdon Sibley in 1887. It was while ransacking and then bringing to order the collections of the Boston Public Library and the Harvard College Library that Winsor first drew together his knowledge of the sources of the American Revolution, including the maps. As a freshman at Harvard, his diary relates, he had prepared a lecture on the Northern Campaign in the Revolution, for which he painted some "diagram like maps."[40] But it was in his *Readers Handbook of the American Revolution 1761–1783* (Boston, 1879), that he made not only his first substantial effort, but *the* first substantial effort, to bring the maps of the Revolutionary War under bibliographical control. In that volume of 328 pages there are 34 sections on maps (some only a

38. For bibliographical information on Winsor, see Horace E. Scudder, "Memoir of Justin Winsor, L.L.D.," *Proceedings of the Massachusetts Historical Society,* 2d ser., 12 (1899): 457–82; and Joseph Alfred Borome, "The Life and Letters of Justin Winsor" (Ph.D. diss., Columbia University, 1950).

39. Justin Winsor, *History of the Town of Duxbury, Massachusetts . . .* (Boston: Crosby & Nichols, 1849).

40. Scudder, "Memoir," p. 464.

PART ONE/HISTORIAN

sentence or two, others a page or more) describing printed maps, maps in books, and manuscript maps, along with their locations.

That book was a necessary background for his next work, *The Memorial History of Boston*, a vast compendium in four volumes, still very useful, and one of the first cooperative histories in America, published in 1880–1881. As general editor of *The Memorial History*, he said, he "secured seventy writers, endeavored to unify their contributions, and aimed to complete publication in two years. It was completely finished in twenty-three months."[41] There were giants in the land in those days!

In these volumes, Winsor provided the editorial apparatus—essays on sources, and the like—foreshadowing his later cooperative work, *The Narrative and Critical History of America*. The *Memorial History* apparatus includes two extensive lists of maps of Boston and its environs, in one of which appears the Battle of Bunker Hill. There Winsor listed and critically compared several maps, each of which had gone through various transformations as they were used again, and again, and again. I quote at length to illustrate the painstaking cartobibliographical detail he affords the student:

> Lieutenant Page [whom Winsor identifies in a footnote] made an excellent plan, based on a survey by Montresor, of the British Engineers, showing the laying-out of Charlestown. The successive positions of the British line are indicated on a smaller superimposed sheet. This was issued in London in 1776, called *A Plan of the Action at Bunker's Hill on the 17th June, 1775, between His Majesty's Troops under the Command of Major-General Howe, and the Rebel Forces*. The same plate; with some changes, was dated April 12, 1793, and used in Stedman's *American War*. It was re-engraved, reduced, by D. Martin, substituting American for Rebel and Breeds for Bunker's in the title, with a few other changes in names, and issued by C. Smith in 1797, in *The American War from 1775 to 1783*. See Hunnewell's *Bibliography of Charlestown and Bunker Hill*, 1880, p. 18, where a heliotype is given. It was again re-engraved, much reduced (5¼ × 9 inches), for Dearborn's *Boston Notions*, 1848, p. 156; and soon after, full size, following the original of 1776 in Frothingham's *Siege of Boston*. . . .
>
> Henry de Berniere, of the Tenth Royal Infantry, made a map similar in scale to Page's, but not so accurate in the ground plan. It was called *Sketch of the Action on the*

41. Quoted in ibid., p. 477.

Heights of Charlestown, and having been first mentioned in the *Gleaner,*—a newspaper published at Wilkesbarre, Pa., by Charles Miner,—as found recently in an old drawer; it was engraved, in facsimile, in the *Analectic Magazine,* February, 1818; where it is stated to have been found in the captured baggage of a British officer, and to have been copied by J. A. Chapman from an original sketch taken by Henry de Berniere, of the fourteenth regiment of infantry, now in the hands of J. Cist, Esq. General Dearborn commented on this plan in the *Portfolio,* March 1818 (reprinted in *Historical Magazine,* June, 1868), with the same plan altered in red (19½ × 12¼ inches), which alterations were criticised by Governor Brooks in June, 1818. See *N. E. Hist. and Geneal. Reg.,* July 1858. G. G. Smith worked on this rectified plan in producing his *Sketch of the Battle of Bunker Hill, by a British Officer* (12 × 19 inches) issued in Boston at the time of the completion of the monument in 1843.

Colonel Samuel Swett made a plan (18½ × 12½ inches), based on De Berniere's which was published in his *History of the Battle of Bunker Hill,* and has been reproduced, full size, in Ellis's *Oration* in 1841; and reduced variously in Lossing's *Field Book of the Revolution,* in Ellis's *History,* and *Centennial History;* and in other places.[42]

Alas, there were only a few maps reproduced in this section of *The Memorial History,* mostly by heliotype, the best method of facsimile reproduction then available. I suspect that Winsor's disappointment over their poor legibility led him to changes in his monumental *Narrative and Critical History of America,* published in Boston, 1884–1889. It is the sixth of these eight cooperatively written volumes that concerns us.

This volume comprises eight chapters, two written by Winsor. At the end of most chapters are "Critical Essays" and "Notes" by Winsor, sometimes running nearly as long as the text. Scattered throughout the volume, frequently in these sections but also in the text, are ninety-four maps (more than twice as many as in Carrington), fifty-eight of them reproductions.

While Winsor's maps vary in size, method of reproduction, and quality, they have three important elements in common. First, each map's source is given, usually with a genealogy of the map's various

42. Justin Winsor, ed., *The Memorial History of Boston . . . 1630–1800,* 4 vols. (Boston: J. R. Osgood & Co., 1880–1881), 3: i–ii.

transformations through book after book in the nineteenth century, as illustrated above; second, for each map Winsor indicated whether it was an exact reproduction or a sketch based on the original; and third, he indicated the method of reproduction. Even a casual study of this volume reveals much about Winsor as a cartobibliographer, as a cartographer, and as a frustrated scholar trying to fit maps of varying sizes to a set page size. Let us deal with the frustrations first.

Winsor had devoted a great amount of time to cartography and maps, as we have already seen. In the Massachusetts Historical Society are five large folio scrapbooks with facsimiles of maps (and some originals) that Winsor gathered not only for *The Narrative and Critical History* but also for his later works on Columbus, on the Mississippi Basin, and on the Far West. He was ready to do a nearly definitive work. But book publishers were not up to the job. On Bunker Hill, for example, we know he was an authority, as is shown in his *Handbook* and in his *Memorial History of Boston*. But in the chapter concerning Bunker Hill and Boston in *The Narrative and Critical History*, not one of the seven maps or the one view is as informative as he would have liked.

First appears a drawing, based on a tracing (provided him by Lossing) of the original manuscript sketch made from Beacon Hill of Charlestown following the battle. He had used a later engraving of this for *The Memorial History*, but here he wanted to get closer to the original. It was reproduced as large as his page permitted. While it does convey the sense of immediacy, the details are difficult to distinguish, and the manuscript handwriting is illegible to middle-aged eyes.

There follow: first, a sketch of Charlestown peninsula from the plan by Montresor, which is almost useless; second, a cut of the Charlestown Heights Battle plan from the *Analectic Magazine*, that, as reduced, has a legend so small Winsor had to have it set in the text on the following page; third, a full page reproduction from Stedman's *History*, showing Boston and Bunker Hill, which is much clearer than the preceding map; fourth, a reduced reproduction from the Atlas accompanying Marshall's *Life of Washington*, far inferior to the original; fifth, a map of Boston and vicinity taken from a photograph of a map in *Almon's Remembrancer*; sixth, a sketch based on a manuscript in the Library of Congress entitled "A Draught of the Town of Boston and Charlestown . . . 1775," which, while attractive, is merely an illustration here because it really cannot be read without magnification; and finally, a quite legible detail from Page's *Plan of the Town of Boston* (London, 1777) showing the British lines of the Boston Neck, but again with the legend requiring resetting in the text.[43]

These frustrations, I believe, led Winsor to become his own cartographer. They led him to try to produce pen and ink drawings, with lettering and numbering of his own, that, when reduced photographically and subsequently reproduced (by linecut, a process developed in the 1880s), would be intelligible, or at least legible to the reader. How he did this can be inferred from an examination of his scrapbook volumes in the Massachusetts Historical Society. In that work are an extended note by Winsor and two maps of the Brandywine campaign. The original map, which was Washington's, Winsor found "much crumpled and torn" in the Pennsylvania Historical Society. He had a facsimile tracing made of it, and then reduced the facsimile photographically to see how clearly the legend and detail would show. That reproduction is in his scrapbook. He then retraced it, simplifying the detail considerably. He then placed printed numbers on the map corresponding to the location of Washington's notes on the original, and these notes were then printed separately in the text.[44] In all, Winsor produced thirty-six maps by this method.

One other example of Winsor's cartobibliographical work in *The Narrative and Critical History* should be mentioned, for it shows how careful he was. The map is of the Battle of Guilford, 15 March 1781. A comparison with the original—that is, with Faden's map printed in 1787—reveals a reduction in size and, of course, the use of only black and white. Also lost are Faden's trees and underbrush. But otherwise the maps are identical, at least to the untrained eye. Wrote Winsor:

> Sketched from Faden's map (March 1, 1787), which is the same as the map in Tarleton (p. 108), with the same date, and Stedman, ii. 342, with slight changes, dated Jan. 20, 1794. It is followed in the maps in *Mag. of Amer. Hist.* (1881), p. 44; in R. E. Lee's *Lee's Memoir,* etc., p. 276; and Caruther's *Incidents* (Philadelphia, 1808), p. 108; in Lossing's *Field-Book,* ii. 608. There are among the Faden maps (nos. 52, 53) in the Library of Congress two MSS. drafts of the battle,—one showing the changes of the position of the forces. Johnson (*Greene,* ii. 5) gives five different stages of the fight, and G. W. Greene (iii. 176) copies

43. Justin Winsor, ed., *Narrative and Critical History of America,* 8 vols. (Boston and New York: Houghton Mifflin & Co., 1884–1889), 6: 197–211.

44. "American Maps, Vol. III 1750–1885," Justin Winsor Papers, Massachusetts Historical Society.

them. His lines vary from the description of Cornwallis. Cf. Carrington's *Battles* p. 565; Hamilton's *Grenadier Guards* (ii. 245); *Harper's Monthly*, XV, 162, etc. Ed.[45]

Winsor, then, emerges as the most significant nineteenth-century cartographer and cartobibliographer of the American Revolution. He reproduced more maps, and, with the exception of Carrington, his own maps are more legible than those of most scholars restricted to book-page size. He experimented with different ways of reproducing maps, settling finally on photographically reduced tracings and eliminating what he considered unnecessary clutter to make the main lines legible, then using the linecut method of reproduction. Winsor compared different maps and different accounts in arriving at his final delineations, much as modern scholars edit a manuscript that has various versions to establish the text. He provided (unlike Carrington) documentation for each map, and he prepared a systematic cartobibliography for each battle.

The Coming of Scientific History

If the work of Justin Winsor marks the culmination of nineteenth-century historical cartography, it also represents a significant departure from the mapmaking of Lossing and Carrington. The last decades of the nineteenth century were formative ones for the historical profession. The days of the patrician amateur were clearly numbered: an ambitious group of university-trained men were endeavoring to bring order and professional standards to their discipline. Viewing the works of earlier historians as romantic and subjective, these new scholars wanted to place history on a "scientific" basis. Winsor was among this group.[46]

The scientific basis of such scholarship derived in part from Darwinism, which had a tremendous impact on all aspects of American thought. In history, the impact took the form of environmental determinism. Rather than seeing American history as the unfolding of providential design or as the development of Teutonic institutions, the so-called scientific historians believed that environment was primary in shaping human thought and behavior. Frederick Jackson Turner, of course, was the preeminent spokesman for this point of view. Winsor too was influenced by this outlook, and he concluded

45. Winsor, *Narrative and Critical History*, 6: 540.
46. John Higham, with Leonard Krieger and Felix Gilbert, *History: The Development of Historical Studies in the United States* (Englewood Cliffs, N.J.: Prentice-Hall, 1965), pp. 6–25, 92–103.

that mapmaking must be a necessary part of historical analysis. His systematic appreciation for cartography thus contrasted significantly with the more antiquarian—and nationalistic—concerns of Lossing and Carrington. Winsor expressed his views about the importance of environment in this way: "I would not say that there are no other compelling influences, but no other is so steady."[47]

There remains to be made a brief foray into the twentieth century in anticipation of Barbara Petchenik's essay. I wanted to find out whether twentieth-century historians of the Revolution relied on nineteenth-century cartographers and cartobibliographers. With the help of Professor Don Higginbotham of the University of North Carolina, I chose eight military histories published between 1909 and 1972.[48] Of the eight works, all but one, Howard Peckham's *War for Independence*, have maps. In the others, the number of maps varies from a low of eight to a high of sixty-three—in Francis Vinton Greene, *The Revolutionary War and the Military Policy of the United States*.

The two works published earliest, Steele's *American Campaigns* and Greene's *Revolutionary War*, are the only ones that follow, in a limited way, the cartobibliographical principles developed by Winsor. They cite works by Carrington, Henry Johnston, and Fiske, all from the nineteenth century, as sources for their maps. The remaining six moderns do cite nineteenth-century works in footnotes and bibliographies. Here the most enduring works appear to be studies of individual battles, such as those by Charles Coffin, Henry Johnston, and Richard Frothingham.[49] Willard M. Wallace's *Appeal to*

47. Quoted in Ray Allen Billington. *Frederick Jackson Turner: Historian, Scholar, Teacher* (New York: Oxford University Press, 1973), p. 113. See Billington's discussion of the intellectual background of the frontier thesis in chap. 5, pp. 108–31.

48. Matthew Forney Steele, *American Campaigns*, 2 vols. (Washington, D.C.: B. S. Adams, 1909); Francis Vinton Greene, *The Revolutionary War and the Military Policy of the United States* (London: John Murray, 1911); Willard M. Wallace, *Appeal to Arms: A Military History of the American Revolution*, (New York: Harper & Brothers, 1951); Christopher Ward, *The War of the Revolution*, ed. John Richard Alden, 2 vols. (New York: Macmillan Co., 1952); John Richard Alden, *The American Revolution, 1775–1783* (New York: Harper & Brothers, 1954); Howard Henry Peckham, *The War of American Independence: A Military History* (Chicago: University of Chicago Press, 1958); Don Higginbotham, *The War of American Independence: Military Attitudes, Policies, and Practice, 1763–1789* (New York: Macmillan Co., 1971); and Marshall Smelser, *The Winning of Independence* (Chicago: Quadrangle Books, 1972).

49. Charles Carleton Coffin, *The Boys of '76: A History of the Battles of the Revolution* (New York: Harper & Brothers, 1876); Richard Frothingham, *History of the Siege of Boston . . .* (Boston: C. C. Little & J. Brown, 1849), *Battle of Bunker Hill*

Arms and Christopher Ward's *War of the American Revolution* were the heaviest users of such materials.

The two most recent works, by John Richard Alden and Don Higginbotham, probably point to the future, for they depend even less than their predecessors on nineteenth-century histories. This is indicative of the growing body of twentieth-century secondary literature on the Revolution: the increased attention being given to archival sources, the shift away from stories of battles to other aspects of military-social history, and the greater availability of contemporary maps today than at the beginning of this century. Thus nineteenth-century cartography appears to be falling into disuse. For the most part, it is of only antiquarian interest.

In my opinion, however, Justin Winsor, at least, will be consulted as long as no better critical cartobibliography exists. And, indeed, his volume 6 was recently republished, in 1972, as *The American Revolution* (New York: Lands End Press). Even so, the cartobibliographical material thus reprinted needs redoing: after nearly a hundred years, it cannot stand as definitive. *Sic transit gloria mundi.*

(Boston: Little, Brown & Co., 1889); and Henry Phelps Johnston, *The Campaign of 1776 around New York and Brooklyn . . .* , Memoirs of the Long Island Historical Society, vol. 3 (Brooklyn, N.Y.: Long Island Historical Society, 1878), *The Yorktown Campaign and the Surrender of Cornwallis, 1781* (New York: Harper & Brothers, 1881), *The Battle of Harlem Heights, September 16, 1776, with a Review of the Events of the Campaign* (New York: Published for Columbia University Press by Macmillan Co.; London: Macmillan & Co., 1897).

›8‹

AMERICAN STUDIES TODAY—THE

MIDDLE OF A REVOLUTION (1969)

Towner was a close watcher of trends in scholarship. His conception of his job, first as editor and then as librarian, required it. He did this essay summing up the trends in American historical scholarship of the 1960s at the same time he was working on the rationale for a research library (selection 9) and the plan for the future of the Newberry (selection 11).

It is easy to spot trends years later; it is much harder while you are living through them. The "revolutions" he identified now seem obvious: the vast editorial projects of the writings of the "founding fathers," the microform technologies that decentralized the use of huge bodies of primary sources, and the paperback revolution that changed classroom teaching. His reading of the breakdown of the paradigm of "consensus" history seems prescient. It was not predictable at the time.

What Towner was too modest or too politic to say was that the new wave of social history owed a debt to scholarship he had joined in pioneering.

WHEN THE INVITATION TO ATTEND this important Conference came, I was particularly delighted. It released in my mind a perfect jumble of things I should like to talk about with Japanese scholars and librarians concerned with the study of America. Alas, I fear that very little order has been made out of that perfect jumble. Among the things I thought of was one of the first important books I read in my special field of American history, Roy Hidemichi Akagi's *The Town Proprietors of the New England Colonies*, published in Philadelphia in 1924 and still the standard monograph on the subject. Another

"American Studies Today—the Middle of a Revolution." From the first Japan–U.S. Conference on Libraries and Information Service in Higher Education, Tokyo, 1969. In *University and Research Libraries in Japan and the United States*, ed. Thomas R. Buckman, Yukihisa Suzuki, and Warren M. Tsuneishi, 137–43 (Chicago: American Library Association, 1972). Reprinted with permission.

was a recollection from the period when I was editor of the *William and Mary Quarterly: A Magazine of Early American History* between the years 1955 and 1962. The most rapidly growing subscriber among foreign countries was Japan, and Japanese readers often wrote to me with queries and requests for help. Now there are twenty-two Japanese subscribers to this quite specialized historical magazine. Quite clearly, an interest in American studies is no new phenomenon in Japan.

When one attempts to describe and analyze the state of American studies today, one must attempt to describe the middle of a revolution, a very difficult thing to do. It is like other revolutions; one is not sure when it started, where it is going to end, and just what stage of it one is in. Moreover, there are several revolutions going on at once. But perhaps, if we look back over the past twenty-five years, we can grasp some of the essentials of some of those revolutions pertinent not only to American history as a discipline but also to American history and literature as a collecting area for libraries.

First and most significant, there has been a revolution in the interpretation of American history by students of that subject. It is not easy to describe succinctly and, as with the other revolutions, the end is not in sight. But that does not prevent our trying. Prior to World War II, American historiography was dominated by the great Populist or Progressive historians. They were Charles A. Beard, Vernon Louis Parrington, and Frederick Jackson Turner. Much of the history of America written in that period was a working out, in one way or another, of the broad themes these men had laid down in their key works. Broadly speaking, their interpretations pictured American history as a struggle between the haves and the have-nots; between the rich and the well-born, the creditor, the businessman, and the slaveholder, on the one hand, and the agrarian, debtor classes, often in combination with urban workers, on the other.

The period of American history, for example, that saw the creation of the nation—the separation from Great Britain and the laying of the foundations of the present government, that is, the period from 1763 to 1789—had a widely accepted interpretation handily described as the Becker-Beard hypothesis. These men saw the American Revolution not only as a fight for home rule but also as a fight over who should rule at home. Lined up against each other were not only the patriots and the British—the goods and the bads, respectively—but also, within American society, the poor against the rich, the West against the East, the agrarian classes against the commercial classes—also the goods and the bads. In colony by colony, state by state, this was found to be the case. The Revolution itself, it was held, was led from above but pushed from below.

The Articles of Confederation, which provided for a great deal of local autonomy, were found to be the perfect expression of the Revolutionary spirit, and the Constitution that came in 1787 was in turn a perfect expression of a Thermidorian reaction. It was viewed as the instrument of the creditors, the Eastern merchants, the bankers, and the traders, who designed it to keep power out of the hands of the common people. From this vantage point, the rest of American history was viewed as the struggle of the farmers and workers (and slaves) to wrest economic and political democracy from the reluctant hands of the rich and well-born. In short, it was the working out in the ages of Jefferson, and Jackson, and Lincoln, and Roosevelt, and Wilson of the Declaration of Independence's statement that all men are created equal.

After World War II the historians who had been trained in the old Populist or Progressive school still taught this interpretation, not only of the Revolution, but of American history in general. A new generation of historians put all this under attack, however, again using the Revolution as an example. The seemingly solid and durable Beard-Becker interpretation of the internal revolution was undermined from every side, and the walls came tumbling down. Beard's classic *An Economic Interpretation of the Constitution*, for example, was the subject of two major assaults: one by Robert E. Brown, who took the work chapter by chapter and refuted its findings, and the other by Forrest E. McDonald, who did all the research Beard said ought to be done and found Beard wanting. Studies of the British Empire, of the origins of the Revolution, of the colonies and states before, during, and after the Revolution revealed that the Beard-Becker hypothesis was too simplistic, too unsophisticated, too wrong to hold the period together. Their interpretation of the Revolution fell into chaos, from which no single historian or group of historians has been able to rescue it.

What arose in the 1950s instead of the old Populist-Progressive view of American history has been labeled, not too inaccurately, I think, as "consensus" history. That is to say, some of the leading historians, Daniel Boorstin, for example, tended to emphasize the common grounds, the common ideas, and the agreements of the American people throughout their history and to de-emphasize the sharp conflicts so well described by the earlier historians. To what extent this transformation of American history was the product of a felt (if unperceived) need of Americans to draw together in the face

of an implacable foe in Eastern Europe and in the face of unprecedented world responsibilities for which we were not clearly prepared, it is hard to say. Future historians will undoubtedly explore
this aspect of the American mind relentlessly, but we are still too
close to it, probably too much a part of it, to be able to understand
what happened and why. But that there was a major shift in emphasis can hardly be ignored.

I want to pause here in my necessarily sketchy and crude description of the revolution in interpretation. That revolution is continuing, and there are some new developments, but they can be discussed better after we examine some of the technical revolutions of
the last twenty years with regard to the availability of historical and
literary materials.

For two decades, much of what has been written in American history, and, I suspect, in American literature, might be described as
deeper and deeper analysis of smaller and smaller points. Partially
this is a consequence of the great proliferation of historical and literary studies. It has often been almost antiquarian in character—a
study of the past without direction from the questions of the present. But one salutary aspect of this intensified study of America's
past has been a turning to great editorial projects. These decades
have certainly been the second great age of editing in America, ri-
valing the great age in the nineteenth century which saw the publication of so many documents in American history. There are some
important pre–World War II precedents that one ought to touch on
if space were not limited, but we can start with the greatest editorial
project of them all, *The Papers of Thomas Jefferson*, edited by Julian
P. Boyd. This project proposes to edit and publish not only all the
letters and other writings of Thomas Jefferson, but also all the letters *to* Thomas Jefferson. Hence the word "Papers" rather than
"Writings" or "Works" in the title. When completed, this project
will run to some fifty volumes, and it will be, undoubtedly, the
greatest documentary biography ever written.

Following the lead of the Jefferson project, there are now, as you
know, several other great series, including the papers of James Madison, Benjamin Franklin, the Adams family (not just one generation
but four), Alexander Hamilton, John Jay, John Marshall, and, soon,
George Washington. Altogether there will be some 250–300 volumes of the papers of the founding fathers. Other publication projects, including the debates on the Constitution, both in the Philadelphia Convention and in the state conventions, the papers of the
first Congress, and the like, will make the Revolutionary era possi-

bly the most fully-reported period in the history of any country. Nor is this development confined to the Revolutionary generation. Other historical figures, such as Polk, Wilson, Theodore Roosevelt, Franklin Roosevelt, Grant, and Lincoln, are or have been subjects of editorial projects of greater or lesser magnitude.

It will come as no surprise to this group when I say that editing has also become a major preoccupation of students of American literature. The "new bibliography," as exemplified by the work of Professor Fredson Bowers of the University of Virginia, has made the establishment of a text—which is a necessary preliminary to subject editing—an immensely complicated and scientific affair. One needs to learn a whole new technique and a whole new language to comprehend the method editors have evolved. Using this method, the Modern Language Association—some 26,000 members strong— has set up a vast editorial project to make available, often for the first time, editions of the complete works of the great nineteenth-century American literary figures. Nathaniel Hawthorne, Edgar Allan Poe, Herman Melville, Walt Whitman, Mark Twain, William Dean Howells, Ralph Waldo Emerson, Henry David Thoreau, Stephen Crane, and Washington Irving are marching in ever-growing sets across the shelves of every university and college library in the land. Some 220 volumes are planned. When the works of these literary figures have been exhausted, no doubt other authors will be subjected to the same editorial process to provide the best possible edition of their literary works. Editing, in short, has become a major preoccupation in the scholarly world concerned with American studies, literary as well as historical.

Concurrent with the editorial revolution, there have been technical revolutions in methods of reproducing materials that are stupendous in their consequences. Let us look again at the period of early American history for our examples. Thirty years ago it would have been nearly impossible to go beyond a master's degree, if indeed that far, in early American history without visiting for several months those great Eastern libraries where the printed and manuscript records of seventeenth- and eighteenth-century America are concentrated. Harvard, Yale, and Princeton, the Library of Congress, the Massachusetts, New York, Pennsylvania, and Virginia historical societies, and the great private libraries, such as the American Antiquarian Society in Worcester, Massachusetts, or the John Carter Brown Library in Providence, Rhode Island, were musts on the lists of every student of early America.

Now, however, a revolution has been taking place. Microfilm and other forms of microprint, Xerox and other forms of copying, and photo-offset printing—all partially responses to the tremendous market created for all forms of printed material by the fantastic increase in the number of students and faculty members in our colleges and universities—have made it possible to write a creditable dissertation in early American history in almost any university in the land.

For example, as you all know, the great bibliography of materials printed in America before 1800 is that compiled by Charles Evans at the turn of the century. This chronological list of all published books and pamphlets has been an indispensable tool since the first volume came out. Now, of course, thanks to the American Antiquarian Society, almost all these books can be seen in any university library on microcard. Similar projects have made the newspapers and magazines of early America equally accessible, so that for an expenditure of probably under $25,000 any library in the world can have at its disposal everything published in what is now the United States prior to Thomas Jefferson's first term as President.

Further, much of the material published by historical societies and state governments in the nineteenth and early twentieth centuries pertaining to early America, long out of print, is now being reprinted in one form or another. The great demand for this kind of material by new libraries and the fact that the originals usually are printed on poor paper has created an economic market that will not be denied. For a well-spent $100,000 or so and a great deal of bibliographic searching it will soon be possible to have available everything except the unpublished manuscripts concerning early America in one's university or college library.

And even that exception has increasingly become subject to exceptions. I have already mentioned the project to edit and print the papers of the Adams family, but in anticipation of that publication venture, the Adams Papers Trust and the Massachusetts Historical Society, some fifteen years ago, made available for purchase by any library the entire great body of Adams papers on microfilm. More recently the National Historical Publications Commission has begun the systematic publication on microfilm of important manuscript materials pertaining to American history wherever they may be found, in private or public institutions, throughout the land. Sitting in my study in Chicago, I can read even now the papers of many of our presidents, along with some of the important parts of the manuscript collection of, for example, the Massachusetts Historical Society, such as the papers of Timothy Pickering and Robert Treat Paine.

These developments, of course, were necessarily preceded by years and years of work on finding aids for manuscript materials, among which should be mentioned Philip Hamer's *A Guide to Archives and Manuscripts in the United States* (New Haven, Conn.: Yale University Press, 1961); the Modern Language Association's *American Literary Manuscripts* (Austin; University of Texas Press, 1960); and, of course, the great ongoing *National Union Catalog of Manuscripts.*

The rapid growth of the availability of materials on American history and literature has, of course, put a vast burden upon college and university libraries. Not only have costs of individual items gone up significantly, but, more important, the number of items published in any given year pertaining to American history and literature and culture has grown staggeringly. Concurrent with this revolution, however, has been a paperback revolution liberating both the teacher and the student from the restrictions of any given library's holdings and, at the same time, eliminating the libraries' need to purchase large numbers of copies of single books for course work. A single copy of most books, or at most two, is really all that is necessary. Teachers in American studies now build their courses around paperback books, and students can now afford libraries that their professors at one time could not get or afford. My own children, for example, have larger libraries than I had when I started teaching twenty-three years ago.

The increasing numbers of students and professors studying American history, literature, and culture is reflected not only in a greater output of books (which a library must acquire) but also in a great output of articles and other materials published in periodicals. As a consequence, not only has the circulation of such established magazines as the *American Historical Review,* the *William and Mary Quarterly, PMLA,* and the *Journal of American History* increased greatly, but also the number of new magazines has increased. Periodicals specializing in American Jewish history, American labor history, the history of the American Negro, the histories of various states, and in such new disciplines as American studies are a few that come to mind at once. These new periodicals produce an added strain on any library attempting to provide resources for American studies. Clearly, students and scholars need to have access to all periodical literature, if only to avoid the unnecessary duplication of effort in their researches.

This means that old libraries are faced with quickly expanding budgets for periodical literature and that new libraries not only have to acquire the current magazines but also must somehow acquire back issues of old ones. This latter problem is being met by technological advances in reprints. Many magazines, such as the *William and Mary Quarterly*, are now available through such organizations as Kraus Reprints, Inc. and on microfilm. Reprinting, in fact, has become a major industry within the printing industry.

I mentioned in connection with the growth of periodical literature the subject of American Studies with a capital *"S."* This is a phenomenon whose *major* growth I associate with the postwar period. No one except its initiates are quite sure exactly what "American Studies" means, and some of us who are not initiates are not sure that the initiates know. At its best it indicates that we must have training in literature as well as in history, in architecture and in the history of science—a kind of cultural anthropology of modern man—if we are to understand American society in all its complexity and richness. It is a kind of "area-study" approach like that developed in the United States for enriching our understanding of other areas by bringing to bear on them all the techniques and resources of many disciplines. At its worst, one suspects it to be a manifestation of hyperpatriotism and neoisolationism sponsored by a few idiosyncratic rich men who believe that concentration on American Studies is a necessary antidote to such strange foreign *isms* as Communism and Socialism. However one interprets American Studies, its existence surely reflects the fact that America has become a major world power—"the new Romans," as a Canadian recently called us. America is a subject worthy of intense preoccupation and study, if not just for its intrinsic merit, then simply because it has become the most powerful (and perhaps most dangerous) nation on earth.

Into this peaceful, if industrious, scene of "consensus history," major editing projects, proliferation of monographic studies, new technologies of reproduction, and the growth of American Studies, now intrudes the rude and ugly face of controversy, which, I suspect, will do much to revitalize the study of American history and (perhaps) of literature as well. To go back to my opening question of interpretation, I refer to the continuing revolution in the meaning of America's past as understood by America's present. This revolution is not easy to describe.

Recently I was chairman of the American Historical Association's Annual Meeting Program Committee, which had responsibility for organizing some seventy-five scholarly sessions. In my brief report on that program, I opened by saying that someone said history doesn't teach us a damn thing about the present; instead the present tells us the kind of questions we have to ask of the past. I think this is true, and the critical problems American society is now trying to face have not only opened up new fields of historical inquiry, they have also begun to subject the so-called "consensus" history to a hard-hitting attack from what is now called the "New Left."

New fields of inquiry, rejuvenated old fields of inquiry, concern first of all the great domestic problems of American society. Urban studies are now being pushed on almost every American campus. There is a growing interest in the history of the family. Negro history has become transformed into black history, and black history programs, with black instructors, books written by blacks, and classes attended by blacks, seem now to be the sine qua non for survival of any academic administration or, indeed, institution. But perhaps more important than any other current problem facing American society has been the ruthless, unhappy, and tragic mistake of Vietnam. This war has produced a greater division in American society than anything since the American Civil War. Without question, without fear of being proved wrong, I predict that in the future, if we have a future, we will view the war in Vietnam as a great watershed in American intellectual and cultural history, as well as in politics and international diplomacy.

As a consequence of the failure of American society to solve its domestic problems (partly, I think, or even in large part, because of its tremendous involvement in Vietnam), the youngest generation of American historians have found my generation's writings sterile expressions of the Establishment. At its best our historical writing is found to be irrelevant, and at its worst it is viewed as a mask for an imperialist, aggressive, exploitative, capitalist society. The consensus which they see it depicting they believe to be imaginary, and its authors are to them the witting or unwitting tools of an industrial-military complex which dominates the society. There have not been many products of this historical view—it is not yet a school—and I know of none in the field of literature as yet, though they will come.

Among the works of the "New Left" historians are two collections of essays that deserve careful examination: Barton J. Bernstein's *Towards a New Past: Dissenting Essays in American History* and Alfred F. Young's *Dissent: Exploration in the History of American Radicalism*. The latter work is a perfect example of today's problems informing our view of the past, in this instance, the protest movements that began with the civil rights issue. Dissent is important today. It is important, therefore, to demonstrate a tradition of dissent to give it a kind of legitimacy that the more conservative elements in our society would deny. Bernstein's book, on the other hand, gathers essays by historians who question, from the Revolution to the present, the received interpretations of the past.

If the consensus historians can be characterized as those who stress the wide range of agreement among Americans throughout our history, the "New Left," as revealed in these works, can be characterized as those who stress the points of conflict. These conflicts, in their view, have not necessarily resulted in improvement in American society. The consensus historians view American history as a general upward spiral toward greater democracy, toward a better life for everyone, toward greater improvement for the downtrodden. They are optimistic, in short. The New Left is pessimistic in its view of the outcome, thus far, of American history and is sometimes inclined to believe that a fundamental reconstitution of American society may be necessary if wrongs are to be righted and democracy prevail.

The temper of this different emphasis can be gauged from a recent review by one of America's great historians, Professor C. Vann Woodward of Yale, author of the widely read and influential *Jim Crow in America* (among other books). Woodward's liberal credentials are impeccable. Like the rest of us, he accepted the liberal interpretation of the antislavery movement which reduced the great abolitionist William Lloyd Garrison to the level of a noisy troublemaker, intransigent, radical, and therefore ineffective in bringing about the actual abolition of slavery. It was the antislavery moderates that accomplished that goal, they said; Garrison, if anything, may have been an impediment. A recent study—*Means and Ends in American Abolitionism: Garrison and His Critics on Strategy and Tactics, 1834–1850*, by Eileen S. Kraditor—finds in Garrison's very intransigence, his uncompromising unwillingness to be a moderate on the subject, his insistence on being heard, the stuff of a hero.

As Vann Woodward put it in his review of this book:

> His big thing was that abolitionism was a *radical* and not a reform movement, that slavery, and the social dogmas that justified it so thoroughly permeated American society and government, North as well as South, that the

eradication of the institution and its ideological defenses
... was a root and branch operation. On that he never
equivocated.

Garrison warned that slavery was a sin and that, if the Constitution
supported slavery, then the Constitution ought to be destroyed, and
the society which fed on slavery ought to be reconstituted. As Vann
Woodward points out, our new self-conscious awareness of the extent to which we are still a racist society makes the recently revised
interpretation of Garrison seem painfully and tragically true.

As I said at the beginning of this brief essay, where the revolution
in interpretation of American history will end no one can tell. It is
possible that America will see itself a little more clearly as a consequence of the "truths" the New Left is trying to see and to make
American society see. On the other hand, we may not pay sufficient
attention to this new view of ourselves. That is, we may not pay
sufficient attention *in time*, and our own imperfect understanding
of ourselves and our past may lead to our undoing. This great noble
experiment which had, and may still have, so much promise for
mankind, will then end in failure. It would not be mankind's first
failure. It could be mankind's last.

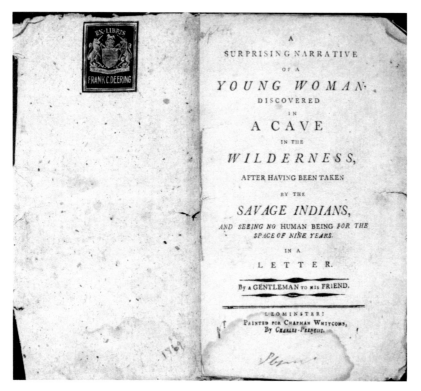

A Surprising Narrative of a Young Woman Discovered in a Cave in the
Wilderness, after Having Been Taken by the Savage Indians (Leominster,
[Mass.]: For Chapman Whitcomb þy Charles Prentiss [1799]). From the
Frank C. Deering Collection, purchased 1967.

American sheet music (left to right): *The Red Rose Rag* (New York, 1911); *At the Centennial Galop* (New York, 1876); *Chicago Express March Two-Step* (Chicago, 1905); *The Frisco Rag* (New York, 1909). From the J. Francis Driscoll Collection, gift and purchase, 1967.

LOOK HERE!
Horses Wanted!
FOR WINTER HERDING!

J. P. McKISSICK and W. H. MOORE
Will take horses for winter herding, from any point on Wood River, at any time upon application. advantages over all parties in the same business, as follows:

FIRST.—Three hundred and twenty-five head already running upon a good range.

SECOND.—We have sixty head of broke saddle horses for our own use. Will take care of all horses intrusted to our care and guarantee that they will be returned to their owners without saddle or spur marks, from wintering or use.

MARK IT!

Our Range is below the Malad and in the "Clover Creek Country."

Bunch Grass in Abundance and an Easy Place to Hold Stock.

DON'T NEGLECT THE OPPORTUNITY

Very Respectfully Yours,
McKISSICK & MOORE.

Look Here! Horses Wanted! For Winter Herding! J. P. McKissick and W. H. Moore Will Take Horses for Winter Herding, from Any Point on Wood River . . . [Shoshone(?) Idaho, 188(?)]. Purchased from the Everett D. Graff Bequest, established 1964.

Map of Hacienda de Santa Ines (1569). In manuscript collection of some 250 documents relating to the estate, 1567–1744. Purchased with assistance from the Arthur Holzheimer Fund, established in 1982.

LE SECRET DV
IANSENISME
DE'COVVERT
ET REFVTE'
Par vn Docteur Catholique.

TROISIE'ME EDITION.

Auec des Reflexions sur la response des Iansenistes.

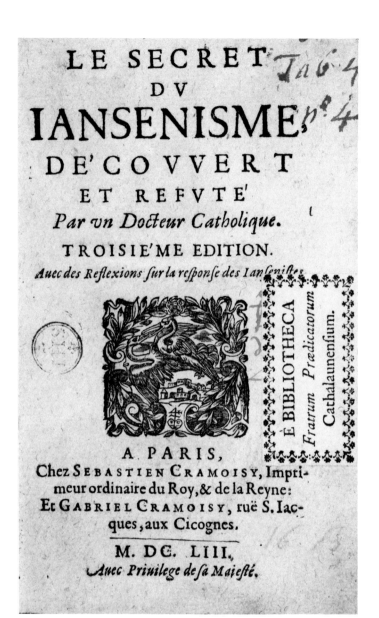

A PARIS,
Chez SEBASTIEN CRAMOISY, Impri-
meur ordinaire du Roy, & de la Reyne:
Et GABRIEL CRAMOISY, ruë S. Iac-
ques, aux Cicognes.

M. DC. LIII.
Auec Priuilege de sa Maiesté.

Le secret du Jansenisme, de'couvert et refute' par un docteur catholique (Paris: Sebastien Cramoisy, 1653). From the Jansenist Collection, purchased 1968.

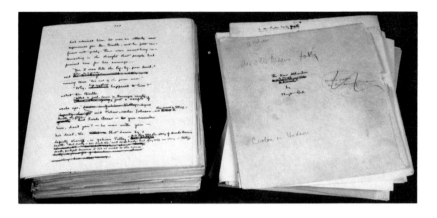

Floyd Dell, *An Old Man's Folly*. Author's autograph manuscript. Purchased from the Lloyd Lewis Fund, established 1985.

George Taylor and Andrew Skinner, *Survey and Maps of the Roads of North Britain or Scotland* (London: D. Wilson & G. Nicol, 1776). Purchased from the Andrew McNally Fund, established 1980.

Selected editions of *Moby Dick* (clockwise): first English edition (London, 1851); Newberry-Northwestern edition (Evanston and Chicago, 1988); Finnish edition (Helsinki, 1957); Serbian edition (Belgrade, 1969); edition with illustrations from the John Barrymore movie (New York, 1925); Icelandic Classic Comic Book edition (Rekjavik, 1956); Urdu edition, New Delhi, 1959). From the Melville Collection, established 1965.

"Rural Sport: Or, a Peep at a Lancashire Rush-Cart, 1821." Woodburytype in Richard Wright Proctor, *Memorials of Manchester Streets* (Manchester: Thomas Sutcliffe, 1874). Purchased from the Burgess Fund, established 1973.

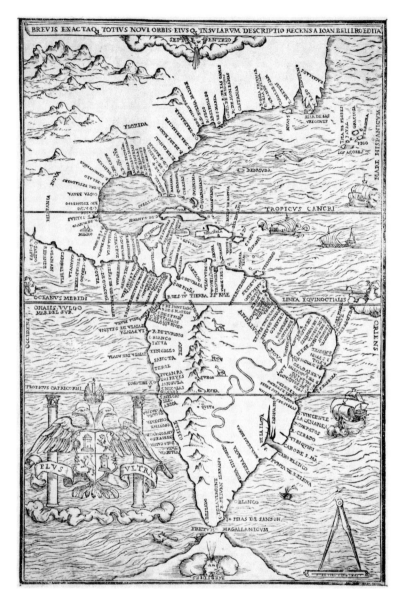

Jean Bellère, *Brevis exactaq[ue] totius novi orbis eiusq[ue] insularum descriptio* (Antwerp, ca. 1544). From the Franco Novacco Collection, purchased 1967.

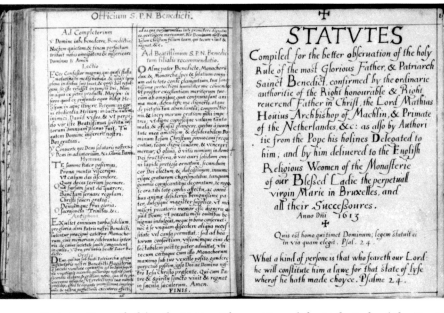

Statutes Compiled for the Better Observation of the Holy Rule of the Most Glorious Father & Patriarch Sainct Benedict ... Anno Dñi 1613. Manuscript, probably from Abbey of Our Blessed Lady the Perpetual Virgin Mary in Brussels. From the Recusant Collection, purchased 1968.

Oszvald Pelbart Themesvari, *Pomerium Quadragesimale* (Augsburg: Johann Othmar, for Johann Schoensperger, 1502). Purchased from the Samuel R. & Marie-Louise Rosenthal Fund, established 1972.

François Piquet, manuscript book, with prayers and hymns in the Mohawk language, used at Piquet's mission at Ogdensburg, New York, 1750–52. Purchased from the Rudy L. Ruggles Fund, established 1986.

Guillaume Del'Isle, *La France* (Paris: Del'Isle, 1703). From the Johan Gabriel Sack Collection, purchased by the Newberry Library Associates, 1968.

"God Presiding over the Fall of the Angels," in Jacques Legrand, *Livre de Bonnes Meurs*, illuminated manuscript, Flemish, before 1478. From the Louis H. Silver Collection, purchased 1964.

Autograph manuscript, Napoleon Bonaparte to his son, Prince Eugene de Beauharnais, St. Cloud, 14 May 1810. From the William M. Spencer Collection, given 1979–85.

Autograph letter, signed, Thomas Jefferson to George Watterston, Monticello, 3 January 1816. From the Herbert R. Strauss Bequest, 1975.

The Damnation of Theron Ware, or Illumination, by Harold Frederic, poster by J. H. Twachtman. From the Stone and Kimball Collection, purchased 1970.

II

LIBRARIAN

★

PAST IMPERFECT: THE USES OF A

RESEARCH LIBRARY

The occasion often dictates the form of discourse. One unappreciated form at which Towner was a master was the afterdinner talk to a general audience. The audience expected to be humored with a certain number of anecdotes, if not jokes, then was willing to endure some serious thoughts on a general subject with broad appeal.

In this talk, given numerous times, Towner took on the task of justifying the purposes of a research library, and answering the question of why scholars are constantly rewriting history or reinterpreting literature. He had been shaped in his own scholarship by the tides of the 1940s and 1950s; he understood the way the scholarship of American history was being reshaped by the movements of the 1960s and 1970s. Unlike some traditional scholars, he welcomed them as opening the discipline to new questions.

Towner gave this talk to several audiences between 1968 and 1976: the Huntington Library, the New York State Historical Association, the Newberry Library Associates, and the State Historical Society of Wisconsin, among others. He was constantly revising it, inspired by new examples of scholarship. We have taken a version he delivered in 1974 and added footnotes identifying the books and articles he referred to.

I WANT TO TALK WITH YOU tonight about the uses of a research library. I have used the words "Past Imperfect" in my title as a "grabber," as the Madison Avenue types say, but it is really more serious than that. By "Past Imperfect" I mean that our knowledge of the past—whether of literature, history, music, or philosophy—is, indeed, imperfect. It follows, so it seems to me, that it is the indispensable and primary use of a research library to preserve the records

From an unpublished typescript, Towner Papers, Newberry Library Archives.

of the past so that research can make our knowledge less imperfect than it is. Any other purpose of a library, however appealing, can only be secondary.

Do not mistake me. I love books as objects. Like any other librarian, collector, or bibliophile, I dearly love to see those handsomely bound, beautifully printed, carefully preserved, and damnably expensive works lined up on the shelves. The Beinecke Rare Book Library at Yale, for example, is beautiful, not just because of the handsome marble walls (so thin the light shines through), not just because of the massive olive-wood tables (a royal privilege to work on), but really because one can see from the foyer a breathtaking bookcase, six stories high, with thousands of books stacked up behind the glass.

And, like any librarian, I love to report the acquisition of a Shakespeare quarto, a Western guidebook, or an important incunable. I love to mix with that rare and curious tribe, the bookmen, to listen to their arcane stories of deals, of quixotic and secretive collectors, of auctions, of foolish librarians, and the like. But all these are only part of the story, the iceberg's tip that gleams so brightly in the sun.

No, contrary to what we librarians sometimes like to think, the real uses of a research library are not ordinarily fulfilled by the bookman. A research library does not exist for the pride of the collector, the enhancement of the rare book dealer, or, indeed, for the vanity of the librarian. However important these individuals are, in their symbiotic relationships with research and rare book libraries they are the means to an end, not the end itself; the end is *research.* To preserve the records of the past and to make them available for scholarly research are the real uses of a research library. Sometimes that obvious fact is forgotten in the excitement of adding the latest rare bird to the collection.

To answer your unvoiced questions at this point, let me hasten to assure you that I know that the muses, or goddesses, of historical and literary research have feet of clay. The fact that a lot of trivial research gets done, and then, worse luck, gets published, no one knows any better, perhaps, than the research librarian who helps the scholar do it, who often reads various drafts of what has been written, and who then must choose from the glitter of newly published books that which is gold to purchase for his library.

We librarians are well aware of the many articles and books on bad research (and worse teaching) that have come from the presses, and that are in part reflected, for example, in the decline in history classes. One such work, *The Dissenting Academy,* edited by Theodore Roszak, has such chapters as: "On Academic Delinquency," or "The Scandal of Literary Scholarship," and such opening sentences as: "Of the death of Academic Literary study as a serious enterprise, few seem to be aware."[1] In fact, the groves of academe are accused on every hand of sprouting the stunted growth of such research as that caricatured in the *New Yorker* a few years ago. Entitled the "Exegesis of St. Nick," it took the form of a letter to the editor of the *New York Review of Books* complaining about a review therein.

> Nothing could be more flattering to a scholar [wrote the imaginary correspondent], than to have a work of his reviewed by so eminent an expert as Herman Kronstadt; but candor forces me to confess a total lack of surprise when I discovered that Professor Kronstadt had in fact barely bothered to read my little exegesis of "A Visit from St. Nicholas" (*Clement Moore and the Pre-Keynesian Apocalypse*, Pottawattami A. & M. Univ. Press, $15.), but had chosen instead merely to add some footnotes to his own tediously celebrated post-Freudian studies of the sexually feudalistic substratum in American children's books—a lode that so clearly ran out in the early chapters of his recent *Wynken, Blynken and Nod's Narrenschiff: Anal Archetypes on a Sea of Guilt*. . . .
>
> I think it is typical of Professor Kronstadt's well-known vendetta style of criticism [the letter continues] that he should concentrate in his review upon my careless but entirely insignificant omission of Prancer from the list of reindeer, while he neglects all mention of my fruitful *propositio*, first suggested to me by Dietrich Maltby at the Determinism Workshop of 1961, that "Dasher, Dancer, Prancer & Vixen, Comet, Cupid, Donder & Blitzen" are, in fact, evidence of Clement Moore's desperate need for economic reassurance and moral book-balancing in a time of stress, through the agency of the sudden arrival of two thinly disguised Wall Street law firms on his rooftop. [And so on][2]

Well deserving as some scholarship is of this kind of spoofing, a knowledge of history and literature protects the research librarian from being devastated by it. He knows that bad scholarship *and its critics* have always been a part of the library scene. One needs only

1. Theodore Roszak, ed., *The Dissenting Academy* (New York: Pantheon Books, 1968).

2. Roger Angell, "Exegesis of St. Nick," *New Yorker*, 24 December 1966, 28.

to recall Swift's *Gulliver's Travels* and Gulliver's visit to the academy in Laputa to be reassured on that point. Wrote Swift nearly three hundred years ago: "The first Professor I saw was in a very large Room, with Forty Pupils about him. . . . Every one knew [he said] how laborious the usual Method is of attaining to Arts and Sciences; whereas by his Contrivance, the most ignorant Person at a reasonable Charge, and with a little bodily Labour, may write Books in Philosophy, Poetry, Politicks, Law, Mathematicks, and Theology, without the least Assistance from Genius or Study."

Swift then described an ingenious machine, operated by several of the students, which turned out words and phrases copied down by the others. "Six Hours a-Day the young Students were employed in this Labour," Swift continued, "and the Professor shewed me several Volumes in large Folio already collected, of broken Sentences, which he intended to piece together; and out of those rich Materials to give the World a complete Body of all Arts and Sciences."[3]

Just to make the record complete, I should point out the obvious fact that librarians themselves deserve, and get, the same kind of spoofing. One of the most delightful occurs in a novel by Julian Moynahan, entitled *Pairing Off*.[4] At one point, the hero, a librarian named McCormick, contemplates having to catalogue a dusty collection of five thousand pamphlets dating from seventeenth-century England. "The crown of the undertaking," thinks McCormick, "would be a printed bibliography issued *at the library's expense* in a fine edition of three or four hundred copies."

With these anecdotes, I hope I have established my credentials as a true skeptic and now I would like to return to those scholars who illustrate my theme positively, "Past Imperfect: The Uses of a Research Library."

There are four reasons why I say that knowledge of our past is indeed imperfect.

First, there is always some aspect of our past that deserves our attention but that has thus far escaped serious investigation. Depending upon the quality of the mind that is engaged in the investigation, and the quality of library resources available, these corners can be of purely antiquarian interest or of major historical importance. In the hands of most people, for example, a study of *unemployment* in Jamestown, Virginia, in the early seventeenth century

3. Jonathan Swift, *Gulliver's Travels: An Authoritative Text*, ed. Robert A. Greenberg (New York: Norton, 1970), 155–56.
4. Julian Moynahan, *Pairing Off* (New York: William Morrow, 1969).

would turn out to have about as much social significance as an unpublished genealogy. But in the hands of such a scholar as Edmund Morgan at Yale, it becomes an exciting analysis of the whole Protestant work ethic in Elizabethan and Jacobean England, a subject of compelling interest today when our so-called middle-class virtues are—no doubt justifiably—under attack.[5]

The second reason for reexamining the past is that some hitherto unknown or restricted source material has just become available and, because of its importance, requires reexamination of the subject to which it relates. A recent and obvious example on a national scale is the opening of the manuscript schedules of the 1900 Federal Census, with all their consequences for social history. Another example, on a less cosmic scale, is the recently available Malcolm Cowley archive at the Newberry Library. His vast acquaintance with twentieth-century authors and his role as a critic and a commentator on the literary scene combine to make the collection a literary mine. Perhaps even more appropriate for a librarian to mention is the opening up of old sources because of the publication of a new guide. I have reference to Leo Lemay's labor of love, *A Calendar of American Poetry in the Colonial Newspapers and Magazines.*[6] If a half-dozen dissertations do not result as a consequence of this guide, I shall be very much surprised (and, perhaps, pleased).

The third reason for reexamining the past is that new techniques allow us to reexamine old evidence and come up with new answers. A special and rather esoteric example is that of the late Allan Stevenson, sometime Fellow of the Newberry, who developed, through his great knowledge of watermarks and the history of papermaking, along with the use of radioactive isotopes, a technique for dating very early books. In his last book, to the chagrin of the Pierpont Morgan Library, he proved that their great work, the Constance Missal, does not, after all, antedate the Gutenberg Bible.[7] Perhaps more important, new techniques in the field of historical demography, largely imported from France, require the reuse of old materials to rewrite the history of population growth and its causes, family structure, marriage ages, the distribution of poverty, and the like.

5. Edmund S. Morgan, "The First American Boom: Virginia 1618 to 1630," *William and Mary Quarterly*, 3d ser., 28 (1971): 169–98.

6. J. A. Leo Lemay, *A Calendar of American Poetry in the Colonial Newspapers and Magazines and in the Major English Magazines through 1765* (Worcester, Mass.: American Antiquarian Society, 1972).

7. Allan H. Stevenson, *The Problem of the "Missale speciale"* (London: Bibliographical Society, 1967).

It is not just the availability of new techniques of family reconstitution and data linkage, not just the new technology of the computer, and not just the availability of new census materials that explain the remarkable proliferation of population studies, demographic research, and studies of the family. These techniques, tools, and sources are merely the means, not the causes. Far more important is the understanding of the historian that the unrestricted proliferation of population raises grave problems of public policy, and that the family, as an institution, is in serious difficulty. In other words, *the awareness of contemporary social problems by historians and students of literature is a premier motivation for new research and new writing.*

To elaborate this point further: since the Renaissance, change has become the norm in Western Civilization, now spreading throughout the world. The engine that has driven this change, and made it ever more rapid, is technology. As technological changes are introduced, they usually, if not always, bring about unforeseen consequences in the form of social change. Those unforeseen consequences create problems of lesser or greater magnitude. When those problems become acute enough, they rub the scholar's bump of curiosity; he wants to know their historical origins. And finally, in a time of pervasive government activity, there is often seen to be a connection between public policy with regard to these problems and their historical origins, so that the scholar finds public money to support his pursuit of his own curiosity. Since change is a norm in our society, and since it is constantly accelerating under the impact of the accelerated application of technology, new questions and problems arise faster than we can find the historical antecedents of the old ones. That is why I call our Past Imperfect, or our knowledge of our past imperfect. It will always be so, and that fact creates a continuing role or use for research libraries.

Let me make some obvious illustrations from the past decade. I believe that that decade, beginning with the murder of President Kennedy, will be viewed some day as a great watershed in our history. Assassination and other forms of violence became a common means of attempting to change public policy as well as a blind response to alienation. A tragic, senseless, useless, and criminal war undermined our confidence in our leaders and ourselves and had only one potentially salutary consequence—the possibility that we might come to view ourselves as we truly are. (After Vietnam can we any longer view ourselves as the destined vessel of democracy charged with responsibility of spreading it over the earth?) A surging population bulge made us fearful that man himself was a cancerous growth on the face of the earth, and a growing awareness of the pollution created by our technological civilization made us fearful that our world could no longer be viewed as indefinitely capable of sustaining life. A great social experiment to bring about equality for blacks in our society ended in apparent, if not real, failure. The American Indian, hitherto considered a vanishing race, began to increase in number and seek redress of historic wrongs. A youth culture, promoted if not caused by our indiscriminate breeding, when combined with other factors, such as a rapidly growing divorce rate, the decline of authority, and the failure of we adults to solve society's problems, shook the family to its foundations. At the same time the role of women in that family became a hot social issue. An apparently corrupt administration summed up by Watergate seriously undermined our faith in our being able to govern ourselves, so that neither the presidency nor the Congress can get a favorable vote in our polls. And finally, the energy crisis—accelerated by the oil embargo—brought under serious question, not the *morality* of using GNP as the measure of a great society (that had already been questioned) but the possibility of GNP being used as any kind of measure, because continued growth was likely to disappear as an economic and social phenomenon. One way or another, these are, or will be, the main veins of historical inquiry in this decade.

The evolution of one social problem and the response of the historian is instructive. At the very time of the great Supreme Court case of *Brown* v. *Board of Education*, there was a prevailing historical interpretation of racial discrimination that went something like this. Discrimination, or prejudice against Negroes—as they were then called—was a consequence of their previous condition of servitude, not of their blackness. Oscar and Mary Handlin's essay, "The Origins of the Southern Labor System,"[8] was one of the main planks of this interpretation if only because of what it didn't find. Our perception of blacks as former slaves and present housemaids, bootblacks, yardmen, and day laborers reinforced discrimination. Obviously, Negroes appeared inferior because they occupied inferior positions in our society. With the end of slavery, with the end of legal segregation, and with the growth of economic opportunity, prejudice would gradually end and our race problem would disappear. It was an optimistic interpretation, based in part on the old melting pot

8. Oscar and Mary F. Handlin, "The Origins of the Southern Labor System," *William and Mary Quarterly*, 3d ser., 7 (1950): 199–222.

theory, and our society believed in it and acted on it. If we were to alter those conditions by social legislation, discrimination would ultimately disappear. A most optimistic view. And this was the prevailing view in 1954.

But midway in the midst of the consequent social revolution, when black separatism, instead of integration, became the acceptable social answer, appeared Winthrop Jordan's monumental study, *White over Black*.[9] Stated oversimply, his argument is that the prejudice of whites against blacks was not the consequence of black enslavement, but instead *the prior cause*. A most pessimistic view, and one widely accepted by whites and blacks alike.

But now, two decades after *Brown* v. *Board of Education*, a new interpretation seems to be emerging, and sociologists are leading the way. Contrary to the Jeremiad of Win Jordan, it is now being argued seriously that a revolution *has* occurred since *Brown* v. *Board of Education*. And it is argued on Handlin's terms. That is to say, our new social perception (however unarticulated) of blacks in positions of social acceptability is creating in our rising generation a new image of blacks that may be compatible, eventually, with true social equality, at least for Middle Class Blacks, and what seemed to be a racial problem may once again be viewed as a *class problem*. When that happens, the popular Winthrop Jordan book may be viewed as having obscured the real issue for nearly a generation, and the hated Edward Bonfield—who was stopped from speaking at Chicago last week by a radical mob—may become the darling of the New Left.[10] From this angle of vision, let me nominate the most apt title in historical studies of the entire decade: Barton Bernstein's *Towards a New Past: Dissenting Essays in American History*.[11]

Let us take another current problem, that of violence. We are all greatly concerned about it today, and law and order have become political catchwords. But the very violence that sends voters to the polls to elect policemen as mayors sends historians to the research library. And so we learn, however tentatively, from a new book by a group of historians—part of it written at the Newberry and the Hun-

9. Winthrop D. Jordan, *White over Black: American Attitudes toward the Negro, 1550–1812* (Chapel Hill: University of North Carolina Press for the Institute of Early American History and Culture, 1968).

10. Edward Banfield was prevented from delivering a lecture at the University of Chicago on 20 March 1974 by the Students for a Democratic Society Chapter (*New York Times*, 25 May 1974).

11. Barton J. Bernstein, ed., *Towards a New Past: Dissenting Essays in American History* (New York: Pantheon Books, 1968).

tington—that we have always been a violent society. We have just conveniently ignored it.

As the editors of this work, *Violence in America*, point out, "Americans have always been given to a kind of historical amnesia that masks much of their turbulent past. Probably all nations share this tendency to sweeten memories through collective repression, but Americans have probably magnified this process of selective recollection, owing to our historic vision of ourselves as a latter-day chosen people, a New Jerusalem."[12] So we find that crime, rapine, plunder, and vigilantism are not aberrations but, possibly, partial characteristics of our society. Such revelations, do not, of course, excuse or justify violence today, but they may make us look twice at our proposed solutions. They may make us realize that the solutions advanced either by the hard-handed advocates of law and order or by those who would simply capitulate in the face of threatened violence may be too simple for the complexity of the problem.

Another current social problem—closely related to violence—is protest or dissent. The parades down Michigan Avenue in Chicago, the Freedom Marches, and the draft-card burners send many of us up the walls. But again they send the historians and the students of literature back to the research library. There they find anew that America was *founded* by dissenters. Those seventeenth-century pioneers whom we like to idealize today, were often run out of England because they would not conform; some of their ilk even beheaded their king. And they kept on dissenting. The boys and girls at Grinnell who took off their clothes recently to protest *Playboy* magazine probably did not know it, but they had a good historical precedent in the Quakers who paraded naked in Boston in the seventeenth century because they wanted freedom now. We get furious with our modern day Quakers—like Staughton Lynd who has written a book on nonviolent dissent in American history—partly because we have forgotten our own past, because our historical amnesia has dropped a wall between then and now.[13] It is one of the uses of a research library to enable the historian to breach that wall. What he finds and tells us may be cold comfort, at best, but maybe we can at least understand dissent better by understanding our own history. We may even be less shattered by what we see than would otherwise be the case, and thus avoid overreacting ourselves.

12. Hugh Davis Graham and Ted Robert Gurr, *Violence in America: Historical and Comparative Perspectives* (New York: Bantam Books, 1969), xiv.

13. Staughton Lynd, ed., *Nonviolence in America: A Documentary History* (Indianapolis: Bobbs-Merrill, 1966).

And, finally, this leads us to the generation gap itself. Puzzlement and frustration over the behavior of adolescents sends some of us to the bottle, some to bed with a sick headache, and some of us back to the office where a semblance of order exists. But again, the scholar goes back to the research library.

It takes very little research, even into our own history, to realize that the generation gap is no new phenomenon. It was Samuel Willard, president of Harvard in the eighteenth century, who said that if there was any one thing that would destroy Puritan New England it was the widespread disobedience to parents prevailing at that time. As his text for that sermon he chose the Fifth Commandment ("Honor thy father and thy mother that thy days may be long upon the land which the Lord God giveth thee") which tells us that even in biblical times the generation gap existed—else why the commandment in the first place?

We are always discovering or uncovering a new past. Not, or at least not yet, in the frightening way depicted in Orwell's *1984*, but rather because the new problems we face stimulate new questions about their origins. For example, as we all know, pollution has become a very popular public issue. Do not think for a moment that some historian, somewhere, is not already doing a book on the pollution of the environment by the colonists of Jamestown back in 1607. In fact, in one way, it has already been done in John Cotter's *Archaeological Excavations at Jamestown*[14]—yesterday's pollution is today's archaeology!

Thus, one can run the categories of our society's problems and discontents—the family, overpopulation, ethnic minorities, violence, the presidency as monarchy, the invasions of privacy, alienation, you name them—and we can expect to find historians industriously at work in archive and library asking new questions about our past in new ways.

Almost at random, but not quite, I picked a recent issue of a well-known scholarly journal, the *William and Mary Quarterly*, as an example of how the engine of social change drives our inquiries of the past. The lead article deals with precontact Indian ecology and how it was upset and eventually destroyed by the advent of the white man with his superior technology and his, apparently, more powerful religion. Here, our present concern for the ever-growing

14. John L. Cotter, *Archaeological Excavations at Jamestown Colonial National Historical Park and Jamestown National Historic Site, Virginia* (Washington, D.C.: National Park Service, 1958).

surviving remnant of the original dwellers on this continent, our guilt about stripping them of their land and their culture and about our own disregard for ecology, clearly motivate the article. On a similar tack, the lead note examines the changing historiography with regard to pre-Columbian Indian population in the Americas. Here demographic analysis and Indian history blend, and we learn to our surprise that present estimates include the mind-blowing figure of 100,000,000 Indians in the Americas prior to the advent of Columbus, a tenfold increase over previous estimates.[15]

Another article, undoubtedly inspired by the present cycle in women's on-going search for meaning and equality as persons, reexamines the Antinomian controversy of seventeenth-century Massachusetts and the role of Mrs. Ann Hutchinson, or Ms. Ann Hutchinson as the author calls her. He finds everywhere implicit, if not consciously explicit, Ms. Hutchinson's desire to free women of male domination as a motive equally as important as her more obvious desire to free Christ's spirit from the constraints of Orthodox Puritanism.[16]

Another article—representative of the currently richest vein being mined in colonial history—deals with family structure, population, and mobility in Windsor, Connecticut, in the seventeenth century, and is obviously the product of computer analysis with all kinds of strange quantitative language, such as unadjusted quintiles and selected comparative persistence rates.[17] When this vein has been mined, and when its findings are combined with the previous findings based largely on literary remains, we shall undoubtedly have a much better picture of the family in colonial America than is represented by Calhoun's old book and other old works written by other historians, including myself, and we shall be closer to the truth than we were. But I submit that part of the motivation comes not just from the availability of new techniques and new technologies, but also from the perilous condition in which the family found itself in the 1960s and early 70s.

15. Calvin Martin, "The European Impact on the Culture of a Northeastern Algonquian Tribe: An Ecological Interpretation," *William and Mary Quarterly*, 3d ser., 31 (1974): 3–26.

16. Lyle Koehler, "The Case of the American Jezebels: Anne Hutchinson and Female Agitation during the Years of Antinomian Turmoil, 1636–1640," *William and Mary Quarterly*, 3d ser., 31 (1974): 55–78.

17. Linda Auwers Bissell, "From One Generation to Another: Mobility in Seventeenth-Century Windsor, Connecticut," *William and Mary Quarterly*, 3d ser., 31 (1974): 79–110.

If what I have said so far about the fourth use of a research library leads some of you to conclude that I am guilty of that heinous historical sin of *presentism*, I plead not guilty: I think there is a significant difference between seeking the historical antecedents of a present problem, on the one hand, and judging the past by contemporary values, on the other. Among my listeners tonight, for example, there is a most able historian of early Indian-white relations who, aware of present Indian problems, has tried, successfully I think, to enlarge our understanding of their origins without judging his subjects by contemporary standards. He has been subjected to much criticism because he has sought brilliantly to understand— not defend—the origins of federal Indian policy instead of to condemn it as conscious genocide.[18]

If I were to sum up what I have observed as a librarian (as distinct from what I may believe as a historian), I think the horizons of new knowledge in history and literature are constantly enlarged by all four of the factors I have mentioned: (1) new investigation of old materials, (2) new resources being opened up for the first time, (3) new techniques and technologies, and, most of all, (4) new problems created by technological and social change that are clearly perceived for the first time.

Perhaps I might reclassify that fourth factor as a generalized *search for a usable past*. The blacks, the Indians, the emerging white ethnic groups, women, youngsters—soon our whole society—all seem to be seeking for such a past. A recent undergraduate seminar at the Newberry, exploring the problem of "Alienation and the Search for Community" seems to have been searching for a usable past in this alienated present; Laura X's Women's History Research Center seems to be trying to provide a usable past for women; and the fastest growing teaching technique in history—starting historical study with personal genealogical research—rests on the search for a usable past for the individual.

Individually and collectively, then, we need a usable past. And since as individuals and as societies our changing problems make our perception of our situation constantly different, our understanding of our past will always be imperfect and the uses of a research library will always be necessary and relevant.

18. Bernard W. Sheehan, *Seeds of Extinction: Jeffersonian Philanthropy and the American Indian* (Chapel Hill: University of North Carolina Press for the Institute of Early American History and Culture, 1973).

A HISTORY OF THE NEWBERRY

LIBRARY

Towner wrote this brief history of the Newberry on the occasion of the one-hundredth anniversary of the Library, a year after his retirement. As a capsule history of the Library it is unrivaled. As a record of what Towner accomplished it is an account he, as an editor, would never have approved. It is filled with passive verbs which mask his own active role: a collection "was purchased," the building "was renovated," and endowed funds "have been established." Nonetheless, it gives a sense of the Library Towner had inherited and how it had been transformed.

THE NEWBERRY LIBRARY is a privately-endowed, independent research library concentrating in history and the humanities. Its holdings comprise some 1.4 million volumes, 13,000 separately printed pre-1900 maps, and 4,110 running feet of manuscripts (plus two large railroad archives and the archives of the Pullman Company). The collections embrace Western Civilization from the late Middle Ages to the end of the Napoleonic Era in Europe; from the Era of Discovery to the Age of Revolution in Latin America; and to modern times in North America. Within that temporal, spatial, and subject framework are great areas of concentration supported by both the General and the Special Collections, as is revealed below. Appropriately enough the Library has used "An Uncommon Collection of Uncommon Collections" as its sobriquet since 1965.

To know the history of the Newberry Library is to understand its collections and its character. Indeed, one could reverse that equation and say that to understand its collections and character is to know its history. Unlike its nearest analogs, the Folger Shakespeare Library and the Huntington Library, both based on great collections gathered by their founders, the Newberry Library began, from

From Rolf Achilles, comp. and ed., *Humanities Mirror: Reading at the Newberry Library, 1887–1987* (Chicago: Newberry Library, 1987), 17–26.

scratch, as a collection of money made available in the great era of institution building during the Chicago Renaissance. It was not "created," like a building: rather it "grew," like a tree.

Walter Loomis Newberry (1804–1868), under whose will the Library was founded, died at sea on the way to join his wife and daughters in Paris. He had been an early Chicago pioneer (1831) involved in shipping, commerce, banking, and real estate, the latter being the true foundation of his bequeathed estate. Starting in the 1830s, he had bought land in Chicago "by the acre and sold it by the front foot" and was a rich man in 1868. It was not until the demise of his two surviving daughters, Mary and Julia, and later, in 1885, of his widow, Julia Clapp Newberry, however, that a contingent provision of his will assigning half of his estate, if his children died without issue, for a "free public library," became operative. (Newberry's drive to achieve immortality is illustrated by another contingent provision, an offer to settle a handsome sum on the first born son or sons of either or both daughters if the grandson, or grandsons, took the Newberry surname). Following Mrs. Newberry's death, the Trustees of the estate, Eliphalet Wickes Blatchford and William Henry Bradley, proceeded to establish the Library in 1887, hire its first Librarian, William Frederick Poole that same year, get it incorporated in 1892, and construct the present building at 60 West Walton Street.

Events—equally real and symbolic—between Newberry's death in 1868 and the death of founding Librarian Poole in 1894 significantly shaped, and still shape, the Newberry's collections and its character. First, the Chicago Public Library had been established, in 1876, so that the Newberry Trustees in 1887 were free to create a reference and research library rather than a public circulating library. Probably it was the former that Newberry had had in mind, for his friend William B. Astor had already founded the Astor Library in New York in his father's memory carrying out his father's will. Second, shortly after the Newberry opened its doors, the John Crerar Library was established, in 1893. Between them, the Trustees of the Newberry and the Crerar, in concert with the Trustees of the Chicago Public Library (which Poole had headed), divided up the world of knowledge then deemed relevant to research and reference libraries. Over the next decade, the Newberry disposed of most of its materials in law, medicine, science (including, alas, the great Audubon *Birds of North America* elephant folio), technology, and the hard social sciences, such as they were in those days, and left those fields to the Crerar (where the Audubon was assigned) and other institutions. The Chicago Public Library, in addition to general circulating-library responsibilities, also agreed to collect to research strength in business, law, patents, and fine arts. The Newberry then focused more sharply (and ever more sharply) on the humanities.

In that act of deliberate shaping of the collections, the Library established what became an ongoing tradition of willingness to dispose of duplicate and out-of-scope materials. Even as late as the 1960s it drew on that tradition for its auctions at Sotheby's and Parke-Bernet for disposing of duplicates and its sale to another library of a collection on the Russian revolutionary movement deemed out-of-scope.

The third shaping event was the purchase by the Newberry of the rare book collection of Henry Probasco of Cincinnati, in 1889, before the Library opened its doors. This collection, some 2,500 volumes purchased for $52,924, included incunabula, Shakespeare folios, Grolier bindings, rare Bibles (among them the King James, first edition), ten early editions of Homer, nine of Dante, and eight of Horace, to mention only a few special works. It was the foundation of what has become a major rare book collection. As a consequence, the Newberry "tradition" would include rare books within its scope as well as general research and reference materials.

Although the purchase of the Probasco collection certainly established rare books at the Newberry, which continues to gather them by both individual and *en bloc* acquisitions (as late as 1964, an even greater collection than Probasco's, that of Louis H. Silver, was also purchased), the Edward E. Ayer collection is more characteristic of Newberry acquisitions: it focuses on a broad subject field rather than on books as artifacts, even though it contains thousands of rarities. Ayer was a member of the first Board of Trustees. An avid collector of works relating to the pioneer period in America, he extended his collecting back into Europe and the Age of Discovery, southward to Central and South America, and westward to the Pacific Coast, Hawaii, and the Philippines. Within this broad geographical and chronological pattern, he always focused on the early contacts between aboriginal peoples and the European, and on the discovery, settlement, and emergence to statehood of the states. These are major themes running throughout the Newberry's North American collections. He gave his library of about 14,000 volumes to the Newberry in 1911, continued to add to it himself, and later provided three endowment funds for its maintenance. Today the Ayer Collection holds some 100,000 volumes, 80 percent of which have been selected by successive curators and bibliographers who have shaped it into a rich resource. It is one of the Uncommon Collections of which the Library justly boasts. It is a true—and great—research collection.

Ayer's gifts in the 1910s and 1920s soon attracted gifts and collections of note that were closely related to his subject matter. Trustee William B. Greenlee's excellent gathering of working books on the Portuguese empire to about the 1830s came as a gift in 1937. It beautifully complemented the major Brazilian holdings in the Ayer. A small endowment was later established by his widow. Similarly, in 1964 trustee Everett D. Graff bequeathed his notable collection of Western Americana, along with a purchase fund. Again the collection handsomely complemented the Ayer, in this instance, in the history of the West. These gifts were followed by the 1967 purchase of the Frank Cutter Deering collection of early Americana, which, among other fields, increased the Newberry's Indian captivity narratives by 50 percent and made it the best such collection in the world. The Franco Novacco collection of sixteenth-century Italian printed maps, also purchased in 1967, fit well with Ayer's early map collection and positioned the Library to make a significant contribution in that field (see below).

Free both to acquire collections *en bloc,* by gift or purchase, and to sharpen the collections by disposal of unwanted items, a long series of librarian-scholars has been encouraged by the Trustees to build massive subject-oriented collections in such areas as the history of cartography, the history and theory of music, the Italian Renaissance, colonial Brazil and other Latin Americana, the history of the family, local history, and the history of Indian-white relations, to name only a few of the Library's stronger areas of collecting. At the same time the staff built and maintained a solid foundation in the history and literature of the areas and periods in which the more specialized collections fall. Bibliographies, journals, documentary sets, monographs, biographies, publication series of learned societies, antiquarian and out-of-print works, modern works, and newspapers all help make the Newberry Library a complete reference and research library in its fields.

This freedom to develop major special fields of collecting and research is well illustrated in the John M. Wing Foundation Collection on the History of Printing. Wing (1845–1917), a Chicago printer and newspaper publisher, bequeathed to the Library in 1917 his own collection in printing history, along with a substantial sum to build a major collection in the field under the direction of a custodian.

Three successive and outstanding curators, Pierce Butler, Ernst Detterer, and James M. Wells, have built the Wing Collection into a major, world-class research collection of some 30,000 volumes and several thousand manuscripts that document not only the aesthetic of book design, finely-printed and illustrated books, but also the milestones of technological progress, from Aldus Manutius to today. Included in the Foundation's holdings is an excellent collection of printers' and founders' specimen books, with rare, sometimes unique, examples by Baskerville, Bodoni, and other great type designers.

The Wing Collection is also rich in manuscripts documenting the history of printing, including printers' records, press archives, and papers of such outstanding students and practitioners as Will Ransom and Stanley Morison. Among unusual strengths is an unsurpassed gathering of writing books and letter forms, with first and later editions of all of the most important scribes, as well as manuscripts in their hands. Intellectual dividends of the Wing Foundation printing collection are the thousands of texts (including most of the Newberry's two thousand-odd incunabula) that fit particularly well with the Library's Renaissance holdings. That is to say the samples of printing are chosen from among significant texts, when possible. Among these are first printed editions of works by Dante, Caxton, and many others. Finally, supporting the whole is a first-rate collection of monographs, histories, biographies, and other reference works that open up the Wing Foundation's holdings to its users. Its card catalogue, like that of the Edward E. Ayer Collection, has been published in book form.

By the early 1940s, the Librarians—William Frederick Poole, 1887–1894; John Vance Cheney, 1894–1909; William N. Carleton, 1909–1919; and George B. Utley, 1920–1942—had directed, with the aid of a highly skilled staff, the building of a very substantial collection of some 285,000 titles. This all occurred in a little more than a half century of Library development—a notable achievement.

Their successor, the late Stanley Pargellis, 1942–1962, a historian trained at Oxford and Yale, and a consummate bookman, perceived for the Library three tasks building on those collections, and began a new era in Library development—the second half of its first century.

First, Pargellis sought to augment the existing collections, building primarily on already-developed strengths. He nearly tripled the size of the collection in his twenty years. In doing so, he bought imaginatively and well, taking advantage of books and manuscripts available at low prices in post–World War II Europe and England. In these endeavors, he was ably seconded (and sometimes led) by such very different bookmen as Mabel Erler, Ruth Butler, Felix Borowski, James Wells, and Hans Baron, among others. Samplings from their rich selections are described in the volumes of the *Newberry Library Bulletin* 1944–1962. This area, Stanley believed, would provide his chief claim to fame. And it was an enormous contribution.

Second, Pargellis reversed a long-standing policy that had kept the Library from acquiring manuscripts, except literary works, in large numbers. He did this not only by encouraging the purchase of texts in Renaissance literature and history but also, and more important, by literally inventing two new fields at the Library: the history of the Chicago Literary Renaissance, whose anchor is now the 70,000-piece papers of Sherwood Anderson; and the history of business, a field in which Pargellis was a founding father. He persuaded two great railroads, the Illinois Central and the Chicago, Burlington & Quincy, to place their early records on deposit for use by scholars.

Third, he perceived that the Library's often unknown resources had to be brought to the attention of scholars worldwide. To do this he created the *Newberry Library Bulletin*, a modest fellowship program, and a series of brilliantly conceived and executed conferences, all focusing on the Library's great collections and encouraging their scholarly use.

The imagination and verve that Pargellis brought to his self-appointed tasks is perhaps best illustrated by a spectacular series of Library events that he brought into being two years after his 1942 appointment. In 1944 he inaugurated a series of fellowships, sponsored by a $100,000 grant from the Rockefeller Foundation, to encourage Midwestern studies. With resident scholars available, he inaugurated a series of eight Conferences on American Studies designed not only to illuminate their subjects but also to publicize the holdings of the Newberry. These conferences (and similar ones in English history, French History, American Indian History, and Latin American Studies plus the annual Renaissance Conference) were reported in the newly-established (1944) *Newberry Library Bulletin*, which flourished during his administration and went to libraries everywhere in the scholarly world. To edit the *Bulletin*, he persuaded newspaperman and non-academic historian Lloyd Lewis to make the Library his intellectual home and to help Pargellis create the Library's very important Midwest Manuscript Collection (now Modern Manuscript Collections).

Through Lewis' good offices the papers of such notables as Sherwood Anderson, Floyd Dell, Willa Cather, Octave Thanet, Edward

Price Bell, and Lambert Tree were brought to the Library and Malcolm Cowley's important manuscripts began to be sent here. At about the same time came the railroad manuscripts mentioned above, to which were later added the Pullman Company papers.

Three decades after Lewis' death, Katherine E. Lewis, Lewis' widow, established an unrestricted and substantial acquisition fund in her husband's memory. This was followed, a year later, by a gift of a good sampling of his papers from a friend of the Library and, in 1987, a bequest from Lewis' sister, Louise Lewis, of a substantial endowment to support fellowships in American History. Thus a Pargellis initiative in the 1940s is still blossoming in the 1980s.

The Newberry thrived on what Pargellis achieved by the time of his retirement and in 1962 it capitalized on many of his initiatives. That is to say, it adopted as standing policy the desirability of helping scholars, wherever they may be, to use the Newberry if they need the Newberry. The Library achieves this goal not only in the traditional manner—cooperation with national and international bibliographies, publication of catalogues and checklists and exhibit catalogues based on its own collections, publications of primary resources, microfilm, and Xerox, and extensive telephone and written responses to reference questions—but also by bringing scholars to use the library *in situ*. This was done with funds raised outside the thin endowment, and expenditures increased from $20,000 to $300,000 per year.

Beginning in 1964, to augment the fellowship program inaugurated by Pargellis, the Newberry created a series of programs and centers designed to further increase the effective use of its collections. The first of these was the Kenneth Nebenzahl, Jr. Lectures in the History of Cartography, endowed by the Chicago rare book and map dealer (since become a Trustee) in honor of his (now late) son in 1964. The series of lectures and conferences that have resulted and that reach an international audience, along with the purchase of the Novacco map collection mentioned above, helped lead to the creation of the Hermon Dunlap Smith Center for the History of Cartography in 1971, which was endowed handsomely by Mr. Smith with gifts and a bequest. At the same time as the Nebenzahl series, the Humanities Program of the Associated Colleges of the Midwest (later enlarged to include the Great Lakes Colleges Association) was created in 1965. Then followed the Center for the History of the American Indian, 1971; the Family and Community History Center, 1973; and, most recently, 1980, the Center for Renaissance Studies.

The Research and Education Division, established in the early

1970s under the leadership of Richard H. Brown, not only embraces the above centers and projects, it also administers a large fellowship program and Lyceum program. It has become a center of nontraditional education. To sum up, by 1987 the annual budget for research and education had grown to more than one million dollars. Several endowed funds, in excess of $4.5 million, have been established to support the Division, and it has drawn heavily on the National Endowment for the Humanities since 1968. The innovations begun by Stanley Pargellis to increase the effective use of the collections by scholars had thus become, under his successor, a permanent part of the Newberry's program.

None of the Uncommon Collections nor the Library's Programs that at its centenary characterize the Newberry as a leading reference and research library could have occurred without the strong support of interested Trustees and of the successive Boards as a whole. Indeed, the Library has always had a close, symbiotic relationship with its originally small Board of Trustees. Under the original charter, Trustees were elected for life and the Board (self-perpetuating) was limited to thirteen members. Trustees tended to stay on the Board, once on: of the original thirteen, only four served less than ten years, eight lasted more than fifteen, five more than twenty, and one, John P. Wilson, lasted thirty years, 1892–1922. Several sons succeeded their fathers or grandfathers, *viz.* C. J. Hambleton, Henry P. Isham, George A. Ranney, and John P. Wilson. Through 1964, when Everett D. Graff died, only five men had served as President of the Board: Eliphalet Wickes Blatchford, 1892–1914; Edward L. Ryerson, 1914–1928; Horace S. Oakley, 1928–1929, Alfred E. Hamill, 1929–1953, and Mr. Graff, 1953–1964.

This close-knit characteristic of the Board was enhanced, moreover, by a common interest in books and scholarship on the part of many of its members. To be sure, the kind of civic humanism that characterized Renaissance Florence moved many of the Trustees, and still does; but there has also been a strong particular interest in books. These persons included by 1987 at least two very distinguished booksellers, A. C. McClurg and Kenneth Nebenzahl; several printers and/or publishers, including McClurg again, and Emmett Dedmon, Gaylord Donnelley, Charles C. Haffner III, Andrew McNally IV, George A. Poole III, John B. Schwemm, and George B. Young; several scholars, Ray A. Billington, Sir William Craigie, Eric W. Cochrane, Elizabeth Gebhard, Jean Hagstrum, Neil Harris, Franklin C. Head, Carl H. Kraeling, Lawrence Lipking, Andrew C. McLaughlin, William A. Nitze, Ferdinand Scheville, Bernadette E.

Schmit, and Mr. Young, again; scholarly administrators, Ann Ida Gannon, Lawrence A. Kimpton, and Robert Wedgeworth, Jr.; and, above all, collectors, most of whose collections are now part of the Newberry Library. These latter include Edward E. Ayer (1892–1911); Eliphalet W. Blatchford (1892–1914); T. Kimball Brooker, 1979–); Frederick Ives Carpenter (1913–1925); Suzette Morton Davidson (1972–); David W. Dangler (1983–); Everett D. Graff (1948–1964); William B. Greenlee (1932–1953); Alfred E. Hamill (1928–1953); George A. Poole III (1957–); Rudy L. Ruggles (1964–); Louis H. Silver (1957–1963); Hermon Dunlap Smith (1943–1983); Edward Byron Smith (1970–); and Herbert R. Strauss (1969–1974). Clearly none of these Trustees' interests could be considered casual.

An amendment in 1973 to the enabling legislation of 1892 permitted the Trustees to enlarge their numbers from thirteen up to a maximum of twenty-five. Subsequent revisions in the bylaws changed Trustee terms from life to five years, renewable; set seventy-five years as the retirement age; changed the titles of officers from president and vice-presidents to chairman of the board and vice chairman (necessitating a change in the designation of the director and librarian to president, librarian, and chief executive officer with Lawrence W. Towner, 1962–1986, being the first to bear that title).

These changes recognized the evolution, culminating under President Hermon Dunlap Smith (1964–1975), and continued by his successors Edward F. Blettner (1975–1979), Chalkley J. Hambleton (1979–1983) and Harold Byron Smith, Jr. (1983–) of placing administrative responsibility on the professional staff, reserving to the board the role of policymaking.

One major area of board policymaking concerns the institution's finances. The original endowment by Walter Loomis Newberry paid not only for the construction of the building and the early purchases of books, but also continues to provide approximately 57 percent of the current income from endowment. At approximately $28 million (1986), the total endowment now includes forty-seven additional funds (thirty-four created under Towner's aegis): some designated for books, some for research and education, some for general purposes.

Until 1964 the Library had lived well within its endowment income and had little occasion to raise money on a regular basis. Its total annual cash gifts amounted to something over $4,000 in 1962, for example. However, with the purchase of the Louis H. Silver collection, the drive to upgrade and professionalize the Library's staff, and the development of research and education programs, the Trustees had to play a much larger and more active role in the Library's finances than had hitherto been the case. In 1964–1965, the first fund drive in the Library's history resulted in gifts totaling $1.5 million. At the same time, in 1965, the Newberry Library Associates organization was created, under the leadership of Trustee William R. Odell, and now gives some $300,000 per year. Other gifts, grants, and bequests have raised the annual level of giving to well over $2 million and in some years to over $3 to $5 million. The total annual budget of the Library is over $4 million (1986).

Other policy decisions include the absolutely critical one of choosing to continue as a privately-endowed independent research library, in the present location, a decision made in the period 1959–1962 under the Trustee leadership of Everett D. Graff and the staff leadership of Librarian Stanley Pargellis. Because of strong interest on the part of local universities in absorbing the Newberry, the question of future viability of the Library as an independent institution had been raised. In any event, the Trustees chose independence, and during those years the Library invested more than $1 million in renovating the building and air-conditioning and fireproofing it to protect the collections.

Because the Newberry is a research library with major and irreplaceable collections, the Trustees also adopted a policy early in the 1960s of supporting the developing field of book preservation and conservation, in both practice and research, so that the Newberry has become an important center in this much-needed effort. Built on the tradition of an in-house bindery and a growing awareness of the environmental impact of polluted air on acidic paper, this decision resulted in the appointment of Paul N. Banks in 1963 as Conservator. Under his leadership, the Newberry attained renown in the preservation field. It exhibited that leadership in the construction in 1980–81 of a modern, state-of-the-art bookstack building and the construction of a new conservation laboratory and bindery whose program won endowment under a challenge grant from the Mellon Foundation.

In the early 1970s, concern for the long-range future intensified: the 1959–1962 decision to remain independent and in the same location was reaffirmed; plans were developed for the aforesaid ten-story bookstack building, and a major renovation of the old building was begun. The twofold purpose of the construction and renovation was to provide the best environment for the collections that could be devised, and to create adequate and rationally ordered space for research and education programs and for public programs in the existing structure. The program was completed in time for the centennial. At the end of the first century, the retiring President and Librarian, in characterizing his own (near) quarter-of-a-century tenure, said there were now four components to the Library's historic program: adding to the collections, preserving the collections, providing for their effective use, *and* raising the money for the whole shebang.

A PLAN FOR THE NEWBERRY LIBRARY

(1971)

This is the final document of a long planning process in which Towner lays out his conception of the Newberry and an all-embracing plan for its future. It has the strength that "in-house" memoranda often have: it is cogent, sharpened over several years of discussion and debate. This version is numbered 4.9.

The planning process involved most members of the library staff, who were asked to prepare reports on their specialities, and outside scholars, each of whom was to answer specific questions. Joel Samuels, Deputy Librarian, prepared the reports that translated ideals into architectural realities. The plans were discussed in working committees and rewritten. Towner prepared an overall memorandum which he reworked many times. There were often serious disagreements among the staff, scholars, and trustees on a plan which involved such sweeping changes in the conception and shape of the Library. The overall concept was Towner's, and the process probably served to hone his ideas rather than alter them. Selection 17 in which he reviews his twenty years at the Newberry reveals the extent to which his ideals were carried out.

I. INTRODUCTION

THE NEWBERRY LIBRARY is a great reference, research, and rare-book library in history and the humanities. From its very beginning it was conceived as a library where serious scholars, academic or lay, might pursue their various researches. For breadth of scope, depth within that scope, and size of collections, it is unmatched among the world's privately endowed, independent research libraries. With an eighty-five-year history, with some million-odd volumes and five

From "A Program of Library Development." This is an internal planning report dated 10 September 1971, Towner Papers, Newberry Library Archives. Several pages at the end estimating sources of financial support have been omitted.

million manuscripts, with four endowed collections, with several funds dedicated to special subjects, and with a long-established commitment to scholarly research and publication, its future is determined very much by its past.[1]

Consequently, the Newberry will remain and grow as a great reference, research, and rare-book library in history and the humanities. It will continue to select, acquire, preserve, and make available the record of the past. And it will continue to grow in greatness as effectively as it can for the service of scholarship and the dissemination of knowledge.

But that is not to say that the Library has been or is only a library in the narrowest sense of the word. Its real character may be located somewhere along a scale whose opposite and for us, abstract, *extremes* might be defined as (1), an inert mass of materials waiting patiently to be used by the regular or occasional scholar-visitor on demand, and (2), an organized group of scholars in history and the humanities who happen to have a good library at their disposal.

When one stands up close, the Newberry does appear to be a library that, because of its excellent collections and the ease of access to them, attracts individual scholars in ever-increasing numbers. Indeed, it will continue to recognize that most research and writing in history and the humanities is done by the individual scholar, self-motivated, seeking answers by himself to questions he has himself posed. Further, it will continue to seek funds to make it possible for such individual scholars, wherever they are, to have both time and opportunity to gain access to the great and growing collections. Thus, it will continue and expand its role as a research library parallel to, and often connected with, the academic community, predoctoral and postdoctoral, as well as being an advanced research library for the lay public. This is the Library in its most traditional sense.

However, when one stands back far enough, one gains a somewhat enlarged perspective on the Newberry. That perspective enables one to perceive the Library as one of several varieties of educational institutions—museums, colleges, universities, academies, institutes, and independent libraries—all sharing a common objective. That

1. For a brief resume of the Library's history and collections, see L. W. Towner, *An Uncommon Collection of Uncommon Collections: The Newberry Library* (Chicago: Newberry Library, 1970, 1971). A detailed history of its early years is to be found in W. L. Williamson, *William Frederick Poole and the Modern Library Movement* (New York, 1963), 138–184. [See also Towner's "A History of the Newberry Library" reprinted as selection 10 above.—Eds.]

objective is the enlargement of mankind's knowledge and the sharing of that knowledge with as large an audience as is practical for the kind of institution it is.

This latter vision of the Library as an educational institution obtained almost from the start. The first Librarian, William Frederick Poole, established what came to be known as the Newberry Library University Extension Centre, which provided formal courses in such fields as the American Revolution, the Romantic Poets, the Novel, the History of Political Parties, and Shakespeare. More recently, during the Librarianship of the distinguished historian and bibliophile Stanley Pargellis, 1942–1962, the Library developed programs designed to increase the *planned* use of the great collections which by that time had been created. With a grant from the Rockefeller Foundation, for example, Pargellis established a fellowship program for Midwest studies (in connection with the newly created and now great Midwest Manuscripts Collection); he developed the Newberry Library Fellowship program; he created the Newberry Conferences, which were designed to stimulate research in such fields as Negro History, American Indian Studies, the Renaissance, Military History, and Business History; he created the *Newberry Library Bulletin,* which often published the results of such conferences; and he encouraged the book publications program. In other words, to adopt a partly anachronistic metaphor, throughout its history the Library has been viewed not merely as a memory core with millions of bits of information stored therein waiting for random recall, but also as an educational institution with a programmed method for the retrieval and use of that memory.

Over the past decade, the development of "programmed research" has accelerated even while the individual "random" scholarly use of the Library has increased and the support for individual research, through a revised fellowship program, has grown. Planned exploitation of the Library's holdings has taken several forms in this decade. Among them are the Newberry Library Seminar in the Humanities of the Associated Colleges of the Midwest, the Northwestern-Newberry edition of the *Writings of Herman Melville* (planned to train editors as well as to produce books); the "Atlas of Early American History"; the Committee for the Study of History; and, most recently, the Center for the History of Cartography (which will soon have its own endowment of some $600,000.00). Not to be overlooked in this summary of planned use of our major collections is the systematic effort to stimulate the offering of graduate seminars, by local universities, in fields where the Newberry is outstanding.

Chicago, Northwestern, Loyola, Roosevelt, Illinois (Circle), and Illinois (Urbana), as well as the Big Ten through its Committee on Institutional Cooperation, are universities that have taken advantage of the opportunities we have offered.

Each of the programs thus far developed at the Newberry has been based on the character and quality of our research materials, demanding no departures from (although sometimes an enriching of) our existing collections. Each of them has been and is, for the most part, self-sustaining, requiring little or no direct financial contribution from the Newberry without equivalent return. In fact, it has been a key part of the strategy of their development that, as they increase our visibility and support within the community, they make the greater growth of the Library *as a Library* more possible than would otherwise be the case.

The future holds promise of a further series of short- and long-term projects and centers. We distinguish the two, because a project has a definite concrete result and a foreseeable termination in mind (e.g., the "Atlas of Early American History," or the *Writings of Herman Melville*), while a center has an ongoing, and somewhat less concretely definable, purpose (e.g., the Center for the History of Cartography). As one contemplates the various centers and projects (established or only under consideration), there emerges an awareness that, while quantitatively the Newberry will simply be deepening its commitment to "programmed research" (loosely defined), qualitatively a subtle alteration will be taking place. The Library will be moving further along the scale towards a combination of a collection of collections and a more permanent and somewhat more organized group of scholars than now obtains. That community might be described as one large enough, however impermanent its individual components are, to maintain at the Library a "critical mass" of scholars.[2]

This community could well take the form of an Institute for Advanced Study in History and the Humanities (an idea advanced, in different form, as early as 1960). Such an institute would serve, in the first instance, as a kind of holding company for the various projects and centers created at the Newberry. (In effect, we already have it.) Second, it would serve as a generator of new projects and centers, with minimal seed money to bring to the Newberry scholars with ideas that look both appropriate and promising, not only with regard

2. By which I mean, of course, enough scholars in different fields and with different intellectual baggage to stimulate creativity among themselves and the staff.

to the intellectual results but also their potential for achieving independent support. (In effect, we nearly have it.) Finally, it would provide long-range fellowships to distinguished scholars whose contribution to the world of knowledge would be enhanced by being at an independent research center rather than at a major university. (I cite Dr. Hans Baron, Distinguished Research Fellow, 1965–1970, as an example.)

Thus, the future of the Newberry lies along three interdependent lines of development. First, it must and will continue to grow in greatness as a collection of collections. This growth, in turn, will continue to attract, in growing numbers, the individual scholar, academic or lay, pursuing serious research. Finally, it will continue to seek support for "programmed" research—centers and projects—that may result in the necessity of establishing a formal administrative structure to hold them, conceivably to be known as the Newberry Library Institute for Advanced Study in History and the Humanities. The sections which follow seek to elucidate the consequences of those recommendations and possibilities.

2. COLLECTION DEVELOPMENT

The Newberry will, of course, remain a library. As such, it will seek to define its role as a collector and preserver of library materials more sharply than it has in the past, placing its highest priorities on those fields where it is already so great that it attracts not only the local scholar but also the national and international scholar. In those areas it will seek to be complete, regardless of the form the library materials take—manuscript, contemporary book, reprint, or microprint. In turn, it will place its lowest priorities on those fields where the Newberry is merely of casual reference quality, already superseded by other libraries, especially those in the greater Chicago area.

Only in its priority fields of greatness, as we come to define them, will the Newberry seek the primary materials of research, whether rare books, manuscripts, published documentaries, maps, or newspapers. At the other end of the scale, for its lowest fields of priority, it will probably stop buying, and in some very select cases it may well eliminate whole sections by sale or exchange. In between these extremes will be large and important areas where growth in primary acquisitions by purchase, at least, will almost cease entirely, but where secondary literature will continue to be added.

There will be three exceptions to this increasing concentration: Bibliography and Reference materials, Methodology, and Areas of

Special Consideration. In Bibliography and Reference, we will concentrate most heavily in history and the humanities, of course. But recognizing the arbitrary nature of the division of knowledge into compartments, we will continue to seek to open the door bibliographically to all of mankind's knowledge. Thus, our already strong collection of general bibliographies and general reference works will be augmented, even as we continue to give first priority to having *everything* appropriate to our special fields. The second exception— Methodology—will be to develop more systematically than we have a collection of those seminal works in the humanities and social sciences, regardless of their chronological and geographical bounds, that provide new approaches and insights to the general subjects our collections embrace. A book that may focus on the Chinese family, but which provides new questions or new methods of analysis of the historical family, will be as appropriate as a standard monograph in the middle of our chronological, geographical, and subject specialities. The third exception—Areas of Special Consideration—will develop when convincing arguments are made, which can be supported financially, that a major subject held by the Library must be extended chronologically and/or geographically in order to make the collection "complete," or to make it significantly more useful to an existing or anticipated program.

The above exceptions aside, the thrust of our acquisition policy is to build greater concentrations of research materials, using as our criteria for setting priorities our primary and secondary fields of greatness. This policy is easier to state than it is to carry out. But over the past several years much duplicate and out-of-scope materials (most notably in the latter category, the Bernstein Russian Collection) has been disposed of. More recently, nearly six months of systematic discussion has laid before the staff the dimensions of the problem of setting priorities if not all the priorities themselves.[3]

One should not mistakenly infer, from our intent to set more rigid priorities than have obtained in the past, that the future of the Li-

---

3. A brief statement of our collecting policies is now in draft. It can be supplemented by *An Uncommon Collection of Uncommon Collections* (1970, 1971); by the much more detailed description, accurate at its time, in *Handbook of The Newberry Library* (1938); by the issues of the *Newberry Library Bulletin*, 1942–1971; and by scores of special bibliographies, checklists, and exhibition catalogues. Planned is a detailed guide for staff use from which will emerge brief guides in published form for public distribution; for example, The History of Cartography at the Newberry Library. [The "General Guide to the Collections of the Newberry Library" was compiled in loose-leaf form and copies are now available in the reading rooms.—Eds.]

brary includes a decision to live within our present book budget, constricted as it is by rising costs and the greatly increased rate of publication. On the contrary, this policy envisages ever-larger resources being spent on a better-defined collection so that the greatness of the Library will continue and grow, and so that its usefulness to scholarship may be continually enhanced.

Three examples (among many that might be given) where augmentation of funds for acquisition are needed will serve to illustrate the point. The advisory council for this planning study has strongly recommended that the funds for the purchase of *current* publications—books of all kinds, periodicals, and continuations—are presently too limited at the Library (we budgeted $80,000 in fiscal 1971). It seems quite clear that we will need to double this sum if we are to catch up and then keep up. The second example concerns subject-area special funds, particularly for the purchase of out-of-print, rare, or unique materials. While the Library has several such funds now, it has been seven years since the last special book fund was established (Everett D. Graff, 1964). Such funds should be especially attractive to would-be donors, and in our continuing program of library development we need to seek ways of showing, better than we do, what a capital gift, of say $20,000, can do over a period of ten years. The third example concerns the strategy of collection buying. At present, because we do not have a reserve and consequently have to raise the money for a major collection *after* we know we want it, we are not in a position to bargain over prices. As in real estate, one cannot get an option at a price lower than the asking price, because such an option automatically sets the lower price for the next prospective customer. While we expect to have to continue to raise money for exceptional purchases (as in the case of the Recusant Collection in 1970, $100,000), a fund needs to be established to pay the interest on money we might borrow should we succeed in getting a significant price reduction on the basis of a firm cash offer, raising the funds after the purchase is completed. I am fully persuaded that such a system should be tried and that, if tried, it might work very well under proper Trustee guidance.

As the second and third examples imply, the Library will continue to be a repository for books as artifacts as well as texts. We are, after all, a major rare book and research collection. Our special book funds will continue to be used to buy manuscripts, rare books, and other editions contemporary with their authors where they can be found. But further additional purchases made in the field of antiquarian books and older manuscripts and maps will have to come from special resources raised for that purpose. The General Fund book budget, even though enlarged, as it must be, will be used mostly to purchase books in print and appropriate reprints in whatever form they may be available.[4]

Because we will continue—and emphasize—our role as a preserver of particular books both as texts and artifacts, greater attention will have to be paid to preserving what we have than has been the case in the past. Eventually, hundreds of thousands of dollars will have to be expended in an expanded program for the repair of books, manuscripts, and maps in both the Special and General Collections. It is a complex problem requiring hundreds of thousands of individual decisions.

As a general rule of thumb, those books and maps printed before 1840 will be scheduled, mostly on a routine basis, to get the treatment necessary to preserve them indefinitely. This is a simple thing to say, but it is a vast, while not always urgent, undertaking. It involves individual repair work as needed, proper storage, dusting, and, in the case of leather bindings, periodic oiling.

For those works created in book form or manuscript form after 1840, however, a complex series of decisions will soon have to be made about their need for preservation. This is because of their relatively rapid deterioration—the consequences of bad paper, high acid content, bad bindings, and heavy use. Those materials published contemporaneously with the events they describe or, in the case of literature, in the lifetime of the author will be treated as primary materials worthy of being preserved in their original state. Works that are compilations from previous ages as, for example, the five volumes in six *Records of the Governor and Company of Mas-*

4. A corollary, incident to the better definition of our collections, is that our cooperation with local research libraries will have to be increased markedly. This fact is not an unmixed blessing. If we assume responsibility for a field, we will have to fulfill that responsibility. Responsibility will include both finding the money to buy the requisite works (as another first priority on our book budget) and also making the materials available to those readers the cooperating libraries ordinarily admit. In the past we have done neither task systematically. On the other hand, such cooperation will make available to our resident readers—from near or far—the vast library resources of the Chicago area, another six to ten million volumes. With certain exceptions, we will continue to follow Polonius's advice to Laertes—"Neither a borrower nor a lender be"—but there are other and more appropriate forms of cooperative use. We have helped create, and are joining, an Illinois Regional Library system to explore fully what can be done.

sachusetts Bay, created in the seventeenth century but not printed until the nineteenth, may be replaced with modern reprints as they become available.

Manuscripts, of course, will be treated on an individual basis. Literary manuscripts, including letters, will be preserved, but post-1800 business records (for example, the letter books of the Chicago, Burlington & Quincy Railroad) may well be microfilmed and then allowed to deteriorate unless some cheap mass deacidification process is developed.

Thus, the long-range goal of the Library's collection policies will be to sharpen, augment, and preserve in good usable condition an increasingly valuable collection of collections that will draw scholars from all over the world.

3. USE OF THE COLLECTIONS—ADMISSIONS POLICIES AND READERSHIP

Perhaps the most difficult (and sometimes disagreeable) task the Library has is to plot the point where the line of maximum efficient present use of the collections crosses the line representing the responsibility to preserve the collections for future use. The number of factors to be kept in mind is substantial, and their relative weights are difficult to determine. To confound the issue, both the number of factors and their relative weights change over time. Finally, in exercising judgment about where that point of use versus preservation is at any given moment in time, one is not only subject to grave miscalculation but also to charges of intellectual snobbery, elitism, racism, and other forms of mortal sin. Nonetheless, one must have a policy with regard to the use of the collections even if that policy were to be open to all comers.

Our present policy may be divided, for the sake of further discussion, into two categories: a policy for academic use, and a policy for lay use. Academic use assumes that the libraries available to students and faculty scholars are arranged in a hierarchy of quality, value, and use. The student, whether high school, undergraduate, or graduate (up through the Master's degree) is expected to exhaust the resources of his high school, public, college, or university library before he turns to the Newberry, where he can be admitted for specific research (but not general reading) purposes. Machinery exists for determining the appropriateness of such use of the Library by such persons, and provisions have been made recently to assure us that that machinery will not delay for even a day the necessary use by such persons. Further up the scale, doctoral candidates, teachers, and professors (in other words, qualified senior researchers) are admitted on request.

Lay use of the Library falls into two groups. The largest of these lay groups is comprised of persons working in the genealogy collection, most of them tracking down their family trees. (Some ten thousand persons in the past five years). Such persons are admitted on request without regard for their background in the use of libraries or research materials.

The second group is a small but growing miscellany: book lovers and collectors; serious researchers, some looking up minor points that can be cleared up in a day, others undertaking long-range research and writing projects; and professional but nonacademic researchers—encyclopaedia employees, professional genealogists, editors, and the like. All these persons are admitted on request, if our collections are appropriate.

The glaring discrepancy in this policy with regard to academic and lay readership is, of course, the use of the genealogy collection. And this discrepancy requires a digression here. Users of the collection come in large numbers (about a third of our readership); they are mostly unfamiliar with the use of libraries, card catalogues, and research materials; they call for great numbers of books which they use for only a few moments; they need (but we cannot afford to give) a great deal of help; and the materials they use, mostly printed in the nineteenth century, are fragile, out-of-print, expensive to reproduce, and *of great use to scholars.* A currently ongoing survey of ten thousand of them, while as yet incompletely tabulated, indicates that they are terminal users (that is, they do not go on to become students of history after they have finished their family trees), and they do not generally make the results of their researches publicly available.

If the final results of our survey bear out these preliminary findings, and if an appropriate solution to meet beginning user needs can be found elsewhere, we will recommend that the Library take the necessary steps to bring the qualifications for admission of amateur genealogists in line with those for all other readers. That is to say, we may wish to require that the beginning researcher in genealogy do his research elsewhere, so he can demonstrate that he has exhausted the resources available to him in other local libraries and that he knows how to do genealogical research. (It should be noted that such a decision, while logical and consistent, would have repercussions that need careful study and evaluation.)

While we envisage a possible diminunition of readers in genealogy, we expect an increase in academic and lay scholarly readers for the following reasons. First, the numbers of undergraduate and graduate students, along with the numbers of faculty, will continue to increase in the immediate Chicago area as population increases. Second, the changing character of education in history and the humanities, which now places far greater emphasis on wide reading and original research than it did ten years ago, makes the Newberry a greater necessity than ever to a larger number of students, not only on the graduate level but also on the college and sometimes even on the high school level. Third, the policy of building to strengthen our great research collections will attract more scholars from outside the Chicago area. Fourth, the development of more projects and centers will increase the intensive use of the Library. Fifth, the augmented services we plan to introduce (see below) will attract some scholars who would not otherwise come to the Library on a regular basis. Finally, the increase in the general educational level of society, the increase in leisure time, and the greater visibility of the library will attract more lay scholars.

In sum, it seems safe to say that our readers will increase gradually but regularly unless we curtail beginning genealogy research. If we do make that change, the immediate consequence will be an initial decrease but one that will be made up, eventually, by more readers whose use is appropriate to the collections.

4. USE OF THE COLLECTIONS—A COMMUNITY OF SCHOLARS

Implicit in the Newberry's collections and admissions policies is the creation of an ongoing Community of Scholars in history and the humanities. This goal has been made explicit in the Director's *Annual Reports* of the past several years, in the published and unpublished (if widely uttered) public speeches[5] of the staff, and in our recently published guide, *An Uncommon Collection of Uncommon Collections: The Newberry Library*. It has also been implicit in staffing policies and in the kinds of programs that have been emphasized the past several years. It should come, therefore, as a surprise to no one who is at all familiar with the Library.

This Community of Scholars, present and future, has and will have a variety of relations to the Newberry Library. Some will be

5. For example, the various versions of my "Past Imperfect: The Uses of a Research Library," read in Tokyo (1969), the New York Historical Association (1970), the Huntington (1970), the Newberry Library Associates Fifth Annual Meeting (1970), and the Wisconsin Historical Society (1971). [A somewhat later version is printed in this collection as selection 9, above.—Eds.]

permanent, or semipermanent, others will be short term. Some will have a formal relationship to the Library, others very informal. Some will be part of the operating staff, others will be members of the staff of projects, of centers, or of other educational institutions. But all will be members of our Community of Scholars in history and the humanities.

The most permanent of these groups is the Staff. As it is presently constituted, that Staff not only represents a change from nine years ago, it also represents the direction we expect it to move in the future. Nine years ago there were three Ph.D.'s on the Staff, one of them not in a special field of the humanities but rather in the technical field of library science. Today there are five Ph.D.'s, with specialities in Renaissance History, Early American History, Nineteenth-Century American History, Economics, and Geography. In addition, there are three Ph.D. candidates with specialties in English History, American Literature, and Latin American colonial history. Several other members of the staff have Master's degrees in subject specialties, along with advanced degrees in library science.

This Staff is not only one that is competent to serve in such library capacities as the selection of library materials, administration, and public service, it is also a research and writing Staff with special interests that cover many of the Library's collecting fields and that result in regular scholarly publications, as our *Annual Reports* indicate.

Closely allied to the Staff are the staffs of projects and programs already in existence, including the Center for the History of Cartography (with its Atlas project), the Melville project, and the Newberry Library Seminar in the Humanities. These programs alone bring to the Library on a temporary basis (fifteen weeks to several years) many other members of our community of scholars. For example, in the fall of 1971, there are six Ph.D.'s (two in Early American History, one in Geography, and three in English Literature), four Ph.D. candidates (three in Early American History, and one in English Literature), and sixteen college seniors. All of these scholars are using the Library intensively.

Also closely linked to the Staff are those persons who, from time to time, are awarded senior and junior fellowships or grants-in-aid for intensive use of the Newberry. Ordinarily these are persons for whom neither the physical access to the Library nor the time to use it would be available without financial support from the Library.

The next most frequent scholarly users of the Library are those from the greater Chicago community who regularly use the Library as their research home. These persons are ordinarily faculty and Ph.D. candidates, sometimes M.A. candidates, from the local universities and colleges, but they also include lay scholars. At the present time, these regular users of the Library are assigned some ninety-two carrels, studies, and reserve shelves in the Library for long-term intensive use.

Less immediately a part of the Library's Community of Scholars, but often likely to become part of it, are those graduate students whose professors teach graduate seminars here, using not only the space provided by the library but, especially, using for short periods of time, and quite intensively, our special holdings in such fields as Tudor History, Early American History and Literature, Renaissance History and Literature, Cartography, and the like. (Some of the faculty who do the teaching at the universities are primarily members of the Library staff, thus providing another tie that binds our scholarly community together.)

The future of the Newberry Library will be determined by how well we succeed in serving this ongoing Community of Scholars, in augmenting this Community of Scholars, and in tying this Community of Scholars to the Newberry Library. To accomplish these purposes we must continue to seek to provide the best collection we can, the best service we can, as good working conditions as we can, as much money for grants-in-aid, fellowships, and publications as we can, as many ideas for projects and programs and centers appropriate to the Library's holdings as we can, and as much outside support from foundations and individuals for those projects as we can.

To the extent that we are successful in achieving our purposes, we will not only be increasing the number of individual scholars attracted to do their own work on an individual basis, we will also be creating a series of projects and programs and centers, some permanent, some temporary, some solely the product of Newberry sponsorship (with the help of foundations), others the joint project of two or more sponsors. Thus, in the process of improving our "services," in the broadest sense of the word, the Library will move further on the spectrum away from the *abstract* extreme of an inert collection awaiting the demands of the scholar and toward the equally *abstract* extreme of a community of scholars who have a library at their disposal. In short, a new kind of educational institution will be in process of creation.

For purposes of discussion, we have given this "new kind" of educational institution a tentative name, The Newberry Library Institute for Advanced Studies in History and the Humanities. As a formal institution, it may never be realized, but as a Community of Scholars with a good library, it already exists, or, at least, much of it already exists.

First of all it would include many of the local and visiting individual scholars pursuing independent research who use the Newberry Library regularly and intensively. Those whose work falls within the main research fields of the Library's holdings would be designated Fellows of the Institute, as follows:

Resident Jr. Fellows	Local Scholars below the level of the Ph.D.[6]
Visiting Jr. Fellows	Out-of-town Ph.D. candidates, on stipend
Resident Fellows	Local Scholars above the level of the Ph.D.[7]
Visiting Fellows	Out-of-town Scholars above the Ph.D., on stipend
Senior Fellows	Fellows on extended visit for a year or more on stipend[8]
Distinguished Research Fellows	Fellows on more or less permanent and full-time appointment, with or without stipend

All of these Fellows, because their work is directly related to the main thrust of the Library's collection and because they are judged especially competent scholars, would have special privileges, *in varying degrees*, depending on *their* needs *and* the Library's resources. These services could include parking privileges, private studies, access to the Fellows Lounge, limited stack privileges, typing and Xerox facilities, support for publication, travel and research grants, and moderately priced housing. In addition to the above perquisites, Fellows of the Institute would be allowed, and encouraged, to give graduate (and in some cases undergraduate) seminars at the Library for credit at local universities and colleges, their students having, at least for the duration of the courses, reading privileges at the Library. Some of the Fellows would be allowed, and indeed encouraged, to give scholarly (but not necessarily academic) courses open to the general public for pleasure and instruction in a renewed effort to provide continuing adult education.

Already, in the above description, existing elements at the Library—fellowships, grants-in-aid, and publications—become part of

6. This category often does now, and in the future will, include staff members assigned to at least one-third time for study and research.
7. Ibid.
8. Ibid.

an incipient Institute for Advanced Study. But an important series of programs already in existence would be also included. These are the ongoing Melville Project, the Center for the History of Cartography (with its constituent elements, including the Nebenzahl Lectures and the Atlas of Early American History project), the Newberry Library Seminar in the Humanities of the Associated Colleges of the Midwest, *The Newberry Library Bulletin* (in perhaps revised form), and the Newberry Library's annual Renaissance Conference.

Three incipient programs for which we have high hopes of outside funding before the end of fiscal 1972 would also be incorporated. They are the Center for the History of the American Indian, the Center for the History of the Family, and the Center for Humanities Education (which promises to have its own journal, entitled *History Education*, sponsored by the American Historical Association). Other suggested programs and centers include a Center for the History of the Book, a Center for the History of Linguistics, and a Center for Continuing Education in History and the Humanities ("Adult" Education).

The creation of an Institute for Advanced Studies in History and the Humanities at the Newberry, in short, is all but formally underway. Were it to be formally established, it would perform in a twofold capacity: *first*, as a "holding company" to administer and supervise the Community of Scholars and the programs already in existence; *second*, as an initiator and funder (largely from outside resources) of new and appropriate programs. Its own endowment need not be large, except in ideas. How would it come about?

Experience can, indeed, be misleading, but the Library's experience in creating the Center for the History of Cartography may be very instructive and perhaps cause for optimism about the other centers and programs as well as about the potential of the Institute. In the case of the Cartographic Center, the basic elements are susceptible to analysis. They are:

    1. A very strong and growing collection of Library materials in the field. This is an absolute prerequisite.

    2. A demonstrable need.

    3. A strongly felt interest on the part of the scholarly world.

    4. A series of component parts already in existence that could be put together.

    5. An interested donor or donors.

When I arrived at the Newberry in 1962, we already had a truly great collection in the history of cartography. Within two years we had developed two of the Center's constituent parts: a publication program with the Society of the History of Discoveries and the Kenneth Nebenzahl, Jr. Lectures in the History of Cartography. We then added two major map collections in 1967 and 1968, the Novacco Collection and the Sack Collection. We had had, by that time, two formal scholarly discussions at the Library on the need for a center. This need was certified by the adoption of the Center by the Big Ten universities and Chicago. An appropriation of a reserve fund of $50,000 (earmarked for the Atlas of Early American History), made by the Library Trustees, enabled us to persuade the Institute of Early American History and Culture of Williamsburg, Virginia, to bring the Atlas project (with its $90,000 funding) to the Library. By the spring of 1970, the Atlas had additional funding totaling $76,000 from two foundations. Meanwhile, we had brought Dr. David Woodward, a specialist in cartography, to the Library, first as a Fellow and consultant, then as curator of maps. Thus, by 1971 we were in a position to attract a pledge of some $600,000 to endow the Center.

If this pattern were to recur for the larger Institute for Advanced Studies, most of the elements are already in existence, and it is time for an endowment. The time is also ripe because of the need for educational and research options outside the traditional university structure, a need which is widely felt and is finding some response from major foundations.

Formal institute or no, our Community of Scholars in History and the Humanities will continue to change and grow, and as we plan our building addition and our alterations within the present building, we must be sure that the planning reflects the possibility, indeed the probability, of change in the predicted direction.

5. THE BUILDING PROGRAM

The building "Program," of which this projection of the "Future of the Newberry Library" is a part, is based on several key assumptions. The first two assumptions are implicit in the preceding pages. They are that the Library will continue its independent existence as a research and rare-book library in history and the humanities—a decision made at the time of the renovation in 1959–62 and mutually agreed upon when I came to the Library in 1962—and that its independence is justified and must continue to be by its collections and its programs designed to exploit them. A third assumption is that the present building, ideal as it is for people (and it is) although less than ideal for books and other library materials, will be retained. A fourth assumption is that the *key* resources of the Library are its precious Library materials—the endowment might be lost and recovered, the books could not.

On the basis of the above assumptions and the thinking that lies behind them, a list of priorities for a building program logically emerges. Those priorities, in descending order, are as follows.

1. *The erection of a modern, fireproof, air-conditioned, and efficient stack building adjacent to the present building.* In order to understand this need, a bit of history has to be remembered.

William Frederick Poole, the founding Librarian of the Newberry, was brought to the Library from the Chicago Public Library after an already distinguished career as librarian and historian. He was a strong-willed and persuasive leader, and he fought for and won the right to determine (with several compromises) the physical character of the Library building. He was one of the last major librarians to argue for the old library concept of a series of reading rooms surrounded by collections of books within easy reach. Thus, at the very time when other libraries were turning to the modern stack principle, Poole designed a building whose result can be seen today— books located in thirty-four separate locations behind twenty-four locked doors on six different floors and stored in dark and gloomy stack areas with great amounts of wasted space between stack and ceiling. The consequent impossibility of adequate security control, effective organization, and efficient service in and from the stacks is a burden the Library has carried too long and which it is now time to remove.

In addition to inefficiencies and inadequate control, the collections are subject to three additional hazards. While the renovation of the building a half generation ago made the building as fireproof and as pollution proof as this old building can be, the books are still subject to damage from fire, from water, and from pollution. From fire, because there is much woodwork and inflammable substance (not counting the library materials themselves), because the steel columns which support much of the weight of the building are subject to collapse at certain temperatures, and because the heating plant is immediately adjacent to the Ayer vault and the Ayer stacks, holding one of our greatest collections. From water, because fire will bring water and because the plumbing in the attic subject to freezing and bursting is a real, if remote, hazard to several million manuscripts and several thousands of books. From pollution, because while this old building can be adequately air-conditioned for people, it cannot be for books. Temperature and humidity controls are within tolerable limits, but soot and other forms of air pollution cannot be kept out.

Finally, the need for an addition in the form of a book stack arises out of the growth of the collections, which has already required the renting of space for one major collection, the Pullman Company archives.

2. *A new heating plant and an expanded air-conditioning capability.* The present boilers are more than thirty years old and have been nursed along far beyond their normal life expectancy. The air-conditioning capacity probably could not handle the extra cubic feet envisioned for the addition to the present building.

3. *A reallocation and re-renovation of the space in the present building.* In adding stacks, we would recapture some 47,000 square feet of gross floor space. In addition, if plans materialize for moving the bindery-conservation complex to a new location (outside the building and organized as a joint venture on the part of several libraries), we would recapture some 4,500 feet. Finally, if the ACM offices move from the Library, as we expect they eventually will, we can recapture an additional 4,800 square feet. In short, approximately half the existing gross floor space will become available.

This situation will allow a flexibility in planning the rational use of space within the present building, a possibility open only once before, when the Library was first built. (In 1959–1962, space was already at a premium, tradition had frozen a certain organization in the staff and the facilities, and no comprehensive program was written by the staff. It was a sensible and beautiful renovation, and most of the expenditure, which went to mechanical features, viz. air-conditioning, elevators, fireproofing, was spent on permanent improvements.)

During the past nine years, the Administration has followed a deliberate policy, not only of seeking a more efficient organization of the Staff, but also a more efficient use of the space. A corollary purpose has been to so break the cake of custom that the Staff would become used to change as the norm rather than stasis as the norm. Examples abound, but perhaps the most dramatic and far-reaching are the consolidation of the Special Collections and Rare Book Reading Rooms into one administration and one room. Similarly, the Local and Family History Room on the third floor was moved adjacent to the Main Reading room on the second floor. Thus, even though we have reached almost the end of physical flexibility in the present building, the present Staff is highly flexible and ready for positive changes that will lead to greater efficiency and better service.

At this writing, all the specifics of the changes that should take place in the administrative and physical organization of the Library have not been determined, but the goals have. These include:

1) The establishment of a Reference and Bibliographical Center bringing together our card catalogue (the public catalogue) and, from the stacks and other locations, our thousands of reference and bibliographical tools, now so difficult of access. On that floor will be our main reference desk, our subject specialists, and our cataloguing and order department.

2) A new Special Collections and Rare Books reading room in immediate proximity to all the Special Collection stacks and a consolidated vault

3) A new Map Reading Room in immediate proximity to the appropriate materials

4) A Micro-Text Reading Room

5) A Main Reading Room embracing both the general reader and those users of the genealogical collection who will continue to be admitted

6) An enlarged and more commodiously furnished Study Carrel Room

7) A vast increase (up to a total of perhaps 100) in the number of private studies

8) A series of flexible project and center rooms

9) A series of seminar rooms

10) A consolidated photo lab

11) An enlarged and more efficient business office

4. *Fourth in the list of priorities is an addition to the present building of a combined exhibition hall, lecture hall, dining facility, staff lounge, and readers' lounge.*[9] This complex is highly desirable. Libraries, with the exception of the Beinecke at Yale, have too little addressed themselves to the problem of exhibition space. Usually it is an afterthought, stuck in a corridor someplace, ill conceived, ill lighted, inadequately ventilated (the cases, that is), and therefore a failure. There will be some exhibition space in the old building, but

9. Depending on the finally determined space needs, part or all of this complex could be in the present building. For examples, lounges and kitchens could be in the basement, the lecture hall and exhibition space could be on the first floor west (requiring, however, the removal of some pillars), and the large dining area could be omitted. It will also depend on how attractive such a complex would be to a donor or donors.

what is needed is a newly conceived, flexible, and exciting exhibition space where major exhibits can be mounted. A well-thought-out and richly developed exhibition can be a major magnet to attract use of the collections. In designing the space for such exhibitions, we have much to learn from museum people, architects, and the advertising business.

We also need a lecture hall where an expanded series of lectures can be held, where music from our collections can be performed, and where our outstanding drama collection can find occasional modest production. The Associates would be able to meet there, and community groups would find it useful.

Below the lecture hall, and surrounded by the exciting and provocative exhibitions we intend to mount, there should be a room where occasional large dinners can be served and large meetings not suitable to a lecture hall can be held, and which will be adjacent to a modern kitchen that can be used by both caterers and staff (and which might serve as a soup-and-sandwich kitchen maintained at noon for both readers and staff).

5. *A fifth element in the building program will be a parking facility.* Much of the present parking space will be taken up by the stacks and the lecture hall. Parking facilities (with size determined by the minimum necessity for staff and readers and by the minimum requirements of the law) will have to be planned either under the new buildings or on land to be acquired nearby that is suitable for institutional parking.

6. *A sixth element in the building program will be a solution to the problem inherited from the first librarian and the first board of trustees, the unfinished appearance of the building when viewing the East, North, and West elevations.* The stacks and lecture hall solve much of the problem on the West and North, but the East, from which most viewers see the building, would still look unfinished. Now is the time to do it, if ever. Its cost would be justified on aesthetic grounds alone, especially in view of the recommendation that the present building be considered the permanent structure for the Newberry. It may be that the solution will be essentially cosmetic, but it may also be that additional useful space can be added so that part of the cost can be charged to operational functions.

6. The Cost of Greatness

The "Future of the Library" sets out an ambitious program. It is my opinion that it is not, however, a new departure but rather a logical extension of the Library's development over the past eight decades.

And it is no more ambitious than the library deserves. With a collection of some million books and five million manuscripts that can be conservatively estimated to have a worth of some $200 million; with a reputation solidly built as a great research library and as a world leader in developing new library programs for privately endowed independent research libraries; and with a history which reaches back, through Walter Loomis Newberry, to the founding generation of this great city, its needs *can be met.*

The costs of this program are yet to be estimated, but they will be high. The costs of not embarking upon it, in my judgment, will be higher still. Therefore, we must go forward.

It would be embarrassing to write the words, "Therefore, we must go forward," in an essay addressed first to all to the Library's Trustees, who ultimately are responsible for the financial soundness of the Newberry Library, were it not for the fact that the Staff is prepared to share that burden as much as it can. We are confident that, over the past several years, we have prepared both the national foundations and the local community to regard us in a light different from, and more favorable than, the past. And we have laid plans ourselves, however unfruitful they may turn out to be, to help finance the future. Currently, for example, having found a major foundation unwilling to help libraries more than it already has, we have joined with three other private independent research libraries in proposing a general matching grant program, for capital, that may possibly prove out. In any event, we have little doubt but that the major national and local foundations know who we are and the extent to which we deserve support.

At this writing, largely because the cost of the additions have yet to be determined, we do not have figures on the costs of the outlined "Future of the Library," although we do, of course, have some idea of the costs.

[Two tables indicating possible funding sources have been omitted—Eds.]

It could be that, when all the figures are entered in the above tabulation and added up, the total to be raised over a period of years from a variety of sources would amount to from ten to fifteen million dollars. If that is the case, my answers to the shocked reader would be: (1) that is less than people have contributed to the Newberry in the past, and (2), THIS GREAT LIBRARY DESERVES TO BE USED TO ITS FULLEST POTENTIAL. I think it can be. But we have to want it to happen. As Captain John Smith wrote three hundred and fifty years ago:

"Seeing honour is our lives ambition: and our ambition after death, to haue an honourable memorie of our life: and seeing by noe meanes wee would be abated of the dignities and glories of our predecessors; let vs imitate their vertues to bee worthily their successors."

EVERY SILVER LINING HAS A CLOUD:

THE RECENT SHAPING OF THE

NEWBERRY LIBRARY'S COLLECTIONS

The acquisition of major *en bloc* collections monopolized Towner's energies in his early years; for a new librarian they were his testing. For those who think the process of buying a major collection is simple—or dull—Towner's account of the Newberry's purchase of the Louis H. Silver Collection in mid-1964 for $2,687,000 will be revealing. The decision to buy required decisions to sell to meet the costs. In the long run it also meant far more attention to fund-raising to build endowment. Creating the Newberry Associates was part of this process. This account written several years after the event does not quite recapture the adrenalin that flowed among the librarians, curators, and trustees who were part of the enterprise. A movie that Sotheby's made of the record-breaking Silver sale does.

CHICAGO'S NEWBERRY LIBRARY has been much in the news of late—much in the news for a library, that is. Chiefly this is because we have been doing a great deal of spectacular buying and selling, for which we have been both applauded and hissed. The adding and subtracting, we believe, has been far more than mere activity, it has significantly increased our collections in the only way that, at this juncture in time, it could have been done. And we are satisfied that the net result is on the positive side of every ledger we can devise. But there have been some debits to record in arriving at that net: thus my title, "Every silver lining has a cloud." This paper tells about some of the linings and some of the clouds.

From A. N. L. Munby and Lawrence W. Towner, *The Flow of Books and Manuscripts: Papers Read at a Clark Library Seminar, March 30, 1968* (Los Angeles: William Andrews Clark Library, University of California, Los Angeles, 1969), 35–50. Reprinted with permission.

But first a warning. In 1948 Richard C. Hofstadter published his stimulating book *The American Political Tradition and the Men Who Made It*. In a chapter on Herbert Hoover occurs a sentence I have never forgotten and which is worth quoting as a warning against drawing any generalizations about the proper conduct of libraries or librarians from what I say today: "There are times when nothing is more misleading than personal experience . . ." *Caveat Emptor!*

In order to understand the buying and selling that has been going on recently at the Newberry Library, one has to know a little of the institution's background. Its present greatness as a research library, which started long before today, goes unquestioned, and scholars who know it and use it are quite likely to compare it with its two great sister institutions, the Folger and the Huntington. There are, indeed, many similarities. Like them it was named after an entrepreneur, like them it was privately (and generously) endowed, and like them it is off campus—it is an independent institution.

It is at this point, however, that the similarities end and the differences begin. And it is the differences that make the Newberry uniquely great. The Huntington and the Folger, and indeed, most privately endowed, independent research libraries, began as collections of books, whereas the Newberry began as a collection of money. Whatever books Walter Loomis Newberry had—and there is evidence that he had a good gentleman's library and was actively interested in libraries and historical societies—were consumed by the great Chicago fire, three years after his death in 1868. In fact, no direct descendant, and not even his widow, ever saw the institution which bears his name. The Library was created because of a contingent provision in his will that was to become operative only on what must have seemed an unlikely prospect—that his two daughters would die without issue.

In 1887, the contingent provision was invoked, for the two daughters had already died, young and unmarried, and the widow, Julia Clap Newberry, died that year. A public library was already functioning in Chicago, and the Newberry Trustees elected to create a reference and research library rather than a general circulating library. Shortly thereafter, the will of John Crerar provided a second, similar library, so that the Newberry became even more specialized, devoting itself to the humanities and turning over to the Crerar its medicine, law, and science books. These included the elephant folios of John James Audubon's *Birds of America* and *Viviparous Quadrupeds*—a fact that should give the bravest or most foolhardy librarian pause as he shapes his collections by disposing of out-of-scope materials.

Since the time of that painful experience, the growth of the Newberry's collections may best be described as the gathering together, by accident as well as design, of an "uncommon collection of uncommon collections." The Library was not built according to a conscious architectonic plan. Instead, like almost all libraries, it grew; and it grew partly, at least, as the consequence of fortunate and often unforeseen opportunities seized upon when they presented themselves—there is no better time.

That the Library grew rather than having been built can be illustrated best by the consequences that followed the great gift from Edward E. Ayer in 1911 of 21,000 books and manuscripts—now grown to more than 80,000—relating primarily to the American Indian and his early contacts with the whites. It was this collection, with its works on Latin America, that led to the gift of the Greenlee collection in Portuguese metropolitan and imperial history; it was Ayer's works on the West that, in part, led to the bequest of the great Everett D. Graff collection of Western Americana in 1964; it was the Ayer early Americana and, especially, its Indian material that made us purchase the Deering collection with its Indian captivity narratives in 1967; and it was the Ayer materials on cartography—starting with the great Stevens collection of Ptolemys—that made it necessary for us to buy the Franco Novacco collection of maps of the sixteenth century in 1967 and the Sack collection of seventeenth- and eighteenth-century maps in 1968.

The care and feeding of these special collections would alone tax the resources of a private library, but they by no means exhaust the Newberry's list of special collections and, therefore, obligations. At least two others should be mentioned, on each of which we could easily expend our entire ordinary annual appropriations for books and manuscripts. The first of these is our great collection of books, manuscripts, and scores on the history and theory of music, now numbering over 160,000 items. Supported in part since the 1930's by the Oakley Fund, this is a major research area at the Library, and it requires specialists for selecting items to acquire and for cataloging those that are acquired. The second collection is the John M. Wing Foundation in the history of printing. Numbering some 23,000 items, it includes most of our incunabula as well as a small but very important selection on calligraphy. It too requires the bibliographic knowledge of a specialist, regular trips to Europe, special cataloging skills, and the like.

Most of our special collections have endowment funds to support them, never large enough, of course, and they have to be supplemented from our general funds, but they do have endowments. Demanding as they are on our resources, however, they represent less than half our titles and only the skeleton of our collecting responsibilities. I need only mention our important Renaissance holdings, partially covered in special collections, to make my point. To be sure, Ayer, with its interest in the expansion of Europe, its travel accounts, and its cartography; Oakley, with its early music and music theory works; and Wing, with its early texts and printing, are significant resources for the study of the Renaissance, but we are also a great general library on the Renaissance, covering Italy, especially, but with major holdings elsewhere on the Continent and in England, and we have had a specialist bibliographer in that field since 1949.

And so it goes for the entire Library. When I arrived in 1962, we covered (and still do, for the most part) the history, literature, philosophy, and music of Western civilization from the Middle Ages to the end of the Napoleonic era in Europe, to the end of the nineteenth century in England, to the Revolutionary period in Latin America, and to the present in North America. No library without access to tax money or alumni giving can possibly cover in depth that wide-ranging a field. This is especially so if it tries, as we do, not only to keep up with current books, bibliographic tools and other reference works, and periodicals, but also to buy scholarly out-of-print works, antiquarian and rare books, and manuscripts. In 1962, we had, at most, an average of $130,000–$150,000 a year to spend on books at a time when many university libraries were spending $1,000,000.

The problem we faced—a *polylemma*, really; it was too complicated to be a mere dilemma—was how to cut our obligations, thus allowing us to concentrate on our strengths and at the same time to increase absolutely the funds available for purchases. This is what the buying and selling are all about. We have had some successes in solving both of these problems. We have gotten rid of some obligations and books, and we have upped our acquisitions since 1962 to a precariously held average of about $800,000 worth a year, *including* gifts and bequests.

But, so far, the cutting has not gone deep enough and the increase in expenditures is on too precarious a foundation to give us satisfaction on either count. That is why I say that every silver lining has a cloud.

We have ceased to be a general reference library and have eliminated many current periodicals of only contemporary interest; we have stopped buying materials pertaining to the period after World War I, except for the Middle West; we have tried, with intermittent success, to stop buying badly researched genealogy on poor paper; and we have gotten out of the sea of Russian history, where we only had our feet wet. But a great deal more cutting is called for. Possible candidates are oriental materials, nineteenth-century English history and literature, some fields of nineteenth-century American history, and non-Western linguistics. For a library like ours, chronological, geographic, and the very broad term "humanities" are not sharp enough definitions to permit the continued building of great research collections in this age of rising costs and proliferating publication. As for the annual value of our acquisitions, our average since 1962 is a remarkable increase, true, but it is due largely to the year 1964, when we added $2,000,000 net by purchase and $1,000,000 by bequest. Without that year, our average has only a little more than doubled. Not enough.

A closer look at some of our transactions, our buying, and, particularly, our selling over the past six years, will illustrate how our successes have had their attendant problems. It would be profitable to me, and possibly to you, if I had the time and the ability to make a systematic economic analysis of those transactions. Alas, I am afraid that I have neither. Instead, I have to approach them as a historian. Each of the decisions was made not only in the general context of reinforcing our strengths and cutting our obligations, but also in a particular context of time and events that very greatly affected each decision made.

For example, take a look at the decision to purchase the great Louis H. Silver Collection in mid-1964. That important step depended on several immediate factors and influenced several other decisions, so that to analyze the purchase in a vacuum rather than to describe what happened would lead to inevitable distortion. We very possibly would not have bought that collection for $2,687,000, as we did, had it not been for the fact that Mr. Everett D. Graff had died earlier in the spring and that we mistakenly assumed *his* collection would produce some $500,000 in duplicates to help us pay for the Silver books. Similarly, we would have had to put a lot more of the Silver collection, duplicate or not, on the block in London in the fall of 1965—a year and a half later—had we not been as successful as we were in our fund drive in 1964 and 1965, started as an anticipated and welcomed consequence of the dramatic purchase of the Silver collection. Again, we would not have sold our Russian collection when and where we did, although we had decided to get out of that field—dormant at the Library for years—had we not felt when we started negotiations that we would need the money to replenish the treasury after the Silver purchase. And we might have delayed our sale of Graff duplicates—held in the spring of 1966— had we not needed the money to replenish the treasury and to prepare for the coming Thomas W. Streeter sales, and had we been willing either to compete with Streeter or wait until 1970 when those auctions will be over.

The interrelatedness of these various transactions and their role in shaping our collections is well illustrated by our two big auctions. As the book world well knows, we sold our Silver duplicates at Sotheby's in the fall of 1965 and our Graff duplicates at Parke Bernet in the spring of 1966. These auctions, resounding successes, also illustrate my statement that every success has its attendant problems.

Mr. Silver's library was a combination of two kinds of collections. On the one hand, he collected very heavily in the literature of the Renaissance; on the other, he gathered books and manuscripts of important works, high spots, regardless of their subject or period. In combination with the Newberry's holdings, most of the Silver Renaissance materials—the bulk of the collection—made a great deal of sense, but some of the other materials were peripheral to or outside our major fields. Thus, the science books, the Hebraica, some of the isolated autographs, some of the later eighteenth- and nineteenth-century materials, and some of the association copies were either outside our collecting strengths or too expensive (in relation to our other needs) for us to keep, or both.

Immediately after we got the collection, therefore, we prepared to dispose of the duplicates and the materials furthest from our needs. At the same time we were exploring the best method for their disposal. In the latter connection, we visited and corresponded with scores of persons: book dealers, librarians, and auction houses. We asked the advice of rare-book men at Yale, Harvard, the Morgan, the Folger, the Huntington, and other libraries. We spoke or corresponded with book dealers in Chicago, New York, New Haven, Boston, San Francisco, and abroad. We talked with Parke Bernet, Christie's, and Sotheby's. The majority advised that—unless we would sell directly to them—the best method would be to sell at auction.

While we were in the process of coming to that conclusion, the two major auction houses were combined—Sotheby's of London gained control of Parke Bernet. The only question left, then, was *where* to sell the Silver duplicates—in London or in New York. Again we took the advice of dealers and librarians. Again there was agreement, though by no means unanimity. It was argued that we would get better prices for the European and English materials if we sold them in London and better prices for the American materials if we sold them in New York.

Consequently, during the visit of the Grolier Club to Chicago in May 1965, the Newberry announced that it had made a treaty to dispose of a major part of its duplicates through a series of sales with Sotheby-Parke Bernet. The first sale was to be in London, the second probably in New York.

Meanwhile, we had been working steadily at the Library to select the works for the first sale. Several meetings of the Trustee Book Committee were devoted to discussion, first, of the criteria to use in selecting works for sale and, second, of specific works themselves. Staff members, far more qualified than I, prepared recommendations, not one of which was made without painstaking examination, leaf by leaf, of each work chosen. Arguments developed among the staff members, tempers flared, and feelings were hurt, but finally the recommendations were made. On those recommendations I made my decisions. Those decisions, right or wrong, were *my* decisions and *my* responsibility. None was taken lightly.

The final list of works chosen for sale was published, of course, in the catalog which Sotheby and Company prepared for the auction held November 8 and 9, 1965. It was a splendid affair. The first day, grossing $462,316.40, is still the best record for a single session of printed books at auction, and the two days' gross of $808,914, while not a record, is a "damn good average," as they say. Believe me, it gladdened our hearts, for we had confidently hoped for a gross of only somewhat over $500,000.

But, in order to achieve that figure, several non-duplicate, possibly in-scope works had to be sacrificed, including the great Chatsworth copy of the Jenson *Biblia Latina* on vellum; a Kilmarnock Burns, uncut; the manuscript of Shaw's *John Bull's Other Island* (which I had the pleasure of seeing recently at the University of Texas); the block book, *Ars Memorandi;* and a letter of Galileo's.

Why did we sell them? The answers are very complicated, but, briefly, they involved both bibliographic and economic considerations. We had other great incunabula on vellum; we felt the Kilmarnock Burns was too fragile for use by scholars, a true collector's item; the Shaw manuscript was outside our field of manuscript collecting—in the modern period we collect only Midwest authors; our present block book is a better representative of the genre than the *Ars Memorandi;* and the Galileo letter was an isolated item, of little research value as a lone example.

There was also a strategic economic reason. Edwin Wolf II points out that thirty-two, or less than 10 per cent, of the 369 lots sold at our Silver auction accounted for 65 per cent ($541,540) of the gross return. Quite clearly, if we had not sold those thirty-two works, among which were the five I mentioned, the sale would have been a failure. Not only would we not have grossed the $541,000 the thirty-two brought, but the remaining lots might not have brought the large number of buyers to the sale prepared to spend money.

For example, Warren Howell came all the way from California to attend the auction. But I wonder if he would have if those thirty-two lots had not been for sale. He spent $127,673 for thirty-eight works, but $86,240 of that was for only four items. One of the four, the Coverdale *Bible,* was indeed a duplicate and a less desirable copy than the one we kept. One was indeed out-of-scope, the Semmel-weis work on puerperal fever. One was a non-duplicate, sold because we felt it was too expensive for us to hold in that condition—the Kilmarnock Burns. And one was pretty much out-of-scope and *very* expensive, Petrus Apianus's *Astronomicum Caesaeream* (1540), a signed gift copy from Tycho Brahe. The point is, that without those four books to buy and the other big ones to try to buy, would Mr. Howell have come at all? If he had not—and he was an underbidder on several lots—would the sale have been as successful? I doubt it. We would not now be able to say, as we can, that, whether we sold a Silver copy or a Library copy, in most instances the sale price was higher than what we paid for the Silver copy.

On the other hand, despite our regret over giving up several fine books, twenty manuscripts, and forty-six non-duplicates (of which fifteen were out-of-scope), on balance we feel very good about the whole transaction. This is so because in 1964, when the staff and I recommended the original purchase to our Trustees, we said that there was only about $800,000 worth of the $2,687,000 library that we *absolutely had to have* to be happy, and that the rest, *if dire necessity forced it,* could be sold. Instead we were allowed to keep over $2,000,000 worth.

In retrospect, I am even more persuaded now than I was in 1964 that the purchase of the Silver collection was the right thing to do. Silver had been a Newberry Trustee, he had built his collection parallel to ours (there was, after all, nearly 45 per cent duplication), and in buying the collection we added many, many really great books and manuscripts, especially in the Renaissance and in English literature. The negative consequences of losing it, moreover, would probably have been even greater than were the positive consequences of getting it. Can you imagine waking up to those headlines?

But buying it certainly changed the nature of my position, probably permanently, for the $2,687,000 had to be recovered, especially since it came on the heels of a $1,250,000 renovation of the building. We have raised $1,400,000 in capital, we have created a 500-member friends group who are contributing about $40,000 a year—the income from another $1,000,000—but we are probably now committed to periodic fund-raising programs for the first time in Newberry's history. The time and energy this absorbs from the staff is considerable, and it is not easy to determine the long-range consequence for the Library of such distractions from our more scholarly pursuits.

The Graff collection arrived at the Newberry the same month in 1964 that the Silver collection was delivered. This was a gift, a collection of some 10,000 volumes, worth well over $1,000,000, filled with works duplicated in our Library, and coming with the donor's authorization to sell the duplicates provided we retained the better copies. In addition, Mr. Graff left a fund of $100,000 for book purchases and still other funds for the publication of a catalog. Here, it seemed, was a silver lining without a cloud.

Yet, when it came to the Graff sale, there were disappointments. First, many of the duplicates in our collection were not in very good condition—Ayer, in particular, had not been the discriminating collector Graff was—and they could not be sold at auction. Second, many of the supposed duplicates turned out to be variants, not to be sold. Third, the duplicates chosen to be sold included but few really big books and a very large number of almost run-of-the-mill items. The latter were often lotted, and, at auction, brought prices that were disappointing.

In the Graff sale, in other words, the pattern of the Silver sale was greatly exaggerated. A few books carried the whole sale and the weaker books did worse than in Silver. As Mr. Wolf again pointed out, of the 765 lots (not books) in the Graff sale bringing $230,187, eleven accounted for $107,350, or almost half of the gross. And of those eleven, two, the Eliot Indian *Bible* and Morton's *New England's Memorial*, brought $50,000, or more than 20 per cent of the total. It appears, therefore, that we might have done better if we had put only the first session's books on the auction block and sold the others through a dealer. Certainly we would have done as well. It was almost a dealers' holiday, made more so by the unfortunate decision of the auction house to divide the catalog into four sessions, each with its own alphabet, and to publish it without an index. If we had stopped at the first session, with its 151 lots selling for $170,000, we would have been better off. I do not call the sale a failure, but its success is clouded.

Our relative success in selling at auction has not persuaded us, in short, that auction is always the best way to sell. We have tried another method, that of selling out-of-scope books directly. Our Russian collection, gathered largely by Léon M. Bernstein and acquired in 1956, was sold to an eastern university for $150,000 in 1966, at about the time of the Graff sale. We will never know, of course, if this was the best price, but we believe it was a fair price, and perhaps that is the best price. We had received one offer of $100,000 from a dealer and it was tempting, but we appraised the collection ourselves—first by trying to estimate what we would have to pay on the current market, and second by figuring what the actual cost had been, including compounded interest on the money laid out in buying and cataloging the collection—and established the higher price. Both we and the buyer are satisfied.

The cloud in this silver lining is that we tried very hard to sell the collection to a local institution which was not quite ready to take the plunge, but might be now, two years later. Should we have waited? We did not, because the pressures generated by the Silver purchase and, equally important, by other desirable collections coming up, required a shorter timetable.

Two of those collections we bought in the summer of 1967—the Frank C. Deering collection of early Americana and the Franco Novacco collection of sixteenth-century separately printed Italian maps. The Deering collection we had to buy, if only because it contained some five hundred narratives of Indian captivity, a narrow field in which we were already preeminent and are now unassailable. But about three-fourths of the books in the collection—including many of the narratives, a set of Jesuit Relations, and a Rosier— were duplicates, a fact which gave us pause. The late John Hayward in the *Book Collector*, Robert Pirie in the *TLS*, and Sanka Knox in the *New York Times* had already scolded us for selling the Silver duplicates, and while we were not gun-shy yet, we did not want to become so, either.

But the seductive quality of the Deering collection overcame our reticence. We really did want those narratives, plus the fine copy of

John Smith's *True Travels* (ours had a facsimile plate); the first edition, first issue of Filson's *Map of Kentucke*; a grand copy of the great *Atlantic Neptune*; and the manuscript, in the author's hand, of Daniel Gookin's "An Historical Account of the Doings & Sufferings of the Christian Indians, 1676–7–8," among other choice items.

In this instance, we worked out in advance of the purchase an arrangement to sell the duplicates to Kenneth Nebenzahl, Inc., so that within thirty days after we passed our check to the sellers we had nearly half of the purchase price safely back in our bank account. If I were a true entrepreneur, I would probably have recommended that we keep the books for several years and then turn them on the market—certainly we would have gotten better prices. But for two basic reasons, I did not.

In the first place, we wish to avoid becoming book dealers ourselves. This is a highly specialized profession and I know for sure that I am not qualified. We recognize our interdependence with the fascinating lot of men and women from whom we buy, and we have learned to value that interdependence highly. But I do not want them to become librarians, and I do not want to become a dealer. The other reason is that we did not want to tie up the entire purchase price waiting, for example, for the Streeter sales to end—because we were then negotiating for the Franco Novacco collection of early cartography, which we bought concurrently with the Deering Library.

The Novacco purchase is a truly great collection that we are proud to add to our already very strong holdings in the field. As Signor Novacco said, speaking of the maps we bought, "This is the important section of my collection. I spent thirty years looking for them and collecting them, as they were scattered all over Europe. I am confident that my Collection constitutes an 'unicum' of extraordinary interest, not only for cartographic history, but also for the history of art and human civilization. These maps, nearly all printed between 1530 and 1570, are the link between the primitive cartography of Ptolemy and the great Atlases of the end of the sixteenth century."

Naturally, we did not take our collector's word in evaluating these maps but sent two experts to look at them—I had already seen them and was impressed by their beauty—and we also got an opinion from R. A. Skelton, then Superintendent of the Map Room, the British Museum, who had this to say of the Italian printed sixteenth-century maps in the collection: "The Novacco Collection stands alone and is unsurpassed even by the oldest national libraries. It may be said with some confidence that in this class no collection of equal scope, variety, and completeness could ever again be assembled."

But what of the atlases and books that were in the collection and that we could not afford to buy? Aye, there's the cloud, for while many, many were duplicates, if we had had the money in 1967 we could have gotten them all and sold the duplicates ourselves, paying far less for the ones we wanted than what they will sell for at auction. As Kenneth Nebenzahl recently pointed out, a Lafreri Atlas was sold at auction in the fall of 1967 for more than four times what was generally considered to be a realistic pre-sale estimate. Where will the money come from?

That, of course, is always the question in every library, and it is getting to be a bigger question every year, especially for the non-tax-supported, non-affiliated libraries. Our answer is partly shaped by the experiences of the past six years, as I have related them above.

First, there must be a continued shaping of the collections, so that what money we have will be used to concentrate on fewer and on better-defined areas of collecting. This, I think, may be the most important single task facing us. It is a never-ending task and one that requires great knowledge and foresight. This shaping will be reflected in our readership—the curtailment of genealogists and of master's-degree candidates and faculty researchers outside our special fields of interest, with a concurrent increase of users in our special fields of greatness. Modern transportation, modern methods of reproducing materials, and the tremendous growth of university libraries will relieve us of some of our current fields of responsibilities, because we will no longer be the only available research library for the hundreds of scholars who now rely on us.

Second, we shall certainly continue to sell duplicates and out-of-scope materials. Between our Ayer collection and our general collection, for example, there are a vast number of duplicates, and in such recently acquired collections as the Novacco and (one I have not mentioned thus far) the J. Francis Driscoll collection—83,000 pieces of American sheet music—there will be still more. While I do not expect great returns from such sales—too few glamour items and too much cost in locating duplicates and decataloging them—they will produce a small, steady income, and put the duplicate books where they will be more useful.

Third, I expect that we will continue to raise capital for endowment in order to augment our income. An increasing amount of that, I trust, will come from our Associates over the years, for with them we have created an active, generous "alumni," as it were, but we will continue to rely on corporate gifts as well.

Fourth, we will continue and enlarge our Associates' program of annual giving. They have already bought two important smaller collections for us—the library of a late Italian humanist, named Pietro Angeli (Barga), which includes his own books, his annotated library, his manuscripts, as well as works about him, and, with the help of the Trustees, the map collection of an eighteenth-century Swedish nobleman, Baron John Gabriel Sack, comprising some 1500 seventeenth- and eighteenth-century separately printed maps.

Fifth, the Newberry, like so many institutions, is seriously reexamining its investment policies. We shall undoubtedly move toward a much higher percentage of equities and a more active investment program, so as to assure the growth of our endowment and income to keep up with the inflationary forces loose in our society.

If we do all these things, then surely we will have effectively put our house in order, and perhaps then we will have a silver lining without a cloud—until we buy more big collections, with more duplicates to dispose of, of course.

›13‹

"WRECKING" HAVOC: CONSERVATION

AT THE NEWBERRY

In this talk at a conference of the American Library Association in 1974 Towner described the major programs in conservation the Newberry had launched and their underlying assumptions. In the course of his arch tribute to Paul N. Banks, the resident conservator, Towner revealed one of the secrets of his success as an administrator—his capacity to appoint first-rate people, give them full rein to do their job and stand by them, no matter how much they rubbed him the wrong way.

The talk was vintage Towner. One of the panelists, Captain George Cunha, instead of reading his paper, talked for an hour off the cuff. Cunha, the conservator at the Boston Athenaeum, was a traditionalist with unmasked contempt for the scientific approach Banks was pioneering at the Newberry. Towner let him have it.

Conservation flourished at the Newberry under Banks who went on to Columbia University where he headed the country's first graduate program in library conservation. Ten years after this talk the problem of conservation at the Newberry was still so overwhelming Towner said he "felt like the little Dutch boy with a finger in the dike."

"Wrecking" Havoc: A Talk Given at a Conference of the Rare Books and Manuscripts Section, American Library Association, Charlottesville, Virginia, July, [sic], 1974 (Chicago: Glistening Water Press at the Newberry Library, 1976–77). This booklet was set in type, printed in an edition of twenty-five copies, and bound at the Library as an avocational exercise under the direction of Paul N. Banks by the conservators in his department: James C. Dast, Gary L. Frost, Barclay W. Ogden, Sherelyn J. B. Ogden, and Jeffrey M. Rigby.

[Author's note:] *The author wishes to state that this paper is printed unexpurgated, as it was uttered in June of 1974. The conditions were inauspicious for judicious and restrained discourse, because a previous paper by Captain Cunha had been discarded in favor of off-the-cuff remarks that I found irritating—their targets were not there to defend themselves. He, therefore, apologizes for resurrecting something that might better have remained buried.*

UNLESS I HAVE GOTTEN my library association alphabets hopelessly confused, I believe this is the fourth or fifth time I have had the opportunity to make an ass out of myself before this group since 1962, when I was suddenly made a librarian. While I am always best when speaking unencumbered by the facts, I assure you that you can expect a most spectacular performance today, because the R.B. and M. section of the A.C.R.L. of the A.L.A. has finally conclusively established the Peter Principle—I have finally reached the level of my incompetence.

When Ms. Vesta Lee Gordon wrote me on 7 November 1973 asking me to moderate this session and—horrors—possibly to allow my remarks to be published, I responded swiftly with a "no." Let Paul Banks do it, I said; anything I would have to say would be his words in my mouth. She responded negatively, and I correctly inferred that instead of wanting the word from the horse's mouth, they . . . [Towner's ellipses].

I want you to know that I did not succumb to Miss Gordon's blandishments without certain assurances: (1) They would have Mr. Liebert's paper well in advance, so that I could ruminate upon it; (2) it would be possible to arrive by air the same day the conference opened, instead of a day earlier; and (3) they would get the local D.A.'s office to take the heat off the massage parlor next door. ALAS, none of these promises were fulfilled. Mr. Liebert's paper was literally delivered Sunday; I had to arrive Saturday; and my flatteringly suspicious friends on the university faculty warned me about the parlor!

The fact that I am talking at you a fourth or fifth time illustrates one of the hazards of public speaking. One has only so many jokes and they really cannot be repeated. And there are several rather amusing hazards of public speaking I could tell you about, but will not, because I have done so before.

But there is a new one, I've just discovered, and that I will pass on to you: Never agree to follow Fritz Liebert. It is bound to be an anticlimax! My best comment on his paper would be a steal from a speech he gave at the Newberry Library, when we invited him out to kick off our fund drive to raise $2,687,000 to pay for the Louis H. Silver collection back in 1964. He said, "all I can say is, Wow." Well that is all I can say. While I might have said what he said Sunday much better than he, I agree with every word.

In fact, as I listened to Fritz on Sunday, I was reminded of a great introduction by Professor Bergen Evans of the late Dixon Wecter. He told of two Indians sitting on a rock in New Mexico in 1945 as the first atomic mushroom cloud rose on the horizon where ordinarily the Indians picked up smoke signals from a distant but friendly tribe. Said one Indian to the other: "I wish I'd said that!"

At any rate, after hearing Mr. Liebert's informed, witty, and erudite remarks, I decided it would be an act of supererogation to repeat them, saying at each paragraph, I agree, I agree. Instead, I have decided to focus on one remark of his and one malaprop of Captain Cunha—it may be just a mispronunciation, but if it was, it was a pregnant mispronunciation. So I entitle my remarks, halfway through them by quoting Mr. Cunha's twice repeated words, how to avoid "Wrecking Havoc."

It is here that Fritz Liebert and Captain Cunha really seem to come to grips. Mr. Liebert makes it a first principle that, in our capacities as temporary custodians of the record of the wisdom of the ages, we should not allow ourselves in 2025 to be known as the barbarians of the 1970's. Never do the irreversible in repairing, restoring, or conserving those monuments that are not *ours*, but are only our temporary responsibilities. To me, this bespeaks an admirable conservation that, would to heavens, had been understood and acted upon the past 100 years as vulgar bindings were fastened on to newly-cropped copies of John Smith, as Scotch tape was liberally spent in ruining the 17th- and 18th-century records in the Massachusetts Archives known as the Felt Collection, and as Indian drawings were lovingly glued to high acid paper for preservation's sake in the Edward E. Ayer Collection.

In juxtaposition, Captain Cunha excoriates those "self anointed" scholars purveying the "rubbish" that conservation is a science and who thus warn about rushing in to take out tonsils, adenoids, and appendices as preventive medicine, when the operations are really so simple and so prophylactic. Just buy a bottle of Canada Dry Soda and some milk of magnesia tablets, he says, mix well, cool overnight, and deacidify your own documents. I hope that his unspoken, but soon-to-be published, remarks suggest that the pH factor should be tested first, that one might wish to make sure the ink is not soluble in his Cunha cocktail, and that no prussian blue, for example, is present (for when it has been alkalized it will turn, gradually, to a light tan). I can only assume that Captain Cunha's do-it-yourself exhortations misrepresent him, and at his worst. For otherwise I would send not even a Rapid Transit Transfer to him to be restored without the mixed emotions of seeing my mother-in-law drive my new Cadillac off a cliff.

It is not polite in a scholarly gathering such as this to be so impolite. I assure the good Captain that I do not attack him, only his philosophy, as orally expressed at this conference. Since he is in charge of a major co-operative venture of immense importance to us all, I pray that he misrepresented himself. But the issue is too important to be polite about it. And since he threw down the word gauntlets of "self anointed" and "rubbish," let me represent the challenged since they are not here to defend themselves.

I am relieved to be able to say at this point, that having informed Captain Cunha of my strong reservations about his oral presentation and having urged him to stay to hear them, he left a copy of his paper for me to read. It is much more conservative than he came across orally in its do-it-yourself approach and I feel constrained to offer an apology, not for attacking his remarks but for not having had a chance to read his paper before attacking his spun off remarks.

I am not qualified to judge the quality of his scientific analysis of our problems or of his solutions. However I do feel qualified to comment on the main thrust of his *written* argument, and I agree with it.

The burden of conservation—both preventive and curative, is indeed an administrative problem. No conservator can help unless we administrators are determined to help ourselves. The technical and scientific knowledge, while still in a state of an emerging science and art—is ahead of our (we librarians') willingness to apply it. I think of a fairly recent bestseller entitled the *Agony and the Ecstasy* as an apt description of our situation. We tend to embrace the ecstasy of acquiring that latest incunabulum, but we avoid the agony of providing it with a proper environment, of restoring it, and of conserving it.

The second major idea in Mr. Cunha's printed paper is a restatement of the old adage that an ounce of prevention is better than a pound of cure. The creation of a secure physical environment—secure from fire, water, diurnal variations in humidity and temperature, outside pollutants, careless staff, and wreckless readers—will probably do more to stay the forces destroying our books, and at less cost, than any individual or mass treatment yet devised. In that regard, I refer you to Paul N. Banks' article "Environmental Standards for Storage of Books and Manuscripts," in the *Library Journal* for February 1, 1974.

Indeed, at the Newberry, we air-conditioned and "fire proofed" our eighty year old building in 1959–62, and we have just completed architect's drawings for a new stack building that could house 95 percent of our collection. Specifications call for an ideal temperature of 60 degrees and ideal humidity of 50 percent; reinforced poured concrete construction; no water; and elevator shafts, stairwells, and all other vertical "chimneys" that carry fire and smoke from floor to floor, are to be outside the security perimeter. In short, just a heavily insulated box. It will be the best environment we can devise.

Besides responding to Messrs. Liebert and Cunha, I am charged with talking about in-house restoration. I will not bore you here with all the details of what we try to do at the Newberry, but let me say something about our work in general. First, we do have a resident Conservator, and we consider it a major staff position at the Newberry. He and the head of our Conservation Lab are one and the same persons, Paul N. Banks. We hired Banks in 1963, when he was running his own bindery in lower Manhattan. It was a stroke of genius. Banks is the most opinionated, arrogant, intransigent, insufferable, and uncooperative, son of a bitch I have ever known. He is one of three staff members in twelve years who have really told me off (I forget for what), and I would trust him absolutely with any manuscript, book, illumination, work of art, or rapid transit transfer we have. The reason is that Banks' basic philosophy is the same as Liebert's: if you don't know, don't do it: never do anything that is irreversible. One of Banks' greatest attractions is that he knows when he doesn't know.

Backing up Banks, and usually at loggerheads with him, is the best head of a small bindery for buckram and other standard bindings—eager to take over more and more leather binding and repairs until the Conservation Lab is left with paper conservation. He is our John Dean. In his own way, he is as arrogant as Banks and, consequently, conservation and binding at the Newberry Library are not easy subjects. In fact if we could set up a cooperative conservation center that ran the whole gamut from stamping, to original binding, to rebinding, to restoring, it would be an immense relief to me to ship both these characters off. They would run the best conservation center in the world if they didn't strangle each other.

Anyhow, we do in-house conservation and we recognize philosophically, if not administratively, that conservation problems are not just a rare book problem, they run like a cancer through our entire collection of 1,300,000 volumes and 5,000,000 manuscripts. Conservation is a spectrum, not a series of boxes. So we run a full spectrum conservation program. For example, Banks has the responsibility to see to it that every aspect of conservation, including the humidity and temperature in our stacks, is monitored. This includes the quality of buckram binding, the quality of leather binding, the storage of books and manuscripts, the exhibition of library materials, and *the decision not to act.*

More than that, we also feel deeply we have an obligation to help develop conservation as a professional field, as a science and an art. Consequently, Banks has the responsibility, and the time, to do research, to write, to teach, and to consult. My guess is that at least one-third of his time is devoted to such activities, including teaching an introductory course in conservation for librarians at the Graduate School of Library Science at the University of Illinois in 1971 and 1973—that Captain Cunha failed to mention on Sunday—and including in-house training of conservation specialists who now work at the New York Public Library and the Library of Congress as well as at the Newberry. For years he has been working to establish a formal education program for conservators, as distinct from conservation specialists, but as yet to no avail.

While Banks goes much further than Liebert, by claiming we should spend at least as much money on conservation as we do on acquisitions, we do not meet his standards. But we do spend a great deal more than Mr. Liebert's formula of one cent for each dollar of acquisitions. Our conservation budget for 1973–74 for salaries alone is more than ten percent of our entire salaries budget and equals about thirty three cents on the dollar for acquisitions. We charge each of our book funds not only for acquisition costs, but also for conservation costs, despite the howls of protest from the custodians of those funds.

And we do have a plan, however insubstantial it may seem. Years ago, in addition to supporting some of Dr. Richard Smith's research, we had him do a profile of our general collection and the acid content of its paper as well as the fold factor. We then worked out a basic formula for applying the results which, because of the cost, has never been formally adopted, but which is nevertheless being implemented within the limits of our financial resources. It recognizes that, despite the fact we are a library of record, and all records are equal, some records are more equal than others. Thus, our great local and family history collection, which was in as bad condition as the New York Public Library's five years ago, is now revitalized by $300,000 worth of bound Xeroxed copies that will last 300 years instead of thirty. That's at the lower end of the scale, preserving the word not the artifacts. At the other end, we have a $14,000 grant from the National Endowment for the Arts to conserve our great 19th-century Indian drawings on lousy paper. Similarly, we had a resident art conservator for twelve months who cleaned and conserved most of our great Indian oil portraits.

But after 10 years of modest Herculean efforts (that must be a contradiction, but is real), I know that I am just a little Dutch boy with his finger in a dike. All we have really done is to identify the major desiderata in conservation. In our opinion they are:

1. The development of a formal, university-connected training program for conservators to establish the profession on a solid foundation.

2. The training of a large number of conservation specialists in paper conservation, book repair, rebinding, and fine binding.

3. The creation of a series of regional cooperative conservation centers, such as Captain Cunha's, that will realize the economies of scale inherent in having a large staff of specialists who can develop a production line for the repair of rare materials.

4. A major breakthrough in deacidification and (it is to be hoped) restrengthening of paper as exemplified in the dissertation of Richard Smith, by the experiments of the Barrow Research Laboratory outlined by Mr. Walker on Sunday, and by experiments in the Library of Congress.

When these goals have been achieved, we will then be able to have a proper blend of in-house preventive conservation and centralized cooperative restoration. Both are badly needed.

THE ART OF THE ANTIQUARIAN BOOK

DEALER

This review of the memoirs of David Randall, an antiquarian bookdealer, and founding librarian of the Lilly Library, is a tribute to the breed. As one of the chief buyers of rare books in Chicago, Towner rapidly got to know antiquarian bookdealers in the city and in time throughout the world. They were his antagonists, in one sense, because the Library's budget forced him to strive for the best deal possible. But their passion for books and learning and their eagerness to show him good stuff were to his liking, and he formed lasting friendships with many. He thought of the bookman as an indispensable "catalyst" in extracting rare books from one collection and placing them in another.

BACK IN THE DAYS when young men signed indentures of apprenticeship, their contracts usually included the words, "the art and mystery of . . ." whatever trade they were being apprenticed to. Perhaps no other words—and both are necessary—describe as well the trade of antiquarian book dealer. One cannot learn it in college, but only by an extensive apprenticeship. Formal courses in such fields as literature, history, and languages, in fact, any and all fields of knowledge, from the most general to the most esoteric, all help, of course. But antiquarian bookmanship is an "art and mystery" not susceptible to formal analysis for instruction and learning: one must live it to learn it.

This fact illustrates both the weakness and the strength of David Randall's memoirs of nearly three decades as a rare book dealer, 1929–1956. On the one hand, there is no sustained organizational pattern to them. Sure enough, he begins at the beginning, with his informal apprenticeship, and he ends at the end, with his ties to the

A review of David A. Randall's *Dukedom Large Enough* (New York: Random House, 1969), in *Chicago Daily News* (30–31 August 1969).

great collector J. K. Lilly, Jr., that resulted in his appointment to the Lilly Library at Indiana University. But in between there is a potpourri of anecdotes about authors (dead or alive), individual great books, collectors and collections. On the other hand, because the memoirs are anecdotal rather than analytical, and because, as a rare book dealer, Mr. Randall handled a large number of great books and manuscripts in many collecting fields, under a variety of circumstances, and coped with many important collectors, every bookman, whether collector, librarian, auction house employee, or dealer, will find them of great interest.

If one thinks of the scholarly article, monograph, or biography as the end result of a process that begins with research in libraries and private collections, then he will not understand the world of the bookman, as most scholars do not. The bookman's world of activities precedes that of the scholar, although it often draws upon scholarship and often draws scholars into its orbit. But one can be a vigorous user of libraries, a historian, a university professor, and an editor of a scholarly journal without really penetrating or being very cognizant of the bookman's world. But if one becomes a librarian who cares for the collections that bookmen create, then all the little bits and pieces of bookmanship floating below the horizon of consciousness come into view.

This is what David Randall's book is all about: how and why men (and institutions) get excited about certain authors, books, manuscripts, and collections, and about such esoteric things as first issues of first editions, the difference between uncut and unopened, the meaning of cancels, the relative value of an autograph letter signed and a letter signed, and the like.

The role of the dealer in all this is quite simple. He is the catalyst. He must extract from one collection the books and manuscripts he wishes to place in another. He sells these items for more than he pays for them and lives off the difference. In the process, he travels widely, meets fascinating people, eats great meals, drinks great wines, handles the truly great written and printed products of civilization, and becomes erudite, urbane, and once in a while, rich. Rare books is one of the last strongholds of the individual entrepreneur.

But don't resign your job to become an antiquarian book dealer. It takes capital, my friend, and it takes a long and expensive—for somebody—apprenticeship. You must have a tremendous appetite and memory for what seems to be trivia—"points" they are called— about thousands of books. You must have a gambler's instinct about what will sell and what will not: you must be prepared to reinvest what you make on successful deals in other books and manuscripts you may not move for years. You must have considerable knowledge of the contemporary scene—who are the people and institutions collecting what, or who ought to be collecting what—along with an even greater knowledge of what is collectable. You have to be prepared for the fact that your best laid plans to place a book or a collection where it ought to be can be circumvented by the present owner, by the competition, by the state of the stock market, by the bullheadedness of a librarian, by the reluctance of a given set of trustees, and by the failure of your own bookman's instinct. And when you come to write your memoirs, your best stories are likely to be the ones against yourself.

It is into this world that David Randall takes the reader with candor and good humor. There are few alive today better prepared to do so.

GENEALOGY AT THE NEWBERRY: THE

SERVICE THAT CAME IN OUT OF THE

COLD

Towner's handling of the Newberry's genealogy collection is an example of turning a problem into an opportunity—one of his favorite phrases. The Newberry had the best collection of genealogy and local history in the Midwest. Genealogists, when he arrived, put in the largest number of "user-days" at the Library. But the books in the collection were literally falling apart, and the yield to scholarship from the genealogists was disproportionate to the costs.

The first Towner came to New England in 1686 and Bill's father had compiled the family genealogy, but Bill was no ancestor worshipper. As a scholar of New England, however, he learned the value of genealogies in tracing obscure people.

In this talk before the Chicago chapter of the Mayflower Society he describes the way the Newberry literally rescued its genealogy collection from decay and then turned materials intended for one use into the data base for the Family and Community History Center. Under the direction of Richard J. Jensen and later directors these materials were then put to creative scholarly use for a burgeoning subfield of social history.

IT IS ALWAYS a dilemma for a public speaker as to whether it is worse to speak before dinner, when everybody is waiting for a cocktail, or after dinner, when everyone is falling asleep. But your Governor, when giving me instructions tonight said, "Your job is to talk, Bill, and theirs is to listen. If they finish before you do, you can go home."

When my children were young, I used to drive them to distraction by saying "you know, in two or three steps you can get from any one

"Informal Remarks on the Service That Came [in] Out of the Cold: Genealogy at the Newberry Library, 1962–1983," *Mayflower News* (Society of Mayflower Descendants in the State of Illinois) 20, no. 1 (May 1984): 2–4. Reprinted with permission.

thing to any other thing, just using logic and your imagination."
They just couldn't understand the marvelous "logic" with which I
moved from one subject to another. The one I remember particularly
is asparagus, because we had one daughter who hated asparagus, and
she always hid it in her shoe rather than eat it. I remember her trying
to distract me by asking, "How do you get from asparagus to the
man in the moon in three steps?" I said it was very simple. Asparagus comes in sticks, doesn't it? Right. And you use a stick for pole-
vaulting, don't you? Right. Well that is one hell of a pole vault for
the man in the moon. (It *was* kind of disgusting, I admit, but they
liked it).

Well I am sort of doing that tonight. I have brought along a series
of odds and ends, and I am going to try to put them together into a
story. Here is a stone, and here is an issue of *Psychology Today* from
April, 1981. Here is a xerox of a title page of a recent publication
from the Newberry. Here is a letter to the editor of the *New York
Times Magazine*, October 13, 1957. And here is a copy of the first
folio volume published in America, Samuel Willard's *Compleat
Body of Divinity*, Boston, 1726. It took two printers to do it, as no
one printer had that much type. (They got into trouble with the
pagination, for there were about 50 pages where the numbers over-
lap.) These are the items I am going to try to pull together tonight.

I am not a Mayflower descendant, so far as I know. Last night I
pulled off my shelves the *Log of the Mayflower*, and three different
editions of *Bradford's Journal*, Samuel Morison's edition, the great
two-volume edition published by the Massachusetts Historical Society, and the first printed edition, published by the State of Massachusetts in the nineteenth century. Then I pulled out the genealogy
my father did of our family and looked at the early wives of the first
three Towners in this country. We came in 1686, a little bit late for
the *Mayflower*. And I couldn't find a single name that looked like it
was a name that had been on the *Mayflower*, so I gave up. I didn't do
a thorough genealogical research, in other words. But I am sympathetic. I am a fellow traveler of you *Mayflower* descendants.

As evidence of that I have the letter I mentioned to the Editor of
The New York Times Magazine for October 13, 1957. I was at that
point an arrogant young man (now I am an arrogant old man) teaching at the College of William and Mary at the time of the 350th
anniversary of Jamestown. Some Virginians were claiming Virginia
was the cradle of democracy and at the same time working diligently to obstruct *Brown* v. *Board of Education* trying to keep the
schools segregated. A distinguished editor of *The Richmond Times*

Dispatch, Virginius Dabney, wrote an article in *The New York Times Magazine* in which he said he couldn't understand why Americans paid so much attention to the Pilgrims. After all, the people of Jamestown got here first. Jamestown, not Plymouth was the cradle of democracy.

That made me pretty irritated. And, as I say, in my arrogance, I wrote back. "It might have occurred to Mr. Dabney that almost every section if not every state on the seaboard has had its local boosters, not only among editors but among historians. But more important than undue local pride in assessing the Pilgrims' hold on American views of the past is the fact that the Pilgrims' story appeals to the image of our better selves which we would like to keep untarnished. Those pious and simple folk were largely moved by non material forces to hazard their lives and their families' lives in the new world. It was the overriding consciousness of their obligation to God and their desire to worship him according to the best light that brought them here. Not gold. Not land, not empire. That is their mystery and that is their attraction for us."

That letter made me sort of *personna non grata* in Williamsburg, Virginia, believe me. So that's where I start. I am a fellow traveler of you *"Mayflowers,"* even though I am not qualified to get on the ship.

On last October 15, just a month ago, Rachel and I buried the mortal remains of our eldest son, 31 years of age, in a little Wisconsin river town across the Mississippi from Winona, Minnesota. His headstone is on the family plot that I bought when—my father and mother having died—I became a representative of the oldest generation in my family. There in a country cemetery in Trempealeau Township, when I am buried at last, will lie my son, Larry; his father Lawrence; his grandfather, Earl; his great grandfather, Elmer; his great, great grandfather, Johnathan; and his great, great, great grandfather Aaron—all in one little country graveyard. Nearby is the farm that Aaron homesteaded in 1857 and which has been occupied by a Towner ever since. This stone I brought along is from that homestead's barn.

Aaron himself, 1800–1873, was the sixth generation Towner in America, having been preceded by Gershom, another Gershom, Phinneas, John, and finally, Richard, who came from Sussex County in England to Guilford, Connecticut, in 1686 where he named Towner's Swamp and Towner's cave. Legend has it that he lived in the cave in the swamp. Now Richard, my progenitor in this country, had a second son besides John, named Benjamin. It was in Benjamin's line for eight generations that the swamp, the cave, the land,

and the home, stayed until ten years ago. The son of the last owner, the same generation as my father, but separated by eight generations from their common ancestor, walked into my office about five years ago, and, except for six inches in height, he was a dead ringer for my father. Eight generations! And it wasn't just I who thought so. My daughter, who happened to be passing the door said, "He looks just like grandpa." So genealogy means something to me!

I suspect the interest hit me about the same time it hits most of us who cannot claim famous or infamous ancestors: when we become the oldest and want to know who we are and where we came from. I think, in fact, that the pressure to know who we are and where we came from is increasingly powerful as each generation matures in this century. I say that, because we seem to have a less and less certain future.

When I was a kid there were two great oceans there, and we felt invulnerable behind those oceans. But we are no longer invulnerable. The national resources of this country seemed to be limitless and virtually untouched. But we now know we have squandered those resources, not only our own heritage but our children's heritage. And we are but 45 minutes from a possible final holocaust. Because of these things, we have a less and less certain future, every generation. And so we look for a more certain and more usable past.

We all know, as well, that for the last twenty-five years the great institution of the family has been under constant and unremitting assault. (Among those who assaulted it were my four oldest, then adolescent, children of the 'sixties. Now two of them are married, have three children each, and think the family is the greatest thing since ice cream.) A description of the changed attitudes in our society towards the family occurs in the magazine *Psychology Today* (April 1981)—one of my artifacts for tonight. Daniel Yankelovich, in a very fascinating article called "The World Turned Upside Down," reports that a generation ago 75–85% of American families consisted of a male breadwinner, a mother, and children at home. Today, it is just about the reverse. The family has indeed changed.

I have to admit that I have not always felt this sympathetic towards genealogy. I was trained as a professional historian by professional historians in the 1940s. I shared their disdainful attitude towards genealogists and patriotic societies, the latter so sadly misrepresented and caricatured by one grossly vulgar act, the refusal of the Daughters of the American Revolution to allow the great Marion Anderson to sing in Constitution Hall in 1936. As a liberal historian of the 1940s, I didn't like the memory of that.

So when I came to the Newberry in 1962, too young to have a personal interest in genealogy and carrying with me at least the residue of a prejudice against it learned in graduate school, the genealogical collection and those who used it seemed to represent a problem rather than an opportunity. Even the arrangement at the Newberry Library seemed to agree with that assessment. The genealogical reading room was on the third floor, almost hidden from the public, isolated from the "scholars" who used the second floor. They didn't have the public card catalog available to them, for that was on the second floor. They only had a "catalog" for the genealogy collection. The late and dearly-lamented Joseph Wolf (whom we called Sir Joe, for he was indeed made a Knight of Malta because of his great knowledge of heraldry), and his handmaiden, Ellen Chase, of indeterminate age, a great person, presided over that collection and provided the only real access to it.

At first blush that seemed fair enough. Only genealogists were admitted without any determination of their skill in the use of a library, without any academic attainment to their credit, and without any requirement that they be working on some research project appropriate to the Newberry Library that might potentially enlarge or alter the received knowledge of the day. Their work was purely personal, almost never got published, and often seemed designed only to qualify them for admission to a patriotic society or societies because of the accident of birth, not because of any inherent virtue or performance.

This attitude of historians towards genealogists—and the return hostility—didn't really exist in the nineteenth century, when history and genealogy were little different from each other in method and when they were both the province of gentlemen scholars, not of professional historians.

But towards the end of the nineteenth century, as the influence of the German universities came to this country, and the seminar was introduced into the university, and history became a profession, and the people who taught history in the universities were no longer professors of moral philosophy but professors of history, history itself became professionalized, and genealogy was left out in the cold. An orphan. Worse than that, a changeling, an abandoned child on the front steps of academe.

But my own interest in genealogical materials and local history and vital records had been stimulated by my interest in the family as a socializing institution for the poor, the non-English Europeans, the criminal, the unskilled, the debtor, the Indian, and the Black. It was the family that incorporated these people into Puritan society in the seventeenth and eighteenth centuries, through the institutions of apprenticeship, poor apprenticeship, indentured servitude, penal servitude, and Indian and Black servanthood and/or slavery. All were incorporated into Puritan society through the family.

Which brings up Samuel Willard's *A Compleat Body of Divinity*, 250 expository lectures on the Assembly's Shorter Catechism. There we find that under the Fifth Commandment, "Honor thy father and thy mother that thy days may be long upon the land which the Lord thy God giveth thee," this *summa theologica* of New England thought discusses *the order that lies in society:* the governance of husband over wife, or parent over child, and of master over servant. So I used this work to help explain how the Puritans viewed the family as a socializing institution.

This copy is very badly damaged. I spent maybe a dozen Saturdays on Cornhill Road in Boston looking at this book and lusting for it when I was a graduate student. Finally the bookseller said "Would you like to buy that book?" and I said "Yes, but I can't afford it." He said "it is in terrible shape." And I said, "I know." He said, "it smells." I said, "I know, it's moldy." "It's got worm holes in it." I said, "I know." "Half the title page is missing." I said, "I know." "Would you give me five dollars for it?" I said, "I sure would."

So when I came here I was able to view the genealogical collections and the genealogists from my own experience in doing research on the family, per se, and see the collection and the genealogists as an opportunity rather than as a problem. It is still my dream, before I retire, to harness the historian and the genealogist to the same yoke to plow the fields of history together, in the harmony of a mutual endeavor.

A lot of people who were doing genealogical research at the Newberry when I first came here didn't believe that. There were all kinds of rumors circulated around that I was anti-genealogy. And, indeed, we did have a very serious report made by a very good librarian, recommending that we either go out and raise a hell of a lot of money or else get rid of the collection. The books were falling apart. A lot of the books that you people used in order to determine your right to stand up when Mr. Brewster's name was read were falling apart, because they were printed on bad nineteenth-century paper, filled with acid and because they were abusively overused, not read, just used. You could go up to our reading room on any Saturday after we had had the "invasion" and look at the floor. You would see confetti spread from one wall to the other. Those books were just crumbling apart: they were a disaster.

As a consequence of that disaster, as you may know, we have become one of the leading libraries in the country in the field of book conservation. *We had to,* for three-fourths of our collection was at risk.

And we have been recognized for that leadership, for example, by the Pew Memorial Trust, which gave us $250,000 to establish our new conservation lab and bindery on the fifth floor, one of the finest facilities in the world. Our former Conservator is running the first degree program in the field of book conservation at Columbia University and New York University. The Andrew W. Mellon Foundation has challenged us to raise $1,200,000 to endow our conservation program. And our new $6,500,000 bookstack building is designed to deter or slow down the process of book deterioration by maintaining a constant temperature of 60°F and a relative humidity of 50%.

So we have spent a lot of money to preserve what we have and what you need. But there was no funding for new books. There was little apparent interest—we test marketed the genealogy department and we got very little response. We wrote to everybody who had been in the department one year and asked if they didn't want to form a special society to support the Genealogical Collection. Some people were willing, but not enough to warrant doing it. And no support from the opposite side, that is from the foundations that support scholarly research.

We tried very hard to get a program going in the history of the family that would galvanize the Rockefellers, the Carnegies, and the Mellons into supporting research in this field at the Newberry. We brought Sigmund Diamond, a very distinguished historian from Columbia University, for a semester. We brought William R. Taylor, a very distinguished historian at the University of Wisconsin, now at SUNY, Stony Brook, for a year. But nothing happened. Then, after about ten years, all of [a] sudden everything began to happen. Joe Wolf, negotiated a treaty with the Ft. Wayne and Allen County Public Library that was endeavoring to establish a genealogical collection. They xeroxed thousands of volumes of our sick books and gave us xerox copies on permanent and durable paper, sturdily bound. That saved the core of the genealogy collection, step one! Then, we moved the genealogical reading room to the second floor, right next to the Main Reading Room. That was step two. Then we were lucky and we got some people to give us endowment funds to buy books; the Kenneth L. Burgess fund of $100,000; the Mark Morton fund of $50,000; the Frank H. Woods fund of $25,000. These were the first endowment funds for that purpose and *that* was the third step. (Eventually, a bequest of $500,000 will be made available for local and family history to buy books and to support research.)

The fourth step was to create from among professional historians the Family and Community History Center started about ten years ago. The Center has raised over $2 million in grants for various research and education projects, including teaching 500 historians how to use the computer in quantitative analysis in doing historical research. Through its Chicago Metro History Fair, the Center has reached high school students in more than 100 high schools in this city (last year alone, 4,000 students participated) to introduce them to the joy of doing family and neighborhood history so that they won't think of history as just a bunch of dates to remember, but rather as a method of inquiry.

Currently we have two research grants in the Family and Community History Center. One is to study the French in Illinois in two communities in the nineteenth century and the other is to study the origins of the working class in Chicago, 1850–1870. And we have had two grants of $50,000 each from the Dr. Scholl Foundation to endow the Center.

In the future we have to get direct access to that fantastic microfilm collection of local records that is in the mountains back in Utah. I am sure many of you have been to Salt Lake City and used the Mormon Library with the huge number of microfilm readers. (We could use some more at the Newberry, by the way). Now you either have to go to Salt Lake City to get access to them or you have to go to a temple library and order them by mail. But there seems to be a little bit of glacial movement towards having them available through research libraries.

I seem to have one artifact left over. Ah, yes, it is a xerox of the title page of a recent Newberry publication, an index to our multivolume checklist of maps of the Midwest printed before 1900. Here is a guide, and a location symbol, to every known map covering the whole or a part of the Midwest from the first map down to the end of the last century. What a useful tool this should be for you, along with our study of midwest county boundary changes from 1790 to 1970! Between these two tools, you should be able to locate a lot of ancestors!

So in the future, we will continue to harness the energy of genealogists (and their sense of inquiry and of mystery and their question marks) and the historians together in joint enterprises to find out the answers to questions we have to ask about the past. And I take great pride in the fact you can look into the Main Reading Room today and you can't tell a genealogist from an historian—they are not separated, they are both using the card catalog. (The genealogist may be using more books—otherwise you can't tell one from the other). And I think, therefore, it is fair to say that genealogical service at the Newberry Library is a service that has come in out of the cold. Thank you.

16

AN END TO INNOCENCE

For a librarian who had devoted his life to building "a community of scholars," the "plague" of thefts in the library world in the 1980s was painful. This essay is as engrossing as the detective work the thefts unfortunately entailed.

Towner, a tough-minded idealist, asks librarians to accept their own responsibility for their plight. Deeply conscious of the experience of the United States in the forty years of Cold War he worried whether "the security measures, like national security measures [will] possibly destroy the liberty we seek to defend." But in posing the question this way, he helped librarians to think through ways of coping with the problem that would not destroy the trust on which the scholarly community was built.

IN THE QUARTER CENTURY that I was a librarian, from 1962 through 1986, vast changes occurred in the library world. The period was really a series of revolutions in which hardly an aspect of librarianship remained unaffected. Think of it—computers and preservation technology; drastic changes in funding sources, dollar value, and material costs; tenure-driven demands on research libraries; and copyright issues.

Most of these stresses and strains can be quantified in millions of dollars. But one evolving change—with its own costs—has potentially graver and more insidious consequences than any of the others. It is the emergence of the theft of library materials as a plague throughout the world of libraries.

This change, marked by the increased vulnerability of library materials to theft, is illustrated by the case of Charles Merrill Mount, a Washington, D.C., writer and artist and an alleged manuscript thief. As the story was summed up in the *New York Times* (Oct. 13, 1987), Merrill was charged with the interstate transport of manu-

From *American Libraries* 19, no. 3 (March 1988): 210–13. Originally delivered as the keynote address at a Conference on Library Security at Oberlin College, 20 September 1983. Reprinted with permission.

scripts from the Library of Congress and the National Archives, where he was "well known" as a "registered researcher."

As Daniel Boorstin, then Librarian of Congress, put it, "A scholarly eminence and Ph.D. degree is no certificate of virtue." But it used to be!

Dean Neal, executive director of the Society of American Archivists, was paraphrased in the same *Times* story as saying that "the trust formerly placed in the scholar and the air of collegiality that has been a hallmark of the academic and archival world are both rapidly disappearing." "We've been burned too many times," he added.

"Too many times" is indeed the key. One has only to remember the remnants of book chains that once secured books to reading tables in ancient libraries to know that book theft is no new phenomenon. It is as old as books themselves. But what was once only an endemic disease has in a quarter of a century become a virulent epidemic of unknown proportions.

The theft of unique manuscripts and maps, rare books, and even of current books and journals puts obstacles in the way of learning and scholarship, sometimes forever and universally, other times temporarily and locally. It steals from the many for the use of the few, whether it be for illegal resale or private use. And we are all the losers. What had been gathered and preserved for public purposes is stolen for the most selfish of reasons. This alone is intolerable and needs to be stopped.

TRUST IS THE REAL VICTIM

But in a larger sense, the real victim of book theft is far greater than the disappearance, temporary or permanent, of materials for study and research. The real victim is trust—that fragile net that for so long and so lovingly has held the library, its staff, the scholarly user, the book collector, and the bookseller together. It is trust that sustains all those whose purpose it is to collect, preserve, and make freely available our common human heritage so that scholars can constantly redefine and reinterpret our usable past. As we permit that priceless trust to dissipate, we all become losers, and the Republic of Letters is itself imperiled.

The most terrible loss occasioned by book thefts, therefore, is in the fullest sense spiritual. Trust is replaced by mistrust. This is a moral tragedy. It is so acidic, so destructive, and it is becoming so pervasive that it may well destroy what we most desire to defend. At best it will be—already is—terribly costly; at worst it is making us view each other not as concerned friends engaged in a common task, but rather as potential enemies, an attitude that can undermine our common purpose: the advancement and dissemination of knowledge.

How can this be happening? It would be easy to blame only those dishonest individuals, those numerous discovered and as yet undiscovered thieves who steal from us all. And certainly our major tasks are to track them down and to stop them, and to reduce the opportunity for additional thieves to appear and operate among us. To go to the other extreme, we might lay the blame for this tragedy on the corrupt, materialistic, and amoral society in which we live—on the times themselves.

Librarians Share the Blame

Whatever the cause, I want to share with you my feeling that we librarians must certainly assume a significant part of the blame for the thievery in our midst. An indifference compounded by innocence, ignorance, and complacency has allowed and even encouraged the current wave of thefts from our precious heritage. We are too belatedly coming to realize, as J. W. Griffith reminded us in the April 1978 *American Libraries*, that "Book losses in [our libraries] . . . probably aren't as bad as . . . [we] think. More than likely, they are much worse." So catch the thieves we must, stop the thieving we must; but to do this we librarians must put our own houses in order. Let me illustrate from my own experiences.

In the early 1970s, asked to preside over a session on security held among rare book librarians, I developed a 52-point questionnaire to circulate in advance among the participants, with a promise that I would eventually disseminate the quantified results. But the results of that questionnaire—which did not even include the basic question "Do you require positive identification of all readers?"—were so devastating (one librarian wisely refused to respond) that I could only summarize them orally at the conference and then lock them up, eventually to destroy them.

Certainly *then*, if to a lesser extent *now*, we librarians were guilty of neglect. We embraced the prevailing idea of mutual trust; or we were unwilling to risk offending our readers or alienating our staff; and, even if our eyes were opening, we were unable to turn up the new dollars, or unwilling to transfer the old dollars, so as to provide truly adequate security.

I believe my former institution in the 1960s may be instructive in this regard. Shortly before I left for the Newberry Library in 1962, readers we "knew and trusted" were allowed to work in our rare books stacks. This changed when a dealer returned a book that he had once sold to us, which had been subsequently sold back to him by a respected reader—I believe a gentleman of the cloth—who had worked in our collections. Did we prosecute the reader? No; we simply closed those stacks to all readers, and to this day I do not know if that thief knows that we know.

When I arrived at the Newberry, the only guard was a retired policeman at a small desk at the door, who presumably checked readers' tickets and examined their briefcases. But the back door was unlocked and unsupervised, and was used by staff and "old-hand readers" alike. Fortunately, we had closed book stacks and a non-circulating collection.

But our closed book stacks—rare books, special collections, and general collections—were then scattered on six floors in a block-long building behind 23 locked doors. Pages, paid at the minimum wage, had virtually unsupervised access to them. The general collections stacks were also open on a need-to-use basis to some trusted readers. The books from the general stacks were paged through public corridors and elevators. Key blanks to the locks were available at the local hardware stores!

Positive identification was not required of persons who claimed they were Ph.D. candidates, or professors, or genealogists. Only the undergraduate and the occasional high school student was required to have a letter of introduction. Staff could carry grocery bags and even wrapped packages in and out with minimum scrutiny.

In the 1960s, then, our complacency about thefts, *even when we learned of them,* left us far too vulnerable. To this day, I do not completely understand that complacency, although certainly I shared it. Part of it stemmed, I believe, from the advice of legal counsel, who seemed to advise us against legal action for fear of false-arrest suits, or who believed that evidence for conviction would be unobtainable. Dismissal of an employee or barring a reader from admission was about as far as we were advised to go without hard, red-handed evidence, and even those actions could not be taken on mere suspicion.

Part of that complacency stemmed from a perhaps understandable misconception on our part: as humanists, we felt that persons we suspected of thievery were not really thieves, but emotionally disturbed persons who, when confronted with their acts—and not prosecuted—might avoid such transgressions in the future. How could a lover of scholarship be a book thief? In retrospect, how could we have been so innocent?

Like other libraries, we were in the 1960s—and still are, of course—more vulnerable to our staff than to our readers. How did we handle the problem?

Brown-Bag "Borrowing"

The case of one problem employee was particularly disturbing. There was enough evidence in that person's desk to indicate that the employee and the employee's roommate lived in a make-believe world of conspiracy that involved their writing incoherent letters to civic leaders, university presidents, and even one of our own trustees with accusations of the most unlikely behavior. During intensive and excruciatingly painful questioning, the employee broke down and wept before us, admitted "borrowing" uncataloged books by carrying them out hidden in bags of groceries. The books were returned and the employee was dismissed, but *not prosecuted*. It was a terrible experience.

In a second instance, a well-read member of our custodial staff was alleged to have dozens of Newberry books in his apartment. If I remember correctly, when we inquired of counsel concerning a search warrant, we were dissuaded from pursuing the matter. The evidence—if any—was too flimsy, and the possibility of a suit too likely; so we dropped it. He eventually quit.

In a third instance, a staff member was discovered removing printed call letters from the spines of some books. Little explanation was offered for that bizarre behavior, but again we were advised against going to the police, and, since the employee was leaving the library, *nothing* was done.

Thus, in three cases in the 1960s, we were too soft-hearted, indeed *too soft-headed* to prosecute. Did we come close to misprision of felony in these cases? It doesn't bear thinking upon in the dark of the night.

Rarely Rough on Readers

Nor were we tougher with our readers in the 1960s. We never did identify or catch the reader who was seen tossing a book out a window to a confederate. All of our windows are now locked. We didn't bar an old-time reader whom we knew was borrowing and returning books he was using for his dissertation; we just told him to stop. And despite the provocative suggestion of one suspected thief, we did not strip-search him—he had acted suspiciously in Special Collections and was probably the one who "wet-stringed" a title page from a rare pamphlet. We simply confronted him with our suspicions and banned him from the library. (We later learned that several libraries and booksellers had also banned him from *their* premises.)

A more recent case shows that we are tougher now than we were in the '60s, but it also illustrates how time-consuming the catching of a thief can be. An excepted version of our security officer's report is given in the accompanying box. I have changed the names, since the case is still open.

How long it has taken us all to wake up. At the Newberry we started getting religion when the "brothers" (two thieves disguised as monks) stole the atlases and other books from Yale; when the Gutenberg Bible was dropped into the Widener Library's center well by a would-be thief; when the professor from Tulane stole maps from us, among others; and when two maps were removed from early editions of our Champlain voyages, along with other similar maps from other libraries.

Our conversion to the true faith was completed more recently when it was revealed that some $500,000 worth of rare books and manuscripts had been stolen from a local library, apparently over a period of years, with the apparently innocent connivance of a now-deceased staff member.

The dollar cost of this security consciousness is already high and it will grow higher. It will eat into our budgets for service and acquisitions. But I will not—in fact, dare not—reveal publicly the steps those costs include. I can mention a security audit, a high-security stack building, a full-time professionally experienced security officer, significant annual costs for collections insurance, a planned regular program of shelf reading, stack attendants for the few readers admitted to the stacks, greater surveillance in the reading room, and far greater surveillance at the exit desk.

But even with these measures, we will still be vulnerable not only to the clever and determined thief but also to our own staff, people we work with every day, whose birthdays and weddings and new babies we celebrate, whose deaths we mourn, and who are united with us in their dedication not only to scholarship but also to the institution we jointly serve. Are there thieves among us? Oh God, we do not know. What it would cost in dollars, and even more important, in morale, to test our staff by one of various methods available—polygraph or so-called pencil and paper test—can only be imagined.

To Catch a Thief: What's Involved
A Security Officer's Report

On Saturday, December 18, 1982, the following book was taken from the Special Collection Reading Room: *The Epistles of Jacob Boehme.*

The book was paged and delivered to a gentleman who signed into the Library as Mr. George Dumond at 12:17 p.m. The book was not returned to the Reading Room desk.

On Monday, December 20, 1982, the missing book was reported to me. A search of the admission applications revealed no application for the name George Dumond; however, I found an application for a Mr. Gene Dulane with similar handwriting. The address for Mr. Dulane was in the same area of the city as the address listed on the call slip for Mr. Dumond. . . .

Mr. Dulane had claimed academic affiliation with the University of Chicago; but the University of Chicago had no such person listed as a faculty member, staff member, or student. Mr. Dulane had presented an Illinois Driver's License when applying for his card on July 17, 1982, and I confirmed his address with the Department of Motor Vehicle Registration. On December 20, 1982, I sent Mr. Dulane a letter via certified mail which was returned unclaimed on January 7, 1983.

On December 29, 1982, after receiving no response from Mr. Dulane, and after being unable to contact him by phone, I called the Chicago Police Department. The Police Officer . . . filed a case report on the stolen book . . . The case was assigned to the Chicago Police Department Area 6 Investigators . . . On January 4, 1983, an Investigator delivered the original documents (call slip, sign-in sheet, and Application for Admission) to the Chicago Police Department Crime Laboratory. On January 25, 1983, the Chicago Police Department Crime Laboratory issued a report stating that in their opinion all items submitted for examination were completed by the same person. On Saturday, January 21, 1983, Mr. Dulane came to the Library and he was refused admission by the Kiosk Attendant and by the Duty Officer.

On January 28, 1983, I signed a complaint in the Circuit Court of Cook County, Branch 42, charging Mr. Dulane with felony theft. The case has been continued several times, and a felony warrant is currently outstanding. . . .

On May 9, 1983, the book was returned to the Library . . . through the United States mail. The binding had been broken and the bookplate had been removed. There is an incoherent sentence penciled on a blank leaf in the back of the book. I am holding the book while the Chicago Police Department Investigators decide whether to have it sent to their Crime Laboratory.

To be sure, most of our security costs can be measured in dollars. But how can we measure the human costs of the now-pervasive suspicion of readers, staff, and of book dealers?

I can only give you an example. While I was still in charge of the library, we had to dismiss a staff member for *non*-security reasons. On the date we told the staff member of the dismissal—*not on the date it was effective*—we canceled stack access for the remainder of that person's tenure. What caused me to impose that humiliation? Was it fear that, even though a known lover of books, that person might damage or destroy or steal the rare books otherwise still accessible? What did that act do to that person? What did that act do to me? What does that act do to all of us?

For us it imposes a dilemma. Can we afford to introduce Orwell's *1984* into a library dedicated to the humanities? Worse yet, can we afford not to? Will library security measures, like national security measures, possibly destroy the liberty we wish to defend?

The answer to that question, like the assurance of salvation to the Puritans, is probably unknowable. But as the late Perry Miller wrote about those Puritans in *The New England Mind: The Seventeen Century*, the elect "are to be saved for trying, not for succeeding, whereas the reprobate are eternally damned, not for failing, but for not trying."

Let us all try, in this Republic of Letters, to join the elect, for trying, and avoid being among the damned, for not.

17

AN EXCITING AND INCREDIBLY

REWARDING TWENTY YEARS

In this annual report for the year ending 30 June, 1982, Towner summed up twenty years at the Newberry. The report can be read in conjunction with selection 11, "A Plan for the Newberry Library" of 1971, to measure the extent to which he had achieved his goals. Almost all the major projects had been completed save for the renovation of the "old Library building" which would be completed by the time of his retirement in 1986.

THIS *Annual Report* COVERS MOST OF my twentieth year as operating head of the Newberry Library. I am confident of my arithmetic, because my twin sons will be twenty on August 30. My wife Rachel and I and our then four children drove into Chicago from Cambridge via Williamsburg on the 28th of August, our furniture arrived on the 29th, our fifth and sixth children were born on the 30th—one a complete surprise—and I started as Librarian on September 1, 1962. It was a busy week.

It seems appropriate to review the main trends of the Library's development in that twenty years under the leadership of four Trustee Chairmen—Everett D. Graff, Hermon Dunlap Smith, Edward F. Blettner, and Chalkley Jay Hambleton—and with the support of a dedicated board of Trustees, a splendid staff, and philanthropists and book lovers—individuals, corporations, foundations, and the National Endowment for the Humanities—in greater Chicago and throughout the nation. They have all been aiders and abettors in accomplishing what we collectively chose to do.

It is a truism that a living library is never complete. It must regularly augment its research materials and the tools that enable them to be used effectively—modern scholarly works—if it is to remain vital. On a modest annual book budget (varying from $200,000 to

From *Newberry Library Annual Report for Year Ending 30 June 1982*, 2–5.

$350,000), the Library has added by purchase, gift, and bequest, by individual title and by *en bloc* acquisition, library materials worth some $15 million since 1962. I can only mention a few of the major acquisitions here; but in reading them, one should never overlook the importance of painstaking book selection, one by one, by skilled bibliographers. Theirs is the true scholarship in action. My role has largely been confined to helping with the acquisition of collections, both gifts and purchases.

Pride of place still goes to the 1964 purchase of the great Louis H. Silver collection of Renaissance literature and English literary first editions, for $2,687,000, and to the bequest of the splendid Everett D. Graff collection of Western Americana, valued in 1964 at $1.2 million. That was a big year! From the duplicates later sold at auction in London and New York, we raised money that was largely spent on still other acquisitions.

There following the Deering Collection of early Americana; the Driscoll Collection of American sheet music; the Novacco Collection of 16th-Century Italian printed maps and the Sack Collection of 17th- and 18th-Century maps; the Alfred Cortot collection of music theory; continuation of the Malcolm Cowley papers; the Stone and Kimball Collection; the Recusant Collection; the Pullman Company archives; the transfer from deposit status to gift status of the archives of the Chicago Burlington & Quincy Railroad; the Herbert R. Strauss Collection of Jefferson materials; the William M. Spencer Collection of Napoleon manuscripts; the Jane Dick Collection of the manuscripts of Katherine Mansfield; the John P. Wilson Collection on the Southwest; the Helen Heller collection of Frankliniana; the Hermon Dunlap Smith Collection of Midwest maps—with more to come; and the Edward Byron Smith collection of Americana and Kelmscott Press books. And these are only the high spots. Here, it would be a grievous fault not to single out the chief instigator and abettor in all these, James M. Wells.

To acquire books, manuscripts, and maps places a burden on a library to preserve them. Under the inspired and dogged—even cussed—leadership of our former Conservator, Paul N. Banks, the Newberry in these years earned a world-wide reputation for the conservation of library materials. The boldest statement of that leadership is our new state-of-the-art bookstack building, surely the envy of librarians elsewhere. But there are other signals as well: the regular raiding of our Conservation staff by institutions all over the country; the research, writing, and education Banks has performed and is performing (including the Directorship of the first degree program in the field at Columbia and New York Universities); the $250,000 grant from the Pew Memorial Trust for the construction of a new Conservation Center on our fifth floor, and the Andrew W. Mellon Foundation $600,000, one-to-one challenge grant to endow our Conservation program.

Adding books and preserving them is only one side of librarianship. The other side is to assure their effective use—no small task when a library consists of "an uncommon collection of uncommon collections" of research materials gathered in great depth, and when its audience is not just local, not just regional, not even just national, but also international. The Trustees have always recognized effective use as a responsibility we must meet; so our annual Research and Education budget has grown from some $20,000 in 1962 to often over $1 million. Richard H. Brown has played a key role in this development for the past decade.

Since 1962, we have developed six major programs, all funded by new endowment or spendable grants, all raised in addition to the Library's endowment and annual giving in 1962. The Fellowship program has grown from $20,000 to about $200,000 a year. A cooperative undergraduate humanities program, begun in 1965 with a $250,000 grant from the Carnegie Corporation of New York, now embraces twenty-five colleges from Colorado to Ohio and is tuition-driven. Our first research center was started with a handsome $600,000 gift from Hermon Dunlap Smith for the Center for the History of Cartography that bears his name. We have since added the Center for the History of the American Indian, now modestly endowed; the Family and Community History Center, even more modestly endowed (with its subsidiary Chicago Metro History Fair available to high school students throughout the metropolitan area); and the Center for Renaissance Studies, now a cooperative venture with the Folger Shakespeare Library and sponsored by midwestern and eastern universities, as well as by the National Endowment for the Humanities.

But an equally significant statement of the Trustees' determination to provide for effective use is the plan for renovating the old Library building for better people use. In it we will serve more readers more effectively than ever before, and with it, we will reach a far wider public constituency than has ever been possible—with two handsome exhibition halls, a lecture and concert hall, and access for the handicapped. When completed, it, like the bookstack building, will stand as a symbol of what the new Newberry is all about. Joel L. Samuels, who wears many hats, is providing the leadership in planning and implementation for this task, as he did so ably for the bookstack building.

All of these extra-endowment projects have and will continue to cost more money than we had available in 1962. A few statistics will make the point. The number of endowed funds has grown from thirteen in 1962 to thirty-five in 1982. In 1962 our gifts were running at about $5,000 annually. For the past several years we have usually exceeded $2 million in unrestricted gifts, bequests, grants, and endowment donations. Much of this new money has come from Trustees, who generously open their purses to accomplish our goals. The Newberry Library Associates, begun in 1965 and now 1,800 strong and growing, presently give at the rate of more than $150,000 annually. Virtually every major (and many a smaller) foundation in Chicago has been generous to the Library, as have more than fifty corporations. Non-Chicago foundations—Andrew W. Mellon, Carnegie, Ford, Rockefeller, Rockefeller Brothers, Pew, Bush, Kresge, and Exxon—to mention only the most generous—have also given crucial support. They, along with the National Endowment for the Humanities, a major benefactor, have stimulated our growing national recognition.

So it has been an exciting and incredibly rewarding twenty years for me, and, I like to think, for the Trustees, for my colleagues on the staff, and for the readers as well, who have especially benefited. With an inspired board, doubled in size by a legislative amendment; a talented and dedicated staff, who give endlessly in so many ways; a surpassingly great collection of collections, and a host of friends, we have accomplished much, and we are gearing up—under the leadership of our new Chairman, Harold Byron Smith, Jr.—to celebrate our Centennial in 1987, preparing to offer a *new* Newberry Library that will be ready for a second century of service to scholarship in the humanities.

I take great pride in what all of us have accomplished while my twins grew to manhood. As the late Everett D. Graff said to me in 1962, when the Trustees offered me this position, "Bill, you are a lucky young man." He was right, and at sixty, I still feel like a lucky young man. Few have had so many opportunities to seize as they come along—the very best time, always.

III

COLLEAGUE

★

›18‹

RAY ALLEN BILLINGTON

Ray Allen Billington (1903–1981) was Towner's doctoral director at Northwestern University. In 1963, when Billington retired to become senior research associate at the Huntington Library, Towner delivered what he called "A Personal Appreciation" at a surprise farewell party of The Westerners in Chicago, May 27, 1963.

IN THE SUMMER OF 1951, I sent a first chapter of what became my doctoral dissertation to Professor Ray Allen Billington of Northwestern University. The subject of that chapter was the kinds of anti-social behavior that kept servants in colonial New England in hot water with their Puritan masters: I called these acts "Servant Protest." There was one kind of behavior, however, which I really did not know how to treat. I had first thought of including it in a chapter on the servants' leisure-time activities, but since religion and education were already under that rubric, it seemed better to label this particular activity as protest after all. To this day I am prepared to defend my decision, but I must admit that labeling fornication as a form of protest against the conditions of servitude is debatable.

From out West, where he was gathering first-hand information on buffalo-chip fires and the mountain men, Mr. Billington returned the chapter accompanied by a letter of searching criticism. But the real message was on the margin of the page where I had attempted to link fornication and protest. In Ray's crabbed script were two short words, "Some protest!" Working with this man has never been dull.

Ray Allen Billington began his academic career at the University of Michigan. There he wrote for the university newspaper until a double entendre, which today would hardly cause a raised eyebrow, led him to finish his undergraduate work at the University of Wisconsin, in 1926. He went on to take a master's degree at Michigan

From *Westerner's Brand Book* (Chicago Corral) 20, no. 4 (June 1963): 25–27. Reprinted with permission.

in 1927, and a doctorate at Harvard University in 1933. As an under-graduate at Wisconsin, he had been introduced to the study of the West by the great Frederic L. Paxson, and, at Harvard, he continued this interest under Professors James Blaine Hedges and Frederick L. Merk, the latter a student of Frederick Jackson Turner. I believe it was the connection with Professor Hedges which led Ray to make a decision for the Frontier as his chief field of research—but that decision came later.

At Harvard, Ray did his major work with the senior Arthur Meier Schlesinger, one of the historians most responsible for turning the eyes of the profession to social and intellectual history as proper fields of investigation. Under Mr. Schlesinger's direction, he wrote a dissertation entitled "The Origins of American Nativism, 1800–1844." This dissertation had its start as a term paper, was enlarged to a seminar paper, and in 1938 ended up as a book, *The Protestant Crusade, 1830–1860: A Study of the Origins of American Nativism* (New York, 1938). It was re-issued in 1953. This book is important for two reasons. First, it is the standard work in the field, a rare accomplishment for even a revised doctoral dissertation. Second, it provides a valuable key to the kind of scholar, teacher, and man Ray Allen Billington is.

Ray's study of American Nativism is a carefully documented analysis of Nativism's origin and growth, its social, political, and intellectual ramifications, and its temporary eclipse by the issue of slavery. In it he satisfies all the canons of scholarship. At the same time, implicit in the book is a rebuke to all of us. American Nativism, an anti-Catholic, anti-immigrant movement, was but one brand of the various intolerances we Americans have been subject to, and victims of, since the founding of this nation. Perhaps no people lives up to its highest ideals; certainly we often have not. For every great enunciation of human right, for every great decision in favor of democracy, there have been—and no doubt will continue to be—specific and deeply-rooted denials of human dignity on the part of one group or another towards other individuals or groups in our society. In this particular case, no one, it seems to me, could read *The Protestant Crusade* without becoming aware of similar intolerances within himself.

In fact, wherever one turns in the writings of Ray Allen Billington, evidence is to be found of his interest in social and intellectual history combined with an equal interest in what may be called the problem of making democracy work. In the field of social relations, for example, nothing has disturbed the past decade so much as the problem of prejudice against the Negro. In Ray's edition of the hitherto unpublished *Journal of Charlotte L. Forten* (New York, 1953), written by a sensitive Negro woman of the mid-nineteenth century, we find his intellect, his sympathy, and his sense of outraged justice united. In the introduction he writes as follows: ". . . racial consciousness endows Miss Forten's *Journal* with an importance in the twentieth century that it scarcely enjoyed in the nineteenth. Enlightened individuals today have dedicated themselves to a crusade for equality and human decency. Yet how few among them—how few among the non-persecuted—that is, can know the effect of prejudice on its victims. Miss Forten's *Journal* makes this terrifyingly clear. . . . No believer in the golden rule can read that record today without re-awakening to the need for decency among men."

Many of Ray's social and political views are explicit in the first textbook he wrote along with two friends from Harvard days, *The United States: American Democracy in World Perspective.* (New York, 1947). Here three American historians placed our historical development in the context of world history in a text written for undergraduates. The experience of the war had taught thoughtful Americans that we live in one world, that the oceans no longer represent a barrier but a highway between us and the Old World, and that threats to democracy and human dignity abroad are threats to democracy and human dignity at home, and vice versa. This textbook, no mere recounting of the oft-told story of American history since 1492, is a highly interpretative book designed not to confirm the prejudices of its readers but openly to challenge them. The foreword boldly proclaims: "Our object has been a liberal book that places the story of democratic development in the United States continuously in more universal perspective." A more conventional book would have sold far better, but it would not have been nearly as interesting to write or as important to read.

It can be said, then, that Ray's interest in social history and his vital concern for strengthening the best of American values have been supported by and grown out of his professional life as an historian. But more than that, anyone who knows Ray knows that he has actively sought to forward the cause of democracy in this country, devoting his time, his intellect, and his fortune to that cause again and again. He has successfully united the man of research and contemplation with the man of action. Without question, this has been true since the writing of his doctoral dissertation in the early 1930's.

While he was revising that dissertation as a young historian at

Clark University, an event occurred which had a tremendous impact on his professional career. He was approached by a publisher to share in the writing of a great book on the West, an authoritative survey, a synthesis of what had been written about the West. Flattered to be asked to participate, but deeply involved in writing *The Protestant Crusade*, he turned to his mentor for advice, just as his students now turn to him. He was advised that to be associated with Professor Hedges in the writing of a badly needed book in a field in which he was already trained was an opportunity too good for a young historian to miss. With this encouragement in hand, Ray agreed to participate. Before long, however, his colleague was forced to withdraw almost completely from the project and the publishers thereupon asked Ray to do the book himself. Again Ray was urged by his mentor to go on to complete the job. This he did with the help of a John Simon Guggenheim Memorial Foundation fellowship.

The result, *Westward Expansion: A History of the American Frontier* (New York, 1949), is now the standard work on the history of the West in these United States. Its original edition had six printings, and in 1960, it was brought out in a new and revised edition. Wherever the history of the West is taught or read, this book must be reckoned with. More important, the writing of *Westward Expansion* committed Ray to years of research in Western history, a field in which he is now the pre-eminent authority.

We need take only one other book as an example of how Ray's work in Western history has brought him fame. In 1953–54 he was Harold Vyvyan Harmsworth Professor at Oxford. There he carried the story of the American West to so many English ears that, I understand, there are today nearly as many Western enthusiasts in England as in America—Teddy boys in chaps, they call them. It was while at Oxford that he wrote the first draft of *The Far Western Frontier, 1830–1860* (New York, 1956) as a volume in the *New American Nation* series. Enthusiastically reviewed by professional historians, this book has also achieved considerable acclaim in non-academic circles. All one has to do is read the chapter on the mountain men to see why this is so. Amazing to relate, an Italian edition, *La Conquista del Far West*, appeared in 1958, thus conjuring up visions of the Mafia adapting scalp-lifting to the needs of their society.

Three projects on Western History go with Ray as he leaves Northwestern University for the Huntington Library. He is currently editing a twenty-volume series on the American frontier. In addition, he is editing some of the correspondence of Frederick Jackson Turner, whose essay on the closing of the frontier turned so many historians to that subject. Finally, he is writing what will become the definitive study of Turner's life.

This, then, is some kind of measure of Ray Allen Billington as a scholar: eminent authority on the great Westward movement in American history, a respected scholar in the field of intellectual and social history, and a thought-provoking critic of the American past. These characteristics make him intellectually stimulating to work with, but they are not the whole story. I would like to tell you a little of what it is like to be his student.

I began work with Ray Billington in 1946, taking two lecture courses, a two-quarter seminar, and a reading course with him, and writing my dissertation under his direction. In addition, I was a teaching assistant for him one year and a paper grader for two years. I think I know my man as a teacher.

The perfection of Ray's lectures is legendary. They are beautifully organized, impeccable in style—though based only on notes—uttered with a rhythmic delivery, and timed to the second: the last word almost invariably rolls out as the bell rings. As history and as art, they are a joy not to be forgotten.

In a lecture course, he is a hard taskmaster. A great generalizer himself, he requires of his students the ability to generalize in turn, for history must not be just dry facts; it must have meaning. At the same time, generalizations must be backed up with the facts. I can still remember the pain experienced in preparing for his exams; I would not like to prepare for another.

A worse discipline than his exams was his seminar. Picture, if you will, eight ambitious graduate students, each aware he is being measured against the others, each aware that how well he does in the seminar may well determine how much support he will get from his professor and his university. Each student has picked a topic for research and, during the next six months, will present two papers for criticism not only by the professor but also by two student critics whose grades are to be determined in part by the acidity of their criticism. Each bibliographical reference, each quotation, and each footnote, is sure to be checked; every awkward sentence is sure to be caught, and every unsupported assumption is sure to be blasted.

All this, of course, was preparation for writing a dissertation. Unlike many professors, Ray took dissertation students in many fields, rather than sticking just to his own speciality, Western history. Some wrote in the colonial period, others in the twentieth century. In my own generation there were such subjects as Jeffersonian Republicanism in New York State, 1790–96; biographies of Louis Agassiz and Ignatius Donnelly; a study of the Medical Society of Chicago; an analysis of the Ku Klux Klan in Indiana during the twenties; a history of Methodist camp meetings in the old Northwest; and an examination of the Social Gospel in the late nineteenth century. Ray's own wide interests and his desire to have his students pursue theirs led him down many strange paths. Moreover, unlike some dissertation directors, he neither picked the subjects for his students nor laid our the research in neat little blocks. That was our job: flounder we must, and flounder we did.

The statement that we were left to flounder suggests that Ray lacks interest in his students, but nothing could be further from the truth. Whether on campus or off, his students were always his concern. I have in my files, for example, scores of letters that have followed me wherever I have gone, not only while still a graduate student, teaching and writing on my dissertation, but also after the work for the degree was completed.

I recently spent an evening re-reading many of those letters in preparation for what I wanted to say tonight. In almost all of them, I discovered, a pattern repeats itself again and again. That pattern, I think, is rather interesting.

The opening sentences or paragraphs are invariably words of praise, of boosting, of reassurances. Nothing could be more typical, for as I look back over the years of my relationship with Ray, I realize how often I have drawn strength from him, from his optimism, from his faith in his fellow man, from his essentially positive view of men and situations.

The middle part of the letters usually deals with the particular point at issue. A chapter that needed some revision, a job that was opening up, a bit of advice to pass on to the neophyte in the profession. Here too is something typical of the man, for once he has assumed professional responsibility for a student, that responsibility never ends. This is a major key to his strength as a professor. Every position I have ever been considered for in the scholarly world has somehow, and usually to a great extent, involved Ray Allen Billington.

At the end of almost every letter comes the clincher. Almost always he closes with a quotation from some learned colleague. Perhaps it is something he had heard at a convention, or on a train, or in the history department at Northwestern. But always it hits just the right note. Let me give you but one example:

There was a young knight from Parma
Paying court to a medieval charmer
Quoth the maiden demure
Your pardon, I'm sure
Would you mind removing your armour.[1]

What I am trying to say, I think, is that in the academic world, if one is lucky, one has a second father–his major professor. One part of that professor's job is to train his students well, a part which ends when the degree is taken. The other part, more rarely fulfilled, is to follow his students' careers from beginning to end, shaping when he can and sharing the defeats along with the victories. In my opinion, Ray has fulfilled his roles magnificently.

Recently I had the privilege of toastmastering a dinner of Ray's graduate students given in Ray's honor at the occasion of his presidential address to the Mississippi Valley Historical Association and his appointment as Senior Research Associate of the Huntington Library. Some twenty-five of us were there. It was a remarkable experience for us all. Each of us went that evening secure in the knowledge that his own relationship with Ray, unlike that of the others, was unique, and each of us felt somewhat condescending toward the others present. After more than three hours of reminiscence—one by one—around the table, we came away wiser men. Just as each of us had gone to the dinner convinced he was something special to Ray, beyond the others, so each of us left knowing that Ray's affections were big enough to include us all as especially loved. Probably that is why he is especially loved in turn.

1. Slightly bowdlerized.

CLIFFORD KENYON SHIPTON

Clifford K. Shipton (1902–73) was director of the American
Antiquarian Society and, as Towner reveals in this obituary, his
unofficial dissertation advisor and warm friend.

CLIFFORD KENYON SHIPTON was one of those rare men who know
themselves so well, and who like reasonably well enough what they
see, that they can allow themselves to know other men. This was
true of Ted whether he was writing of his old friends from
eighteenth-century Harvard or opening himself to his twentieth-
century friends in that triangle of his affections—Shirley Center,
Boston, and Worcester.

It was this strength of character and this knowledge of self from
top to bottom that gave him the measure of other men and that
make his chief personal monument, the volumes of *Sibley's Harvard Graduates*, forever useful. He measured those men and he left
in the volumes a yardstick of himself, so that one can see the measure as well as the measured. Tory and Whig alike will know the
men because they will know the *man*. One quotation will illustrate:
James Warren's 'difference with his colleagues,' Ted wrote, 'arose
from his simplicity and lack of perspective, qualities essential in a
good revolutionary.'

Ted Shipton was born on August 5, 1902, the son of George and
Edith (Kenyon) Shipton of Pittsfield, Massachusetts. He graduated
from Harvard College, class of 1926, and proceeded directly to the
M.A. in History in 1927. In that same year, on June 11, he and Dorothy Boyd MacKillop were married. They had three children, Ann
Boyd, Nathaniel Niles, and George Mackay. Ted taught for a year or
so at Brown University, but he did not care much for the classroom,
and he returned to it only briefly and extracurricularly but twice
again in his career, at Harvard and at Clark.

His dissertation, which earned him the Ph.D. at Harvard in 1933,
became Volume IV of *Biographical Sketches of Those Who At-*

From *Proceedings* (American Antiquarian Society) 84, pt. 1 (1974): 24–29. Reprinted with permission.

tended Harvard College (Cambridge, 1933), Ted having in 1930 already become John Langdon Sibley Editor of the Massachusetts Historical Society. He was appointed Custodian of the Harvard Archives in 1938, a post he continued to hold (and work at one day each week) after he moved to the American Antiquarian Society. He served the Society as Librarian from 1940, getting under way that enormous contribution to scholarship, the Readex Microprint edition of Evans's *American Imprints Through 1800,* which he finished after he became the Society's Director in 1959.

Ted retired as Director of the American Antiquarian Society in 1967, as Custodian of the Harvard Archives in 1969, and as Sibley Editor of the Massachusetts Historical Society on December 4, 1973, the day he died. He will be remembered and valued as long as men study early American life and letters.

Ted's well-fathomed self gave him a portable identity independent of the chair in which he was sitting. And it took a formidable selfhood to allow him to give himself so unremittingly to three loves that would never bear his name—making the Antiquarian Society's collections not only greater but far more available to others than they had been, producing that magnificent resource that will always be informally known as Evans, and researching and writing fourteen volumes of the now misnamed *Sibley's Harvard Graduates.*

Even Ted's seeming inconsistencies resolve themselves from the right perspective. He could be irritatingly protective of the unique materials and the unique combinations of materials at the American Antiquarian Society. Graduate students, especially those arriving unannounced by the carload, say from Columbia, to 'ransack the library' were not welcomed with open arms, and not merely because Ted resented New England history viewed from New York, although he occasionally did. He was genuinely concerned that the Society's precious materials not be worn out in 'exercises' for the Ph.D. Even those who felt well accepted could be stopped, as I was from reading Increase Mather's manuscript diary, 'because I've read it and there is nothing in it for you.'

However, this custodial conservatism led Ted to the monumental task of making available to everybody everywhere all the books published in America through 1800, wherever they were extant. Starting with the some 39,000 titles listed in Charles Evans *American Bibliography,* he organized a search through more than 250 libraries to find and microfilm the originals. That effort not only eliminated the errors in Evans but also helped identify another 10,000 titles. They are all included in Shipton and James E. Mooney, *National*

Index of American Imprints Through 1800: The Short-Title Evans, ([Worcester], 1969) which serves as the key to the Microprint edition. The protection of the originals by their multiplication and wide dispersal and the resultant 'democratization' of research in early American history and literature were Ted's only, and for him truly sufficient, rewards, which he valued equally as he read the articles and books that poured forth in the sixties, based in part on his great bibliographical and micro-publishing accomplishments.

The various elements of Ted's life, and the way they fitted together—like horseshoes overlapping on the stake—could be sensed best in his and Dorothy's rambling home in Shirley Center. He was rooted in the soil of small-town New England; his woodpile, his gardens, his chickens, and his flowers and trees and shrubs were a part of his independence.

In his study, there was the smell of damp ash in the Franklin fireplace, there was a fine working library in New England history ready to hand, and there was box after box of notes for *Sibley's Harvard Graduates.*

But to lure him forth, there were freshly-gathered fruits and vegetables, cats and dogs to be let in and out, and friends and relatives who came for conversation and Dorothy's special tea and unmatched molasses slab cookies. There were, also, the claims of the village.

I got to know Ted Shipton because he was New-England Puritan enough to believe that useful work was this world's best healer. In 1949, he had set Catharine Barton Mayo, then recently and tragically widowed by Lawrence Shaw Mayo, to work on *Additions and Corrections* to Mayo's edition of Thomas Hutchinson's *History* and, that finished, to transcribing Hutchinson's correspondence in the old Massachusetts Archives, where Kitty and I met. Learning that I was somewhat at sea on my dissertation, she dragged me reluctantly to Ted at the Harvard Archives early in 1950.

He listened to my problem with patience and kindliness and then made a suggestion: Read all eight volumes of the *Records and Files of the Quarterly Courts of Essex County, Massachusetts.* Report back in a *week* with the questions the reading raised.

That was the beginning. Two years later, having in the meanwhile been sent to every county court house in the state, having been forced through every issue of every newspaper and hundreds of sermons, but still baffled by one aspect of my research problem, I turned to him for additional sources. 'You have reached the place in your work where you have got to stop research,' Ted wrote on November 19, 1952. 'The problem now is to make it available. The secret of accomplishing anything in the historical field is *controlled superficiality and sloppiness.*' (Italics mine).

He shared this secret with a larger audience in the introduction to his *New England Life in the Eighteenth Century: Representative Biographies from Sibley's Harvard Graduates* (Cambridge, Mass., 1963). It bears repeating:

'At the outset, I calculated that I might live to get from the Class of 1690 to that of 1800. . . . The research material I divided tentatively into three classes. The first, consisting of such general sources as newspapers and diaries, is of such bulk and low specific yield that it could be used only if searched for all hundred and ten classes at one time. I now have something like *a quarter of a million eight by five slips* of such material in my study.' (Italics mine)

More intensive work was reserved for the particular classes in a particular volume—Class Two, Ted called it; and the most intensive work was for a single biography, Class Three. 'If progress is to be made on a biographical project of this magnitude,' he continued, 'it is essential that work be kept going constantly at all three levels and a definite schedule of producing printer's copy maintained, even if it means abandoning the search of some low yield sources.' That is what he meant by 'controlled superficiality and sloppiness.'

And he meant what he said. In the introduction to the *National Index of American Imprints,* one can sense the hard-driving Ted, determined to get the big job done, letting the chips of small errors and omissions fall where they may. 'Consequently,' he wrote, 'these volumes are not a canon of American printing, but a tool which other generations can use to make definitive bibliographies.'

And again, in the brief, almost off-hand introduction to *Sibley* XVI, the last volume published before his death, he wrote: 'After forty years and thirteen volumes there is nothing new for the editor of this series to say by way of introduction. The only systematic change in this volume has been the extension of the practice of not delaying the work to wait for the recovery of mislaid portraits and manuscripts. There is now a crew of eager, and very able, young historians working in this field who will be glad to take care of any omissions of significance.'

Well, he is gone now, and there are going to be great omissions of great significance needful to be taken care of, not so much in the work he did, but in the work he left undone.

When one reaches his fifties, the members of the generation that nurtured him begin to be gathered one by one to their fathers, and it is a sad thing to lose them. Clifford Kenyon Shipton was one of those who nurtured me, along with many other younger scholars, and there is little consolation for letting him go.

But ten years ago, sorry to learn of a mutual friend's death, Ted wrote that he was 'pleased that it came to him when he was in full possession of his faculties and in full flight of his activities. That is the way he would have wanted it.' Ted spent the day before he died finishing the work on *Sibley* XVII: so let his words be his proper epitaph and our grief's end.

>20<

LESTER JESSE CAPPON

Lester J. Cappon (1900–1981) was the former director of the Institute of Early American History who retired to head the *Atlas of Early American History* project at the Newberry (1968–1976). At the time of his death, he was a Senior Research Fellow. Towner wrote this tribute for the memorial service to Cappon at the Newberry in 1981.

STRIDING BRISKLY UP RUSH STREET after dinner on August 24, twenty-eight days before his eighty-first birthday, Lester Cappon dropped dead on the sidewalk, we like to think in full stride, as usual: there was no way he would die in bed.

Distinguished Research Fellow, emeritus, of the Newberry Library, Lester habitually put in a six-day week—editing the manuscript journals of Jared Sparks; writing articles and reviews; playing the piano for his own delight and the delight of others; entertaining at dinner or being himself entertaining at dinner; dressed always to the nines; and being secretly generous with his time and substance.

Within the two weeks prior to his death he completed (and got accepted for publication) a brilliant article summing up nearly fifty years' reflection on the archival profession. The very day he died, he completed a manuscript draft review of *The Cartography of Northern Virginia*.

My connection with Lester Cappon began in 1955 when, after an interview at the Boston Athenaeum (10½ Beacon Street) he gambled on a brand-new Ph.D. and made him Editor of the *William and Mary Quarterly*, published by the Institute of Early American History and Culture in Williamsburg, Virginia, of which he was the new Director.

His connection with the Newberry Library began in 1968, when he became Senior Research Fellow. Subsequently he edited the *Atlas of Early American History: The Revolutionary Era, 1760–1790* (Princeton University Press, 1976), one of our most praised and

Beethoven and Bourbon: A Celebration of Life. Lester Jesse Cappon, September 18, 1900–August 24, 1981 (Chicago: Newberry Library, 1981).

prized publications. A five-year, $2 million project, he finished it exactly on schedule. He was seventy-five years old. By the *Atlas'* publication date, July 4, 1976, Lester was hooked on the Newberry and the great city of Chicago, whose winter climate he abhorred, but whose Library and music he felt he could not live without. While he kept a house in Williamsburg, and voted (Democratic) in Virginia, his home had become Chicago.

The Beethoven Piano Sonata performed in his memory this afternoon is played on the piano he bought for the Library so its great music collections could find expression and be shared by others. But his first love remained history, and he established, anonymously (until now), a $100,000 endowment for historical editing at the Newberry.

Lester also loved bourbon, especially Virginia Gentleman. He was himself a Virginia gentleman by adoption, and we think it fitting that we should celebrate his life today not only with Beethoven, but also with bourbon. We also celebrate it with his picture, wearing a much abused hat that saw the white waters on rivers all over his beloved West, in Canada, and in Alaska.

HERMON DUNLAP SMITH

Hermon Dunlap Smith (1900–1983) was a member of the
Newberry Library's Board of Trustees from 1943 to 1983 and
president and chairman from 1964 to 1975. Towner wrote this
appreciation in 1972 on the occasion of the dedication of the
Hermon Dunlap Smith Center for the History of Cartography
which Smith had richly endowed.

THE NEWBERRY LIBRARY has a long tradition of winning the support
and assistance of people who are interested in learning and in advancing the cause of scholarship. We have been blessed with numerous civic-minded benefactors who have given us time, and books,
and money. Among the many who come to mind are three especially—Edward E. Ayer, William Brooks Greenlee, and Everett D.
Graff—all of whom collected maps and other materials which made
the Hermon Dunlap Smith Center for the History of Cartography a
logical necessity.

Another of the Newberry's traditions is that of attracting to its
Board of Trustees men who are generous and far-sighted and sage,
men who value the heritage of the past and work to conserve it, men
who are also open-minded, and willing to accept new challenges and
new responsibilities as they are presented. I count myself fortunate
to be responsible to men such as these and especially to have the
privilege of working closely with the man who has made possible
the Center we are dedicating this evening.

Hermon Dunlap Smith—widely and affectionately known as
Dutch to a host of friends throughout the world—is a remarkable
man, as I need not tell you. A native Chicagoan, he attended the
Francis Parker School and Harvard College. After graduating in
1921, he served for a few years as a banker, and then shifted careers
to insurance and became associated with Marsh and McLennan,

"An Appreciation of Hermon Dunlap Smith," in *The Hermon Dunlap Smith Center for the History of Cartography at the Newberry Library, Dedication Proceedings,
November 1, 1972* (Chicago: Newberry Library, 1973), 2–5.

Inc., where he stayed until he retired as Chairman in 1966 and as Chairman of the Finance Committee in 1971.

His business career was a demanding and satisfying one, but he still has found time to take on a great many outside assignments: membership on the Board of Overseers at Harvard University; Trustee of Radcliffe College; Chief of the Price Adjustment Section of the Air Force during World War II; Chairman of the National Merit Scholarship Corporation; Trustee of the University of Chicago; Director of Encyclopaedia Britannica, Inc. (to whose volumes he also contributed the article on Henry Dearborn); Chairman of the Adler Planetarium Board and of the Chicago Community Trust; President of the Field Foundation of Illinois and of the Board of Trustees of The Newberry Library—a chairman of chairmen, if there ever was one.

But it is the Presidency of The Newberry Library's Board that I wish to dwell upon, since it is in this connection that I can speak with considerable authority and with a great deal of respect, admiration, and affection.

Mr. Smith became a Trustee of The Newberry Library in 1943, nearly thirty years ago. In 1954 he became First Vice-President of the Board and, on the death of Everett D. Graff in 1964, he was elected President.

I first met him when I came to Chicago to be interviewed for the Librarianship of the Newberry, in 1962. I had heard a good deal about him before then, especially in connection with Governor Adlai Stevenson and his quest for the Presidency. But, as an American historian, I was also aware of his book, *The Revolutionary War Journals of Henry Dearborn*, and I had heard vaguely that he was interested in maps and collected them. Even in my unsophisticated state—a young man who then knew little about what former Dean Moody E. Prior of Northwestern has called the contingent world—I recognized in Mr. Smith on that occasion the mark of the enabler: the kind of man who helps others get things done that need doing.

During my first two years at Newberry I found these preliminary judgments to be correct. But it was in 1964, when we suddenly became aware that we might acquire the library of the late Louis H. Silver, another Newberry Trustee, that I really began to appreciate his qualities—the ability to appraise a situation correctly and to act quickly on that appraisal; the ability to become enthusiastic himself and to convey his enthusiasm to his fellow Trustees and to the community at large; a willingness to take responsibility and to persuade others to help share that responsibility. A year later, when we were deciding how to handle the disposal of the duplicates and out-of-scope books (and chose to send them to auction in London), he backed us up, on the Board, in the community, and even in the Letters to the Editor column of the *New York Times,* in reply to an unfriendly reporter.

At that same time we launched our first fund drive to raise money to pay for the Silver collection and to replace the money we had spent a few years earlier to renovate and air condition the building. Again Mr. Smith proved himself knowledgeable and sure in the ways of men and institutions, whether things were going well (as they generally were) or badly (as they occasionally did).

And so it has gone, for almost a decade, during which the Library has made great progress and planned for greater. Let me instance but a few of our accomplishments under the warm sun of Dutch's encouragement and support. Some seven and a half million dollars' worth of books and manuscripts and maps added within the decade; some two million dollars in capital gifts; nearly two and a half million in grants for programs, including our Seminar in the Humanities, our Atlas of Early American History project, our Center for the History of the American Indian, our program for the Study of the Family in Historical Perspective; our new Andrew W. Mellon Fund for research and publication; the creation of the Newberry Library Associates, nearly eight hundred strong, who contribute annually more than $60,000 for books, fellowships, and publications; three residences, one for the Director and two for visiting scholars; a new pension system and a generous program of fringe benefits, including medical, life, and total disability insurance; and strong encouragement for our plans to expand the building to keep up with our growing needs. The list goes on, but I will not, for I have already persuaded you, I am sure, that any encomium I might heap on Dutch Smith's head is well deserved and is merely carrying coals to Newcastle.

Meanwhile, however, Mr. Smith was dreaming dreams of his own. We had great maps; we finally had a map curator; and, thanks to the generosity of another man (and his wife), present this evening, we had the Kenneth Nebenzahl, Jr. Lectures in the History of Cartography. We needed the means to pull all these together, to augment them, and to develop a Center for the History of Cartography where the international community of historians, cartographers, and collectors could be brought together to work together in a most interesting and important field.

Eighteen months ago, I received a telephone call from Mr. Smith saying that he'd like to discuss a serious matter. We made an appointment, and I went downtown with slightly sinking heart, wondering whether I had finally tried his patience too much, whether our most recent request, whatever it was, had proven to be the proverbial straw.

I don't think I have ever had a pleasanter surprise. He wanted to ask a question: Would the Library accept a considerable gift—in my opinion, a princely gift—from an anonymous donor to establish the first Center in any known institution for the History of Cartography? If so, we might expect to receive a letter in the next few days offering a capital gift with which to begin such a program. Needless to say, I did not hesitate in my answer. At the next Trustees' meeting, the letter was presented to me to read to the Board, and planning began at once for the new addition to this remarkable institution on Walton Street.

It must be obvious to all by now that the Hermon Dunlap Smith Center is only symbolic of what Dutch has done for The Newberry Library. Once again he is being the enabler for an important step forward, with one difference—after a year of persuading he has allowed us to give him credit for it: that is a golden opportunity not to be missed. Therefore in closing I want to read to all of you a quotation Mr. Smith must by now be quite familiar with, for it is my most favored of all quotations. I hope, Dutch, that you will understand that I use it again, not because of any poverty of imagination, or lack of reading, but because it is so entirely apt. It was written by another Smith, one Captain John Smith of Pocahontas fame, who wrote in 1616 a little book entitled *A Description of New-England*, from which I quote: "Then seeing we are not borne for our selues, but each to helpe other, and our abilities are much alike at the houre of our birth, and the minute of our death: Seeing our good deedes, or our badde, by faith in Christs merits, is all we haue to carrie our soules to heauen, or hell: Seeing honour is our liues ambition; and our ambition after death, to haue an honourable memorie of our life: and seeing by noe meanes wee would bee abated of the dignities & glories of our Predecessors; let vs imitate their vertues to bee worthily their successors."

This Hermon Dunlap Smith has truly done. We are grateful indeed.

22

D'ARCY McNICKLE

D'Arcy McNickle (1904–1977), scholar and novelist, was the founding director (1971–1976) of the Center for the History of the American Indian at the Newberry Library. Towner wrote this foreword to the second edition of McNickle's novel, *The Surrounded*, in 1977.

D'ARCY MCNICKLE'S *The Surrounded*, now reissued some forty years after its original publication, is more timely today and ought to reach a far wider audience than when it was published in 1936. It is a moving story of enduring significance. But to predict an improved reception for *The Surrounded* is not to suggest that it missed critical acclaim when it first appeared. On the contrary, Oliver La Farge, the Pulitzer Prize–winning author of *Laughing Boy*, writing in the March 14, 1936, issue of the *Saturday Review of Literature*, placed *The Surrounded* on his "small list of creditable modern novels using the first Americans as theme." Praising the writing as "simple, clear, direct, devoid of affectations, and fast-moving," La Farge judged that the author presented the Indian condition so skillfully that he educated the reader without effort through the sheer force of the story. "Perhaps the most interesting aspect of McNickle's book," wrote La Farge, "is his success in capturing the whole in small compass, by the exercise of a thoroughly artistic selection, and writing of such sorts that the reader is primarily interested in an excellent story as such, and only secondarily in the background, which he gets in proper balance."

This praise in the *Saturday Review* for a first novel must have been heady stuff. La Farge was not only an established writer but also an eminent authority on Indian life and culture, and an associate of the great John Collier, the anthropologist who was then commissioner of Indian Affairs. La Farge was well on his way to earning the sobriquet, "Indian Man," that D'Arcy McNickle used thirty-six years later to title his biography of La Farge.

"Introduction" to D'Arcy McNickle, *The Surrounded*, 2d ed. (Albuquerque: University of New Mexico Press, 1978), vii–xiii. Reprinted with permission.

But the times are surely riper for *The Surrounded* in 1977 than they were in 1936. It is true that federal Indian policy in the 1930s was changing, showing a new respect for, and a desire to protect, the diverse cultural patterns of the First Americans (a policy tragically reversed in the 1950s in still another attempt to eliminate the Indian problem by eliminating the Indians). And in the 1930s, men like Collier, La Farge, and McNickle strained to make the new policy work. But most Americans, even though shaken by the Great Depression, were still too confident of the American dream to be moved by a desire to share the land with those who owned it first. Despite evidence to the contrary, most Americans assumed that the "Indian problem" would go away as the Indians died or were assimilated—if indeed they thought about them at all.

The America of the 1970s, however, is a different America. (Or, if it is not, it ought to be.) Shaken to its roots by the devastating Vietnam war, the revolt of its youth, the expressed frustration and deep anger of its minorities, and the moral disaster of the presidency, it may well be more receptive to *The Surrounded* than was an older generation. No longer confident of the inevitability of its own history, or of the "American way of life," the America of the 1970s may be more sympathetic to other peoples and to their cultures than it was, or at least more understanding of other peoples who may seem also to have lost their way.

The central figure in *The Surrounded*, a young man, half Spanish, half Salish (or Flathead) Indian, named Archilde Leon, represents the dynamic and complex cross-cultural conflicts that had become characteristic of First Americans. He has returned to his reservation for a brief visit, having learned how to support himself, marginally, in the white man's world by playing the fiddle. His father, a successful Spanish rancher-farmer, an early settler in the region, desperately wants him to take up the land as his other Indian sons would not. His mother, a Salish Indian, among the first to accept Spanish Catholicism, lives as an Indian, separate from the father. In her old age and despair she is rejecting what she gladly accepted from the whites and is returning to her pre-Catholic Indian ways. Archilde's young contemporaries, meanwhile, have succumbed to the destructive influence of the reservation way of life, which is pointless, without hope, dissolute. They are all surrounded by an alien world.

Archilde's planned departure from the reservation is delayed by personal entanglements in each of the cultural patterns that make up his life: love for his Indian mother; love for his Spanish father; love for the music he has learned at Indian school and his hope of becoming a true violinist under the tutelage of the old Spanish priest at the mission; and love for an Indian woman, who is totally uprooted and living only for the senses. He never escapes the entrapments. Each in its turn delays his departure until he is destroyed at the hands of white man's law, personified locally by the game warden, the Indian agent, and the sheriff.

The Surrounded is as good as it is because it grew out of D'Arcy McNickle's most deeply felt experiences, because it is informed by his careful study of anthropology and history, and because it is shaped by his artistry. McNickle, indeed, was one of the most interesting and compelling men that I have ever met. Like his protagonist in *The Surrounded*, he was half Indian and half white, biologically. But in his essential self he was both totally Indian and totally "European," a contradiction I had no difficulty in resolving when listening to him, but which I was at a loss to explain when he was absent. Perhaps it was that he was simply human.

I could visualize him as a free-lance writer in New York City; as an effective administrator in the Bureau of Indian Affairs; as the founding chairman of the Anthropology Department of the University of Saskatchewan in Saskatoon; and as the founding director of the Newberry Library Center for the History of the American Indian. At the same time I could visualize him sitting in an interminable tribal council waiting patiently, with timeless understanding, for resolution through consensus of some difficult Indian issue. I have been at dinner with him at Washington's famous Jockey Club, where he elegantly selected the proper wine for the meal; and I could imagine him selecting with his hands, from a common pot, a choice tidbit of venison "illegally" shot that day on an Indian reservation.

Born in 1904 at St. Ignatius, Montana, on the Flathead Indian Reservation there, McNickle was a member of the Confederated Salish and Kootenai Tribes. At an early age, and against his and his mother's desires, he was sent away to the federal Indian boarding school at Chemewa, Oregon. There, he remembered, he and his schoolmates were given corporal punishment if they lapsed from English into Indian tongues.

At the age of seventeen, he began four years at the University of Montana, followed by a year at Oxford University. His higher education, which temporarily cut him off from his Salish background, was financed, symbolically enough, by the sale of his own Indian land rights under the Allotment Act of 1887. At Oxford in 1925–26, and later at the University of Grenoble in 1931, he must often have wondered who and what he was, having separated himself from his ancestral people and their lands.

But McNickle's *The Surrounded*, his first book, reveals who and what he was and what he remained—a man with the breadth of intellect to live in two worlds, with the compassion to love them both, and with the talent to write so effectively about where they tragically intermesh that he could share his experience with others.

That he could see and have compassion for both sides in the historical tragedy of Indian-white relations is not to suggest that Mr. McNickle was without passion. On the contrary, he was a man of great passionate concern. It was a concern not only for his own particular Indian people, but also for all First Americans. And his histories reveal that passion: *They Came Here First* (1949, 1975); *Indians and Other Americans* (with Harold E. Fey, 1959, 1970); *The Indian Tribes of the United States* (1962); and *Native American Tribalism* (1973). Indeed, so far as I know, everything he wrote was about the First Americans, their culture, and their history. Their plight as the surrounded people absorbed his life.

Just as McNickle's first novel reveals the sources of his passion, so his second novel, *Runner in the Sun* (1954), symbolizes, for me at least, how he responded to it. *Runner in the Sun*, unlike *The Surrounded*, is set in prehistoric times, or at least before the arrival of the white man. Its story is simple. It tells of an Indian boy, called Salt, who is sent by his people on a long journey, he knows not where, to bring back he knows not what, to save his people from some dimly perceived disaster whose origins are not understood. He brings back, almost by accident, a new breed of corn, along with experience about the world outside, and wisdom, so that in the end his people "lived in peace and supported one another."

Until his death in October 1977, D'Arcy McNickle was himself a Runner in the Sun. When he left St. Ignatius, he embarked on a long and dangerous intellectual journey from his people. But he carried with him always a remembrance of their plight. And through his life and works he brought back to them the seeds of knowledge and understanding and wisdom hard won in an alien culture so that First Americans everywhere might live in peace and support one another.

23

EVERETT DWIGHT GRAFF

Everett D. Graff (1885–1964), president of the Newberry's Board of Trustees from 1952 to 1964, contributed his world-class collection of Western Americana to the Newberry. Towner wrote this short biography at the request of the *Dictionary of American Biography.*

EVERETT DWIGHT GRAFF (Aug. 7, 1885–Mar. 11, 1964), steel company executive, book collector, and philanthropist, was born in Clarinda, Iowa, the son of Valentine Graff, the proprietor of a successful clothing and dry-goods business and a state legislator, and of Nancy Elizabeth Fairley.

After attending public schools in Clarinda, Graff entered Lake Forest College in Illinois, from which he graduated in 1906. He then joined Joseph T. Ryerson and Son, a steel company, with which he remained for his entire business career, being named president in 1937. In 1935, Ryerson merged with Inland Steel Company, becoming a wholly owned subsidiary of Inland. Graff was a director of both Ryerson and Inland until his retirement in 1952.

Graff married Verde Alice Clark on Nov. 19, 1918; they had three children. Their home contained works of art and a major collection of Western Americana. These two interests led Graff to serve as trustee and president of both the Art Institute of Chicago (1954–1958) and the Newberry Library (1952–1964).

Graff would probably be remembered only by his family and friends were it not for a passion for books that resulted in the establishment of the Everett D. Graff Collection of Western Americana at the Newberry Library. As a book collector he had high standards. While he relied heavily, especially at first, on the great Americana book dealer Wright Howes, his acquisition files are a roster of Americana dealers from coast to coast.

Between 1940 and 1950, while still engaged in the steel business,

From *Dictionary of American Biography,* suppl. 7, 1961–65 (1981): 294–95. Reprinted with permission.

Graff took brief book-hunting trips with Howes. They sought books in Illinois and Iowa, as far south as Mexico, and in the Pacific Northwest. Howes frequently placed advance advertisements in local newspapers along the way so the book dealer and book collector could pursue their respective interests.

Reflecting on his association with Graff, Howes said:

> Most western collectors have been satisfied with trying to cover some *one* phase of this fascinating subject—overland narratives, the fur trade, the cattle trade—or some *one* state, some *one* region. . . . The insatiable curiosity and interest of the collector we are discussing was content with nothing less than the uncompromising aspiration of covering the *whole*. He has tried to assemble every basic and significant printed source relating to every important event, every phase of human activity, in all the vast interior regions of the United States—throughout the entire sweep of its pioneer and earlier periods. . . .

Howes's judgment of Graff was shared by the rare-book specialist Colton Storm, who called Graff "one of the finest book collectors I have ever known." The Western historian Ray Allen Billington agreed with Howes and Storm, concluding that, with the addition of the Graff Collection, "the Newberry Library, already rich by virtue of the [Edward Everett] Ayer Collection, joins the very front rank among depositories specializing in Western history. . . ."

Graff's contribution to the Newberry was not limited to his bequests of his collection and of a fund to maintain it. He used his leverage to further the general interests of the library as well. Under his leadership the Newberry declined an invitation to merge with the University of Chicago; thus it remained independent and on Chicago's Near North Side. It was also under his leadership that the library, in 1959–1962, modernized its facilities, adding air-conditioning and fireproofing to protect the collections. Full of energy and of plans for the library, at age seventy-eight, Graff continued his activities even after a serious stroke. He died in Rome, en route home from Greece. Until his death he worked with Colton Storm on the catalog of his collection, which was published in 1968.

> [The Everett D. Graff Papers, which include extensive correspondence concerning his collection, fragments of genealogies on both the paternal and the maternal sides, a brief start of an autobiography, and seven typescript journals of book-hunting trips with Wright Howes, are in

the Newberry Library. Articles by S. P. (Stanley Pargellis), Colton Storm, and Ray Allen Billington dealing with Graff and the collection are in *The Newberry Library Bulletin*, Dec. 1960. See also Colton Storm, ed., *A Catalogue of the Everett D. Graff Collection of Western Americana* (1968).]

IV

SPOKESMAN FOR
THE HUMANITIES

★

24

SOME OF MY BEST FRIENDS USED TO

BE UNIVERSITY PRESS DIRECTORS

Towner had the happy capacity to criticize people and make it stick without offense. Here he lays into university press directors in an article that was originally delivered as a talk to the Association of American University Presses in 1975.

They listened, one suspects, because he appealed to their ideals in a publishing world they knew was surrendering to the marketplace. Towner, speaking from a wide range of experience dealing with university presses, identified several areas where they had abdicated their responsibilities to scholarship and offered a menu of possibilities. Some of Towner's best friends continue to be university press directors.

MY CAREER HAS TOUCHED on four aspects of the scholarly publishing world. As a professor, I both used books in teaching and wrote for scholarly publications. As an editor of a scholarly journal, I made decisions on what should be published. As a librarian, I now make decisions on what publications should be acquired and, on a small scale, what kinds of research and publications should be subsidized. One would think, from this twenty years' tangential experience, that I should be able to throw light on the problems of scholarly publishers and, by illuminating them, help to solve them. Alas, all I can do, I am afraid, is add my confusions to others'.

Twice during the last twelve months I have written to university presidents in attempts, not entirely vain—or at least not yet in vain—to ward off dissolution of their university presses in the face of serious financial difficulties. My arguments were, I am sure, quite traditional and hardly need to be repeated here, except that they may provide a background for some of my uneasiness about the actual performance of university presses as I see it.

I pointed out to these presidents that universities, unlike under-

"Some of My Best Friends Used to Be Press Directors," *Scholarly Publishing* 7 (1976): 113–20. Reprinted with permission.

graduate colleges, exist, or ought to exist, primarily for the advancement of knowledge and as privileged sanctuaries from which to communicate that knowledge, regardless of its reception in the community at large. While a primary means of communicating that knowledge is through the classroom, an even more important way is through publication, in journals and in books, and otherwise. It follows that, so long as a university pretends to fulfil its primary function—the advancement of knowledge—it must establish and maintain its own press, or it must have such direct and unrestricted access to another press that its own faculty can be measured not only by the books they publish but also, as members of press boards, by the books they select to be published.

It could be argued, then, that since a university press attempts to represent all the disciplines of a good university in its publications, it is, in fact, universal in its intellectual responsibility. The press, like the university library, should have priority claims on university monies. Better to let an academic department or program die than to let the university's press or its library languish, let alone perish.

A press, I pointed out, should not be viewed as an important matter of prestige, of PR, like a football team. On the contrary, a press should be viewed as an integral and vital part of scholarship. To be sure, a professor's findings and ideas get tested by his students and even by his colleagues in his own community, but not until he publishes, as Messrs Fogel and Engerman are finding out with their book, *Time on the Cross*, does the process of criticism and refinement reach a conclusion. In short, without publication, not only is the communication process aborted, so also is the research process, because the research is not submitted for free criticism in the marketplace of ideas.

I would go even further—and here I imagine most scholarly publishers will disagree—by saying that the first obligation of a university press is to publish the worthwhile works of its own faculty, rather than to try to enhance its own prestige by publishing the works of other scholars perhaps of greater reputation. To be sure, certain great university presses, like certain great universities, are of such quality or have such well-developed fields of specialty that they attract manuscripts as magnets attract filings; but if a university press is not making publication available to its own faculty for worthwhile manuscripts, it is failing its university.

Further than that, I would argue that the same responsibility is especially due its younger faculty, who desperately need to publish what they think they have learned. It is far more important in the total research process, if less prestigious, to publish the first book of a scholar to get his ideas examined and him established, than it is to compete—with higher overheads (design, advertising, royalties, etc.)—for the books of established scholars who often can get commercial publication of their works.

It follows, then, that it is irrational to expect any but a few university presses—if indeed any—to earn their own way through sales. They must be subsidized, and heavily subsidized, if they are to function as an integral part of the academic world. To give up a press because it has to be subsidized, or because its subsidy has to be increased in inflationary times, makes no more sense than to stop buying books or providing service at the university library. The academic process gets aborted at either end.

Finally, I argued that, in today's publishing world, university presses are even more important than they were in the 1960s, the heyday of academic publishing. Both commercial publishing and commercial sales of books, it seems to me, are following other aspects of our economy and our society. The chain bookstores, the book clubs, and the ownership of publishing houses by monster corporations that often look only at the bottom line, threaten, it also seems to me, the marketplace of ideas. It is the obligation of university presses, as plural agents in a pluralistic society, to keep open to our society the free flow of ideas as expressed in books.

My defence of university presses, while enthusiastic, is not without qualification. But speaking as I do, uninformed by the facts, I hope you will forgive my errors of omission and commission, just as I would those of scholarly publishers who happened to be talking about research libraries.

My qualifications on the performance of university presses can be approached in two ways. First, by a simple recounting of disappointing, or at least revealing, experiences; then by a brief attempt at a kind of analysis.

Item: As a director of a research library I have had to shift a series—that of the Renaissance English Text Society—from press to press, three in all, so far, because the directors found this worthwhile project uneconomic.

Item: As a council member of the American Historical Association, I argued we should find a university press, familiar with journal publication, to publish the *American Historical Review,* rather than handle our own advertising, printing, and distribution. I was proven embarrassingly wrong. No truly significant savings and no demonstrable increase in circulation could be argued for.

Item: As a member of the advisory committee of a fifty-volume series of state histories for the American Association for State and Local History, I argued that this was a natural for a university press. I was wrong. No individual press was interested, even though we were paying the authors (so no royalties were involved) and hiring an editorial staff, and a designer. A commercial press is doing it.

Item: As a colonial historian, convinced of the importance of and need for a new edition of the works of Captain John Smith, I thought a university press would surely be able to publish it without subsidy. We have a distinguished editor and are subsidizing the research. Instead, it is taking the combined resources of a learned society, a library, an institute, and a corporation to subsidize the manufacture and publication by a university press.

Item: Even though our collection of Indian captivity narratives is the best in the world, and well known, it was to a small commercial publisher that we turned to bring out, as we are next year, 212 titles in facsimile with an introductory volume by one of the country's leading scholars.

These random reflections about bemusing experiences may indeed be the real causes of the following remarks about university presses seen through the eyes of a research librarian.

I have to say that university presses are pricing us out of the current book market. I am not sure of these data, but one of my colleagues in the library world has calculated that over the past ten years current book prices have increased 10% per year, compounded, or some 238%. Our book budget at the Newberry Library has perhaps increased 50% in that period and, as a result, in order to attempt to keep up with current books, including continuations and serials, we can no longer buy antiquarian books on our operating budget, but must buy them only from special funds. And, while we are still able to acquire most current books in certain of our major fields, such as the Italian Renaissance, the American Indian, the history of printing, nineteenth-century American literature, and the history of the American West, we have to be very, very selective elsewhere. Unlike you, and unlike university libraries, we have no consumers to whom we can pass on these extra costs—the costs stop with us. We either have to raise more money or not buy. If we do not buy, to whom will you sell? The captive market allegedly represented by libraries just isn't there any more.

We all suffer, I suppose, from the post-Sputnik educational boom and bust. And just as universities and colleges failed to read or heed the distant early warning signals in the late 1960s, so, I gather, did the university presses. The foreseeable declines in the growth rate, and eventually in the growth, of colleges and universities were also forecasts of a declining market for books. What none of us could foresee, of course, was the inflation-depression that currently compounds our economic problems.

But I have to ask if university presses didn't, to a significant extent, bring this problem—now so compounded by a declining market and inflation-depression—on themselves?

First it is my unsubstantiated impression that, at least as early as Sputnik, presses began going 'big time.' They first of all became more concerned—or as much concerned—with the package as with the contents, as though McLuhan were right and the medium were the message. As a result, overheads for recruiting manuscripts, design, printing, paper, dustjackets, and advertising went up and keep going up.

Second, presses created staffs and procedures that acted as production lines that had to be fed—*sometimes*, perhaps, regardless of whether the food was palatable. As chairman of the AHA Beveridge prize committee, for example, I came to the conclusion in the mid-1960s that any book, good or indifferent—sometimes bad—could be published without subsidy; and we switched the prize money from free publication to an author's award to get him started on his next book.

Third, in competition for manuscripts among themselves and with commercial publishers, university presses increasingly offered royalties and other inducements to authors who were already rewarded enough, both psychologically and financially, by the mere fact of publication. Those who insisted on royalties could have switched to commercial publishers, relieving university presses of that burden.

Fourth, presses failed to co-operate among themselves to find a way significantly to improve the efficiency of distribution and thus reduce overhead costs per book sold. In co-operation with their chief market—university libraries—it seems to me, the presses might have set up a joint venture to establish bibliographical control over all books in print, and to distribute university press books from a central warehouse with centralized billing. Such a venture could have expanded to include commercial books in print, and, through its contacts in the book world and by the use of reprography, could have supplied a copy—microfilm, microfiche, Xerox, or printed—of any book wanted by any college or university anywhere. Perhaps the presses might have undertaken such services if they had viewed themselves less as competitive entrepreneurial ventures and more as service institutions designed primarily to enhance scholarship. But they didn't, and their warehouses were full.

The end results, of course, were the book sales of this decade. If it is true that architects cover their mistakes with ivy, and doctors bury theirs, then it can be said that in the 1970s university presses remainder theirs.

If the above liabilities are only partially true, they are serious, and I think that in the seventies the presses must find ways to remove them if they are to survive. But this is not my only concern, as a research librarian, with the performance of university presses.

While these presses as a group have published an extraordinary number of monographic works, studies, and biographies in the last twenty years or so, and while they have properly over-burdened themselves economically with documentaries (such as the founding fathers series) and editions (such as the Editions of American Authors series—Melville, *et al.*), my experience, at least, has been that, unlike the more ephemeral monographs, such research tools as bibliographies, documentaries, and editions have always required subsidies from authors, editors, and the supporters of their research. The Newberry Library alone has had to subsidize—by more than $150,000 in the past ten years—the manufacture of such important works as bibliographies, check lists, the Melville edition, the Publications of the Renaissance Text Society, the Publications of the Society for the History of Discoveries, and our own series—the Nebenzahl Lectures in the History of Cartography—or they wouldn't have been published. Soon we will be subsidizing a major bibliographical guide on Indian-white Relations, from 1607 to the present, and a new edition of the works of Captain John Smith in three volumes.

A second area, of non-economic irritation, concerns dissertations. Somehow the university presses seem to have concerned themselves only with the top of the iceberg of research and writing. Admittedly, some, maybe many, of the thousands of dissertations produced this year will deservedly be forgotten. Admittedly, many will ultimately be published. But the vast majority will moulder in departmental or university archives untouched, and unread, except by the author and the author's committee.

Now this is not all bad. In the first place, the training the authors got will not necessarily be wasted, even if they don't apply it in teaching or in scholarly research. In the second place, many dissertations will be boiled down to articles (instead of being inflated into unnecessary books) and as articles will subject their basic ideas to scrutiny in the marketplace and possibly draw attention to the originals. Still, at an average cost of from $5,000 to $10,000 for two years of research and writing (not counting professors' time), a great deal of expensive research gets buried each year. Surely the university presses have some obligation to help this material surface.

It seems to me that university faculties and university presses should be very concerned about this problem. And they ought to get together, through bodies like the Association of American University Presses, the American Historical Association, and the Modern Language Association, to find a satisfactory and equally prestigious substitute for the present form of book publishing for these and other worthwhile manuscripts that cannot hope to be issued as printed books, especially in the 1970s.

For example, I recently suggested to one university press—without success, because the costs were too high—that there ought to be a journal to review American History dissertations. Such a venture should have several good results. First, it would improve the quality of dissertations, because a doctoral committee would know that a scholar outside its department and university would be reviewing its seal of approval. Second, it would help identify those dissertations that ought to be reworked for publication as books. Third, it would bring young scholars quickly to the attention of the academic world. Fourth, it would make the information and ideas in those dissertations recoverable before publication as a book. Fifth, it would help lead to a narrowing of the prestige gap between an unpublished dissertation and a published work. And sixth, it would lead libraries to encourage the kind of on-demand publishing represented by Xerox University Microfilms. Despite the high per-copy price, I believe that libraries would systematically purchase dissertations and other works in this form if they were adequately reviewed.

The utility and economy of on-demand publishing of this kind, and the success of Xerox University Microfilms in developing it over the past thirty years, lead to my next criticism of university presses. With certain exceptions, it seems to me, university presses have been concerned more with the package than with the substance, leaving to commercial entrepreneurs the development and exploitation of other-than-book-or-journal-publishing. The printed page, not the information on it, has beguiled them.

I instance such major, even revolutionary, publishing ventures as Clifford K. Shipton's microcard edition of the Evans bibliography—

all the books published in America before 1800; and University Microfilms' two major projects—the doctoral dissertations and the Pollard and Redgrave *Short Title Catalogue.* In fact, the list of businesses that have invested heavily to make scholarly materials available for study and research in forms *other than the printed page* is bewilderingly large. Among them, Xerox University Microfilms, Bell and Howell, 3M, the *New York Times,* Research Publications Inc., Readex Corporation, Encyclopaedia Brittanica, etc., are but a few. But where were the university presses? They were strategically located—as commercial ventures were not—within the university-research community to find out what was needed, to identify the scholars who could say where it was and how it should be organized, and to work closely with librarians and other scholars in the production process.

Why didn't the university presses join together to set up a major project to capture this field of publication? I don't know. If they had, we libraries that are called the 'have libraries' would probably not have felt it necessary to load commercial production costs by charging permission fees to reprint our unique or rare materials; we could have worked out adequate bibliographical control, so as to avoid the mistakes of commercial ventures; and we would have had better quality control. Thus the chaos that now exists in the microprint industry might possibly have been avoided.

That university presses have virtually ignored this field is also, I believe, a function of their placing too much emphasis on prestige—for fine design, for important authors, and on the tradition of book publication—rather than seeking to publish in the most economical form both the materials for research and the results of research that would make them demonstrably necessary even to the most economy-minded university administrator.

In sum, universities, libraries, and university presses are all in trouble today. To a certain degree, those troubles come from economic and social forces beyond our control—declining school population, inflation, depression. But all of us, not the least libraries, failed to heed the warning signals of the 1960s and, even more important, made mistakes of commission that led us to where we are today. If we are to survive, we will have to identify those mistakes and, if we can, rectify them. Otherwise I do not think society will be interested in bailing us out simply because we exist.

INDEPENDENT RESEARCH LIBRARIES:

"TRULY NATIONAL LIBRARIES"

In this testimony by Towner before a congressional committee in 1973, the Independent Research Libraries Association (IRLA) made its first national public appearance. The association took shape in 1971–1972.

The fifteen libraries who formed the association included institutions founded in the eighteenth century that were older than the republic, a host of institutions like the Newberry a century or so old, and the famous New York Public Library whose research collections are privately endowed. Yet as a body they had little public recognition and had lost out on the expansion of federal funds to libraries—to university or public libraries.

The National Endowment for the Humanities soon after its inception in 1966 began to respond to their needs, and IRLA supported expanded appropriations for the NEH. To make the case for federal support, Towner stressed as examples precisely the kind of programs Newberry had developed.

STATEMENT OF DR. LAWRENCE W. TOWNER, DIRECTOR, NEWBERRY LIBRARY, CHICAGO

I am Lawrence Towner, Director of the Newberry Library in Chicago. I am delighted to be here and to have the opportunity to appear before this Joint Subcommittee.

I suppose I was selected because I am probably the oldest of the directors—and therefore more expendable—and partly because the Newberry has benefited so greatly from the National Endowment in the several programs that we have instituted at the Newberry over the past several years, and partly, I suppose, just for comic relief.

"Statement" and "Testimony," in U.S. Congress, Senate Committee on Labor and Public Welfare, House Committee on Education and Labor, Joint Hearings, *National Foundation on the Arts and Humanities Amendments of 1973*, 93d Cong., 1st sess., 6–8 March 1973, 733–38.

I would like to summarize briefly the gist of the testimony that I have submitted as a representative of the Independent Research Libraries Association. I can do so very quickly by saying essentially it is a paradox that this Nation faces with regard to its independent research libraries.

Since World War II, it has been very clear national policy that the colleges and universities of this country should make higher education available to every qualified individual—regardless of race, sex, or even financial condition—so that he or she could improve himself or herself and make a contribution to our society.

This national policy has resulted, as you know, in a tremendous increase in the number of undergraduate and graduate students in our colleges and universities, and a tremendous increase in the faculty trained to teach them, to write the books they would read, and to enlarge their understanding of the humanities.

The other side of the paradox is that the libraries of last resort for research for these professors and graduate students are the independent research libraries.

Independent, as Secretary Wirtz said, because we are not appendages of any university or other institution and because we receive neither institutional funds from universities as university libraries do nor public funds from taxpayers as public libraries do.

Research, because of the very nature of our collections, which have been gathered, as Secretary Wirtz said, over the last 163 years almost entirely as the result of private resources.

This paradox is that despite our national educational policy that places a great burden on our libraries, we have been largely ineligible for any public support to meet the increased demand for services, the increased costs of labor and staff, and the tremendously increased costs of books and manuscripts.

We had been almost completely ineligible for any public support from the national government, until the National Endowment for the Humanities stepped into the breach with certain judicious grants that have enabled us to accomplish some of the things independent research institutions ought to accomplish.

It has enabled us to take on a role of research institutions somewhat larger than the ordinary character of a library—that is, we are becoming independent research libraries with independent research programs. So we are very happy to appear here to support the National Endowment for the Humanities in its request for reauthorization and for increased finances.

We feel that the National Endowment is vital to our activities, and we hope that the Congress in its wisdom will appropriate even larger funds than are being requested, because we feel we need all the help we can get.

The National Endowment's role in helping us goes beyond the individual dollars they give us. In most cases the grants they have given us have been matching grants, and we have had to raise a dollar for every dollar they give us. But even beyond that the recognition by this great National Foundation in the Arts and Humanities has given us an increased visibility in the local communities—which are primarily responsible for supporting our activities—that has enabled us to raise more money than ordinarily would have been the case.

(The prepared statement of Dr. Towner follows:)

*

Ladies and Gentlemen, I am Lawrence W. Towner, Director and Librarian of the Newberry Library, Chicago, Illinois. I am here as spokesman for fourteen libraries throughout the country, recently joined together in an informal organization called the Independent Research Libraries Association (IRLA).[1] We wish to give our strongest support to the reauthorization and increased funding sought by the National Foundation on the Arts and Humanities and its division, The National Endowment for the Humanities, as expressed in S. 795 and H.R. 3926 and in substantially similar bills introduced by Senator Jacob Javits and Congressman Albert Quie.

Let me speak first, however, as a scholar-teacher, an occupation which absorbed my energies for sixteen years before I became director of a library. I was trained as a specialist in Early American History, at Northwestern University. I have taught, both undergraduate and graduate courses, at several colleges and universities, including Northwestern, the University of Chicago, MIT, the College of William and Mary, and Radcliffe College. For six years I edited *the* scholarly journal in my field, *The William and Mary Quarterly: A Magazine of Early American History.*

As a scholar-teacher, an occupation I still have the privilege of

1. American Antiquarian Society, Worcester, Massachusetts; American Philosophical Society, Philadelphia; John Crerar Library, Chicago; Folger Shakespeare Library, Washington, D.C.; Linda Hall Library, Kansas City, Missouri; Historical Society of Pennsylvania, Philadelphia; Henry E. Huntington Library, San Marino, California; Library Company of Philadelphia, Philadelphia; Massachusetts Historical Society, Boston; Pierpont Morgan Library, New York; Newberry Library, Chicago; New York Academy of Medicine, New York; New York Public Library, New York; Virginia Historical Society, Richmond.

exercising occasionally, there is no doubt in my mind about the signal importance for humane learning and its dissemination of the National Endowment for the Humanities. In a society such as ours—whose ideals express the loftiest aspirations for mankind's freedom and self-expression, but which nonetheless is most renowned for its material culture, its technology, and its science—support for the humanities should have a high national priority. Yet until the creation of the National Foundation on the Arts and Humanities, there was not a single agency of the Federal government that had the encouragement of the humanities as its primary objective. At a time when science, for example, was properly getting millions for its support, history, literature, philosophy, and the other humane studies were admitted only at the back door. Ironically, history often had to rely for the few crumbs it got on the social science division of the National Science Foundation.

The National Endowment for the Humanities, therefore, came as a new dawn for the humanities; and its help has been very important. Never more important than today, however, for universities and colleges, as this Subcommittee well knows, are caught in a crisis that may wipe out many of them. This crisis has already significantly lessened the opportunity for employment, for research, and for publication on the part of hundreds of Ph.D.s turned out in response to society's demands for more scholar-teachers. The National Endowment for the Humanities can be crucial in this transition period by supporting individual research and larger programs that effectively use our current surplus of trained scholars while at the same time enriching our cultural heritage.

But I can speak most concretely, and most appropriately, about the growing importance of the National Endowment for the Humanities to the group of libraries I represent today. Since most of us are libraries in the humanities and since most of us are cut off from other sources of Federal support, the Endowment is of particular importance to us.

We have placed on the table a package of materials—statistics and brief statements—from our individual libraries that we hope you will examine at your leisure. But let me observe in summary, that we hold in our collections more than twenty million volumes, a large percentage of them rare and costly, and more than forty million unique manuscripts dealing with the history and literature of Western Civilization. These library materials represent a priceless asset of the American people, gathered together through private efforts, and preserved and made available to scholars, whether academic or lay, throughout the nation.

The libraries I represent are called "independent," because they are neither subordinate agencies of universities nor dependent upon taxes, as public libraries ordinarily are. They are called "research" libraries, because their primary rôle is to provide the research materials for scholars who interpret the past to us and enlarge our understanding and appreciation of humane values as expressed in the literary and other written records of mankind. Finally, because our collections reach beyond the bounds of a single city, state, or region, and because our readers come from every state in the union, as well as from abroad, we are truly national libraries, serving a national clientele, and a national purpose.

Our independence is both a boon and a liability. It is a boon, because we add to the number of non-governmental agencies that, in competition with all levels of government, keep our society open and free. Moreover, our independence and our freedom from the constraints of parental institutions allow us a greater flexibility and opportunity to innovate, within the limits of our means, than otherwise would be the case. Our independence is also a liability because unlike university libraries, we have no alumni to draw upon for support, and unlike tax-supported institutions, we cannot depend on public funds to meet our budgets. Instead, the money we need for operations, for acquisitions, for building expansion, and for programs must come either out of our endowments or out of monies we raise, *almost always from the private sector.*

In this situation, The National Endowment for the Humanities represents an important, even crucial, exception for us. Hitherto cut off from Federal funds earmarked for educational purposes because we are not included in the Congressional definition of educational institutions, we have begun to expect and get some help from the National Endowment. This is so because the Endowment's successive chairmen and staff members, humanists themselves, have perceived the important rôle we can play in furthering their objectives. They know how vital we are to humanistic endeavor, because they themselves have been nurtured on our collections. They recognize the freedom to innovate that our independence gives us, and they value its existence. They understand that by helping us they are helping all institutions and all individuals engaged in humanistic research, writing, and publication. Finally, they anticipated the changes we are now undergoing as we become a good bit more than

INDEPENDENT RESEARCH LIBRARIES 257

"mere" research libraries, but instead, important educational institutions in our own right, often working alone, but equally often working in co-operation with other more formal educational institutions.

Let me give but two concrete examples. It took imagination and courage on the part of the National Endowment to make its two challenge grants to the New York Public Library, the greatest in our membership. The ability to perceive the need, and more important, to act upon it quickly, was humanistic statesmanship of high order; and the National Endowment deserves great praise for those acts of wisdom.

I can speak more authoritatively of our own experience at the Newberry Library. With the help of the National Endowment we have maintained an advanced level undergraduate seminar in the humanities with twelve fine private colleges organized as the Associated Colleges of the Midwest. We have acquired and made available a significant collection of books and manuscripts dealing with the subject of religious liberty, a fundamental ideal of our society. We have supported, with the Institute of Early American History and Culture of Williamsburg, Virginia, a major research project whose first product will be an Atlas of the American Revolutionary Period, 1760–1790. This publication, we believe, will be one of the finest products of the Bicentennial celebration of our Nation's birth. And we have inaugurated, this last fall, a Center for the History of the American Indian, designed to anticipate, and therefore alleviate, the kinds of problems that arose in the recent spread of Black Studies programs—too few trained scholar-teachers, and inadequate library resources. Altogether, we have received some $1,500,000 from the National Endowment, *half of which was raised from the private sector in response to their challenge grants.*

Five observations should be made with regard to the above-mentioned programs. First, in all cases, they originated at an independent research library because it had the necessary library resources already collected. Second, in all cases they were co-operative programs, doing something better and less expensively than single institutions could have done separately. Third, in all cases they bring men and women together for varying lengths of time whose experience in the programs will eventually enrich several institutions, not one. Fourth, while in two instances, private funds got them started, none of them could have been sustained without the kind of money only the National Endowment has. And finally, all of them attracted as much, or more, money from a variety of private sources.

In the Newberry's case, thus, and increasingly in the cases of other members of the Independent Research Libraries Association, the National Endowment has become crucial to our effective operation in meeting the growing opportunities to serve. We shall become eventually, I believe, library nucleii around which are built great research institutions.

But even today we need funds for almost every aspect of our operations—acquisitions, binding, conservation, construction, fellowships, and publications. Most of these we expect to raise in a carefully orchestrated combination of local support and grants from national foundations. But our ability to do so will be greatly enhanced by the judicious support on select occasions by the National Endowment for the Humanities.

We are confident that, if the Endowment is generously funded, our institutions will get a fair share. We are confident, not only because we have experienced the Endowment's imaginative perception of our needs and opportunities, but also because we have experienced the Endowment's careful scrutiny as they examine individual proposals, and we are sure we can compete.

We urge this Subcommittee, therefore, to support the authorization bills before you, and, when the time is ripe, to support generously the necessary appropriation.

26

ON "PURE SCHOLARSHIP" AND
"PUBLIC PROGRAMS"

From the inception of the National Endowment for the Humanities, there was a difference of opinion among its advocates as to how much support should go to "pure" scholarship and how much to "public programs." Senator Clairborne Pell of Rhode Island, the "father" of the Endowment, favored the approach of the National Endowment for the Arts which put heavy emphasis on public programs by the state arts councils and in 1976 introduced an amendment to push the NEH in this direction.

In a letter to Senator Pell whom he held in high regard, Towner justified support for "pure" scholarship, defending it from the charge of "elitism." Towner made the same case for so-called esoteric humanities research that scientists made for the National Science Foundation: the ultimate but unpredictable benefit of basic research to society.

The issue has been recurrent in the history of NEH, and there is no reason to think it will disappear.

Dear Senator Pell:

Your recent remarks on the National Endowment for the Humanities, as reported in the *Chronicle of Higher Education*, are deeply distressing and leave me truly bewildered. In a letter to you dated September 20, 1975, I described the Endowment as "a bright star in the often murky American skies," perhaps the only bright star; and I now greatly fear that your apparent disenchantment with the agency (and its present chairman) leaves it more exposed to congressional neglect and disfavor than ever before. If its father mislikes it, who can love it? I hope, therefore, that this letter, unsolicited and unprompted, may help to lift your wrath a bit.

It would be less than candid of me to fail to say that I have a strong

Letter to Claiborne Pell, 17 February 1976, Towner Papers, Newberry Archives.

personal interest in the continued growth and success of the National Endowment. As a citizen, a scholar, a former teacher, and now head of a great research library in the humanities, I can hardly lay claim to objectivity when it comes to the NEH. Still, I think my frank assessment, discounted for special pleading, may be of some value to you as you review your position.

My earlier letter argues *against* the so-called Pell Amendment. It is an honest letter, in that it says what experience had led me to believe. Yet, I almost did not send it, because I feared that I was not privy to your motives in offering the amendment. There was the possibility that you had in mind a grand design for securing the Endowment's congressional support by mandating a distribution of some of its funds to all fifty states—a motive and a plan that I would have applauded and endorsed *in that context*. Nonetheless, I concluded that my letter, stressing the overall importance of your creation, would only increase your determination to proceed on your own course. I sent it, therefore, because I did not feel competent to make the political judgment.

But I do feel competent to make some observations on your remarks as reported in the *Chronicle*. It is ironic that your criticisms of Mr. Berman and the NEH should, by implication, focus on the same area—public programs—where he has received the most criticism in the scholarly world, *but from an opposite point of view.* Your criticism is that not enough money has gone to the general public and that too much has gone to scholars and to academe. Academic criticism—such as it is, and it grows less—invariably focuses on the (to us) immense sums going to public broadcasting, courses by newspapers, state humanities councils, and the American Issues Forum (to the last two of which I have donated hundreds of hours), instead of to research and higher education in the humanities. That field had been virtually ignored (unlike the sciences) by the federal government until you funded the NEH. I think it fair to say, therefore, that the NEH, under Mr. Berman's direction, has not only given great and important support to so-called elite studies, it has also led hundreds of scholars—sometimes reluctantly—to seek ways to make the humanities directly and immediately "available" to the out-of-school public.

In reality, however, there is no real dichotomy between "elite" studies on the one hand, and public programs on the other. Just as scientific research, such as that supported by the National Science Foundation, no matter how esoteric, ultimately affects the public directly, so also do humanistic research, experimental educational programs, library support programs, and the like. I feel confident in that observation, for as the head of a research library used primarily by advanced scholars, I constantly have to face the question of so-called elitism, not only when seeking public support but also in justifying the only life I have.

But I know that the research done here, like the research done through the support of the National Endowment for the Humanities, will alter the perceptions of history and of literature and, ultimately, of the life of millions of people who will never step inside the Newberry's doors, just as millions will never step inside the government-supported accelerator laboratory at Batavia, Illinois. The impact of these "esoteric" studies is greater than one immediately perceives. Historians, students of literature, philosophers—to name only the most obvious humanists—respond as congressmen and senators do to the perceived problems of our times. Indeed, like poets and artists, they often perceive the problems before they have become acute enough to engage the attention of the Congress. A simple cataloguing of major issues before our society, it can be said with assurance, is not a bad guide to the cutting edge of humanistic scholarship today: the problems of the blacks, Indian-White relations, ethnic communities and their relationship to the dominant culture, the disintegration of the family, sexual mores, the ghetto, housing, violence and other forms of crime, education, social values, women in society, alienation, the poor, agricultural policy, foreign policy, war, ecology, religion in American life, civil liberties—the list goes on.

To be sure, some research that humanists do, like some research scientists do, *is* esoteric and remote—"pure" scholarship: the connections with reality may be so remote they cannot be perceived. A "Golden Fleece" award, for example, might well be bestowed upon a computer analysis of the numbers of actors required to fill the parts in a series of Shakespeare's plays. Yet such a study could determine how large an Elizabethan company of actors had to be, thus *when* a particular play was first performed, and thus a clue as to when the play was written. That might be research that would keep a great teacher (who teaches teachers of Shakespeare, who, in turn, will reach thousands and thousands of students) charged up to teach Shakespeare effectively, because the research satisfies his curiosity. Thus, even this extreme example of esoterica can be justified, if one needs to justify it. (It was not an NEH project, by the way.) But, to belabor my point, the scholarship that goes on in a research library today, will tomorrow, or the next day, be reflected even in grade school textbooks used by millions of students.

I would not make the comparison myself, but since you made it, invidiously, I should, in closing, address the problem of the popular programs of the Endowment for the Arts versus the scholarly focus of the Endowment for the Humanities. Two observations should be made. First, the participation you see in the arts is *viewer* participation—watching in other words. The viewers are not, themselves, dancing, painting, or performing music. The nearest equivalent to viewers in the humanities is listeners at a lecture; and it would be simple to put on thousands of lectures, though not so simple to get people to listen. Instead, the humanities requires participation— discussion, reading a book, doing research—a significant commitment. Second, the mechanisms for popular communication (i.e., visual communication) in the arts already exist—museums, orchestras, ballet companies, opera companies, and the like (enhanced by T.V.), and they have strong support from the general public who pay to *see*. But the mechanisms for participation in the humanities will have to be created (except for schools, colleges, and libraries). People won't pay to see a scholar writing a book, alas. It seems to me that the NEH has sought with considerable vigor and imagination to create those mechanisms that *will* directly involve the public.

In sum, the National Endowment for the Humanities is *so* important to the scholarly world, and to the institution that I represent (which also serves the general public), that I beg of you once more to look upon your creation with favor. It has done magnificently well.

Sincerely yours,
Lawrence W. Towner
President and Librarian

27

"WHAT ARE OUR NATIONAL

PRIORITIES, ANYHOW?":

IN DEFENSE OF THE

NATIONAL ENDOWMENT FOR

THE HUMANITIES

In 1981, the first year of the Ronald Reagan administration, the mood had shifted. The president called for drastic reductions in NEH and NEA budgets and for eliminating the National Historical Publications and Records Commission, "while in the same breath" calling for $2.5 billion for a new bomber.

In testifying for IRLA, Towner's mood also shifted. There were times when his job required that he walk a political tightrope; this was not one of them. Defining himself as "a life-long liberal Democrat," he conceded the need for budgetary restraint but asked, "What are our national priorities, anyhow?"

Attempting to reach conservatives on an assumption they supported, Towner stressed the crucial role of the NEH's "challenge" and "matching" grants to "leverage" contributions from the private sector. They had become an indispensable "catalyst," he argued, pointing to the Newberry's experience. Congress restored funds to the two endowments, but the warfare over levels of funding continued through the 1980s.

"Statement" and "Testimony," in U.S. Congress, House, Committee on Education and Labor, *Budget Allocations for the Endowments for the Arts and Humanities, and Museums and Libraries: Hearings before the Subcommittee on Postsecondary Education,* 97th Cong., 1st sess. (2 March 1987), pp. 55–60.

I would like to summarize but for the sake of brevity I will not summarize. I will simply say my testimony has been prepared and distributed. I just make a few observations: the first observation I would like to make is, Leonard Garment, where are you? If President Nixon's Leonard Garment were in the White House with the present President, we would not have this problem. I think it should be Mr. Garment rather than President Nixon who should get credit for the programs in the arts and humanities area.

I would like to quote one paragraph from the "Mandate for Leadership" published by the Heritage Foundation:

> . . . the significance of NEH goes to the heart of American society. American society strives both for liberty and equality. Freedom and justice for all is our credo. But these goals are not always in harmony. Can a modern society achieve their full implementation when they are judged to be in tension? This great question of modern life animates the recent public debate about elitism and populism in the agency's actions. At its best, the NEH stands for excellence, the highest fruit of the pursuit of liberty.

That seems to me to be inconsistent with this document, in the program for economic recovery submitted by the administration to the Congress with regard to the budget.

I think chiefly the inconsistency is because of a misunderstanding on the part of the administration of the role that the National Endowment for the Humanities has played in stimulating support by the private sector. It makes the point here that the Federal Government should not be the answer; that the policy of having it be such has resulted in the reduction of the historical role of the private sector. It is baloney to make that statement. It reflects, it seems to me, instead, the attitude toward the humanities and toward scholarship that Governor Reagan as Governor of the State of California intended when he said, "Why don't we sell the Bancroft Library? It is costing the State of California too much." It may have been Reagan's attorney general who said that.

I contrast it with the attitude of President Kennedy who when he received the first volume of the papers of Thomas Jefferson in an august assembly of American scholars said there had been no time in American history when so many scholars were gathered in one place except when Thomas Jefferson sat alone in his study.

That attitude toward scholarship is the kind of attitude toward scholarship we need to have in the White House.

I have been on a council which is the prime sponsor of the publication "The Papers of Thomas Jefferson, John Adams, James Madison, George Washington, and Benjamin Franklin." Therefore I can speak with some authority on that. I am on three such boards.

The administration's position is embarrassing and it gives the idea, it seems to me, of the attitude of our administration toward culture in general that must be distressing not only to all people who live in the United States but to our friends abroad.

Let me close by quoting my last paragraph.

In conclusion, Mr. Chairman, I would like to reemphasize what I said earlier. We all know cuts have to be made. How they are recommended tells the world much about our President: How they are actually carried out will tell much about the Congress. While it is the President who proposes, it is the Congress who disposes—both are necessary to get a balanced product. We are confident you will see to that. Thank you very much.

[The prepared testimony of Lawrence Towner follows:]

Prepared Testimony of Lawrence W. Towner, President and Librarian, the Newberry Library

Mr. Chairman and members of the Committee, I want to thank you for this opportunity to testify with regard to the National Endowment for the Humanities. As Mr. Simon knows, for he has "committed" research at the Newberry Library in Chicago, I am President and Librarian of a great public treasure that belongs to all the people of these United States. It is a research, reference, and rare book library in history and the humanities, and it is one of fifteen such privately endowed institutions that serve the scholarly-minded public free of charge. [We are represented by the Independent Research Libraries Association, of which I am past chairman and co-founder. Together we hold some 13–15 million volumes and provide, annually, nearly one million research days free of charge. We are: The American Antiquarian Society, American Philosophical Society, The John Crerar Library, The Folger Shakespeare Library, Linda Hall Library, The Historical Society of Pennsylvania, The Huntington Library, The Library Company of Philadelphia, Massachusetts Historical Society, The Pierpont Morgan Library, The Newberry Library, The New York Academy of Medicine, The New-York Historical Society, The New York Public Library, and The Virginia Historical Society.] I can speak on the Newberry Library and its sister institutions with considerable authority, and often do so, even without invitation.

But I also speak with experience, if not with quite such authority, about The National Endowment for the Humanities. I have been friends with its last three illustrious Chairmen: Messrs. Barnaby Keeney, Ronald Berman, and Joseph Duffey; my institution has greatly benefited from the imaginative and fruitful way the NEH has used public money to stimulate private institutions; and I have, in turn, gladly made my time and energy available to help the NEH achieve our mutual goals. In the latter regard, I have read scores of proposals, served on several panels, raised more than $25,000 for the Thomas Jefferson Lectures in the Humanities, served on the Chicago Area American Issues Forum, and was Chairman of the Illinois Humanities Council for three years. These are my bona fides.

While I have been asked to address two questions specifically, I would like to preface my remarks by saying that even a life-long liberal Democrat can see that our economy is in trouble, that inflation is its greatest enemy, and that cutting federal deficits must be a priority on both sides of the aisle. But I also think that we should all suffer, not just the poor, not just the educational establishment, not just the arts and the humanities, but all, even that most sacred of all cows, Defense; and we should suffer equally, in due proportion. It does not seem to me to be equal and in due proportion when the two Endowments' budgets are slated to be slashed so drastically; when the National Historical Publications and Records Commission—the chief support of the publication of the papers of our Founding Fathers, should be zeroed out of existence; and when, almost in the same breath, the President should call for $2.5 billion for a new bomber. What are our national priorities, anyhow? What is it we are defending?

With the above in mind, I would like to address first the question of the impact the proposed cuts would have on leveraging private contributions. In an about-to-be-published article for The American Library Association Yearbook, I speak of the impact of the NEH and its gifts and matching grants and its more recent challenge grants. Historically, they have been terribly important. "Indeed," I say there, "most of us would still be slugabeds waiting for our Trustees to come to our rescue if we had not been rousted out by the challenging opportunities the NEH began providing as early as the late Barnaby Keeney's days." In an article in Humanities, December, 1980, which

I have copied and submitted as an appendix to my written testimony, I say that "The leverage NEH provides is far greater than its actual funding capabilities. Through gifts and matching grants and, more recently, Challenge Grants it has justly come to be considered the main catalyst in stimulating the private sector."

Certainly that has been true at the Newberry Library. Since the first grant we got, during the administration of the late Barnaby Keeney—who challenged us with $50,000 to raise another $50,000 to bring a very important collection of books to America—we have raised several millions of dollars at the Newberry for scholarly programs, library operations (in a crucial three-year period) and for renovation.

With a challenge or gifts-and-matching grant in hand, I have fearlessly entered the offices of trustees, private individuals, foundations, and corporations seeking matching money. Now our donors almost reflexively ask, "Can this be matched in some way?" If my answer turns out to be "no," because the Reagan Administration persuaded the Congress to cut the NEH budget disproportionately to other programs, we will start losing the very support the NEH helped us create.

With regard to the human, community, and other consequences of the Administration's proposals, it is not so easy to be so specific, but let me "for instance" a few "for instances" to suggest the dimensions of the problem.

It takes an act of real imagination for a person who is not himself a scholar to get excited about what happens in a research library. Indeed, if my memory serves me, President Reagan, when Governor of California, suggested that the great Bancroft Library of the University of California be sold to save money—we would gladly have bought it if we could have. Obviously the President was not excited by what goes on in a research library. But I think I can excite you just by talking about one or two programs the NEH has helped us with at the Newberry—my "for instances."

Our Center for the History of the American Indian, now ten-years and three-million dollars old, and sponsored by NEH grants matched by such left-wing liberals as W. Clement Stone (who gave $115,000), is a case in point. The history of Indian-white relations in this country is being rewritten as a consequence of this Center. Post- and pre-doctoral scholars are brought to the Library to use our great resources, to write books and dissertations, and to study so they can be better teachers. High school teachers come in the summer to study Indian history and to work up curriculum units; Indians from

embodied in our own lives and actions. That, after all, is what the humanities are all about: the late Denham Sutcliffe of Kenyon College once asked, "What Shall We Defend?" All of us who call ourselves students of the humanities know in our bones what the answer to that question is. But how shall we defend the humanities in the eighties?

To survive the eighties, and beyond, we will have to be like the sharks—aggressive, tough, and adaptable. We will have to be ready to seize those opportunities that do present themselves and use what resources are available. Both are substantial—far greater than our pessimistic assumptions tell us.

The resources, if we weigh and allocate them prudently and rationally, are sufficient to meet the challenges that constitute our agenda for the eighties. That agenda includes:

- continued encouragement of research and writing,
- continued support of publication in the humanities,
- completion of the great historical and literary editorial projects begun in the fifties, sixties and seventies,
- intensified training in languages and other skills that foster scholarship in the humanities,
- improvement of teaching,
- creating new audiences for the humanities,
- keeping underemployed scholars involved in their disciplines,
- collecting and preserving research materials.

We think of the fifties and sixties as the golden age of academic expansion and assume that today's opportunities are meager and today's resources a pale shadow of that palmy era. But our resources now are, in fact, enormous compared to what was available in those supposedly halcyon days.

In this country we have the largest community of highly educated men and women ever known and a wider variety of educational and support institutions ever imagined, even by the most thoughtful and optimistic educational leaders of the past.

The human resources are unprecedented in numbers and unparalleled in quality of training. Of the 86,000 Ph.D.'s awarded in the humanities since 1920, nearly 45 percent, or 38,420 of the recipients, have been out of school only ten years. Nearly 72 percent, or 61,489, have been out only twenty years.

New employment opportunities in academe are, obviously, sharply curtailed compared with the 1960s. But think of the great reservoir of brain power (every year they seem to get brighter as I get dimmer) those Ph.D.'s represent. One of the greatest opportunities—and responsibilities—of the 1980s is to keep all these men and women linked to scholarship and the humanities, if not to academe—to harness all that intellectual energy and talent.

The educational establishment that we put in place in the post-Sputnik decades is also unprecedented. Admittedly, we tend—with a shudder—to single out the possible demise of colleges in the eighties, and brace ourselves at least for curtailed academic budgets and ventures. But allowing for some institutional failures, and even with a slow-growth or no-growth policy, we have in our society as the decade begins the largest educational establishment and, I think, the finest, to be found anywhere in the world.

Granted, the humanities disciplines will have to work to retain audiences and practitioners in languages, history, literature and the classics. We will have to seek new audiences among the out-of-school adult population with greater purpose and imagination than we have in the past. But these strategies should be perceived as golden opportunities. Without a captive audience, one has to become a better teacher and a better scholar to attract people to one's classroom and writing. That is not necessarily a bad thing.

Back in the fifties and early sixties, relatively few humanities centers existed other than the traditional university departments. The Institute for Advanced Study at Princeton, the Institute of Early American History and Culture at Williamsburg, and the very modest programs at the Folger, Huntington and Newberry libraries were, in a sense, humanities centers. All, however, were the preserves of a small number of scholars who conducted their work in a rarefied atmosphere. New research would, in theory, reach a mass audience one day, much as the nineteenth-century robber barons' money would, it was presumed, trickle down to the masses eventually.

Today, the Rockefeller Foundation has identified a hundred humanities centers in the United States. The most recent, ambitious, and daring is the National Humanities Center in Research Triangle Park, North Carolina.

Also in place, ready to be used, are our peerless library resources, which have been augmented on a vast scale during the past two decades under the aegis of the Higher Education Act of 1966. They are still being augmented—albeit on a lesser scale—under renewed appropriations for that Act. Even the independent research libraries, who until recently were generally ineligible for grants under the Act, were recipients of substantial support from other sources—particularly the National Endowment for the Humanities and such enlightened foundations as the Andrew W. Mellon Foundation of New York. The fifteen libraries who organized to become the Independent Research Library Association, together hold some twelve million volumes and forty-five million manuscripts. They provide more than a million individual research days each year.

Finally, among the premier resources must be counted NEH itself. Its fifteenth birthday, just celebrated, marks a period of unimagined growth and maturity. One need only compare the puny resources at the disposal of NEH when the late Barnaby Keeney was chairman with the resources NEH can marshall today. And NEH's own funding resources only begin to describe the scope of the agency's influence. The leverage NEH provides is far greater than its actual funding capabilities. Through gifts and matching grants and, more recently, Challenge Grants, it has justly come to be considered the main catalyst in stimulating the private sector.

When I contemplate all the resources at our disposal—human, institutional, financial—I can only conclude that in the eighties we should see not a retrenchment of the humanities, but a regeneration; not a blight, but a flowering; not a fall, but a spring.

At my own institution—the Newberry Library—which I use as an example because I know it best, we have been stretching the resources at hand to seize these opportunities. In the process, a scholarly research institution that was private and reserved for the few has become virtually a public institution used—and supported—by the many. The same transformation has taken place at other independent libraries, such as the Folger, the Huntington and the American Antiquarian Society.

At the Newberry, we encourage research and writing, not simply by being there, but also by providing fellowships and supporting research centers in the fields of Indian history, family and community history, the history of cartography, and Renaissance studies.

We promote the acquisition of languages and other skills that are the lifeblood of the humanities scholar today—paleography, quantitative analysis of historical data, and the application of computer technology to historical geography.

We seek to improve teaching by fostering interdisciplinary teaching in the humanities at twenty-five midwestern colleges, by holding summer institutes in the teaching of Indian history and the history of Indian-white relations, and by encouraging the use of the new history in colleges and universities to upgrade the study and teaching of local, community and state history.

We co-sponsor and house the Chicago Metro History Fair, which exemplifies the new history and shows how it can be taught to high school students; we have worked to re-unite history with genealogy—once its respected ally but a field much disparaged by scholars. All these programs are part of an ongoing effort to attract new audiences for the humanities.

We do our best to keep underemployed scholars in touch with scholarship through a modest fellowship program and by providing access to the Newberry's materials and programs. We make the Library a home to Ph.D.'s who are employed outside of academe—whether as attorneys or taxi drivers—and we hire Ph.D.'s for every possible job, including institutional development.

In short, we are not afraid of the 1980s, and to prove it, we are currently raising $12.5 million for the new stack building we are erecting in our present facility. When the stack is completed, our "Uncommon Collection of Uncommon Collections" will have the best environment money can buy and man can devise, consistent with the use of the materials. And when the renovation of the old building is accomplished, the Newberry will have new facilities for our outreach program—classrooms, seminar rooms, a multipurpose conference room, exhibition halls, and a great reference and bibliographical center that will direct serious readers to the world's humanities resources.

At the Newberry, we see our "problems" as opportunities; if we can do it, so can the rest of the humanities community. Vast resources *are* available. We need only concentrate on seizing the opportunities that set our agenda for the eighties.

PUBLISHED WRITINGS OF

LAWRENCE W. TOWNER

1953
Review of *The Public Records of the State of Connecticut, IX*, ed. Albert E. Van Dusen. *New England Quarterly* 26:558–59.

1954
Review of *Gorges of Plymouth Fort: A Life of Sir Ferdinando Gorges*, by Richard A. Preston. *New England Quarterly* 27:274–77.

1955
A Good Master Well Served: A Social History of Servitude in Massachusetts, 1620–1750. Ann Arbor: University Microfilms. Ph.D. diss., Northwestern University.

Prefatory note to *Observations on the New Constitution, and On the Federal and State Conventions*, by Mercy Otis Warren, 3–4. Old South Leaflets, no. 226. Boston: Old South Association.

1956–1962
Editor of *The William and Mary Quarterly: A Magazine of Early American History*, 3d ser., 13, no. 3 (July 1956)–19, no. 4 (October 1962).

1956
Review of *The New England Merchants in the Seventeenth Century*, by Bernard Bailyn. *New England Quarterly* 29:117–20.

1957
"Pilgrims' Appeal." Letter to the Editor. *New York Times Magazine*, 13 October.

1959
"Dedication [to Professor Richard L. Morton]." *William and Mary Quarterly*, 3d ser., 16:163–64.

1961
Editor of *Walter Muir Whitehill: A Tribute*. Williamsburg: Institute of Early American History and Culture. Reprint, with additions, of the Trivia section in *William and Mary Quarterly*, 3d ser., 18:122–25.

Review of *Mr. Blackamore's Expeditio Ultramontana*, introd. Earl G. Swem. *William and Mary Quarterly*, 3d ser., 18:309.

1962

"*Ars Poetica et Sculptura:* Pocahontas on the Boston Common." *Journal of Southern History* 28:482–85.

"'A Fondness for Freedom': Servant Protest in Puritan Society." *William and Mary Quarterly*, 3rd ser., 19:201–19.

1963

"And Prospect." Contribution to Trivia section. *William and Mary Quarterly*, 3d ser., 20:134.

"A Look at an Old Institution by Its New Librarian: The Newberry Library." *Men and Events* (Chicago Union League Club) 39:7–11.

Review of *Colonial Justice in Western Massachusetts (1639–1702): The Pynchon Court Record*, ed. Joseph H. Smith. *William and Mary Quarterly*, 3d ser., 20:325–26.

Review of *Independent Historical Societies: An Enquiry into Their Research and Publication Functions and Their Financial Future*, by Walter Muir Whitehill. *William and Mary Quarterly*, 3d ser., 20:615–17.

Review of *Jefferson and the Ordeal of Liberty*, by Dumas Malone. *Chicago Sun-Times*, 10 February.

Review of *Puritans and Yankees: The Winthrop Dynasty of New England, 1630–1717*, by Richard S. Dunn. *Mississippi Valley Historical Review* 49:688–89.

"A Tribute to Ray Allen Billington," *Westerners Brand Book* (Chicago Corral) 20:25–27.

1964

Review of *John F. Kennedy: The Burden and the Glory*, ed. Allan Nevins. *Chicago Sun-Times*, 31 May.

Review of *The Professional: Lyndon B. Johnson*, by William S. White. *Chicago Sun-Times*, 21 June.

Review of *The South Carolina Regulators*, by Richard M. Brown. *Indiana Magazine of History* 60:203–5.

Review of *A Time for Action: A Selection of the Speeches and Writings of Lyndon B. Johnson, 1953–1964. Chicago Sun-Times*, 1 March.

"The Sewall-Saffin Dialogue on Slavery." *William and Mary Quarterly*, 3d ser., 21:40–52.

1965

Introduction to *As Sweet as Madeira . . . as Astringent as Bordeaux . . . as Brisk as Champagne: Thomas Jefferson on Wines. Facsimile of a Document from the Collection of Herbert R. Strauss*. Chicago: Privately printed.

1966

"The Indentures of Boston's Poor Apprentices: 1734–1805." *Publications* (Colonial Society of Massachusetts) 43:417–68.

Introductory essay to "John Winthrop, a Modell of Christian Charity, 1630." In *An American Primer*, ed. Daniel Boorstin, 8–25. Chicago: University of Chicago Press.

Review of *America's Frontier Heritage*, by Ray A. Billington. *Chicago Tribune*, 9 October.

1967

"Foreword." In *Chicagoans Collect in the Eighteenth Century: An Exhibition . . . on View in the Fellows' Lounge, November 30–December 30, 1967*, 1–2. Chicago: Newberry Library.

Review of *Books in America's Past: Essays Honoring Rudolph H. Gjelsness*, ed. David Kaser. *Library Quarterly* 37:408–9.

1968

"The Newberry Library: A Research Opportunity in Library History." In *Proceedings of Library History Seminar #3*, 1–16. Tallahassee: Florida State University.

Review of *Agents and Merchants: British Colonial Policy and the Origins of the American Revolution, 1763–1775*, by Jack M. Sosin. *Journal of Modern History* 40:138–39.

Review of *The First Emancipation: The Abolition of Slavery in the North*, by Arthur Zilversmit. *New England Quarterly* 41:145–46.

1969

"Association Notes: The New York Meeting, 1968." *American Historical Review* 74: 1457–59.

"Every Silver Lining Has a Cloud: The Recent Shaping of the Newberry Library's Collections." In *The Flow of Books and Manuscripts: Papers Read at a Clark Library Seminar, March 30, 1968*, by A. N. L. Munby and Lawrence W. Towner, 35–50. Los Angeles: William Andrews Clark Library, University of California, Los Angeles. Reprinted as a separate. Chicago: Newberry Library, 1970.

Introduction to *Dressed Always Cleanly & a Little More Than Decently: Thomas Jefferson to His Daughter, June 14, 1787. Facsimile of a Document from the Collection of Herbert R. Strauss*. Chicago: Privately printed.

Review of *Congregational Commonwealth: Connecticut, 1636–1662*, by Mary Jeanne Anderson Jones. *William and Mary Quarterly*, 3d ser., 26:466–67.

Review of *Dukedom Large Enough*, by David A. Randall. *Chicago Daily News*, 30–31 August.

1970

Review of *With Hammer in Hand: The Dominy Craftsmen of East Hampton, New York*, by Charles F. Hummel. *Journal of American History* 56:900–901.

"Some Informal Remarks at a Formal Occasion." On the dedication of the New York State Historical Association Library. *New York History* 51:153–59.

An Uncommon Collection of Uncommon Collections: The Newberry Library. Chicago: Newberry Library. Revised in 1971, 1976, and 1985.

1971

"The Library and the Collector: The Newberry Library." *Library Lectures* (Louisiana State University Library), 14–23.

1972

"American Studies Today—the Middle of a Revolution." From the first Japan-U.S. Conference on Libraries and Information Service in Higher Education, Tokyo, 1969. In *University and Research Libraries in Japan and the United States*, ed. Thomas R. Buckman, Yukihisa Suzuki, and Warren M. Tsuneishi, 137–43. Chicago: American Library Association. A Japanese translation was published in the original conference proceedings, Tokyo, 1969, 139–45.

"A New Life for Western History?" *Westerners Brand Book* (Chicago Corral) 29:57–58.

Review of *Open Shelves and Open Minds: A History of the Cleveland Public Library*, by C. H. Cramer. *Journal of American History* 59:727–28.

Review of *The Poetry of Edwin Muir: The Field of Good and Ill*, by Elizabeth Huberman. *South Atlantic Quarterly* 71:271–73.

1973–1986

"The Director's Corner." Renamed "The President's Corner" beginning with no. 5. In *A Newberry Newsletter*, no. 1 (September 1973)–no. 37 (Fall 1986).

1973

"An Appreciation of Hermon Dunlap Smith." In *The Hermon Dunlap Smith Center for the History of Cartography at the Newberry Library, Dedication Proceedings, November 1, 1972,* 2–5. Chicago: Newberry Library.

"Statement" and "Testimony." In U.S. Congress. Senate Committee on Labor and Public Welfare. House Committee on Education and Labor. Joint Hearings. *National Foundation on the Arts and Humanities Amendments of 1973.* 93d Cong., 1st sess., 6–8 March 1973, 733–38.

"Statement Prepared for the National Commission on Libraries and Information Science." In *In Our Opinion: Regional Hearing before the National Commission on Libraries and Information Science,* 250–51. Springfield: Illinois State Library.

1974

"Clifford Kenyon Shipton." *Proceedings* (American Antiquarian Society) 84, pt. 1:24–29.

1975

"As God Gold Was with the Spaniards." Review essay of *Red, White, and Black: The Peoples of Early America,* by Gary B. Nash. *Reviews in American History* 3:52–58.

1976–1984

"Independent Research Libraries." *ALA Year Books* (1976): 181–84; (1977): 153–56; (1978): 145–47; (1979): 126–29; (1980): 160–61a; (1981): 146–49; (1982): 140–42; (1983): 138–43b; (1984): 159–62.

1976

Creating a New Nation, 1763–1803. Notes on the occasion of the opening of an exhibition. Chicago: Chicago Historical Society.

"Introduction." In *A Summary View of the Rights of British America,* by Thomas Jefferson, [ix]-xxii. Chicago: Caxton Club.

My Dad's a Heartless Creature [by] *Earl Chadwick Towner.* Chicago: Privately printed. (Introductory note to a poem written by his father in 1938.)

"Newberry Library." In *Encyclopedia of Library and Information Science,* ed. Allen Kent, Harold Lancour, and Jay E. Dailey, 19:450–56. New York: Marcel Dekker. Reprinted as *The Newberry Library . . . A Brief History.* Chicago: Newberry Library, 1977. Revised and reprinted as "The Newberry Library." In *Research Institutions and Learned Soci-*

eties, ed. Joseph C. Kriger, 373–78. Westport, Conn.: Greenwood Press, 1982.

"Some of My Best Friends Used to Be Press Directors." *Scholarly Publishing* 7:113–20.

Reprinted in *Newsletter* (American Council of Learned Societies) 26/27, nos. 4 and 1 (Fall and Winter, 1975–76): 2–19.

1977–1986
Newberry Library Annual Reports.

1977
"Wrecking" Havoc: A Talk Given at a Conference of the Rare Books and Manuscripts Section, American Library Association, Charlottesville, Virginia, July [sic], 1974. Chicago: Glistening Water Press at the Newberry Library.

1978
"Introduction." In *The Surrounded,* by D'Arcy McNickle. 2d ed., vii-xiii. Albuquerque: University of New Mexico Press. (In later printings this essay appears, with the same pagination, as an Afterword.)

"The Mapping of the American Revolutionary War in the Nineteenth Century." In *The Mapping of the American Revolution,* by J. B. Harley, Barbara Bartz Petchenik, and Lawrence W. Towner, 111–24. Chicago: University of Chicago Press.

1980
"Turning Problems into Opportunities: Agenda for the Eighties." *Humanities* (National Endowment for the Humanities) 1, no. 6 (December): 3–4. Reprinted as part of congressional testimony in 1981.

1981
Beethoven and Bourbon: A Celebration of Life. Lester Jesse Cappon, September 18, 1900–August 24, 1981. Chicago: Newberry Library.

"Everett D. Graff." In *Dictionary of American Biography,* suppl. 7, 1961–65: 294–95.

"Statement" and "Testimony." In U.S. Congress. House. Committee on Education and Labor. *Budget Allocations for the Endowments for the Arts and Humanities, and Museums and Libraries: Hearings before the Subcommittee on Postsecondary Education.* 97th Cong., 1st sess., 2 March, 55–60.

1982

"True Confessions and Dying Warnings in Colonial New England." In *Sibley's Heir: A Volume in Memory of Clifford Kenyon Shipton.* Publications of the Colonial Society of Massachusetts. Vol. 59, *Collections,* 523–39. Andover: Colonial Society of Massachusetts. Earlier and briefer version, with limericks, printed in "Report" of the Society of the Fifth Line, ca. 1970.

1983

Lawrence Baumann Towner, 1951–1983: In Memoriam, Chicago, September 12, 1983. Chicago: Privately printed.

1984

"Before the Apostrophe." Letter to the Editor. *New York Times Magazine,* 15 January.

"Foreword." In *Gardens of Delight: Maps and Travel Accounts of Illinois and the Great Lakes from the Collection of Hermon Dunlap Smith. An Exhibition at the Newberry Library 29 October 1984–31 January 1985,* by Robert W. Karrow, Jr., and David Buisseret, 4. Chicago: Newberry Library.

"Informal Remarks on the Service That Came [in] Out of the Cold: Genealogy at the Newberry Library, 1962–1983." *Mayflower News* (Society of Mayflower Descendants in the State of Illinois) 20, no. 1 (May): 2–4.

1986

Blair Stewart, 1900–1986: In Memoriam April 11, 1986. Chicago: Newberry Library.

"Introduction." In *A Princely Gift: The Rudy Lamont Ruggles Collection of the Newberry Library,* vii–xv. Chicago: Newberry Library.

"Resolution of the Board of Trustees" and "Quotations for a Biography of a Trustee." In *Eric W. Cochrane: May 13, 1928–November 29, 1985,* [11–15]. Chicago: University of Chicago, Department of History.

1987

"A History of the Newberry Library." In *Humanities' Mirror: Reading at the Newberry, 1887–1987,* comp. and ed. Rolf Achilles, 17–26. Chicago: Newberry Library.

1988

"An End to Innocence." *American Libraries* 19 (1988): 210–13.

"William Phillips." In *Dictionary of American Biography,* suppl. 8, 1966–70:500–502.

1993

Past Imperfect: Essays on History, Libraries, and the Humanities, ed. Robert W. Karrow, Jr., and Alfred F. Young. Chicago: University of Chicago Press.

INDEX

References to illustrations that follow page 122 are denoted by *illus.*

British Museum, 180
Brooker, T. Kimball, 145
Brooks, Governor: cited by Winsor, 106
Brown, John: influence on H. B. Carrington, 99
Brown, Richard H., xxx, 144, 212
Brown, Robert E.: attacks Beard, 114
Brown v. Board of Education, 131–132
Burgean, Esther, 49
Burgess Fund, Kenneth L., 200; *illus.*
Burke, Edmund: influence of *Annual Register* on early American historiography, 91
Burns, Robert: Kilmarnock Burns, 176-177
Bush Foundation: gifts to Newberry Library, 213
business, history of: at Newberry Library, 142
Butcher, Mary, 51
Butler, Pierce: and Wing collection at Newberry Library, 140
Butler, Ruth, 142

Calef, Robert: quoted on confessions, 78
Calhoun, Arthur, 135
Cappon, Lester J.: and *Atlas of Early American History*, xxvii, 89; as mentor, xviii, xxi, xxii; photograph of, 230; Towner on, 229–231, 230 (illus.)
Carleton, William N.: librarian at Newberry Library, 141
Carnegie Corporation: grant to Newberry Library, 212
Carnegie Foundation, Andrew: gifts to Newberry Library, 213
Carpenter, Frederick Ives, 145
Carrington, Henry B.: compared to Winsor, 110; contributions of, 98–103
Carrington, James C.: father of Henry B., 99
Cartography, Center for History of. See Hermon Dunlap Smith Center for History of Cartography
cartography, history of: and American Revolution, 89–111

cartography collections. *See* Smith; Ayer; Stevens; Novacco; Sack
Cartography of Northern Virginia: Cappon reviews, 229
Cather, Willa, 142
Caxton, William: first edition of at Newberry Library, 141
Center for Renaissance Studies. *See* Renaissance Studies, Center for
centers, research. *See* research centers
Chapman, J. A.: cited by Winsor, 106
Chase, Ellen, 197
Chatsworth: Jenson *Biblia Latina*, 176
Cheney, John Vance: librarian at Newberry Library, 141
Chicago, Burlington & Quincy Railroad: collection of at Newberry Library, 142, 156, 211
Chicago Area American Issues Forum: Towner on, 267
Chicago literary renaissance, 138, 142
Chicago Metro History Fair: and family history at Newberry Library, 200; at Newberry Library, 212, 273–274; cited by Towner in Congressional testimony, 269
Chicago Public Library: and founding of Newberry Library, 138–139; Poole at, 164
Christie's, 175
Cist, J.: cited by Winsor, 106
Clark, David Sanders: "Index to the Maps of the American Revolution," 94
Clarke, Alice: confession of, 62
Clinton, Sir Henry: *Narrative of the Campaign of 1781* used by H. B. Carrington, 101
Cochrane, Eric W., 144
Coffin, Charles: cited, 110
Collier, John, 236
Columbia University: conservation program at, 183, 199, 212
Communism: and American Studies, 119
confessions, court: essay on, 56–81. *See also* True Confessions and Dying Warnings
Congress, U. S.: Towner testifies before, 253–259, 264–269

consensus school of historians, xviii; challenged, xxvi; described, 121; discussed by Towner, 114
conservation: as priority, xxxii; at Newberry Library, 183–189, 199
Cooper, Rev. William: execution sermon, 76
Cotter, John: *Archaeological Excavations at Jamestown*, 134
Cotton, John: catechism of, 57
Coverdale *Bible*, 177
Cowley, Malcolm: papers of at Newberry Library, 129, 143, 211
Craigie, Sir William, 144
Crane, Stephen: modern edition of, 116
Crerar, John: will of establishes library, 171. *See also* John Crerar Library
Cullen, Charles T., xv
Cunha, Captain George: on conservation, 183; Towner responds to, 185–189
Cutler, Samuel, 50

Dabney, Virginius, 195
Dand, John: confession of, 63
Dangler, David W., 145
Dante: early editions of at Newberry Library, 139, 141
D'Arcy McNickle Center for the History of the American Indian: at Newberry Library, 162, 212, 234; created at Newberry Library, xxviii–xxix, 143; McNickle as founding director of, 236; support for, 258, 268. *See also* McNickle, D'Arcy
Darwinism: influence on history, 109
Dast, James C., 183
Davidson, Suzette Morton, 145
Day, Abigail, 48
Dearborn, Henry: *Boston Notions*, 105; H. D. Smith writes on for *Encyclopaedia Britannica*, 233
Dedmon, Emmett, 144
Deering, Frank C.: collection of, *illus.*, 140, 172, 179–180, 180; mentioned, xxiv, 211
Dell, Floyd, 142; *An Old Man's Folly*, *illus.*

Detterer, Ernst: and Wing collection at Newberry Library, 140
Diamond, Sigmund, 56, 199
Dick, Jane, 211
dissent: perspectives on, 133
documentary editing: discussed by Towner, 115–116
Donnelley, Gaylord, 144
Driscoll, J. Francis: collection of, *illus.*, 181; mentioned, xxv, 211
Duffey, Joseph, xxxv, 267
Dulane, Gene: and theft of book, 208
Dumond, George: and theft of book, 208
Dunn, William, 47
Dunston, John, 32
Durfee, David, 49

Education in History and the Humanities, Center for Continuing: proposed for Newberry Library, 162
Eliot, Rev. Andrew, 46
Eliot, Rev. John: Indian *Bible*, 178
Emerson, Ralph Waldo: modern edition of, 116; quoted, 92
energy crisis, 131
Engerman, Stanley: *Time on the Cross*, 246
Epistles of Jacob Boehme: theft of from Newberry Library, 208
Erler, Mabel, 142
Essex Quarterly Court: and George Norton's case, 62
Evans, Bergen, 184
Evans, Charles: bibliography of, xx, 117
Exxon Education Foundation: gifts to Newberry Library, 213

Faden, William: map of Battle of Brandywine, 96; map of Battle of Guilford, 108; maps of used by H. B. Carrington, 101
family: changes in, 131; institution of in trouble, 130; studied in Windsor, Ct., 135
Family and Community History Center: and genealogy, 193; at Newberry Library, xxix, 143, 162, 200, 212; proposed, xxviii

The Far Western Frontier, 1830–1860:
Billington and, 220
Felt Collection: Massachusetts Archives and, 185
Fey, Harold E., 239
Fifth Commandment: and generation gap, 134; as theme in execution sermons, 64, 76–77; Samuel Willard's use of, 198
Filson, John: *Map of Kentucke*, 180
Fiske, John: cited, 110; maps in *The American Revolution*, 95
Fiske, Rev. John: and confession, 60
Fogel, Robert: *Time on the Cross*, 246
Folger Shakespeare Library: and Renaissance Center at Newberry Library, 212; as humanities center, 272–273; compared with Newberry Library, xxii, 137, 171; mentioned by Towner, 266; rare book men at, 175
Forbes, Esther: on witchcraft, 63
Ford, Gerald, xv; Towner visits, xxxv
Ford Foundation: gifts to Newberry Library, 213
Fowle, Zachariah: takes apprentice, 36–37
Foxcroft, Thomas: execution sermon of, 76
Franklin, Benjamin: *New-England Courant*, 82; papers of, 115, 266
Franklin, James, 18; and Irish, 79
Freeman, Douglas Southall: map in *Life of Washington*, 95
Frost, Gary L.; 183
Frothingham, Richard: cited, 110; *Siege of Boston*, 105

Galileo: letter of, 176
Gannon, Ann Ida, 145
Garment, Leonard, 265
Garrick, David: study of, 104
Garrison, William Lloyd: interpretations of, 121
Gebhard, Elizabeth, 144
genealogy: at Newberry Library, 193–201. *See also* Wolf, Joseph
generation gap: perspective on, 134
Gookin, Daniel, 180
Gordon, Vesta Lee, 184

Gordon, William: *The History of the Rise, Progress, and Establishment of the Independence of the United States* mentioned, 91
Graff, Everett D.: and Newberry Library, xvii; as Trustee of Newberry Library, 144, 145, 146, 210 (chairman), 211; book fund at Newberry Library, 154; collection of, xxiv, *illus.*, 140, 172, 174–175, 178–179, 211, 240–242; quoted, 213; Towner on, 232
Graham, Hugh Davis: *Violence in America*, 132–133
Granger, Sarah, 47
Granger, Thomas: confession of, 61–62
Grant, U. S.: edited papers of, 116
Great Lakes Colleges Association: program with Newberry Library, 143
Greene (Green), Bartholomew, Jr., 32; publisher of Boston *Gazette*, 83
Greene, Francis Vinton: maps in *Revolutionary War and Military Policy of the United States*, 110
Greene, Nathaniel, 93, 101
Greenlee, William B.: as Trustee of Newberry Library, 145; collection of, xxii, 140, 172; Towner mentions, 232
Griffith, J. W.: quoted by Towner, 204
Grinnell College: protest at, 133
Grolier: bindings at Newberry Library, 139
Grolier Club, 176
Guppy, Ruben, 40
Gurr, Ted Robert: *Violence in America*, 132–133

Haffner, Charles C. III, 144
Hagstrum, Jean, 144
Hambleton, Chalkley J., 144, 145, 210
Hamer, Philip: *Guide to Archives and Manuscripts in the United States*, 118
Hamill, Alfred E., 144, 145
Hamilton, Alexander: papers of, 115; mentioned, 93
Hancock, Rev. John, 46
Handlin, Oscar and Mary: "Origins of

Indians. *See* American Indians
Indians and Other Americans: by
	D'Arcy McNickle, 239
*The Indian Tribes of the United
	States:* by D'Arcy McNickle, 239
Institute for Advanced Studies in History: proposed for Newberry Library,
	160–163. *See also* Newberry Library:
	as educational institution
Institute for Advanced Study, 272
Institute of Early American History
	and Culture, 163; as humanities
	center, 272; Cappon at, 229; influence on Towner, xxi; project with
	the Newberry Library, 258
International Conference of Librarians:
	Towner addresses in Japan, xxvi
Irish: condemned as "criminals,"
	18, 79
Irving, Washington: friend of H. B.
	Carrington, 99; modern edition of,
	116
Irving Institute: H. B. Carrington
	teaches at, 99
Isham, Henry P., 144

Jamestown, Va.: pollution in,
	134
Jansenist Collection: *illus.*
Japan: interest in American history,
	113
Javits, Jacob, 255
Jay, John: papers of being edited, 115
Jefferson, Thomas: letter to Watterston, *illus.,*; mentioned by Pres.
	Kennedy, 265–266; papers of, 115,
	266
Jefferson Lectures on the Humanities,
	267
Jensen, Richard J., 193
Jenson, *Biblia latina*, 176
John Crerar Library, 266; founding of,
	138
Johnson, James, 41–42
Johnston, Henry, 110
Jordan, Winthrop: *White over Black*,
	132
Journal of American History: circulation of, 118

Journal of Charlotte L. Forten: Billington's edition of, 219
Julian (Indian): broadside on execution
	of, 69–71 (illus.), 80–81

Karrow, Robert: Towner thanks, 89
Katz, Stanley: on Newberry Library, xv
Keeney, Barnaby: mentioned by
	Towner, 267, 273; Towner works
	with, xxxv
Kelmscott Press: books of in Newberry
	Library collections, 211
Kennedy, John F., 265; Towner on assassination of, 130
Kenneth Nebenzahl, Jr. Lectures in the
	History of Cartography: at Newberry
	Library, 143, 162, 163; publications
	of, 250; Towner's lecture in series,
	89–111; mentioned, 234
Kilgore, Peggy, 50
Kilmarnock Burns, 176–177
Kimball, Hanibal Ingalls. *See* Stone
	and Kimball Collection
Kimpton, Lawrence A., 145
King Philip's War, 77
Knox, Sanka, 179
Kohn, Hans, 90
Korngold, Ralph, xxxvi
Kraditor, Eileen S.: *Means and Ends in
	American Abolitionism: Garrison
	and His Critics on Strategy and Tactics, 1834–1850* reviewed, 121–122
Kraeling, Carl H., 144
Kresge Foundation: grants to Newberry Library, 213

Laertes: advice from Polonius, 155
La Farge, Oliver: on *The Surrounded*,
	236
Lafreri Atlas, 181
Langdon, John, 46
Laura X's Women's History Research
	Center, 136
Lemay, Leo: *Calendar of American Poetry in the Colonial Newspapers
	and Magazines*, 129
Lemisch, Jesse, xviii
Lenox Collection: H. B. Carrington
	urged to use, 101

Towner, 266; microfilm of manuscript collections, 118; Shipton at, 225

Mather, Cotton: and confessions, 60, 76; and Sewall, 28, 33–34; apprenticeship and, 48; *Magnalia Christi Americana*, 77; on servitude, 4–5, 8, 12–13, 15, 19, 24; on William Perkins, 59; *Pillars of Salt*, 73–74, 77

Mather, Increase, 28; and confession, 78; James Morgan's confession, 64, 73; Shipton prevents Towner from reading Diary of, 225; *The Wicked mans Portion*, 63–64, 65 (illus.)

Matthews-Northrup: map printers, 95

Mayflower Society: Towner addresses, 193

Mayo, Catharine Barton, 226

Melish, John: *Atlas of the War of 1812* praised, 96

Mellon Foundation, Andrew W.: establishes fund for research and education, 234; grants to Newberry Library, 146, 199, 212, 213; supports independent research libraries, 273

Melville, Herman: edition of writings at Newberry Library, xxvii, 116, 150, 159, 162, 250; *Moby Dick* editions, *illus.*

Merk, Frederick L., xviii, 218

Merry, Cornelius, 41

Midwestern studies: at Newberry Library, 142

Millar, W. Graham, 54

Miller, Perry: and Puritan "declension," 56, 77; quoted, 75, 209; mentioned, 42

Miner, Charles: cited by Winsor, 106

Modern Language Association: *American Literary Manuscripts*, 118; and literary editing, 116; and unpublished research, 251

Mooney, James E.: and *Short-Title Evans*, 225–226

Morgan, Edmund S., 14, 39; skillful work of, 129

Morgan, James: confession of, 64, 73–74, 78

Morison, Samuel Eliot: edition of *Bradford's Journal*, 194

Morison, Stanley, 141

Mormon Library, 200

Morse, Sidney Edwards: and wax-engraving of maps, 103

Morton, Nathaniel: *New England's Memorial*, 178

Morton Fund, Mark, 200

Mount, Charles Merrill: and library theft, 202–203

Moynahan, Julian: *Pairing Off* spoofs librarians, 128

National Archives: thefts from, 203

National Endowment for the Arts: conservation grant to Newberry Library, 188; emphasizes public programs, 260

National Endowment for the Humanities: and Renaissance Center at Newberry Library, 212; lay public and, xvii; public programs and "pure" scholarship, 260–263; support for Newberry Library, xxx, xxxi, xxxiv–xxxv, 144, 210, 213; supports independent research libraries, 272; Towner defends, 264–269; Towner testifies in support of, xv, 253–259; Towner writes article for, 270–274

National Foundation on the Arts and Humanities, 255

National Historical Publications and Records Commission: mentioned by Towner, 267; microfilm publications of, 117; Reagan proposes eliminating, xxxiii, 264–269

National Humanities Center, 272

National Science Foundation, 256; pure research and, 260, 261

National Union Catalog of Manuscripts, 118

Native American Tribalism: by D'Arcy McNickle, 239

nativism: Billington on, 218

Neal, Dean, 203

Nebenzahl, Kenneth: as Trustee of Newberry Library, 144; endows lecture series in cartography, xxvii–xxviii; on Lafreri Atlas, 181; Towner thanks, 89

Nebenzahl, Kenneth, Inc., 180

Nebenzahl Lectures. *See* Kenneth
Nebenzahl, lecture series in
cartography
Newberry, Julia (daughter of Walter L.),
138
Newberry, Julia Clap (Mrs. Walter L.),
138; death of, 171
Newberry, Mary, 138
Newberry, Walter Loomis: as founder
of Newberry Library, 138, 168; books
of, 171; endowment of, 145
Newberry Library: and 1971 plan,
148–169; as an independent research
library, xv; as "community of scholars," xxviii–xxxi, 158–163; as educational institution, 149–150, 160–
161; as humanities center, 272–273;
as "uncommon collection of uncommon collections," xxii, 137; at
time of Towner's retirement, xxxvii–
xxxviii; book budget of, 248; book
on violence researched at, 132;
building program of, xxx–xxxi, 146–
147, 163–167; Cappon at, 229; collecting at, 152–156, 170–182; conservation at, 183–189; founding of,
171; genealogy at, 193–201; Graff
Collection at, 240–242; history of,
137–147; Institute for Advanced
Study in History and the Humanities proposed for, 152; Melville edition and, 150; National Endowment
for the Humanities and, xxxi, xxxv–
xxxvi, 253, 258, 268; papers of Malcolm Cowley at, 129; publishing
and, 250; renovation of, xxx–xxxi;
security at, 205; seminar on "Alienation and the Search for Community," 136; Towner's tenure at, xv,
xvi, xxii–xxxi, 210–213; University
Extension Center at, 150; University
of Chicago's proposed merger of,
241; wide range of users at, xxxvi–
xxxvii
Newberry Library Associates, 167; addressed by Towner, 125; and collections of Newberry Library, 170; annual giving of, 182; creation of, 146;
growth of, 213; mentioned, 234
Newberry Library Bulletin, 162; and

descriptions of collections, 142; creation of, xxiii
Newberry Library Seminar in the Hu-
manities, 159
New England Courant: wedding game
printed in, 86–87
*New England Life in the Eighteenth
Century: Representative Biogra-
phies from Sibley's Harvard Gradu-
ates*: Shipton and, 227
New England's Memorial, 178
New Left school: and Edward Bonfield,
132; challenges consensus history,
120; described, 121–122
newspapers: in New England, 82
New York Academy of Medicine, 266
New Yorker: article caricatures re-
search, 127
New-York Historical Society: and early
American history, 92; H. B. Carring-
ton urged to use, 101; mentioned by
Towner, 266
New York Public Library: as member
of Independent Research Libraries
Association, 253; Banks trains con-
servators at, 188; challenge grants to
from NEH, 258; mentioned by
Towner, 267
New York Review of Books: fictional
letter to, 127
New York State Historical Associa-
tion: Towner talks at, 125
New York University: conservation
program at, 199, 212
Nitze, William A., 144
Nixon, Richard, 265
Northwestern University: graduate
study at, xviii–xix, 221–222; pro-
grams with Newberry Library, 150,
151; R. A. Billington as teacher at,
217–223
Norton, George: confession of, 62
Novacco, Franco: map collection at
Newberry Library, xxviii, *illus.*, 140,
143, 163, 172, 179–180, 180, 181,
211; mentioned, xxiv

Oakley, Horace S., 144; collection of,
172–173
Odell, William R., 146

Ogden, Barclay W., 183
Ogden, Sherelyn J. B., 183
Oliver, Daniel, 46
Oliver, John, 46
Orwell, George: *1984*, 134; mentioned
 by Towner, 209
Otis, Samuel: master of apprenti-
 ces, 46
Overseers of the Poor (Boston): appren-
 tices and, 36–38, 48–51; poor laws
 and, 44

Page, Thomas: *Plan of the Town of
 Boston*, 107
Paine, Robert Treat, 46; papers of at
 MHS, 118
paperback books, 118
Paret, Peter: quoted on military his-
 tory, 93
Pareus, David, 26
Pargellis, Stanley: and programs at
 Newberry Library, xxvi, 150; as li-
 brarian of Newberry Library, xvii,
 xxiii, 141–144, 146; on Everett D.
 Graff, 242
Parke Bernet: and sale of Graff dupli-
 cates, 175; sales of Newberry Library
 materials, 139
Parker, John, 93
Parrington, Vernon Louis, xviii
Paxson, Frederic L., 218
Peachey, Thomas, 10
Peckham, Howard: maps in *War for In-
 dependence*, 110
Pell, Claiborne: and NEH funding for
 Newberry Library, xxxi–xxxii; helps
 shape research support policy, xxxvi;
 Towner's letter to, xxxvii, 260–263
Perkins, William: and confessions, 59
Petchenik, Barbara: and Nebenzahl
 Lectures, 89; quoted, 95; mentioned,
 110
Peterson, Sandra, 56
Pew Memorial Trust: grants to New-
 berry Library, 199, 212, 213
Phillips, Samuel, 32
Phips, William, 28
Pickering, Timothy: papers of at MHS,
 118
Pierce, William, 53

Pierpont Morgan Library, 175; and dat-
 ing of Constance Missal, 129; men-
 tioned by Towner, 266
Pillars of Salt: described, 73–74;
 66, (illus.)
Piquet, François: manuscript of
 illus.
Pirie, Robert, 179
Plymouth Colony: confession in, 61
PMLA: circulation of, 118
Pocahontas: proposed statue of, 82–88
Poe, Edgar Allan: modern edition of,
 116
Polk, James K.: papers of being edited,
 116
Pollard, A. W., and Redgrave, G. R.:
 Short Title Catalogue, 252
pollution, 134
Polonius: advice to Laertes, 155
Poole, George A. III, 144, 145
Poole, William Frederick: and New-
 berry Library University Extension
 Center, 150; as first librarian of
 Newberry Library, 138, 141, 164
Pope, Alexander: influence on New
 England verse, 84
Populist historiography: discussed by
 Towner, 113–114
Portuguese Collection. *See* Greenlee
printing, history of. *See* Wing, John M.
Prior, Moody E., 233
Probasco, Henry, 139
progressive school of historians, xviii–
 xix; discussed by Towner, 113–114
protest: at Grinnell College, 133; of
 apprentices, 15–17
Psychology Today: Towner uses in
 talk, 194
Ptolemy, 180
Pullman Company: papers of at New-
 berry Library, 143, 211
Puritanism: and women, 135; modern
 misconceptions of, 86–88
Puritans: and servitude, 3–21, 38–41;
 confessions and, 59–81

Quie, Albert, 255

Ramsay, David: *The American Revolution* mentioned, 91

tion: *Jeffersonian Philanthropy and the American Indian*, 136

Shepherd, Thomas, 29

Sheridan, Gen. Philip Henry: and H. B. Carrington, 101

Sherman, Gen. William T.: and H. B. Carrington, 101–102

Shipton, Clifford K.: and Evans bibliography, 251; and Turner thesis, 58–59; and wedding game article, 87; as mentor, xviii, xix-xx; memorial volume for, 56; Towner on, 224–228

Short Title Catalogue: Pollard and Redgrave's, 252

Sibley, John Langdon: succeeded by Justin Winsor, 104

Sibley's Harvard Graduates: Shipton and, 224–228

Silver, Louis H.: and H. D. Smith, 233; as Trustee of Newberry Library, 145; collection of, xxiv, *illus.*, 139, 145, 170, 174, 178, 184, 211

Simon, Paul, 266

Skelton, R. A., 180; and creation of cartography center, xxviii

slavery: Cotton Mather on, 33–35; executions and, 3–4, 79–80; family and Puritan society, 198; in Massachusetts, 5–6, 19–20, 22–35; John Saffin's case in favor of, 29–32; protests and, 15–18, 20–21; Samuel Sewall's case, 23–27; William Ames on, 27–28

Smith, Bradford, 86

Smith, C.: cited by Winsor, 105

Smith, G. G.: cited by Winsor, 106

Smith, Harold Byron Jr., 145, 213

Smith, Hermon Dunlap: and Henry Dearborn, 233; as Trustee of Newberry Library, 145, 210 (chairman); collection of, 211; endows cartography center, xxviii; Towner on, 232–235

Smith, Capt. John: *General History of Virginia*, 84; publishing works of, 248, 250; quoted, 168, 235; *True Travels*, 180

Smith, Page, 92

Smith, Richard: and conservation at Newberry Library, 188–189

Smith Center for History of Cartography. See Hermon Dunlap Smith Center for the History of Cartography

socialism: and American Studies, 119

Society for the History of Discoveries: publication of, 250

Society of American Archivists, 203

Sotheby's: and sale of Silver collection, 170, 175–176; sales of Newberry Library materials, 139

Sparks, Jared: Cappon edits, 229

Spencer Collection, William M.: *illus.*; mentioned by Towner, 211

Stanly, Bethia: confession of, 61

Stannard, David: quoted, 60

State Historical Society of Wisconsin: Towner talks at, 125

Stedman, Charles: and cartography of American Revolution, 91; cited by Winsor, 105; H. B. Carrington reads, 101; influence on Lossing, 97; map from used by Winsor, 107

Steele, Matthew Forney: influenced by Winsor, 110

Steffen, Charles G., 56, 89

Stevens, Henry Newton: collection of Ptolemys, 172

Stevenson, Adlai, 233

Stevenson, Allan: work of, 129

Stone, Herbert Stuart. See Stone and Kimball Collection

Stone, Hugh: confession of, 78–79

Stone, W. Clement, 268

Stone (H. S.) and Kimball (H. I.) Collection: *illus.*; mentioned by Towner, 211

Storm, Colton, 241–242

Strauss, Herbert R.: as Trustee of Newberry Library, 145; collection of, *illus.*, 211

Streeter, Thomas W.: sales of, 175, 180

Striker, Laura Polyani, 86

Sutcliffe, Denham, 271

Swett, Samuel: cited by Winsor, 106

Swift, Jonathan: *Gulliver's Travels* cited by Towner, 128

Tanner, Henry Schenk: maps of, 96
Taylor, William R.: at Newberry Library, 199
technology: as engine for current change, 130
Thanet, Octave, 142
Thatcher, Rev. Oxenbridge, 46
They Came Here First: by D'Arcy McNickle, 239
Thomas, Isaiah: as apprentice, 37, 51; quoted, xxvi
Thomas, Peter, 37
Thoreau, Henry David: modern edition of, 116
Thurber, James, 49
Time on the Cross, 246
Towner, Aaron, 195
Towner, Benjamin, 195
Towner, Earl, 195
Towner, Elizabeth, 89
Towner, Elmer, 195
Towner, Gershom, 195
Towner, John, 195
Towner, Johnathan, 195
Towner, Lawrence B., 195
Towner, Lawrence W. (1921–1992): and 1974 plan for Newberry Library, 148; and founding of Independent Research Libraries Association, xxxi, 253–259; and Newberry Library collections, 170–182; as after dinner speaker, 125; as editor of *William and Mary Quarterly*, xxi–xxii, 229; as Newberry Library president and librarian, xv; as political activist, xix; Award named for, xxxvi; background of, xvii–xviii; buys Willard's *Compleat Body of Divinity*, 198; chairs AHA Program Committee, 120; chairs Illinois Humanities Council, xxxvi; describes concept of research centers, xxviii–xxix, 158–163; dismal assessment of American society in 1978, xxxii–xxxiii; dissertation of described, xviii; experience at Newberry Library, xxii–xxxi; family of, 195; Fellows' Lounge in Newberry Library named for, xxx; fundraising for Newberry Library, 145; historical essay on Newberry Library, xxxvii–xxxviii, 137–147; letter to Sen. Pell, 260–263; "lust" for rare books, xviii, 198; military service of, xix; Newberry Library accomplishments, 137–147; on book dealers, 190–192; on Clifford K. Shipton, 224–228; on D'Arcy McNickle, 236–239; on Everett D. Graff, 240–242; on genealogy, 193–201; on Hermon Dunlap Smith, 232–235; on Lester J. Cappon, 229–231; on library security, 202–209; on Ray Allen Billington, 217–223; on the humanities in the 80s, 270–274; on trends in scholarship, 112–122; on university press directors, 245–252; plan for defending humanities, xxxvii–xxxviii; published writings of listed, 275–282; skills as administrator, 183; speaks to International Council of Librarians, xxvi; summarizes his years at Newberry Library, 210–213; supports publication of founding fathers' papers, 266; title change, 145; vision of humanities and libraries, xv, xvi; visits White House, xxxv
Towner, Michael, 210
Towner, Peter, 210
Towner, Phinneas, 195
Towner, Rachel, 195, 210
Towner, Richard, 195
Towner Award for the Best Risk-taking Proposal, Lawrence W.: created by Illinois Humanities Council, xxxvi
Townsend, Joseph: map of Battle of Brandywine, 95–96
Townsend, Penn, 29
Tree, Lambert, 143
Trempealeau Township, Wisconsin, 195
True Confessions and Dying Warnings: and predestination, 75–76; as source of social cohesion, 76; changes in genre, 79–81; English antecedents of, 58–59; in church, 60–61; in court, 61–63; literary elements of, 74–75; origins of confessors, 79; Puritan theology and, 59–60
Turner, Frederick Jackson: as a scien-

tific historian, 109; as progressive
historian, xviii; Billington edits correspondence of, 220–221; mentioned, 218
Turner thesis: Shipton on, 58–59
Twain, Mark: modern edition of, 116
Tyler, Moses Coit: on eighteenth-century New England verse, 84

*Uncommon Collection of Uncommon
Collections: The Newberry Library,*
158
*The United States: American Democ-
racy in World Perspective:* Billington and, 219
University of Chicago: invites Newberry Library to merge, 241; programs with Newberry Library,
151
University of Illinois: Banks teaches
conservation at, 188
university press directors: Towner on,
245–252
Upham, Charles W.: and witchcraft
cases, 63
Utley, George B.: librarian of Newberry
Library, 141

Vietnam War: effect of, 130; impact on
American society, 120; mentioned
by Towner, 237
violence, 132–133
Violence in America: message of, 132–
133
Virginia Historical Society, 267

Wadsworth, Rev. Benjamin, 8; on ser-
vitude, 14, 15
Wallace, Henry, xix
Wallace, Willard M.: maps in *Appeal
to Arms,* 110–111
Ward, Christopher: maps in *War of the
American Revolution,* 111
Warren, James, 46
Warren, Josiah, 46
Washington, George: as the American
Ulysses, 91; map of used by Winsor,
108; papers of, 115, 266; mentioned,
93, 100
Watergate, 131

Watterson, George: letter from Jefferson, *illus.*
wax-engraving of maps, 103
Webster, Noah: quoted, 91–92
Wecter, Dixon, 184
wedding game: description of printed,
87–88
Wedgeworth, Robert Jr., 145
Weinberg, Arthur and Lila, xxxvi
Wells, James M.: and collection development at Newberry Library, 211;
and Newberry Library collections,
xxv; and Wing collection at Newberry Library, 140; mission of Newberry Library, xxvi; mentioned, 142
Western Americana. *See* Graff Collection
The Westerners: Towner addresses,
217
*Westward Expansion: A History of the
American Frontier:* Billington and,
220
White House Conference on the Humanities: Towner supports, xxxi–
xxxii
Whitman, Walt: modern edition of,
116
Whitney, Eli, 99
Wigglesworth, Michael: and confessions, 60; on servitude, 15
Willard, Samuel: and Fifth Commandment, 77; *Compleat Body of Divinity,* 194, 198; generation gap and,
134; on confession, 75; on servitude,
5, 8–10, 15, 20
William and Mary Quarterly: availability of, 119; circulation of, 118; issues studied in, 134–135; Japanese
readers of, 113; Towner as editor of,
xxi–xxii, 229
Williams, William Appleman, xxii, 50
Wilson, John P., 144; collection of, 211
Wilson, Woodrow: papers of being edited, 116
Wing, John M.: collection on history of
printing at Newberry Library, xxii,
140–141, 172, 173
Winona, Minnesota, 195
Winsor, Justin: contributions of, 103–
110

Winthrop, John: and confession, 59–60; "Modell of Christian Charity," 77; on servitude, 7, 13; quoted, 79
Winthrop, Margaret, 12
Wirtz, William, 254
Wise, John: and Esther Rodgers, 58
witchcraft cases: confessions in, 63
Wolf, Edwin II, 177, 178
Wolf, Joseph, 197, 199
women: as poor apprentices, 45–46, 48, 49, 51, 53; execution of, 57–58; in New England wedding game, 86–88; Laura X's Women's History Research Center, 136. *See also* Hutchinson, Ann
women's history, 135

Woods Fund, Frank H., 200
Woodward, C. Vann: reviews Kraditor's book on Garrison, 121–122
Woodward, David, xxviii, 89, 163
The Works of Herman Melville: Northwestern-Newberry collaboration, xxvii

Xerox University Microfilms, 251

Yale University, 175
Yankelovich, Daniel: article of cited by Towner, 196
Young, Alfred F.: *Dissent: Exploration in the History of American Radicalism*, 121
Young, George B., 144–145